CARIBBEAN LANDS

John P. Augelli, Editor

LIBRARY OF CONGRESS CATALOG CARD NUMBER: 64-16567

CONTRIBUTORS

JOHN P. AUGELLI
Professor of Geography
and Director of the Center
of Latin American Studies
University of Kansas
Lawrence, Kansas

G. ETZEL PEARCY
The Geographer
U.S. Department of State
Washington, D. C.

A. CURTIS WILGUS
Director of the School of
Inter-American Studies
University of Florida
Gainesville, Florida

ROBERT J. ALEXANDER
Professor of Economics
Rutgers University
New Brunswick, New Jersey

PENROD MOSS
Curriculum Consultant
Dixie School District
San Rafael, California

RICHARD P. MOMSEN, JR.
Associate Professor of Geography
Ball State Teachers College
Muncie, Indiana

RAYMOND E. FIDELER
Editor and President

ALAN ADSMOND
Art Editor

JAMES K. DAVIS
Map Editor

MILDRED M. HOOKER
Manuscript Editor

ANNA DIEDRICH INGALLS
Staff Writer

JERRY E. JENNINGS
Staff Writer

MARY MITUS
Index Editor

RUTH MOEN
Picture Editor

ROSEMARY DENMARK MURPHY
Staff Writer

T. J. O'CONNOR
Staff Writer

CAROL S. PRESCOTT
Manuscript Editor

DOROTHY M. ROGERS
Manuscript Editor

ELIZABETH ANNE SHAW
Senior Manuscript Editor

AMERICAN NEIGHBORS

CANADA
MEXICO
CARIBBEAN LANDS

BRAZIL
SOUTH AMERICA

CARIBBEAN LANDS

JOHN P. AUGELLI, Editor

THE FIDELER COMPANY — GRAND RAPIDS, MICHIGAN

CONTENTS

Lesser Antilles and Bahama Islands

Maps and Charts

Why history and geography are important to you. There are two ways of living. Many people live in ignorance, never quite understanding what is going on around them, or why things turn out the way they do. Others try to find out what is going on in the world, and why. Those who choose the second way generally find life more interesting. They have more opportunities to make decisions for themselves. Sometimes, their decisions may help to bring about changes in the world.

The study of history and geography can help you to live this second way. Knowledge of these subjects will help you have a better understanding of the world events that influence your life and the lives of other people. It will also give you an insight into events in your own country and in your community. With this knowledge, you will be able to make wiser decisions about many things.

The problem-solving method is the best way of studying history and geography. Since you have a serious reason for wanting to understand the important historical and geographical concepts that influence your life, you need to use the best possible study method. You could just read a textbook and memorize answers for a test, but if you did so, you would probably forget much of the information soon after the test was over. Therefore, we suggest a better way of gaining an understanding of historical and geographical concepts. This is the problem-solving method. To use it in studying about the Caribbean Lands, you will need to follow these steps:

Step one. Do some general background reading about a country or region you want to explore.

Step two. Choose an important, interesting problem that you would like to solve about this country or region. Write it down so that you will have clearly in mind what it is you want to find out. (Note the sample problems on opposite page.) If there are small problems that need to be solved in order to solve your big problem, list them, too.

Step three. Think carefully about the possible solutions to your problem and write them down. These possible solutions are called "educated guesses," or hypotheses. You will try to solve your problem by proving that these hypotheses are true or false. Some will be partly true and partly false.

Step four. List all the different places where you might find information to prove or disprove your hypotheses. Now begin your research. Keep notes of the information that is related to your hypotheses. If the information in different sources conflicts, check further and try to decide which information is correct.

Step five. Now study your notes carefully. Have you proved or disproved your hypotheses? What new facts have you learned? Do you need to do further research? Remember that when you started out on this project you were on a search for truth. Do you think you have found it? If so, write a clear, interesting report about your research project. You may decide to illustrate it with maps, pictures, or drawings that will help other people share the things that you have come to understand.

The problem-solving method can help you in two ways. The problem-solving method can help you gain a better understanding of the important historical and geographical concepts that influence your life. It can also help you in another way. By using it, you will learn a way of dealing with problems that will help you throughout life. Many successful scientists, businessmen, and government leaders also solve their problems this way.

Where you can find information for solving your problems about the Caribbean Lands. When you use the problem-solving method, you need all the information you can find to reach a correct solution. Following is a list of some of the places where you can find information about the Caribbean Lands. Perhaps you can think of others.

. . . This Depth-Study Textbook was written especially for students who are using the problem-solving method. It contains four main sources of information: text, pictures, maps, and glossary items. To locate the specific information you want, you may use the Table of Contents, the List of Maps and Charts, and the Index.

. . . Many other history and geography books have chapters about the Caribbean Lands region. These will give you a preview of the countries in this region, which will help prepare you to do deeper research on special problems.

. . . Newspapers and magazines frequently contain articles about the Caribbean countries. It will be helpful if you keep a scrapbook or clipping file of these articles.

. . . Radio and television stations frequently broadcast news and special feature stories about the Caribbean Lands. Listening to and watching these programs will broaden your general knowledge about this part of the world.

. . . Your school and community libraries contain many good sources of information, such as encyclopedias, almanacs, atlases, and yearbooks. The Readers' Guide and the library card catalog will help you find magazine articles and books about the subject you are investigating. Ask your librarian to show you how to use these reference guides. Guard against using out-of-date information.

. . . Other sources of information are museums, people in your community who have visited the Caribbean Lands region, and the Director of Information at each country's embassy.

Sample problems to solve. You may choose between investigating problems about the Caribbean Lands region as a whole, or about one country in this region. The following sample problems are about the region as a whole:

1. The Caribbean Lands region is important to the United States partly because of its location. Why is this true? To solve this problem, you will need to use a globe and some of the maps in this book to find out where the Caribbean Lands region is located. Then you will need to make hypotheses that explain how the location of this region adds to its importance. The following questions suggest two hypotheses:

   a. What facts about trade routes help to solve this problem?
   b. What facts about the usefulness, or strategic value, of the Caribbean Lands to the United States in times of peace and of war help to solve it?

2. Why has there been so much unrest and dissatisfaction in the Caribbean Lands?

   a. What facts about the history of this region help to solve this problem?
   b. What facts about the standards of living in the Caribbean Lands help to solve it?
   c. What facts about Communist activity are helpful in solving this problem?

A GLOBAL VIEW OF THE CARIBBEAN LANDS

If you were an astronaut gazing down at the curved surface of the earth from a space capsule, you would see wide stretches of water and great masses of land. The landmasses are continents. Two of these are very familiar, for you have seen them on maps many times. They are the continents of North America and South America. As you know, most of the United States is located on the North American continent.

The globe above shows that North America and South America are connected by a narrow, zigzagging strip of land. This land bridge is the southernmost part of the North American continent. It is known as Central America.

*Please see Glossary, page 335, for unfamiliar terms.

To the north and east of Central America are many islands. (See globe on opposite page.) A few of them are large, but most of them are very small. Together they make up an island group, or archipelago, called the West Indies.

Central America and the West Indies border one of the largest and most beautiful seas in the world. This is the Caribbean Sea, which is an arm of the Atlantic Ocean. The sparkling, deep-blue waters of the Caribbean stretch for nearly 1,800 miles from east to west and about half that distance from north to south. Because Central America and the West Indies form part of the boundary of this sea, they are known as the Caribbean Lands.

A small region divided into many parts. The globe on the opposite page shows that the Caribbean Lands region occupies only a small area on the earth's surface. Its total land area is smaller than the states of Texas and Oklahoma combined.

Within this small region, there are eleven independent countries and eighteen territories that are not fully independent. As you might expect, none of these countries or territories is very large. Nicaragua, the largest country in the Caribbean Lands, is smaller than the state of Michigan.

A "melting pot" of peoples. More than thirty-four million people make their homes in the Caribbean Lands. These people are not all of one race, nor do they all speak the same language. Some of them are Indians whose ancestors lived in the Caribbean Lands long ago. Others are descended from European settlers, or from Negro slaves who were brought from Africa. There are also people from India and other Asian countries. Through the years, many people of different races have intermarried. As a result, there are millions of people of mixed descent living in the Caribbean Lands today.

The population of the Caribbean Lands is not distributed evenly. In Central America, there are large stretches of wilderness where few people live. On the other hand, some of the islands in the West Indies are among the most densely populated places on earth. Chapters 1, 2, and 6 help explain this uneven distribution of people.

A transportation crossroads. Many important travel routes pass through the Caribbean Lands. As you have learned, this region lies at the place where North America and South America meet. It is also located between the world's two largest oceans, the Atlantic and the Pacific. (Compare globe on opposite page with map on page 16.)

To connect the two oceans, a canal was built across the narrow Isthmus of Panama in Central America. This is the Panama Canal, one of the world's most important waterways. Before the canal was built, ships traveling between the Atlantic and Pacific oceans had to journey all the way around the southern tip of South America. This trip often took many weeks. Today, ships going from one ocean to the other can use the canal in order to shorten the distance they must travel. Thousands of ships pass through the Panama Canal each year.

The location of the Caribbean Lands is important in other ways as well. Many ships traveling between the United States and South America cross the Caribbean Sea. Someday it may be possible to drive all the way from the United States to South America, on the Pan American Highway. A highway that is part of the Pan American Highway network has recently been completed in Central America.

A source of valuable products. The farms, forests, and mines of the Caribbean Lands region supply the world with many useful products. In most parts of the Caribbean Lands, the weather is warm all year long. Farmers can raise tropical crops, such as sugarcane, bananas, and coffee, which will not grow where the climate is colder. Large amounts of sugar and other agricultural products are shipped to countries with colder climates. Mahogany and other valuable woods come from the forests of the Caribbean Lands. Useful minerals, such as petroleum and bauxite, are found in a few areas.

The people of the Caribbean Lands are our neighbors. The countries that make up the Caribbean Lands region are very close to the United States. All of these countries can be reached in a few hours by airplane. Each year, thousands of Americans visit the Caribbean Lands

The Panama Canal connects the Caribbean Sea with the Pacific Ocean. This canal was built by the United States. It crosses the narrowest part of Central America. Each year, thousands of ships from all over the world pass through the Panama Canal.

on vacation or on business, and many people from Caribbean countries travel to the United States.

Trade between the United States and our neighbors in the Caribbean Lands is important both to us and to them. The people of the Caribbean Lands produce many things that we need, and we make many things that these people do not produce in their own countries. For example, the island of Jamaica ships large quantities of bauxite to the United States for use in making aluminum. We in turn export mining machinery to Jamaica for use in extracting this valuable ore. Much of the money needed to operate mines and farms in the Caribbean Lands comes from business firms in the United States. American companies operating in the Caribbean Lands provide jobs for many thousands of people in this region.

The Caribbean countries are extremely important to our nation's defense because they are so near to our shores. The Panama Canal may be used by ships of any nation. In time of war, it has been vital to keep this canal open so that our ships can move easily from one ocean to the other.

The people of the Caribbean Lands face serious problems. Most of the people of the Caribbean Lands do not have as comfortable a way of life as we do in the United States. In several Caribbean countries, the per capita income is less than $200 a year. In the United States, the yearly per capita income is about $2,300. Much of the best farmland in the Caribbean Lands region is owned by a small number of wealthy people or by large foreign companies. The farmers who work on these landowners' estates often cannot afford proper housing, food, or medical care for their families. Many city people in the Caribbean Lands are also poor. They live in crowded slums and lack the food needed for good health.

Many Caribbean countries rely on a single farm crop for most of their exports. For example, El Salvador depends heavily on coffee, Honduras on bananas, and the Dominican Republic on sugar. If the harvest is poor, or if the crop is destroyed by hurricane, plant disease, or other disaster, the people of these countries face severe hardship.

Much of the property in the Caribbean Lands is not owned by the people of this region. Sugar mills, banana plantations, mines, and other sources of wealth often belong to businessmen in the United States or other countries. Many people in the Caribbean Lands region deeply resent these foreign-owned companies. They believe that foreigners are more interested in making money than in helping them solve their problems.

An important problem in many Caribbean countries has been lack of democratic government. These countries have a long history of revolution and dictatorship. In much of the Caribbean Lands region, the people are generally poor and uneducated. They have had almost no opportunity to decide how they are to be governed. Only in recent years have some of the people received enough education to understand the idea of governing themselves. In some Caribbean countries, the government is still controlled by men who are more interested in getting rich in office than in the needs of the people.

The Caribbean countries are threatened by communism. The poverty and discontent in the Caribbean Lands have caused some people to turn to communism as a means of solving their problems. Although the Communists are few in number, they are well organized and devoted to their cause. They are experienced in propaganda techniques and are well trained as leaders. The Communists promise to help the less fortunate people of the Caribbean Lands by a more equal distribution of land and wealth. These promises appeal to landless farmers and underpaid workers.

Many students and other people who are impatient with the lack of progress under their present system of government are also attracted to communism.

In one Caribbean country, the Communists have succeeded in gaining power. On January 1, 1959, revolutionary forces led by Fidel Castro seized control of the government of Cuba. Castro soon began a program to make Cuba a Communist nation under his dictatorship. He refused to allow free elections, and persons who opposed his government were arrested and punished. Castro seized oil refineries, sugar mills,

Fidel Castro, prime minister of Communist Cuba, visiting the Soviet Union. Cuba is the only country in the Caribbean Lands in which the Communists have succeeded in gaining power. The United States is firmly opposed to the spread of communism in the Western Hemisphere.

and other property owned by Cuban companies and foreign business firms. In recent years, Cuba has tried to spread Communist ideas throughout Latin America.

In October, 1962, military activity in Cuba produced a crisis that affected the entire world. United States planes flying over Cuba took photographs showing that the Soviet Union was installing missiles there. If these missiles were ever fired against the United States, they could destroy many of our cities. The president of the United States, John F. Kennedy, ordered a "quarantine," or partial blockade, of Cuba, and demanded that the Russians remove the missiles. For several days, the world was faced with the danger of atomic war. The crisis ended when the Russians gave in to President Kennedy's demand to remove the missiles. However, communism in Cuba remains a threat to the Caribbean Lands and to the United States.

The United States is helping the people of the Caribbean Lands. The United States is trying to show the people of the Caribbean Lands how to raise their standard of living in a democratic way. Our government is anxious to prevent the spread of communism from Cuba to other countries in this region. In 1961, President Kennedy announced a ten-year program of assistance to Latin America. This program is called the "Alliance for Progress." Most Caribbean countries are members of this alliance. The program of the Alliance for Progress calls for spending $20 billion in ten years. This money is to be spent in improving education, health, and housing, and for other projects throughout Latin America. The United States

government will provide about half of the total amount to be spent. The rest will come from other countries and from private businessmen.

The people of the Caribbean Lands are learning to help themselves. Some countries in the Caribbean Lands region have recognized that they cannot rely entirely on outside aid to solve their problems. Puerto Rico, for example, has made a great effort to raise its standard of living. The average yearly income of Puerto Ricans today is about five times as large as it was in 1940. Chapter 25 tells how this was accomplished in a democratic manner through a program called "Operation Bootstrap."

In Central America, a "common market" has been formed. All of the Central American republics except Panama have agreed to cooperate in trading with one another. Taxes are gradually being lowered on goods shipped between countries belonging to the common market. The purpose of the Central American common market is to help these countries expand their industry, and to increase trade between them.

Although some countries of the Caribbean Lands are trying to help themselves, most of them are too poor to succeed without some assistance. The United States can provide guidance for the countries of the Caribbean Lands region. Our nation has the wealth, the technical skills, and the democratic traditions that are desperately needed in this area. In order to provide wise guidance, we must learn as much as possible about our Caribbean neighbors. By studying their problems, we shall be able to see more clearly what must be done to help them find a better way of life.

ARIZONA

NEW MEXICO

OKLAHOMA

UNITED STA

ARKANSAS

TENNE

Mississippi River

MISSISSIPPI

LOUISIANA

ALABA

110°

100°

90°

El Paso

Ciudad Juárez

Chihuahua

TEXAS

Rio Grande

Nuevo Laredo

Laredo

Houston

New Orleans

30°

SIERRA

Torreón

Monterrey

Durango

GULF OF MEXICO

Mazatlán

SIERRA MADRE OCCIDENTAL

SIERRA MADRE ORIENTAL

TROPIC OF CANCER

San Luis Potosí

Tampico

20°

Guadalajara

Mérida

Mexico City

Yucatán

Peninsula

Puebla

Veracruz

Acapulco

M

Oaxaca

E

X

I

C

O

BRITISH

HONDUR

GUATEMALA

HONDUR

Guatemala City

Tegucigalpa

San Salvador

EL

SALVADOR

CENTRAL

NIC

Managua

Lower California

GULF OF CALIFORNIA

California

P

A

C

I

F

I

C

O

C

E

A

N

CARIBBEAN SEA

80°

Colón

10°

Gatun Locks

Gatun Lake

Madden Lake

CANAL

ZONE

PANAMA

9°

Pedro Miguel Locks

Miraflores Locks

Panama City

PACIFIC OCEAN

Scale of Miles

0 5 10 15 20 25

COPYRIGHT BY RAND McNALLY & CO.
MADE IN U.S.A.

110°

100°

90° West Longitude

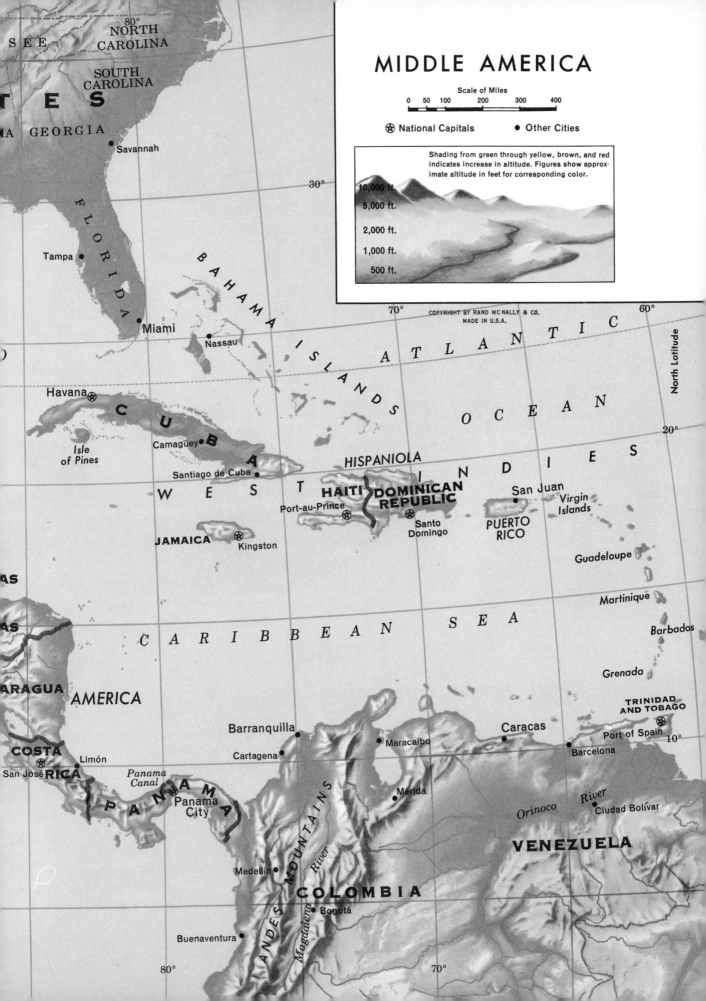

MIDDLE AMERICA

Scale of Miles

0 50 100   200   300   400

⊗ National Capitals   • Other Cities

Shading from green through yellow, brown, and red
indicates increase in altitude. Figures show approximate altitude in feet for corresponding color.

10,000 ft.
5,000 ft.
2,000 ft.
1,000 ft.
500 ft.

COPYRIGHT BY RAND MC NALLY & CO.
MADE IN U.S.A.

SEE

NORTH
CAROLINA
80°

SOUTH
CAROLINA

IA GEORGIA

• Savannah

30°

FLORIDA

Tampa •

• Miami

BAHAMA ISLANDS

• Nassau

70°

ATLANTIC

OCEAN

North Latitude

60°

Havana ⊗

CUBA

Isle
of Pines

Camagüey •

Santiago de Cuba •

WEST

HISPANIOLA

20°

I N D I E S

JAMAICA ⊗
Kingston

HAITI DOMINICAN
REPUBLIC

Port-au-Prince ⊗

Santo
Domingo

San Juan •

PUERTO
RICO

Virgin
Islands

Guadeloupe

CARIBBEAN   SEA

Martinique

Barbados

Grenada

TRINIDAD
AND TOBAGO

AS

AS

ARAGUA   AMERICA

COSTA
San José ⊗ RICA

Limón •

Panama
Canal

PANAMA

Panama
City

Barranquilla •

Cartagena •

• Maracaibo

Caracas •

• Mérida

Port of Spain ⊗

Barcelona •

10°

ANDES MOUNTAINS

Magdalena River

Orinoco

River

Ciudad Bolívar

VENEZUELA

Medellín •

COLOMBIA

• Bogotá

Buenaventura •

80°

70°

CARIBBEAN LANDS
GEOGRAPHICAL DIVISIONS
CENTRAL AMERICA
WEST INDIES:
Bahama Islands
Greater Antilles
Lesser Antilles
Volcanoes in
Central America ▲

0   150   300
Scale of Miles

UNITED STATES

GULF OF MEXICO

ATLANTIC

OCEAN

BAHAMA ISLANDS

MEXICO

GREATER

ANTILLES

CENTRAL

AMERICA

CARIBBEAN   SEA

PACIFIC

OCEAN

LESSER ANTILLES

COLOMBIA

VENEZUELA

The Caribbean Lands region is made up of Central America and the West Indies.

1 Land

Problems To Solve

How do the land features of the Caribbean Lands region affect the people? To solve this problem, you will need to find out what the land features of the Caribbean Lands are like. Then you will need to make hypotheses about the ways in which the land features affect the people in this region. The following questions suggest some hypotheses:

a. How do the land features help determine where people live?
b. How do the land features affect transportation?
c. What facts about volcanoes and earthquakes help to solve this problem?

Information on page 90 and in Chapter 11 will be helpful in solving this problem.

See TO THE STUDENT, pages 6-7.

*Please see Glossary, page 335, for unfamiliar terms.

About 200 miles south of the state of Florida lies the Caribbean Sea, an arm of the Atlantic Ocean. The map on the opposite page shows that the Caribbean is bounded on the north and east by a large group of islands. These island stepping-stones make up an archipelago known as the West Indies. To the west of the Caribbean is a narrow strip of land that forms the southernmost part of the North American continent. This bridge of land joining the continents of North America and South America is called Central America.

Central America: A Land Bridge

Central America stretches southeastward for about 1,300 miles between Mexico and the South American country of Colombia. It varies in width from less than 40 to about 350 miles. Central America is not as large as the state of Texas. Yet within this small area there are six independent countries and a European colony, British Honduras. (See map on pages 14 and 15.)

Highlands of Central America. Most of Central America is mountainous. The

In the highlands of Costa Rica. A rugged highland region with many basins, valleys, and plateaus extends through Central America like a giant backbone. Transportation is a problem in Central America because it is difficult to build roads and railroads over the mountains.

Volcanic peaks bordering Lake Atitlán, in Guatemala. There are many volcanoes in Central America. Some of them are still active. Ashes and lava from volcanoes have helped to make the soil very fertile in many areas of Central America.

map on page 20 shows that a highland region extends through Central America like a giant backbone. Within this region are many ranges of high, steep-sided mountains. In the countries of Guatemala and Costa Rica, some mountain peaks are more than twelve thousand feet above sea level.

The highland region of Central America is a barrier to transportation. It is difficult to build roads and railroads over the rugged mountains. Only a few roads and railroads cross Central America from the Caribbean Sea to the Pacific Ocean.

If you were to fly in an airplane over the highlands of Central America, you would notice many lofty, cone-shaped peaks like those shown in the picture above. These mountains are volcanoes. They extend in a long, irregular chain from southern Mexico into western Panama. (Compare map on pages 14 and 15 with map on page 16.) The volcanoes were formed of lava and ashes that spurted out through openings in the earth's surface.

Many of the volcanoes in Central America have not erupted for a long time, but others are still active. Some

Words to Think With

Caribbean Sea	West Indies	Central America	Pacific Ocean
archipelago	Nicaraguan Lowland	Pacific Lowland	earthquake
Greater Antilles	Lesser Antilles	isthmus	volcano

give off clouds of smoke or steam. At times, a volcano may send a shower of ashes or streams of lava over the surrounding countryside. Through the centuries, some of the ashes and lava have been changed into a soil that is very good for growing crops.

The same forces within the earth that cause these volcanoes to erupt also produce earthquakes in Central America. Earthquakes have destroyed cities and killed large numbers of people. In spite of the danger from earthquakes and eruptions, most of Central America's people live in basins and on plateaus near the volcanoes. Here the

soil is fertile, and the climate is mild. Chapter 2 tells more about the climate of the Central American highlands.

In the northern part of Central America, there are many mountain ranges in

Facts About the Caribbean Lands		
	Approximate Area (square miles)	Estimated Population
Central America	207,900	12,923,000
The West Indies:		
Greater Antilles	81,600	19,103,000
Lesser Antilles	5,300	2,471,000
Bahama Islands	4,400	111,000
Total	299,200	34,608,000

Young coffee trees, shaded by taller banana plants, in the highlands of Costa Rica. In Central America there are many basins and plateaus that have fertile soil and a pleasant climate. Most of the people of Central America live in these areas.

addition to the chain of volcanoes. Some of these ranges extend like crooked fingers toward the Caribbean Sea. (See map on pages 14 and 15.) Between them are deep river valleys. Few people make their homes in this part of Central America. It is hard to travel over the steep-sided mountains, and much of the land is too rugged for farming.

The backbone of highlands narrows in the southern part of Central America. In Costa Rica and Panama, there are small mountain ranges that are not part of the main highland region. These smaller ranges rise from the lowland along the Pacific coast.

Lowlands of Central America. The highland region of Central America is bordered on both sides by fringes of lowland. The largest lowland is a flat, swampy plain that extends along the Caribbean coast of Central America. It is called the Caribbean Lowland. (See map below.) In some places, this lowland is very narrow. In other places, it extends far inland.

Most of the Caribbean Lowland is covered with dense rainforest. From an airplane, the forest resembles a thick, green carpet. In some places, there are patches of grassland dotted with trees and shrubs. These grasslands are called savannas.

Many rivers cross the Caribbean Lowland on their way to the sea. They carry soil that has been washed down

Central America may be divided into highland and lowland regions. The highland region is bordered on both sides by fringes of lowland. The largest is the Caribbean Lowland.

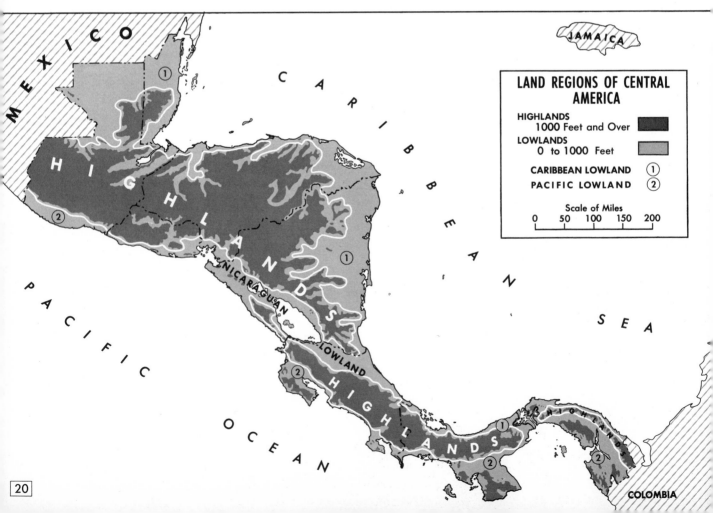

A banana plantation in the Caribbean Lowland. This lowland is a flat, swampy plain. In some places, the water has been drained off the land and tropical crops have been planted. Some of the largest plantations here are owned by United States companies.

from the highlands. Through the years, some of these rivers have overflowed their banks and deposited layers of rich, black soil on the land nearby. Although this land near the rivers is very fertile, much of it is too wet for growing crops. In a few places, people have drained the water off the land and established large plantations. Here, bananas and other tropical crops are grown.

If you were to fly over the Caribbean Lowland, you would not see many towns or farms. Few people live in this densely forested region. Much of the soil is poor for farming, and the climate is hot and humid. You can learn more about the climate of the Caribbean Lowland in Chapter 2.

The lowland along the Pacific coast of Central America is formed mainly of ashes and lava that wind and water have carried from the highlands nearby. This gently sloping plain, called the Pacific Lowland, is generally narrower than the Caribbean Lowland. In several places, it is broken by mountains that extend all the way to the seacoast. The Pacific Lowland has a drier climate than the Caribbean Lowland. In many places, there are savannas where large herds of cattle are pastured. Other parts of the lowland are covered with forests. Sugarcane, bananas, and other crops are grown in some fertile areas.

In two places, lowlands stretch all the way across Central America. These are the Nicaraguan Lowland and a lowland on the Isthmus of Panama.* (See map on page 20.)

The Nicaraguan Lowland is a level plain that extends southeastward from the Gulf of Fonseca, on the Pacific coast, to the Caribbean Sea. Most of it lies less than 350 feet above sea level.

A cattle ranch in the Pacific Lowland of Central America. This lowland is a gently sloping plain broken in several places by mountains.

The Nicaraguan Lowland stretches all the way across Central America. The fertile soil of this level plain is very good for growing crops.

The two largest lakes of Central America, Lake Nicaragua and Lake Managua, are in this lowland.

Rising from the Nicaraguan Lowland like giant anthills are more than twenty cone-shaped volcanoes. Weathered ashes and lava from these volcanoes have made the soil very good for growing crops. The fertile soil helps to explain why many people live in some parts of the Nicaraguan Lowland.

The lowland on the Isthmus of Panama forms a passageway across Central America. Here, the distance between the Caribbean Sea and the Pacific Ocean is less than forty miles. If you were to fly over the narrow isthmus, you would see below you a silvery ribbon of water. This is part of the Panama Canal, an important waterway connecting the Atlantic and Pacific oceans. You can learn more about the canal in Chapter 11.

22

The West Indies:
Island Stepping-Stones

To the north and east of Central America lie the islands of the West Indies. Some of these islands form a chain that separates the Caribbean Sea from the main part of the Atlantic Ocean. Together, the islands of the West Indies make up a land area less than half the size of Central America. Yet they have a much larger population. (See fact table on page 19.)

If you were to fly over the West Indies, you would see that the islands differ greatly from one another. A few of the islands are very large, but others are so small that no one lives on them. Some of the islands barely rise above the sea. On other islands, there are steep-sided mountains that rise thousands of feet into the sky.

The map on page 16 shows that the West Indies may be divided into three main groups of islands. These are the Greater Antilles, the Lesser Antilles, and the Bahama Islands.

In the Virgin Islands of the United States, in the West Indies. Some of the islands of the West Indies form a chain that separates the Caribbean Sea from the main part of the Atlantic Ocean. A few of the islands are very large, but others are tiny and uninhabited.

There are four large islands in the Greater Antilles. The largest islands in the West Indies are Cuba, Hispaniola, Jamaica, and Puerto Rico. Together with the small islands off their coasts, they form the Greater Antilles. (Compare map on pages 14 and 15 with map on page 16.) About nine tenths of all the people in the West Indies live on these four islands.

Cuba. The westernmost and largest island in the Greater Antilles is Cuba. (See Chapter 21.) It is almost as large as all the other islands in the West Indies combined. From northwest to southeast, Cuba stretches more than 750 miles. It ranges from 25 to 120 miles in width.

Most of the land on Cuba is level or gently rolling. The soil is generally good for farming. If you were to fly over the island, you would see many fields of sugarcane and other crops. The large amount of good farmland helps to explain why Cuba has more people than any other country in the Caribbean Lands.

There are three main highland areas on Cuba. Small ranges of low mountains rise above the plains in the western and central parts of the island. The highest mountains are found in the Sierra Maestra, or "Master Range," near the eastern end of Cuba. Some of the rugged peaks here are more than six thousand feet high.

A valley on Cuba, the largest of the four main islands that make up the Greater Antilles. Most of the land on Cuba is level or gently rolling, and the soil is generally good for farming. There are many fields of sugarcane and other crops on this island.

On the island of Jamaica, most of the land is very rugged. About two thirds of the island consists of a plateau broken by valleys and basins.

Jamaica. The island of Jamaica lies in the Caribbean Sea about ninety miles south of Cuba. Most of the land on Jamaica is very rugged. About two thirds of the island is made up of a limestone plateau. This plateau is not level. It is broken in many places by deep river valleys and by large basins. Near the eastern end of the island are steep, forested ridges known as the Blue Mountains, which rise to more than seven thousand feet above sea level. Most Jamaicans live in highland basins or on narrow plains along the coast. Here the soil is fertile, and the land is level enough for farming. (See Chapter 24.)

Hispaniola. To the east of Cuba is Hispaniola, the second largest island in the Greater Antilles. Several ranges of steep-sided mountains extend from northwest to southeast across Hispaniola. Some of these mountains are the highest in the West Indies. One peak

is more than ten thousand feet above sea level. Many of the mountains are covered with dense forests. In some places, the forests have been cleared away, and crops have been planted on the steep mountain slopes.

There are several level, fertile lowlands on Hispaniola. They lie between the mountain ranges and along the coast. In the lowlands, there are many fields of sugarcane, sisal, and other crops. Most of the people of Hispaniola live in these areas.

Two independent countries, Haiti and the Dominican Republic, are located on Hispaniola. Haiti is one of the most densely populated countries in the Caribbean Lands. The Dominican Republic is nearly twice as large as Haiti in area, but it has only three fourths as many people. In Chapters 22 and 23, you can learn more about the Dominican Republic and Haiti.

Rugged mountains on Hispaniola. Several ranges of mountains extend across this island. Some of the mountains here are the highest in the West Indies.

Some of the mountainsides in Puerto Rico are covered with a patchwork of small farms. Others are densely forested. A backbone of mountains extends from east to west through the island.

Barbados is a small, low-lying island in the Lesser Antilles. It is part of a curving island chain that extends from Puerto Rico to Venezuela.

Puerto Rico. To the east of Hispaniola is the island of Puerto Rico. (See Chapter 25.) This is the smallest of the four main islands in the Greater Antilles. A backbone of mountains extends from east to west through the island. Some of the mountainsides are densely forested. Others are covered with a patchwork of small farms. Fringing the island of Puerto Rico is a narrow coastal plain. Farmers grow large amounts of sugarcane in this fertile lowland.

Most of the islands in the Lesser Antilles are very small. If you were to fly southeastward from Puerto Rico, you would pass over some of the islands of the Lesser Antilles. The main part of this island chain curves like a rainbow from Puerto Rico to the northern coast

26

The Islands of the Lesser Antilles

A volcanic island. Some islands in the Lesser Antilles consist mainly of volcanic peaks.

The islands of the Lesser Antilles differ from each other in appearance because they were formed in different ways. Some of them are rugged and mountainous. These islands consist mainly of volcanic peaks. Other islands are flat or gently rolling, and do not rise very far above the sea. Many of these low-lying islands are formed of coral. A few islands, such as Barbados, are part of a mountain range that once extended along the northern coast of the South American continent. They, too, are generally flat and low-lying.

Volcanic islands. Millions of years ago, a mountain range deep under the sea extended from the northeastern coast of South America almost to the Greater Antilles. In this mountain range there were many volcanoes. Through the centuries, the volcanoes erupted again and again, pouring out tons of ashes and lava. As the ashes and lava piled up, the volcanic peaks rose higher. Finally, the peaks emerged above the surface of the sea as islands. Basse-Terre, Dominica, Martinique, Grenada, Saba, and several other mountainous islands were formed in this way.

Coral islands. Among the low-lying coral islands are Anguilla, St. Martin, Barbuda, Antigua, and Grande-Terre. These islands are older than the volcanic islands. They were originally formed in the same way, by underwater volcanoes. Once they looked much like the mountainous islands today. However, wind and rain gradually eroded

their peaks. At the same time, the islands slowly settled back into the sea. When the tops of the volcanoes were completely under the water, coral began to cover them.

Coral is a hard, chalky substance. It is formed by tiny, jellylike sea animals called coral polyps. Most types of coral polyps can live only in clear, shallow salt water where the temperature never falls below sixty-five degrees. The coral polyp usually attaches itself to some underwater surface. It uses calcium from the seawater to form a hard, protective shell around the lower part of its body. This shell is coral. When the polyp dies, the shell remains. Usually many coral polyps live together in a colony. Their shells are joined together, often forming a large mass of coral. Over many centuries, billions of these tiny shells form coral islands or reefs.

Like some of the islands in the Lesser Antilles, the Bahama Islands are also formed mainly of coral. However, these islands were not built on the tops of ancient volcanoes. Instead, they rest on broad banks, or upraised parts of the ocean floor.

Continental islands. Several islands that lie off the northern coast of South America were once connected with that continent. They are part of a range of mountains that extended along the coast of what is now Venezuela. Many centuries ago, this mountain range sank into the sea. Now only a few peaks, worn down by wind and water, remain above the surface. Trinidad, Barbados, Aruba, Curaçao, and a few other islands were formed in this way.

Coral formations. Many of the low-lying islands in the Lesser Antilles are formed of coral.

of Venezuela, in South America. (Compare map on pages 14 and 15 with map on page 16.) Other islands of the Lesser Antilles form a row that extends westward along the Venezuelan coast. There are more than forty inhabited islands in the Lesser Antilles, as well as hundreds of very small islands on which no people live. The islands range in size from Trinidad, which is slightly smaller than the state of Delaware, to coral reefs that are only a few acres in area.

Some of the islands in the Lesser Antilles do not rise very high above the surface of the sea. On most of these islands, the highest point is less than one thousand feet above sea level. Much of the land is flat or gently rolling. Page 27 explains how these islands were formed.

Other islands in the Lesser Antilles are rugged and mountainous. They are formed mainly of high, cone-shaped volcanoes. Some of the mountains on these islands reach heights of more than four thousand feet above sea level. One island, Saba, consists of a single volcano rising out of the ocean like a huge lighthouse. This volcano has not erupted for a long time, and most of Saba's people live in its crater.

The people on some of the mountainous islands still face the danger of volcanic eruptions. The worst eruption took place in 1902, when Mount Pelée, on the island of Martinique, exploded with a tremendous roar and a great burst of heat. About thirty thousand persons in the town of St. Pierre were killed almost instantly. The only survivor was a prisoner in an underground dungeon.

The Bahamas are low-lying islands in the Atlantic Ocean. North of the Greater

Mount Pelée, a volcano on the island of Martinique. In 1902, this volcano erupted and killed about thirty thousand people in the town of St. Pierre. The people who live on some of the mountainous islands in the Lesser Antilles still face the danger of volcanic eruptions.

Antilles, in the Atlantic Ocean, is another large group of islands. From the air, these islands resemble green rafts floating on the surface of the ocean. They make up an archipelago known as the Bahama Islands. There are about seven hundred islands in this archipelago. However, only about twenty of them are inhabited.

The Bahama Islands are low and almost flat. The soil here is formed mainly of coral and seashells which have been ground into tiny bits by winds and ocean waves. Because the soil is shallow, only a small part of the land is used for farming. Many areas are covered with swamps or pine forests. You can learn more about the Bahama Islands in Chapter 27.

The island of San Salvador is one of about seven hundred islands in an archipelago known as the Bahamas. These islands are low and almost flat.

Reviewing What You Have Learned

1. Why do few people live in the Caribbean Lowland of Central America? State two reasons.
2. Explain how the island of Saba was formed. Name two other islands in the Lesser Antilles that were formed in the same way.
3. How have the volcanoes of Central America aided farming in the highlands?
4. The two main divisions of the Caribbean Lands are Central America and the West Indies. How do they compare in area? in population?

Defining Terms

State the meaning of each of the following words. (See the Glossary or a dictionary for more information.) Then write each word in a sentence about the Caribbean Lands.

volcano	basin
rainforest	earthquake
archipelago	isthmus
savanna	lava
plateau	coral

Learning From Maps

Answer the following questions with the help of the map or maps suggested after each:

1. Which country in Central America extends farthest north? Which extends farthest south? (Use map on pages 14 and 15.)
2. Which Central American country has no coastline on the Caribbean Sea? (Use map on pages 14 and 15.)
3. Where does Cuba lie in relation to Florida? What is the approximate distance between the two at their closest points? (Use map on pages 14 and 15 and its scale of miles.)
4. Which Central American country has no land lying in the Pacific Lowland? (Use maps on pages 14, 15, and 20.)
5. In which two Central American countries does the Nicaraguan Lowland lie? (Use maps on pages 14, 15, and 20.)
6. What is the largest island in the Lesser Antilles? (Use maps on pages 14, 15, and 16.)

In San Juan, Puerto Rico, it is sunny and warm even in January. In most parts of the Caribbean Lands, the weather is warm all year round. People generally do not need to heat their homes.

2 Climate

Problems To Solve

How does the climate of the Caribbean Lands affect the people of this region? To solve this problem, you will need to find out what the climate of the Caribbean Lands region is like. Then you will need to make hypotheses about how climate affects the people who live here. The following questions suggest hypotheses:

a. How does climate help determine where the people of the Caribbean Lands live?

b. How does climate help determine the ways in which people make their living?

Chapters 8 and 10 contain additional information that will be helpful.

See TO THE STUDENT, pages 6-7.

It is the first day of January. In New York City, the temperature is twenty degrees above zero. The sky overhead is dark gray, and the air is filled with swirling snowflakes. People hurrying along the sidewalks are wearing heavy coats to protect themselves from the bitterly cold wind.

In the city of San Juan, Puerto Rico, the weather on this January day is very different. Here the sun is shining brightly, and a warm breeze is blowing. Colorful hibiscus flowers are in bloom. Because the temperature in San Juan is eighty degrees, people are dressed in light clothing.

Most of the Caribbean Lands region has a warm climate. In most parts of the Caribbean Lands, the weather is warm all year round. Snow never falls in this region, except on the highest mountains. Average temperatures do not change very much from summer to winter. (See chart below.)

A comparison of the globe on page 8 with the top chart on page 33 helps explain why winters are warm in most parts of the Caribbean Lands. Almost all of this region lies between two imaginary lines called the equator and the Tropic of Cancer. The part of the earth near the equator receives warm sunshine throughout the year. Page 33 explains why this is true.

The warm climate affects the people of the Caribbean Lands in many ways. Because the weather is never very cold except in the high mountains, people generally do not need to heat their homes. The walls of houses are often

COMPARING TEMPERATURES

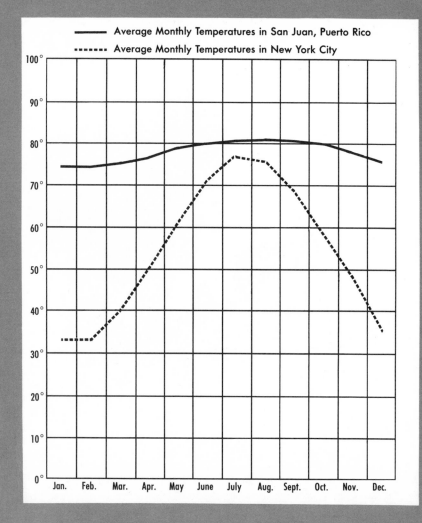

Average Monthly Temperatures in San Juan, Puerto Rico

Average Monthly Temperatures in New York City

As the globe above shows, San Juan, Puerto Rico, is nearer to the equator than New York City is. In New York City, the weather is warm during the summer and cold during the winter. In San Juan, the weather is warm all year round. Average temperatures in San Juan do not change much from one month to another. (See chart at left.) Most other parts of the Caribbean Lands also have a warm climate.

THE SEASONS

The year is divided into four natural periods, or seasons, which we call summer, autumn, winter, and spring. Each season is marked by changes in the length of day and night and by changes in temperature.

The seasons are caused by the tilt of the earth's axis and the revolution of the earth around the sun. It takes one year for the earth to revolve around the sun. On this trip, the earth is always tilted at the same angle to the path along which it travels. The chart below shows how this causes the Northern Hemisphere to be tilted toward the sun on June 21 and away from the sun on December 22. On March 21 and September 22, the Northern Hemisphere is tilted neither toward the sun nor away from it.

The chart on the left shows that on June 21 the sun shines directly on the Tropic of Cancer.* This is the northernmost point ever reached by the sun's direct rays. In the Northern Hemisphere, June 21 is the first day of summer and the longest day of the year.

The chart on the right shows that on December 22 the sun shines directly on the Tropic of Capricorn.* This is the southernmost point ever reached by the sun's direct

A large area around the
North Pole is lighted.

The axis of the earth
is tilted toward the sun.

North Pole

Arctic Circle

Tropic of Cancer

Equator

Tropic of Capricorn

DIRECT RAYS

OF THE SUN

South Pole

A large area around the
South Pole is in darkness.

SUMMER IN THE NORTHERN HEMISPHERE

The chart above shows how the earth is lighted by the sun at noon on June 21, the first day of summer in the Northern Hemisphere.

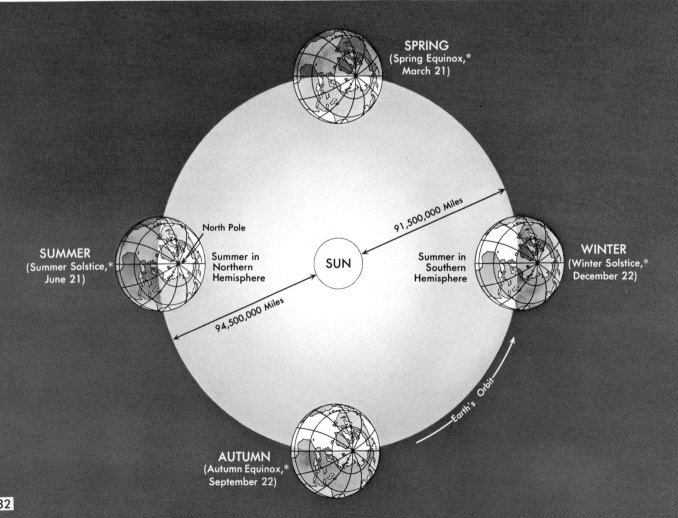

SPRING
(Spring Equinox,*
March 21)

SUMMER
(Summer Solstice,*
June 21)

North Pole

Summer in
Northern
Hemisphere

SUN

Summer in
Southern
Hemisphere

WINTER
(Winter Solstice,*
December 22)

91,500,000 Miles

94,500,000 Miles

Earth's Orbit

AUTUMN
(Autumn Equinox,*
September 22)

OF THE YEAR

rays. In the Northern Hemisphere, December 22 is the first day of winter and the shortest day of the year.

When one hemisphere is tilted toward the sun, the other is tilted away from the sun. For this reason, the seasons in the Southern Hemisphere are just the opposite of those in the Northern Hemisphere. Summer in the Southern Hemisphere begins on December 22, and winter begins on June 21.

Temperatures are affected by the slant of the sun's rays as they strike the surface of the earth. Study the chart below and the picture of Port-au-Prince, Haiti, to see why this is so.

Near the equator, the sun is almost directly overhead throughout the year. For this reason, the weather near the equator is always hot, except in the mountains. In areas farther away from the equator, the sun's rays are more slanted. Therefore, the weather is usually cooler.

Most of the Caribbean Lands region is near the equator. (Compare globe on page 8 with chart at right.) As a result, the climate of this region is warmer than the climate in places farther from the equator.

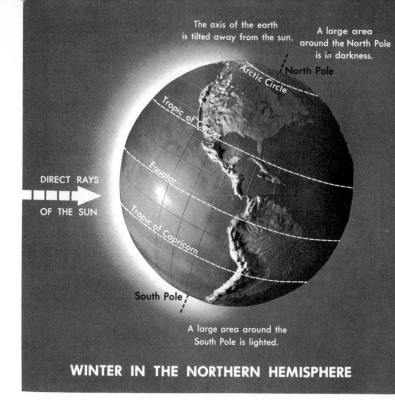

WINTER IN THE NORTHERN HEMISPHERE

The chart above shows how the earth is lighted by the sun at noon on December 22, the first day of winter in the Northern Hemisphere.

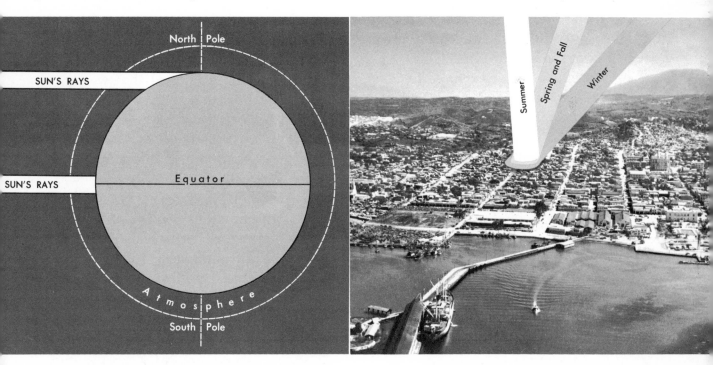

The chart above shows that when the sun's rays strike the earth at a slant, they must travel through more atmosphere than when they strike it directly. This affects temperatures because the atmosphere absorbs heat from the sun's rays. The more atmosphere the rays must pass through, the less heat they retain to warm the earth. This is one reason why regions near the equator are warmer than regions farther away from the equator.

This picture also helps to explain how changes in temperature are caused by the different angles at which the sun's rays strike the surface of the earth. During the summer, the noonday sun is high in the sky. The rays of the sun are concentrated into narrow areas. As a result, they produce much heat. During the winter, the noonday sun is low in the sky. The slanting rays of the sun are spread over much wider areas, so they produce less heat.

made of palm branches or other light materials. Heavy clothing is not needed. Many of the poorer people do not wear shoes or stockings. In most parts of the Caribbean Lands, farmers can grow crops the year around. Some of these crops, such as sugarcane and bananas, cannot be grown where winters are cold. (See Chapter 8.)

Highlands are cooler than lowlands. The only places in the Caribbean Lands that have a cool climate are high above sea level. At high elevations, the air is very thin and does not hold the warmth of the sun. Therefore, the temperature is usually cooler than it is at lower ele-

vations. Each three to four hundred feet of altitude makes a difference of one degree in temperature.

Rainfall differs from place to place. If you study the map at the top of the opposite page, you will see that rainfall is plentiful in most parts of the Caribbean Lands. However, the amount of rainfall is not the same in all places or at all seasons of the year. Some areas receive heavy rainfall the year around. Other areas have at least one dry season. There are a few places where rainfall is always light. Later in this chapter, you will learn more about rainfall in the Caribbean Lands.

Climate in Central America

All of Central America may be divided into three zones according to the height of the land above sea level. These zones are called the *tierra caliente,* the *tierra templada,* and the *tierra fría.* Each zone has a different kind of climate.

The tierra caliente. To learn more about climate in Central America, let's make an imaginary visit to the town of Bluefields on the Caribbean coast of Nicaragua. (See map on page 195.) Although the temperature here is about eighty-five degrees, the weather seems even warmer because the air is so humid. As we walk through the town, our clothing becomes soggy with perspira-

tion. In addition, we are bothered by swarms of mosquitoes.

Suddenly a thundershower begins. Soon it is raining so hard that we cannot see farther than twenty feet. A policeman tells us that it rains like this almost every afternoon in Bluefields. After about an hour, the downpour stops. We walk to the edge of town, where we can see a dense, jungle-like forest stretching out before us. Forests like this grow only where the weather is hot and rainy the year around.

The town we have just visited lies in the *tierra caliente* zone of Central America. In the Spanish language, *tierra caliente* means "hot land." Here

Words To Think With

hurricane	equator	Tropic of Cancer	*tierra caliente*
tierra templada	*tierra fría*	humid	trade winds
orographic rainfall	convectional rainfall		rain shadow

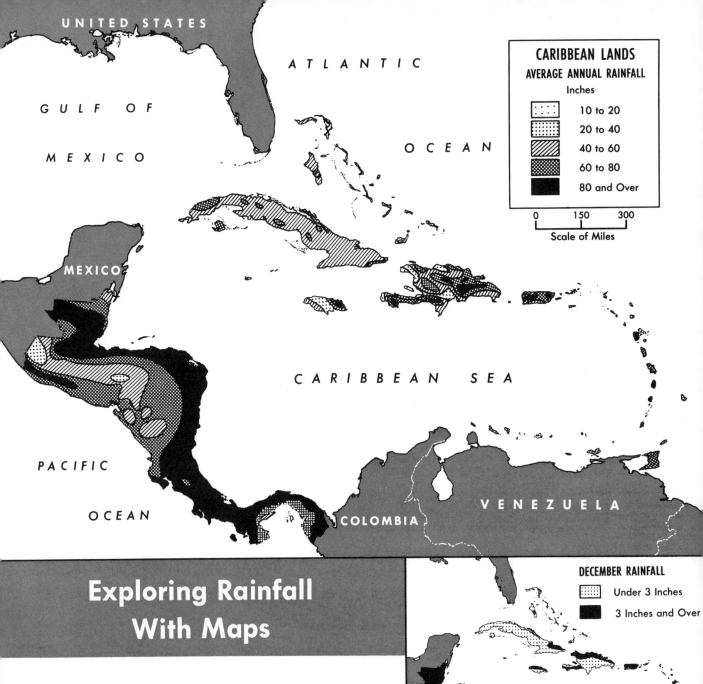

ATLANTIC

GULF OF

OCEAN

MEXICO

CARIBBEAN LANDS
AVERAGE ANNUAL RAINFALL
Inches

	10 to 20
	20 to 40
	40 to 60
	60 to 80
	80 and Over

0   150   300
Scale of Miles

MEXICO

CARIBBEAN   SEA

PACIFIC

OCEAN

VENEZUELA

COLOMBIA

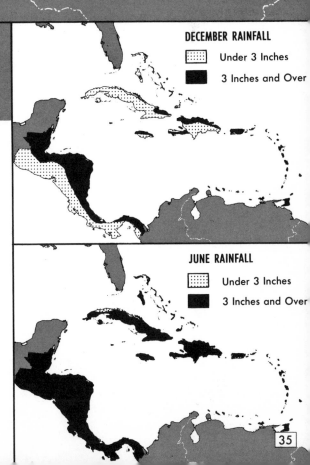

DECEMBER RAINFALL

	Under 3 Inches
	3 Inches and Over

JUNE RAINFALL

	Under 3 Inches
	3 Inches and Over

Exploring Rainfall With Maps

The map above shows that rainfall is plentiful in most parts of the Caribbean Lands. Most of this region has an average annual rainfall of forty inches or more. In the United States, this much rain would provide plenty of moisture for farming. However, the Caribbean region has a warmer climate than most of the United States, and moisture evaporates more quickly. As a result, in many parts of the Caribbean Lands, forty inches of rain a year is not enough to grow most crops.

Some parts of the Caribbean Lands receive more rain than others. Many of the rainier parts of this region lie in the path of moisture-bearing trade winds. Most of the drier parts of the region lie in the rain* shadow of high mountains which shelter them from the moist winds.

The maps on the right show that rainfall differs from season to season in some parts of the Caribbean Lands. On the Pacific side of Central America, rainfall is heavy only during the summer and early fall. During the rest of the year, very little rain falls here.

the weather is hot or very warm during every month of the year. More than half of Central America lies in the *tierra caliente*. This zone includes the lowlands along the Caribbean and Pacific coasts and the highlands up to about three thousand feet above sea level.

<u>Some of the *tierra caliente* receives heavy rainfall all year round</u>. In the part of the *tierra caliente* that lies along the Caribbean coast of Central America, rainfall is heavy during all seasons. Some places receive more than two hundred inches of rainfall a year. These are among the rainiest areas in the Western Hemisphere.

To understand why this part of Central America gets so much rainfall, compare the maps on pages 35, 42, and 43. You will see that winds called the north-east trades blow across the Caribbean Lands generally from the northeast and east. These winds contain much moisture that has evaporated from the Atlantic Ocean and the Caribbean Sea. When the moist trade winds reach the mountains of Central America, they are forced to rise. As they rise, they become cooler and lose some of their moisture in the form of rain. Rainfall produced in this way is called orographic rainfall. (See page 39.)

Not all of the rain that falls on the Caribbean side of Central America is orographic. Some of it is convectional. The causes of convectional rainfall are described on pages 38 and 39.

Because the climate is hot and humid, the Caribbean Lowland* of Central America is not a pleasant place in which

In the hot, humid Caribbean Lowland of Central America, rainfall is heavy all year long. Most of the land here is covered with dense rainforest. This part of Central America lies in a hot zone called the "tierra caliente."

to live. Most of the land is covered with dense rainforest. It is hard to clear away the trees to plant crops or to build roads and railroads. Heavy rains have dissolved most of the plant foods in the soil, so the land is not good for farming. Mosquitoes and other disease-carrying insects live in swampy areas. These are some of the reasons why most of this part of Central America is thinly populated.

Some of the *tierra caliente* has a dry season. The part of the *tierra caliente* that lies along the Pacific coast of Central America has a different kind of climate. Here, too, the weather is hot throughout the year. Rainfall in this part of Central America is heavy only during the summer and early fall. (See page 43.) Very little rain falls during the rest of the year. As a result, the yearly rainfall on the Pacific side of Central America is generally lighter than the yearly rainfall on the Caribbean side. (See maps on page 35.)

The mountains of Central America help to cause dry weather along the Pacific coast. By the time the trade winds blowing from the northeast have crossed the mountains of Central America, they have lost much of their moisture. As they move down the mountain slopes toward the Pacific, they become warmer and absorb moisture from the land. For this reason, the lowlands on the Pacific side of Central America are said to lie in the "rain shadow" of the mountains.

The map on page 43 helps to explain why the climate on the Pacific side of Central America is not dry the year around. During the summer and early fall, moist winds from the Pacific Ocean

On the Pacific side of Central America, little rain falls during much of the year. Rainfall is heavy only during the summer and early fall.

blow northward and eastward toward Central America. When these winds reach the land, they lose some of their moisture as rain.

Because there is less rainfall here, the forests of the Pacific Lowland* are not so dense as those of the Caribbean Lowland. Many of the trees here lose their leaves during the dry season, just as some trees in colder climates lose their leaves during the winter. In many places, there are savannas where large herds of cattle graze.

More people live on the Pacific side of Central America than on the Caribbean side. The climate on the Pacific side is somewhat more pleasant, and it is easier to clear away the forests for farming. In some places, farmers grow cotton, bananas, or other crops. However, the land must be irrigated in order for most crops to grow during the dry season.

The tierra templada. About one third of Central America lies in the *tierra templada,* or "temperate land." This zone includes all of the land between

CONVECTIONAL RAINFALL

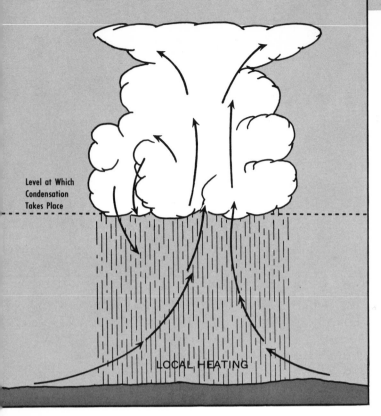

Level at Which Condensation Takes Place

LOCAL HEATING

Two types of rainfall that are common in the Caribbean Lands are convectional and orographic. Convectional rainfall (above) occurs when moist air is warmed, grows lighter, and rises. Orographic rainfall (below) occurs when moist winds are forced to rise because mountains lie in their path.

OROGRAPHIC RAINFALL

Level at Which Condensation Takes Place

Descending Air Becomes Warmer

Moist Air Cooled When Forced to Rise

Nearly all rain is formed when air, which always contains moisture, rises and cools. To understand why this happens, we must know where air gets its moisture, why rising air cools, and what happens when moist air cools.

Where air gets its moisture. Under natural conditions, all air contains moisture. This moisture, called water vapor, is water that has evaporated from the soil, vegetation, rivers, lakes, and oceans. It is mixed with the other gases that compose air, and cannot be seen.

Why rising air cools. As air rises, the weight of the air on top of it decreases. (See page 41.) For this reason the rising air is able to spread out, or expand. As it expands, rising air must push aside the air around it. This requires energy, which uses up much of the air's heat. Therefore, the rising air cools.

What happens when moist air cools. The amount of moisture air can hold in the form of water vapor depends on the temperature of the air. The warmer the air, the more water vapor it can hold. As air rises and expands, it cools. Therefore, the amount of water vapor the rising air can hold decreases. Its excess water vapor must condense. As it condenses, it forms tiny particles of water called cloud droplets. These droplets, as their name suggests, make up clouds.

Cloud droplets combine in several ways to form raindrops. Often droplets fall within the cloud. As they fall, they collide with other droplets, and raindrops are formed. Raindrops are also formed when some cloud droplets turn to ice particles. Other droplets tend to cling to these ice particles until they are heavy enough to fall. As the ice particles fall, they travel through warmer air, which melts them. Thus, they fall to the ground as raindrops. There may be as many as 8 million cloud droplets in a good-sized raindrop.

Types of rainfall. There are three main types of rainfall, which are associated with the reasons why air rises. Sometimes rain falls because of a combination of these reasons.

<u>Convectional rainfall</u>. Air expands, grows lighter, and rises as it is heated. This process, called convection, causes one type of rainfall. As you have learned, air cools as it rises. On very hot days, air rises and cools quickly. If the rising air is very moist, heavy showers may result. Convectional rainfall is especially common in humid, tropical areas, such as the Caribbean

Rainfall

Lands. It often occurs in the afternoon, which is the hottest part of the day.

When convection occurs very rapidly, creating strong currents of rising air, thunderstorms may develop. As rain clouds are formed, the rising air currents sweep them upward, several miles above the earth's surface. Falling raindrops are broken up into fine particles by the rising air. These particles develop electrical charges, some negative (−) and some positive (+). Particles with the same charge collect in different parts of a cloud, or form new raindrops that fall to earth. When the difference in electrical charge becomes great enough, electricity may be discharged between different parts of one cloud, between two clouds, or between a cloud and the ground. This discharge, or flash of lightning, heats the air through which it passes. The heated air expands violently, creating the sound waves that we call thunder. Since it takes about five seconds for a sound wave to travel one mile, a person can tell how far away a storm is by counting the seconds between a lightning flash and the thunder that follows.

Orographic rainfall. A second type of rainfall is called orographic rainfall. This type results when winds are forced to rise because hills or mountains lie in their path. As the winds rise and cool, some of the moisture they contain condenses and falls as rain. (See bottom chart on opposite page.) As the winds flow down the other side of a hill or mountain, however, they become warmer and may evaporate the moisture there. The side of the mountain that receives little rain and loses its moisture is said to lie in a rain shadow. Orographic rainfall is also common in the Caribbean Lands.

Cyclonic rainfall. A third type of rainfall occurs when a mass of warm, moist air rises in a spiral fashion over a mass of cooler and generally drier air. The wind system that results is a type of cyclone. It should not be confused with a tornado, which is a violent, whirling windstorm that travels in a narrow path. Nor should this type of cyclone be confused with a tropical cyclone, which is also a severe storm. When the winds of a tropical cyclone reach speeds of more than 75 miles per hour, the storm is known as a hurricane or a typhoon. (See page 46.)

A cyclone that is associated with cyclonic rainfall is much larger than a tornado, sometimes covering an area as large as one million square miles. The moist air in a cyclone rises and cools slowly enough so that cyclonic rainfall

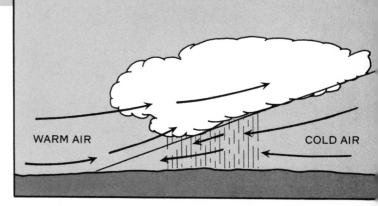

Cyclonic rainfall occurs when a mass of warm, moist air rises in a spiral fashion over a mass of cooler and generally drier air. The area in which two air masses come in contact with each other is called a front. The two main types of fronts are warm fronts (above) and cold fronts (below).

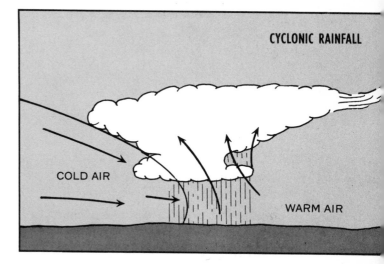

CYCLONIC RAINFALL

usually varies from a drizzle to a long steady rain. In some cases, however, heavy showers and even thundershowers may result.

This type of cyclone develops when two large air masses of different temperatures meet, and the warmer mass rises over the cooler. This usually occurs in the middle* latitudes, where warm air masses from tropical regions meet cold air masses from polar regions. The area in which the two masses come in contact with each other is called a front. There are two main types of fronts, called warm fronts and cold fronts. Usually, one air mass is more active than the other. In a warm front, the warm air mass is more active and rises above the cold air. In a cold front, the cold mass forces itself under the warm mass, causing the warmer air to rise. Cyclonic rainfall results in both cases as the warm, lighter air mass rises.

about three thousand and six thousand feet above sea level. Here the weather is cooler and much more pleasant than the weather in the *tierra caliente*. Daytime temperatures are mild during most of the year. At night, however, it is often so chilly that sweaters or coats are needed.

Not all parts of the *tierra templada* receive the same amount of rainfall. Some mountain slopes facing the moist trade winds receive at least one hundred inches of rainfall every year. Many of these slopes are covered with dense forests. Slopes and valleys that lie in the rain shadow of the mountains receive as little as thirty inches of rainfall a year. Here there are grasslands and scattered groups of small trees and shrubs. In much of the *tierra templada,* rainfall is moderate. There is neither too much nor too little moisture for farming.

In addition to a favorable climate, some parts of the *tierra templada* have soil that is good for farming. Many of the highland basins and valleys are covered with orchards of coffee trees, or with fields of corn and other crops. It is easy to understand why most of Central America's people live in the *tierra templada.*

The tierra fría. To see the effects of a different kind of climate, let us imagine that we are climbing a high mountain in Guatemala. Our hike begins in a forest of pine and oak, about six thousand feet above sea level. As we climb the steep trail, the forest becomes thinner, and we no longer see oak trees. Sometimes we notice a clearing in the pine forest, where an Indian family has planted a small patch of potatoes.

As we continue our climb, the air becomes colder. Now we see only a few small pine trees. Most of the land is covered with grass, on which small flocks of sheep are grazing. Finally we reach the timberline. Above this line, the climate is too cold and windy for any trees to grow. When we reach the top of the mountain, we are more than twelve thousand feet above sea level.

Our hike has taken us into the *tierra fría,* or "cold land." This zone covers only a small part of Central America. It includes all highland areas that are more than six thousand feet above sea level. During the winter months, the temperature here sometimes drops below freezing, and a little snow may fall on the highest peaks. However, none of the *tierra fría* in Central America is cold enough to have snow the year around.

Few people live in the *tierra fría.* Most of those who do are Indians who make a living by raising sheep or by cultivating potatoes and other crops that grow in a cool climate.

On the way to market in the Guatemalan highlands. The high mountains of Central America lie in the cold zone, or "tierra fría." Few people live here.

Pressure Belts and Wind Patterns

Divi-divi trees shaped by trade winds. The trades affect the climate of the Caribbean Lands.

The climate of the Caribbean Lands is affected in part by winds called the trade winds, or the trades. In order to understand what makes these winds blow, we must study the major wind patterns of the world.

Some facts to remember about air. Before we begin to study the formation of these wind patterns, we should review some facts about air. First of all, air has weight. It presses against all surfaces, with weight called atmospheric pressure. Second, warm air is lighter than cold air. When air is warmed, it expands. As it expands, it exerts less pressure on a surface, or grows lighter. It also begins to rise. You know that warm air rises if you have watched small particles of ash swept upward with the heat from a bonfire. On the other hand, when air cools, it contracts. As it contracts, it grows heavy and sinks, exerting more pressure on a surface. The rising and falling of air caused by heat, or by a lack of heat, creates air currents.

The formation of the world's wind patterns. Experts do not agree on how the world's wind patterns are formed. However, the explanation usually given is based on differences between warm and cool areas on the earth's surface. The equator receives more direct rays of sunshine throughout the year than any other part of the earth's surface. These rays warm the land and water, which in turn warm the air. The warm air expands and exerts little pressure on the earth's surface. Therefore, near the

equator there is a low pressure area, called the equatorial low pressure belt.

High above the earth, the warm air that has risen from the equatorial low pressure belt divides into two parts. One part flows slowly toward the North Pole, while the other flows toward the South Pole. Between the 25 and 30 degree parallels in both hemispheres, each warm air mass becomes cooler and begins to sink. As it sinks, it exerts greater pressure on this section of the earth's surface. Therefore, the area near

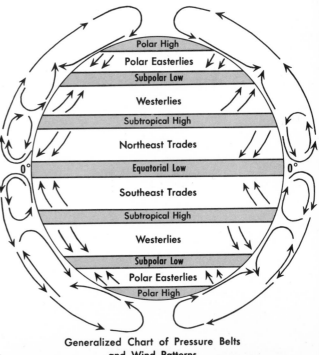

Generalized Chart of Pressure Belts and Wind Patterns

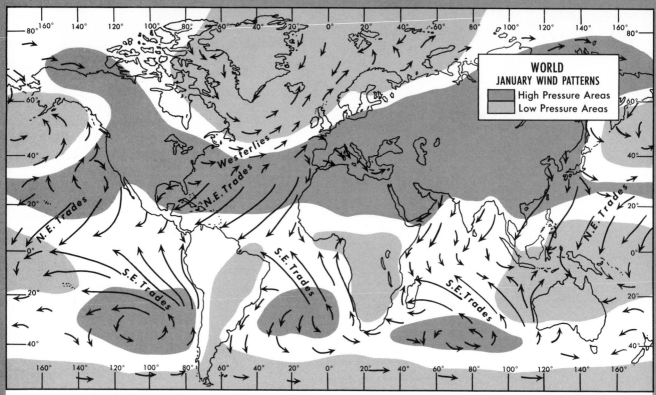

In both the Northern and Southern hemispheres, the trade winds seem to blow generally from east to west, and the westerlies seem to blow generally from west to east. However, there are many variations within these wind patterns.

each 30 degree parallel is called the subtropical high pressure belt. (See the chart on page 41.)

As the warm air cools and sinks in the subtropical high pressure belt, it again divides and moves in two directions. In each hemisphere, some currents flow toward the nearest pole, and others flow back toward the equator. The air currents that flow toward the poles are called the westerly winds, or the westerlies. The air currents that flow toward the equator are called the trade winds, or the trades.

At the North and South poles, the sun's rays are very slanted and bring little heat to the land and water. The air is cold and heavy, forming a high pressure area at each pole. These areas are called the polar highs. The air currents that flow from the polar highs are the polar easterlies. These winds, which travel toward the equator, meet the westerlies at about the 60 degree parallels. As they meet, they form the subpolar lows.

It is important for us to remember that the pressure belts are not formed as evenly as the chart on page 41 shows. It is also important for us to remember that the winds we have mentioned are only the general wind patterns of the

world. Within these patterns, there are many variations.

Wind direction. Notice on the chart on page 41 that the westerlies do not blow directly toward the poles, and that the trades do not blow directly toward the equator. This is caused mainly by the fact that points on the surface of the earth at the equator are moving through space much faster than points at the poles. Take a string and stretch it around a globe at the equator. Now stretch it around the globe at the 60 degree parallel. You will find that the distance around the earth at the 60 degree parallel is slightly more than one half of the distance around the equator. Any given point at the equator must travel more than 1,000 miles per hour to make a complete rotation in 24 hours. Any given point at the 60 degree parallel travels 520 miles per hour to make the same rotation.

Now imagine the westerlies blowing from the 30 degree parallel in the Northern Hemisphere. Although the westerlies are moving northward, they are also a part of the atmosphere that is moving from west to east with the rotation of the earth. At the 30 degree parallel, this speed of rotation is about 900 miles per hour. As the westerlies move northward, they tend to keep up this eastward speed. The farther northward the winds blow, however, the more slowly the land beneath them is rotating, so that the westerlies are moving eastward faster than the land. Because their eastward movement is faster than the movement of the earth's surface beneath them, the westerlies seem to blow generally from west to east.

Imagine the trades in the Northern Hemisphere as they blow from the 30 degree parallel toward the equator. The trades, too, tend to keep the eastward speed of the atmosphere at the 30 degree parallel. Along their way toward the equator, however, the land beneath them rotates faster than the trades' eastward movement. Because the trades are moving eastward more slowly than the land beneath them, they seem to blow generally from east to west. In the Southern Hemisphere, the principles of wind direction are the same. Here, too, the westerlies seem to blow generally toward the east, and the trades seem to blow generally toward the west.

There are many other factors that influence the direction of the wind at any particular place on the earth's surface. One is the changing of the seasons. The equatorial low pressure belt moves to where the sun's rays bring the most heat. In July, for example, the direct rays of the sun are north of the equator, and in January they are south of the equator. Therefore, the equatorial low pressure belt lies farther north in July than it does in January.

The movement of the equatorial low affects wind direction on the Pacific side of Central America. Look at the map showing wind patterns in January. The northeast trades are moving southwestward all the way across Central America. By the time they have reached the Pacific coast, they have lost much of their moisture. Now look at the map showing wind patterns in July. The southeast trades have shifted northward because of the change in location of the equatorial low. They are blowing toward the Pacific coast of Central America. Since these winds have been traveling over the ocean, they contain much moisture. Therefore, the Pacific side of Central America receives more rainfall during the summer than in the winter months.

The changing of the seasons is one of many factors that influence wind direction at any particular place on the earth's surface. For example, the southeast trades blow farther northward in the summer than they do in the winter.

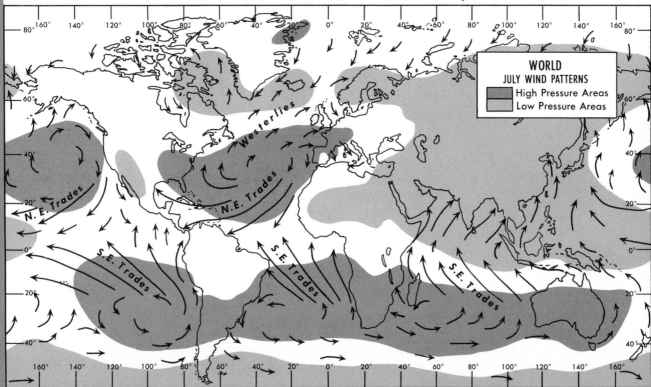

A bright, sunny day on the island of Jamaica. Most places in the West Indies have a warm, pleasant climate. Although the islands lie fairly close to the equator, temperatures are seldom extremely high. Cooling trade winds blow throughout the year in this area.

Climate in the West Indies

Most places in the West Indies have a warm, pleasant climate. Like Central America, the islands of the West Indies lie fairly close to the equator. Here, too, highlands are cooler than lowlands. However, in only a few places are there mountains high enough to be part of the *tierra templada* or the *tierra fría.* There are few large plateaus or highland basins like those in Central America. Most of the people of the West Indies live in the *tierra caliente.*

The climate is more pleasant in the lowlands of the West Indies than in the lowlands of Central America. There are several reasons for this. The larger West Indian islands, such as Cuba and Jamaica, lie farther north than most of Central America. (See map on page 16.) During the winter, masses of cool air from the United States and the Atlantic Ocean sometimes move southward across these islands. They bring cooler weather. Also, most of the islands are cooled by the trade winds that blow throughout the year in this area. Refreshing sea breezes often blow onto the islands from the Atlantic and the Caribbean.

Although the weather is warm the year around, temperatures are seldom extremely high in the *tierra caliente* of the West Indies. The pleasant climate is one reason why many people from the United States and Canada go to the West Indies for their vacations.

Rainfall on the mountainous islands. Anyone who visits the mountainous island of Jamaica in the West Indies will not have to travel far to notice sharp differences in climate. If he drives along the northeastern coast of the island, he will see that the countryside looks fresh and green. There are plantations of bananas, cacao, and other crops that need much moisture in order to grow. More than 130 inches of rain fall on this coastal area every year.

If the traveler drives across the mountains to the city of Kingston, on the southern coast, he will see a different kind of landscape. Although Kingston is only thirty miles from the northeastern coast, the climate here is much drier. There are few trees. Much of the land is covered with brown grass. Cactus plants grow in places that are very dry.

Sugarcane and other crops can be grown near Kingston, but they must be irrigated. Kingston receives only about thirty inches of rainfall a year. Because the hot sunshine evaporates the rainwater very quickly, there is not enough moisture for growing most crops.

Rainfall differs greatly from place to place on Jamaica and other mountainous islands in the West Indies. The north-

ern and eastern sides of these islands lie in the path of the moist trade winds, so they receive large amounts of orographic rainfall. (See page 39.) In most cases, the southern and western sides of the islands are in the rain shadow of the mountains. Therefore, they receive much less rainfall. In these areas, much of the land is used for grazing. Crops are grown only where water is available for irrigation.

Rainfall on the low islands. In Chapter 1, you learned that many small islands in the West Indies are low and almost flat. Here the climate is dry. There are no mountains on these islands to produce orographic rainfall. The rain that does fall here is not adequate for growing crops because much of the water evaporates in the warm climate, and the porous soil does not hold water well. (See pages 35 and 97.) On Curaçao, Aruba, and other islands, salt water from the sea is processed to make fresh water for drinking and other purposes.

Hurricanes often strike the West Indies. It is a warm afternoon in early September. In a small town on the southern

Hurricane damage on Cuba. Much of the Caribbean region lies in the hurricane belt. Hurricanes often strike islands in the West Indies.

Hurricanes

A hurricane, or typhoon as it is called in some parts of the world, is the most destructive storm known to man. It is made up of violent winds that whirl around a calm center, called the eye. The eye is usually about fifteen miles in diameter,* but the entire storm may be as much as five hundred miles across. Such a storm is not considered a true hurricane unless the whirling winds near the center blow at a speed of seventy-five miles an hour or more. The storm itself, however, travels rather slowly, at about fifteen or twenty miles an hour.

Hurricanes form in the tropics, over large bodies of warm water. They are most frequent in summer and fall. North of the equator, hurricanes travel in a northwestward direction until they reach about 25 or 30 degrees north latitude. Then they may change direction and move northeastward. South of the equator, hurricanes move first southwestward and then southeastward. The map below shows where hurricanes are most frequently formed, and the directions they generally follow.

Usually, several hurricanes form each year over the Atlantic Ocean. Some of these storms remain over the sea. Others, however, strike the islands of the West Indies or the coast of North America. The violent winds of a hurricane often cause great destruction of property. Sometimes many people are killed. The enormous tidal waves and heavy rains that come with hurricanes may also cause damage. Fortunately, hurricanes seldom reach far inland. This is because their winds are slowed down by friction when they blow over the land.

ROTATION OF WINDS IN A HURRICANE

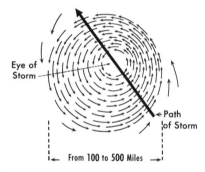

Eye of Storm

Path of Storm

From 100 to 500 Miles

A hurricane is made up of violent winds that whirl around a calm center called the eye. (See illustration above.) In the Northern Hemisphere, the whirling winds of hurricanes and other circular storms blow in a counterclockwise direction. (See chart at left.) In the Southern Hemisphere, they blow in a clockwise direction.

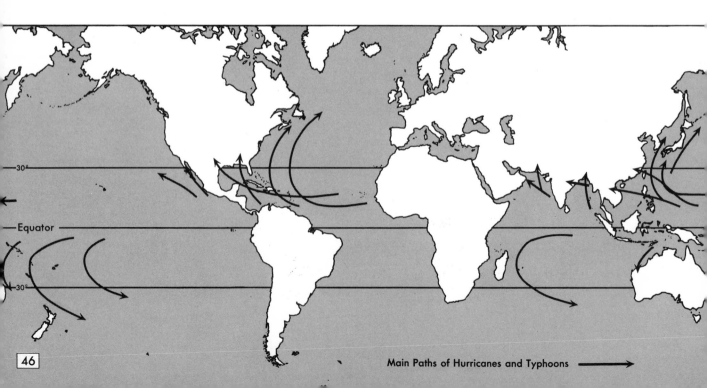

Main Paths of Hurricanes and Typhoons ➝

coast of Puerto Rico, the people are very excited. They have just heard on the radio that a fierce tropical storm called a hurricane is moving northwestward across the Caribbean Sea. Their town lies directly in the path of the storm. People hurry to the store to buy candles, canned food, and other emergency supplies. Some families go to the church or other thick-walled buildings for protection. As the storm approaches, the streets are empty.

At last the hurricane arrives. For a while, the wind is light and gusty. Soon, however, it is blowing at a speed of more than one hundred miles an hour and roaring like a freight train. The wind uproots trees and blows down many wooden houses. It even shakes the thick stone walls of the church. Sheets of blinding rain pour down from the black sky overhead. Huge waves sink several fishing boats in the harbor.

After the storm, the town looks as though bombs had been dropped on it. Several people have been killed, and many more are homeless. It will take much money and labor to repair the damage caused by the hurricane.

Much of the Caribbean Lands region lies in the hurricane belt. Several of these violent storms may strike the West Indies in a single year, between June and October. Occasionally, a hurricane reaches the Caribbean coast of Central America. A hurricane not only may wreck buildings and kill many people, but it also may destroy plantations of bananas, coffee, and other valuable crops. It is no wonder that the hurricane has been called "the dread wind of the Caribbean."

Reviewing What You Have Learned

Choose three of the following statements. Use each as the topic sentence of a short paragraph. In each paragraph, explain why the idea stated in the topic sentence is true. The page numbers after the statements refer to globes, maps, or charts that may be helpful.

1. In most parts of the Caribbean Lands, the weather is warm all year long. (Pages 8, 31, 32, and 33.)
2. The Caribbean side of Central America receives heavy rainfall during all seasons. (Pages 20, 42, and 43.)
3. The Pacific side of Central America has a dry season. (Pages 20, 42, and 43.)
4. The climate is more pleasant in the lowlands of the West Indies than in the lowlands of Central America. (Pages 14, 15, and 35.)
5. Each year, between June and October, several hurricanes may strike the Caribbean region. (Pages 8 and 46.)

Exploring Relationships

1. What two types of rainfall are common in the Caribbean Lands? Explain the causes of each type.
2. Explain why the average amount of rainfall differs greatly from place to place on mountainous islands in the West Indies.
3. In the United States, a yearly rainfall of forty inches is usually enough to grow most crops. However, in the Caribbean Lands this amount is generally not enough for farming. Explain why this is true.
4. Temperatures in the *tierra fría* of Central America are much cooler than temperatures in the *tierra caliente*. State the reason for this.
5. Explain why there is a shortage of fresh water on many islands in the West Indies.
6. Why do the trade winds seem to blow generally from east to west rather than from west to east?

A Carib Indian building a canoe. Indians lived in the Caribbean Lands for thousands of years before European explorers came to America. The Indians had copper-colored skin, high cheekbones, and straight, black hair. Some of them were farmers. Others lived mainly by hunting and fishing.

3 Early Peoples

Problems To Solve

The Maya Indians had the most advanced civilization of all the peoples living in the Caribbean Lands before the Europeans came. **Why was the Mayan civilization so advanced?** In making your hypotheses, consider how each of the following affected the Mayan civilization:

a. the religion of the Maya
b. the people's knowledge of farming methods
c. Mayan handicraft and building skills

Chapter 12 gives more information about the Mayan civilization. You may also wish to refer to outside sources.

See TO THE STUDENT, pages 6-7.

Indians were living in the Caribbean Lands for thousands of years before European explorers came to America. These people had copper-colored skin, high cheekbones, and straight, black hair. Some of them obtained their food by farming. Others lived mainly by hunting and fishing or by gathering food from wild plants.

Some historians believe that there were almost two million Indians living in the Caribbean Lands when Europeans first arrived in this region. The Indians were divided into many different groups. Some groups were very small. Others had thousands of members. On page 53, you can learn where the most important groups of Indians lived.

The Maya

Of all the Indian peoples living in the Caribbean Lands, the Maya were the most numerous. They were also the most civilized. The Maya lived in the northwestern part of Central America and in part of southern Mexico. (Compare map on page 16 with right-hand maps on page 53.) No one knows exactly when the ancestors of the Maya came to this area. However, it is believed that the Maya were living in Central America before Christ was born.

The Maya knew how to grow crops. Unlike some groups of Indians, the Maya knew how to plant and harvest crops. Most of them were farmers. Their main crop was corn, which may have been developed from a type of grass that grew wild in Central America. The Maya also raised such crops as beans, squash, cotton, and tobacco. These crops grew well in the area that the Maya inhabited.

The Maya were able to produce much more food by farming than they ever could have obtained by hunting or by gathering wild plants. In the region where the Maya lived, enough crops could be grown to feed many people. This helps to explain why the Maya

were so numerous. At one time, there may have been almost one million Maya in the area shown on page 53.

Because one man could raise enough food for several persons, not everyone had to be a farmer. Some of the Maya spent their time weaving cloth or making other useful objects, such as baskets and pottery. Others were traders or warriors. A small number of men were priests. The priests not only conducted religious ceremonies but also ruled over the people.

Religion was very important to the Maya. The priests were able to become powerful rulers because religion played an important part in the Mayan way of life. Instead of believing in one God, as most Americans do today, the Maya worshipped many gods. Because most of the people made their living from farming, they particularly honored the gods who could help them raise good crops. Among these were the rain god, the sun-god, and the corn god.

The Maya believed that they must not do anything to displease their gods, or the gods would not help them. When droughts, hurricanes, or other disasters occurred, the Maya thought that the

Words To Think With

Maya	Old Empire	New Empire	Yucatán Peninsula

Lenca	Miskito	Arawak	Carib	Pipil

HOW THE MAYA LIVED

If a traveler could have flown in an airplane over the land of the ancient Maya, he would have noticed many small clearings in the forests. In each clearing, he would have seen a village surrounded by fields of corn, beans, and other crops. To clear the land for farming, the Maya cut down trees with stone axes and burned the trees and brush. Then they planted seeds in holes dug in the ground with pointed sticks.

Homes. Most of the Maya lived very simply. The typical Mayan house was a small hut with one or two rooms and no windows. Its walls were built of poles covered with dried mud, and its roof was thatched with leaves or grass. Inside the hut were low stools, and mats made from reeds. The mats were used as beds.

Food. Although the Maya sometimes hunted turkeys and other wild animals, they seldom ate meat. For their main dish, they usually had thin, flat cakes made from cornmeal. The Maya also ate sweet potatoes, tomatoes, and other vegetables. For dessert, they had honey and various kinds of fruit.

Clothing. Because the Maya lived in a warm climate, they did not wear heavy clothing. Often the men wore only cotton loincloths. The women wore colorful cotton dresses. Priests often wore capes of jaguar skin and huge hats made from brightly colored feathers. The Maya usually went barefoot. However, leather sandals were worn on special occasions.

Games. The favorite sport of the Maya was a game that somewhat resembled basketball. This game was played in a large, walled court. The opposing players tried to hit a rubber ball through a stone ring, using any parts of their bodies except their hands or feet. Because it was so difficult to get the ball through the ring, the game ended when one team scored.

Trade. The Maya traded with each other and with other Indian groups of Central and South America. There was a marketplace in every Mayan city and village. People often came from miles away to exchange goods. Traders walked long distances to a marketplace, carrying goods on their backs. If the market was in a city near a waterway, the traders used dugout canoes to transport their goods.

gods were very angry. Sometimes the Mayan priests sacrificed human beings to make the gods happy again.

The Maya built many beautiful temples to honor their gods. Here the priests held important religious ceremonies. The temples themselves were usually small, but they were often placed on top of steep-sided pyramids made of stone. (See picture at right.)

The Maya built many cities. The Maya often built cities around their temples. There were more than one hundred Mayan cities in Central America and Mexico. In the cities there were large stone palaces and other buildings, as well as temples. These buildings were usually decorated with beautiful sculpture and paintings. In Chapter 12, you can learn more about Mayan art and architecture.

It must have been very difficult for the Maya to build their cities. They had no horses, oxen, or other beasts of burden to carry heavy loads of stone. There were no carts or wheelbarrows, so men had to carry or drag all the heavy building materials. The Maya did not know how to make iron, so most of their tools were made of stone. In spite of these difficulties, the Maya were skillful builders. Many of their buildings are still standing today.

Although the Mayan cities contained many buildings, they had few inhabitants. Usually the only people who ever lived in the cities were priests, who stayed there before important religious ceremonies. Most of the people lived in small villages dotting the countryside. However, they often went to the nearest city to worship their gods or to trade in the marketplace.

51

A Mayan temple at Tikal, a city built by the Maya. The Maya had the most advanced civilization of all the early peoples of the Caribbean Lands.

Mayan priests were skilled in mathematics and astronomy. Measuring time was very important to the Maya. Farmers needed to know the best time to plant and harvest crops. In addition, the Maya believed that each day was lucky or unlucky for certain purposes. Every important undertaking, such as a religious festival or a war, had to be started on a lucky day.

In order to keep track of time, the Mayan priests developed a system of mathematics. They wrote numbers by using dots (. . .) and bars (═══). A dot represented one, and a bar represented five. For example, the number nineteen was represented by three bars and four dots (═══). The Maya invented a symbol for zero long before the zero sign was used in Europe.

To learn more about time, the Mayan priests studied the movements of the sun, moon, stars, and planets. Although they had no telescopes, they became expert astronomers. They could even predict eclipses of the sun.

Symbols carved by the Maya. The Maya developed a more advanced system of writing than any other early Indian group in North or South America.

Using their knowledge of mathematics and astronomy, the Mayan priests invented a calendar. This calendar was different from the one we use today. The year was divided into eighteen months of twenty days each, and a final period of five days. Every fourth year, the final period was six days. The Mayan calendar was more accurate than the calendar that the first European explorers brought to America.

The Maya developed a system of writing. The Maya had a more advanced system of writing than any other early Indian group living in North or South America before the Europeans came. They did not use letters like ours. Instead, words were represented by symbols like the ones shown in the picture at the left. Sometimes, these symbols were carved in stone. At other times, the Maya wrote on paper made from the bark of trees.

What happened to the Maya. The greatest achievements in Mayan art and science were made between about A.D. 300 and 800. Historians call this period the "Old Empire." Among the most important cities of the Old Empire were Copán, Tikal, and Palenque. (See bottom map on opposite page.)

Sometime after 800, the Maya abandoned their great cities in Central America. No one knows why this happened. The people may have left because of diseases, such as yellow fever and malaria. Perhaps after many years of farming, the soil became less fertile and no longer produced good crops. The people may have moved to other areas where the soil was more fertile. Some historians believe that the Mayan peasants revolted against their rulers and drove them out of the area. If that is what

Early Peoples of the Caribbean Lands

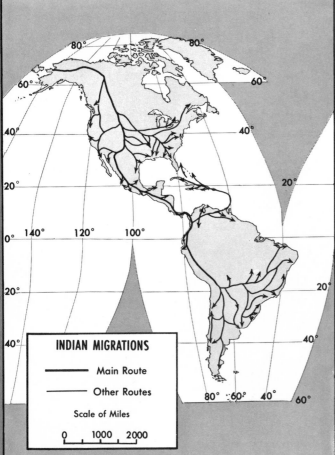

INDIAN MIGRATIONS

—— Main Route

— Other Routes

Scale of Miles

0   1000   2000

Before the white men came, there were Indian groups living in nearly all parts of the Caribbean Lands. The two maps below show where some of these groups lived. Compare the top map with the map on page 16. The Bahamas and the islands of the Greater Antilles were inhabited by the Arawak Indians. The Carib lived in the Lesser Antilles. Central America was the home of many groups of Indians. Except for the Maya, these groups were fairly small.

The Maya made up the largest and most civilized group of Indians in the Caribbean region. These Indians lived in the northwestern part of Central America and in part of southern Mexico. They built many great cities, such as Copán, Tikal, and Chichén Itzá. By studying the remains of these cities, scientists have been able to learn much about the Mayan civilization.

Most historians believe that the people we now call Indians first came to America from Asia. The map above shows the routes that these people may have followed.

Compare this map with the map on page 60. You can see that Asia and North America are very close together in the far north. Here they are separated only by a narrow stretch of water called the Bering Strait. About twenty thousand years ago, the oceans of the world were shallower than they are today. At that time, a bridge of land may have connected Asia and North America. It would have been fairly easy for people to travel from one continent to the other.

The people who came from Asia were wandering hunters. They probably came to America to hunt animals for meat and for skins to make clothing. Some of these people stayed in the far north to hunt such animals as walrus and seal. However, most of them traveled southward to make their homes in warmer regions. Over the centuries, Indian groups settled in many parts of North and South America.

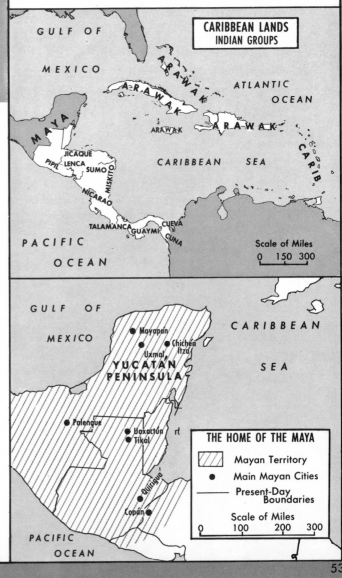

CARIBBEAN LANDS
INDIAN GROUPS

GULF OF MEXICO

ARAWAK

ATLANTIC OCEAN

ARAWAK

ARAWAK

ARAWAK

MAYA

JICAQUE
PIPIL LENCA
SUMO
MISKITO

CARIBBEAN SEA

CARIB

NICARAO

TALAMANCA GUAYMI CUEVA
CUNA

PACIFIC OCEAN

Scale of Miles
0   150   300

GULF OF MEXICO

CARIBBEAN

SEA

• Mayapán
Uxmal • • Chichén Itzá

YUCATAN PENINSULA

• Palenque

• Uaxactún
• Tikal

• Quiriguá

• Copán

THE HOME OF THE MAYA

▨ Mayan Territory

• Main Mayan Cities

— Present-Day Boundaries

Scale of Miles
0   100   200   300

PACIFIC OCEAN

happened, the peasants may have continued to live in villages near the abandoned cities.

During the 900's, a new Mayan civilization grew up in the northern part of the Yucatán Peninsula. (See page 53.) It lasted about four or five hundred years. This period is called the "New Empire." The most important cities of the New Empire were Chichén Itzá and Mayapán. For a while, the Mayan cities of Yucatán were strong and prosperous. Then they began fighting against each other. Later, some of these cities were also abandoned. When the first Europeans arrived, in the 1500's, large numbers of the Maya still lived in Mexico and Central America. However, these people had forgotten most of the great accomplishments of their ancestors.

Other Indian Peoples

Central America was the home of other Indian peoples. Many groups of Indians besides the Maya lived in Central America. (See page 53.) Some of them, such as the Pipil and the Lenca, lived in the highlands. They hunted and fished part of the time, but they obtained most of their food by farming. Other tribes, such as the Miskito, lived in the hot, humid lowlands. These Indians lived mainly by hunting and fishing.

An Indian home. There were many groups of Indians in Central America. Some lived mainly by hunting and fishing. Others grew crops in forest clearings.

The other Central American Indians were not as advanced as the Maya. They had little time for art or science, because they were too busy producing food. Many of them practiced "shifting agriculture." They would make a clearing in the forest and grow crops for a few years. When the soil wore out, they would move to another part of the forest.

Arawak and Carib Indians lived in the West Indies. A group of Indians called the Arawak lived on the islands of the Greater Antilles and on the Bahamas. They were a peaceable people who made their living mainly by farming. The Arawak grew corn, manioc, cotton, tobacco, and other crops. In some dry areas, they irrigated their fields in order to grow crops. Hunting was not important to the Arawak, because there were few animals on the islands.

Most of the Arawak lived in large villages ruled by powerful chiefs. Their houses were small, round huts called *bohíos,* which were made of poles and palm leaves. The houses contained very little furniture. Most of the people slept in hammocks. Unlike the Maya, the

54

Arawak were not skilled at weaving, pottery making, and other handicrafts. However, they did make idols of gold, wood, and other materials. These idols represented the spirits that the Arawak worshipped.

The Carib Indians lived on the islands of the Lesser Antilles. They grew manioc and various tropical fruits, such as pineapples and papayas. Carib villages were usually small, with a large house in the center where all the men ate and slept. The women and children lived in smaller houses nearby. The Carib were excellent sailors. They traveled from one island to another in sailboats that held as many as fifty persons.

Unlike the Arawak, the Carib were very warlike. They killed and ate the men they captured. Our word "cannibal" comes from *Caríbales,* a word used by the Spanish to describe the Carib In-

Carib Indians, who were fierce warriors, lived in the Lesser Antilles. Peaceable Arawak Indians lived in the Greater Antilles and the Bahamas.

dians. The Caribbean Sea is named for these fierce warriors. In Chapter 4, you can learn what happened to the Carib, the Maya, and other Indian peoples after Europeans came to America.

Defining Terms

State the meaning of the following, and relate each to the early peoples of the Caribbean Lands.

Yucatán   *bohíos*
shifting agriculture   Old Empire
Tikal

Finding More Information

Many discoveries about the early peoples of the Caribbean Lands have been made by archaeologists. Archaeologists are scientists who study the remains of ancient civilizations. Their science is called archaeology. Read about archaeology in at least two outside sources. Then write a report in which you answer the following questions:

a. How do archaeologists find and gather the remains of ancient civilizations?

b. How can an archaeologist determine the age of the materials he finds?

c. How does the scientist use the materials he finds, such as tools and carvings, to draw conclusions about the civilization he is studying?

Think and Write

1. Why were other Indian groups of the Caribbean Lands less advanced than the Maya? State one reason.
2. Why was religion so important to the Maya? List two ways by which they tried to please their gods.
3. Who lived in the Mayan cities? Why were these cities important? Give two reasons. Why was it probably very difficult for the Maya to build their cities?
4. Why was measuring time important to the Maya? How did the Maya learn more about time? How did they keep track of time?
5. How were the Arawak and Carib Indians alike? How were they different?

A monument on the island of San Salvador marks the place where Christopher Columbus is believed to have landed on October 12, 1492. Columbus was the first European explorer to visit the Caribbean Lands. He thought that he had reached the Indies.

4 Europeans Come to the Caribbean Lands

Problems To Solve

1. During much of the 1500's, Spain ruled the Caribbean Lands. **Why did Spaniards explore and settle in this part of the world?** To solve this problem, you will need to make hypotheses about how Spanish interest in the New World was affected by the following:

   a. the discoveries of Columbus
   b. rivalry among European nations
   c. the natural resources of the Caribbean Lands
   d. the religion of the Spaniards

2. In the early part of the 1600's, other European nations began to claim parts of the Caribbean Lands. Their colonies became more prosperous than the Spanish colonies. **Why was this so?** In forming your hypotheses, consider how prosperity in Spanish and other European colonies was affected by the following:

   a. the colonists' reasons for coming to the New World
   b. trade with the mother country
   c. wars in Europe

See TO THE STUDENT, pages 6-7.

Shortly after sunrise on October 12, 1492, three sailing ships anchored near a small island in the Bahamas. The Indians who lived on this island had never seen a ship larger than a canoe. They had never seen people with white skin, either, so they stared in amazement at the men who rowed ashore. The strangers knelt on the beach and offered prayers of thanksgiving for a safe voyage. Then their leader drew his sword and claimed the island for Queen Isabella and King Ferdinand of Spain.

The man with the sword was an Italian explorer named Christopher Columbus. For many days and nights, Columbus and his men had been sailing westward across the Atlantic Ocean. To understand their reasons for making this long and dangerous voyage, you must know something about the history of Europe during the 1400's.

European explorers seek an all-water route to the Indies. The map on page 60 shows the continents of Europe and Asia. When Columbus was a boy, it was very difficult to travel from Europe to the eastern part of Asia. No sea route between these areas had been discovered. People had to travel most of the way by land. The journey took many months, and travelers were often attacked by robbers.

Despite the hardships and dangers, Europeans were eager to make this trip. In the countries of eastern and southern Asia known as the Indies, they could obtain spices, silks, and precious jewels. These rare goods could be sold for high prices in Europe.

Columbus and his men knelt on the beach of the island where they landed and offered prayers of thanksgiving for a safe voyage. Then Columbus drew his sword and claimed the island for the king and queen of Spain. In the years that followed, many Spaniards came to the New World.

The Voyages of Columbus

The first voyage. Columbus sailed from Spain in 1492 in search of a sea route to the Indies. On October 12, he landed in the Bahamas, on an island which he named San Salvador. Sailing southward, he discovered Cuba and Hispaniola. When one of his ships was wrecked off Hispaniola, Columbus and his men went ashore. They built a fort, called La Navidad, from the timbers of the wrecked ship. Leaving some men there, Columbus returned to Spain to tell of his discoveries.

The second voyage. Columbus returned to the West Indies in 1493. He discovered Guadeloupe, the Virgin Islands, Puerto Rico, and several other islands. Sailing to Hispaniola, he found La Navidad destroyed by Indians. Columbus started a new settlement, called Isabella. After exploring part of the southern coast of Cuba, he sailed southward and discovered Jamaica. Then he continued exploring the Cuban coast. Returning to Hispaniola, he stayed there more than a year before returning to Spain.

The third voyage. On his next voyage, in 1498, Columbus discovered Trinidad. From there, he sailed along the coast of Venezuela, mistaking it for an island. Then he sailed to Hispaniola. During his absence, a new settlement, called Santo Domingo, had been founded. Columbus remained there and took charge of affairs in the colony. Two years later, a governor sent to Santo Domingo by the Spanish king arrested Columbus on charges of cruelty and sent him back to Spain.

The fourth voyage. In 1502, Columbus was allowed to make a fourth voyage. He sailed across the Caribbean Sea as far as what is now Honduras. For months he explored the Caribbean coast of Central America, still looking for a water passage to the Indies. Then he sailed to Jamaica. Because his ships were leaking badly, he was marooned there for a year. In 1504, Columbus returned to Spain, where he died two years later.

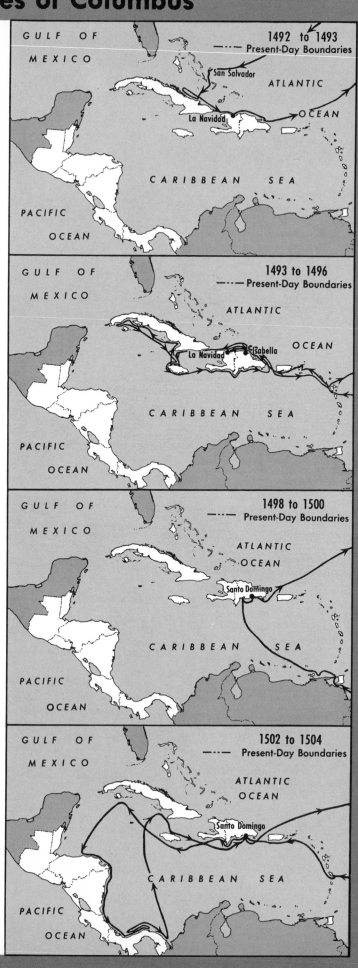

Many Europeans realized that an all-water route to the Indies would be safer and easier than any land route. Early in the 1400's, explorers from Portugal began making voyages southward along the Atlantic coast of Africa. It was not until 1498, however, that a Portuguese explorer named Vasco da Gama reached the Indies by sailing around the southern tip of Africa.

Meanwhile, Columbus was planning to reach the Indies by a different route. Like many other Europeans at that time, Columbus believed the earth was round. He thought that if he sailed westward across the Atlantic Ocean, he would come to the Indies. Columbus spent many years trying to obtain the money for this voyage. Finally, he persuaded Queen Isabella of Spain to supply him with the money and ships he needed.

Columbus sails westward and finds a new part of the world. Columbus and his men left Spain in the *Niña,* the *Pinta,* and the *Santa María.* They first sailed to the Canary Islands, off the northwestern coast of Africa, and stayed there for about a month. Then they sailed westward across waters that had never been explored by Europeans. Day after day passed without any sign of land. The frightened crew begged Columbus to return home, but he refused.

At last, the three ships reached the islands that we now call the Bahamas. During the next three months, Columbus searched for the rich cities of the Indies. (See opposite page.) Then he returned to Spain to report the exciting news of his discoveries.

Although Columbus made three more voyages to America, he never realized that he had found a new part of the world. He thought that the lands he discovered were part of the Indies. For this reason, these islands have become known as the West Indies, and the native peoples of America are called Indians.

Before long, other European explorers were sailing westward to learn more about the lands that Columbus had discovered. They soon found that Columbus had been mistaken about reaching the Indies. To the west of the Atlantic Ocean lay two huge, unknown continents. These became known as North America and South America.

Spain Rules the Caribbean

In 1492, the countries most interested in exploring new lands were Spain and Portugal. The Portuguese were not pleased to hear about Columbus' discoveries. They were afraid that Spain would interfere with their plans to build up trade with the Indies.

To avoid conflict, representatives of Spain and Portugal signed the Treaty of Tordesillas, in 1494. This agreement set up the boundary line shown on the map on page 60. Portugal could claim all newly discovered lands to the east of this line. Spain could claim all new lands lying to the west. Under the provisions of the Treaty of Tordesillas, Spain claimed all of the New World except the easternmost part of South America, which became the Portuguese colony of Brazil.

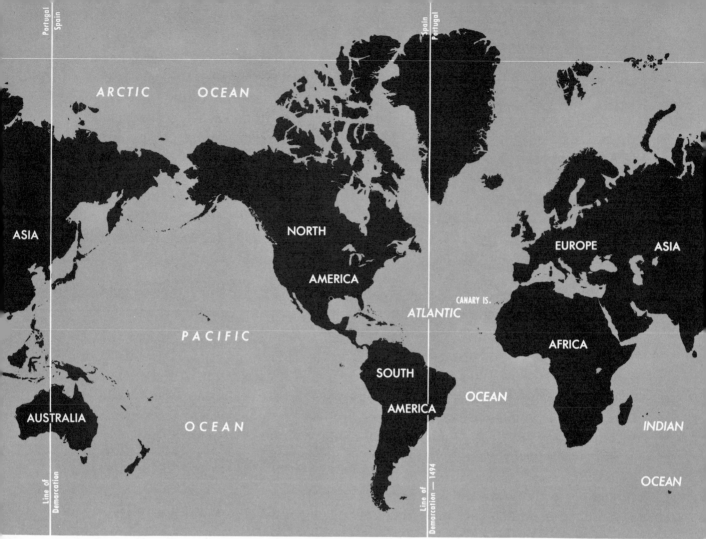

Portugal | Spain

ARCTIC OCEAN

ASIA

NORTH AMERICA

EUROPE

ASIA

CANARY IS.

ATLANTIC

PACIFIC

AFRICA

SOUTH AMERICA

OCEAN

AUSTRALIA

OCEAN

INDIAN

OCEAN

Spain | Portugal

Line of Demarcation

Line of Demarcation — 1494

The boundary line set up by the Treaty of Tordesillas, in 1494, divided the New World between Spain and Portugal. According to this agreement, Portugal could claim all newly discovered lands to the east of the line. Spain could claim all new lands lying to the west.

In the years that followed, many Spaniards came to the New World. Some of them were still looking for a sea route to the Indies. Others wanted to spread Christianity among the Indians. Most of the Spaniards, however, came to the New World in search of wealth. They hoped to find gold, silver, and other valuable goods. The Spanish

explorers also wanted to gain possession of land so that they could set up large estates for themselves.

The rulers of Spain encouraged Spanish settlers to come to the Americas. They wanted Spain to become wealthy and powerful. One way to do this, they believed, was to have colonies that could furnish Spain with raw materials

Words To Think With

Columbus   *audiencia*   Indies   Treaty of Tordesillas

Santo Domingo   Balboa   Cortés   Alvarado   González

pirate   Drake   armada   mother country   trade restrictions

not produced in the mother country. Also, the colonists could buy large quantities of manufactured goods from Spain.

Spaniards settle the Greater Antilles. The first Spanish settlements in the New World were on the islands of the Greater Antilles. It was easy for sailing ships to reach these islands, because they lie in the path of the trade winds that blow southwestward across the Atlantic Ocean. The four main islands of the Greater Antilles were discovered by Columbus during his first two voyages. In 1496, Columbus' brother Bartholomew founded a settlement called Santo Domingo on the island of Hispaniola. From Santo Domingo, Spanish colonists were sent to the islands of Puerto Rico, Jamaica, and Cuba.

The Spaniards who came to the Greater Antilles were interested mainly in becoming rich. Some of them brought seeds, tools, and livestock to start farms.

Instead of farming, however, most of them preferred to look for gold and silver.

The Spaniards found large numbers of Arawak Indians living in the Greater Antilles. (See page 54.) The Arawak were a peace-loving people. They did not have guns, horses, or armor, so it was easy for the Spaniards to conquer them. The Spaniards put most of the Indians to work in mines and on farms.

Within about fifty years after the Spaniards arrived, there were few Indians still living in the Greater Antilles. Some had been killed in battle against the Spaniards. However, most of them had died from other causes. The Spaniards grazed their livestock on the Indians' farmland, so the Indians could no longer raise enough food to eat. As a result, many starved to death. Because the Indians were not accustomed to hard labor, many of them died from

Spaniards mistreating the Indians. The Spaniards found many peace-loving Arawak Indians living in the Greater Antilles. They forced most of these Indians to work in mines and on farms.

overwork in the mines and on the farms. Still others died of smallpox and other diseases that the Spaniards brought from Europe. The Indians had never been exposed to these diseases, so their bodies had not developed any resistance to them.

During the early 1500's, the islands of the Greater Antilles were valuable mainly as "stepping-stones" for Spain's conquest of the mainland. Most of the Spaniards who came to these islands did not remain here very long. Since most of the Indians had died, there was no one to work for the Spaniards. Only small deposits of gold and silver were found on the islands. When gold and silver were discovered on the continents of North and South America, many settlers left the Greater Antilles and went to the mainland in search of wealth. The islands declined in importance.

Central America is explored and settled. Panama was the first part of Central America to be explored by Spain. A Spaniard named Rodrigo de Bastidas discovered the Isthmus of Panama in 1501. In 1513, a brave soldier named Vasco Núñez de Balboa crossed the isthmus and discovered the Pacific Ocean. (See opposite page.) Six years later, the Spanish founded a town called Panama on the Pacific side of the isthmus. From Panama, Gil González and other Spaniards journeyed northwestward into the lands that are known today as Costa Rica and Nicaragua.

Meanwhile, settlers in Cuba were hearing rumors about a rich land that lay to the west. In 1519, a Spaniard named Hernán Cortés set out from

Balboa sighting the Pacific. In 1513, Vasco Núñez de Balboa crossed the Isthmus of Panama and discovered the Pacific Ocean. Later, the Spanish founded a town called Panama on the isthmus. From Panama, Spaniards journeyed northwestward to explore more of Central America.

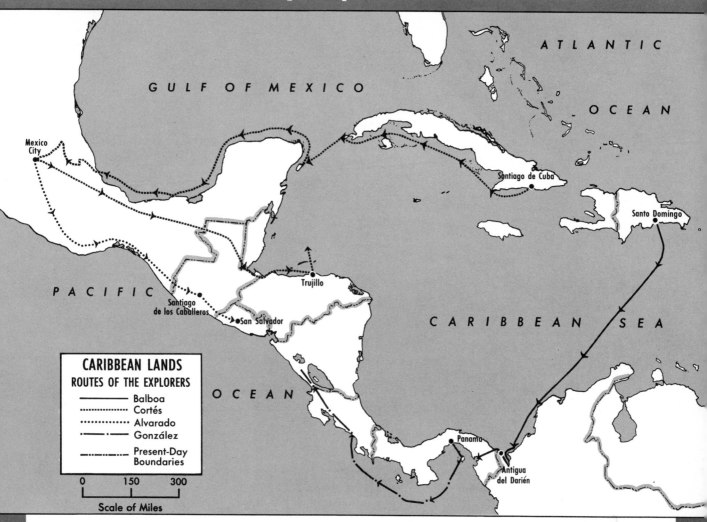

During the 1500's, many brave Spaniards explored the Caribbean Lands. Four important explorers were Vasco Núñez de Balboa, Hernán Cortés, Pedro de Alvarado, and Gil González.

Balboa. In 1509, Balboa sailed from Santo Domingo to the mainland. (See map above.) Here he helped to found a settlement called Antigua del Darién. Balboa heard of a vast sea that lay across the mountains, and in 1513, he and some of his men set out to find it. They struggled across rugged mountains and through swamps and dense forests. Finally, Balboa stood on the summit of a mountain and sighted the Pacific Ocean. When he and his men reached the coast a few days later, Balboa claimed the sea and all the lands bordering it for Spain.

Cortés. In 1519, Cortés sailed from Santiago de Cuba to conquer the land that is now Mexico. After many fierce battles, he and his men defeated the Aztec Indians, who lived near the present site of Mexico City. A few years later, Cortés set out to conquer what is now Honduras. After a very difficult journey, he reached a settlement in Honduras called Trujillo, which had been established earlier by some of his men. Cortés took charge of the settlement and made

improvements so that Trujillo could be used as a port and headquarters for further explorations. After about a year he returned to Mexico by sea.

Alvarado. Alvarado was a Spanish soldier who helped Cortés conquer the Aztecs in Mexico. In 1523, Cortés sent Alvarado southeastward into the rugged land that is now Guatemala. Here Alvarado found several tribes of warlike Maya Indians. Alvarado's army fought and defeated tribe after tribe, and finally gained control of Guatemala. After founding a settlement here, Alvarado marched into what is now El Salvador. Within three years, Alvarado conquered the Pipil Indians of El Salvador and established a settlement called San Salvador.

González. In 1522, González and an explorer named Andrés Niño sailed northwestward from Panama as far as what is now Costa Rica. Then Niño continued exploring the coast by sea, while González traveled by land. González and his men discovered Lake Nicaragua and explored it in canoes, looking for an outlet to the Caribbean Sea. Later, fierce Indians attacked the small band of Spaniards. Greatly outnumbered, González and his men returned to the coast and rejoined Niño. In 1523, both explorers returned to Panama.

An artist's view of colonial life in Guatemala. The Spanish established a number of settlements in Central America. Most of these settlements were in the highlands where the Spaniards found a pleasant climate and fertile volcanic soil.

Cuba to conquer this land, which is now called Mexico. Within about two years, Cortés and his men defeated the Aztec Indians, who lived near the present site of Mexico City. The Spaniards found great treasures of gold and silver in Mexico. They were eager to explore farther and find still more wealth.

From Mexico, Spanish expeditions traveled southeastward into Central America. One of these expeditions was led by Pedro de Alvarado, a soldier who had fought under Cortés. Alvarado and his troops marched through the lands that we now call Guatemala and El Salvador, defeating the Indians they met along the way. Cortés himself explored parts of Guatemala and Honduras.

The Spaniards established a number of settlements in Central America. Most

of these settlements were in the highlands where the climate was pleasant and the soil was fertile. In addition, there were large numbers of Indians in the highlands who could be forced to work for the Spaniards.

In most cases, Spanish settlers avoided the lowlands of Central America. There were few Indians in these areas. The climate was hot and humid, and dense forests covered much of the land. Many Spaniards who went to the lowlands caught yellow fever or other diseases carried by insects. Usually the only settlements in the lowlands were seaports such as Panama.

In Central America, just as in the West Indies, the Spaniards forced the Indians to work for them. Here, however, many Indians survived the Spanish conquest. For one thing, there were more

64

Indians in Central America than in the West Indies. Also, these Indians were usually more accustomed to hard labor than the Arawak had been. Some of the Maya who lived in Guatemala and Honduras continued to live according to their ancient customs. In other parts of Central America, most of the Indians adopted the Spanish way of life. Many Spaniards and Indians intermarried. Their children were known as mestizos, meaning persons of mixed descent.

Although the Spaniards did not find much gold and silver in Central America, they did find areas with fertile soil and a favorable climate. Some of them took up farming. As a reward for their help in conquering Central America, many soldiers were given large tracts of land by the king of Spain. Other Spanish colonists could buy land in Central America for a very low price. Some of the settlers started cattle ranches. Others began to grow such crops as sugarcane and indigo for export to Spain.

Among the Spanish colonists in Central America were many Roman Catholic priests. These men converted thousands of Indians to Christianity. They also founded churches, schools, and hospitals. In Central America, just as in other Spanish territories, the Catholic Church became very wealthy and powerful.

Treasure ships anchor in Caribbean ports. In 1531, a group of Spaniards led by Francisco Pizarro set out from Panama to conquer the land of Peru. This was the home of the Inca Indians, who ruled over a large area in South America. The Inca had developed a great civilization. From mines within their

empire, they had obtained rich stores of gold and silver. Within a few years, Pizarro and his men conquered the entire Inca Empire. They began sending large amounts of precious metals to Spain.

After the conquest of Peru, the Isthmus of Panama became very important to the Spaniards. Gold, silver, and other valuable products were carried by ship from Peru to the Pacific coast of Panama. Then the goods were transported by mules and riverboats to the Caribbean side of the isthmus, where they were loaded on ships for the voyage to Spain. (See map below.) Products from Spain bound for Peru were carried across the isthmus in the opposite direction. Because of its location on this important trade route, Panama became a prosperous town.

Routes of Spanish treasure ships. Large amounts of gold, silver, and other valuable products were shipped from Caribbean ports to Spain.

ROUTES OF THE TREASURE SHIPS

Scale of Miles
0   250   500

A few cities in the West Indies also took on new importance. Ships loaded with treasure from the mines of Peru and Mexico assembled at Havana, Cuba. From there they traveled to Spain in convoys, for protection against pirates. San Juan, Puerto Rico, became an important Spanish military base. Some colonists in the West Indies made a living by providing food and other supplies to passing ships.

By the middle of the 1500's, Spain ruled over an empire that included much of South America and part of North America. The flow of gold and silver from the New World helped to make Spain one of the richest and most powerful nations in Europe.

Other Nations Challenge Spain

France and England are attracted to the New World. Spain's success caused France and England to take a greater interest in the lands to the west. The rulers of these countries wanted a share of the wealth coming from the New World. They refused to believe that Spain was entitled to all of the lands west of the Tordesillas line.

Spain and England were rivals for another reason as well. During the early 1500's, many people in Europe broke away from the Roman Catholic Church. These people became known as Protestants. For many years, there was bitter hatred between Protestants and Catholics. Protestant countries, such as England, and Catholic countries, such as Spain, sometimes went to war against each other.

During the 1500's, bands of English and French pirates began to attack Spanish ships and settlements in the Caribbean region. The pirates found it easy to capture large stores of gold and silver. Spain's navy was too small to give protection wherever it was needed. In addition, the islands and reefs in the West Indies were excellent hiding places for pirates who lay in wait for Spanish ships.

Some of the pirates were openly encouraged by the rulers of England and France. In England, these pirates were known as "sea dogs." One of the most famous sea dogs was Sir Francis Drake, who was knighted by Queen Elizabeth I of England. During the late 1500's, Drake attacked Santo Domingo and other Spanish ports on the Caribbean Sea. Once he captured a Spanish treasure ship in the Pacific Ocean near Panama and took millions of dollars' worth of gold and silver.

Spain's power begins to decline. The raids of English sea dogs on Spanish shipping led to war between Spain and England. In 1588, King Philip II of Spain sent a huge fleet of warships, called an armada, to conquer England. The Spanish armada was defeated by the English navy under the command of Drake and other famous seamen. On their way back to Spain, many ships in the armada were sunk by storms. The defeat of the armada was a great blow to Spain.

Sir Francis Drake, a famous English pirate. During the 1500's and 1600's, bands of English and French pirates attacked Spanish ships and settlements.

During the 1600's, Spain's decline in power continued. There were several reasons for this. Much of the wealth that came from the New World was spent in fighting costly wars in Europe. Also, the Spanish rulers failed to develop agriculture and industry at home. As a result, Spain did not produce as many goods as other countries in western Europe. In addition, Spain was weakened by revolts and religious disputes.

Englishmen and other Europeans settle in the Caribbean Lands. The Spanish had never tried to settle most of the islands in the Lesser Antilles. These islands contained little gold and silver, and they were inhabited by fierce Carib Indians. (See page 55.) Between 1620 and 1650, many of these islands were taken over by people from England, France, and the Netherlands. Most of the Carib died from disease or in warfare against the Europeans.

In 1655, England challenged Spain's rule in the western part of the Caribbean region. English forces captured

Jamaica, an island in the Greater Antilles. Jamaica became a hideout for English pirates who attacked Spanish ships and seaports. One of the most fearsome of these pirates was Sir Henry Morgan, who destroyed the town of Panama in 1671. Using Jamaica as a base, small groups of Englishmen started settlements on the Caribbean coast of Central America. Chapter 16 and pages 186 and 198 give more information about British settlements in this area.

France, too, obtained a colony in the Greater Antilles. Early in the 1600's, French and English pirates settled on the small island of Tortue, just off the northern coast of Hispaniola. (See map on page 250.) There were no Spanish settlements in the western part of Hispaniola, so the French gradually moved into this area. The Spanish government in Santo Domingo was not strong enough to drive them out. Eventually the western part of Hispaniola became the French colony of St. Domingue. (See Chapter 23.)

Henry Morgan and other English pirates used Jamaica as a hideout. Some Englishmen settled on the Caribbean coast of Central America.

Between 1672 and 1733, Denmark gained control of several islands in the Lesser Antilles. These islands were part of an archipelago known as the Virgin Islands. You can learn more about their history in Chapter 30.

Sugar brings wealth to some West Indian colonies. Unlike the Spaniards, the settlers who came from other European countries were very much interested in farming and trade. They knew that various kinds of tropical crops would grow well in the warm climate of the West Indies. By raising these crops and exporting them to Europe, the settlers hoped to make large profits.

At first, some of the colonists grew tobacco for export. Laborers were brought from Europe to cultivate the tobacco fields. However, the European laborers did not work well, and tobacco was not a very profitable crop.

Most farmers in the Lesser Antilles began to grow sugarcane instead of tobacco. They imported large numbers of Negro slaves from Africa to work in the cane fields. The sugarcane was used in making sugar, molasses, and rum. These products sold for high prices in Europe.

During the 1700's, the growing of sugarcane spread to St. Domingue and Jamaica. These colonies became the world's leading producers of sugar. Many planters in St. Domingue and Jamaica grew very wealthy. They owned huge estates and hundreds of Negro slaves.

The British and French colonies in the West Indies brought much wealth to their mother countries. For this reason,

Sugar making. Unlike the Spaniards, settlers who came from other European countries were very much interested in farming and trade. During the 1700's, St. Domingue and Jamaica became the world's leading producers of sugar. Many planters owned huge estates and hundreds of slaves.

they were regarded as highly valuable possessions. The British, for instance, considered Jamaica more important than the thirteen colonies that became the United States of America. European navies fought many battles for control of various islands in the West Indies.

The Spanish colonies are less prosperous. During the 1700's, little sugarcane was grown in Cuba and other Spanish colonies in the West Indies. The Spaniards were not interested in earning money from farming. Most of the colonists did not raise valuable crops for export. Instead, they grew food crops for their own use or raised livestock on large ranches. Because they did not need a large supply of labor, they imported very few Negro slaves.

The Spanish colonies in Central America were not very prosperous either. Like the Spaniards living in the West Indies, most Central American colonists raised food crops or livestock for their own use. It was difficult and costly to transport goods from settlements in the rugged highlands to ports along the coast. Only goods that were valuable and not very bulky could be exported at a profit. Among these products were gold and indigo. Cattle ranchers in Central America could not export much meat, because it spoiled too easily. Instead, they exported hides and tallow.

There was another reason why the Spanish colonies were poorer than those of other European countries. The Spanish colonies had less freedom of trade. As you learned earlier in this chapter, the rulers of Spain wanted their colonies to provide them with as much wealth as possible. To achieve this aim, the

The Spanish colonists in the New World were not allowed to govern themselves. The most important government officials were appointed by the king of Spain. These officials were required to follow the king's instructions in all matters.

The highest colonial officials were the viceroys, who were the personal representatives of the king. Each viceroy ruled over a vast territory. For much of the colonial period, all of the Spanish colonies in the Caribbean Lands except Panama were part of the Viceroyalty of New Spain. (See top map on page 72.) Panama was included in the Viceroyalty of Peru until 1717, when the Viceroyalty of New Granada was formed. New Granada included what are now Colombia, Venezuela, Trinidad, and Ecuador, as well as Panama.

Each viceroyalty consisted of several districts called *audiencias*. Within each *audiencia,* there was a high court appointed by the king. This court was also called an *audiencia*. In some of the districts, a military officer called a captain-general served as governor and head of the military forces. One of the districts that was governed in this way was the *audiencia* of Guatemala. This included a small part of Mexico and all Spanish colonies in Central America except Panama. It was divided into several provinces, most of which later became independent countries.

The palace of the captain-general in Guatemala.

A busy harbor in Barbados, about 1700. During the 1700's, British colonies in the Caribbean Lands were more prosperous than the colonies of Spain.

rulers placed many restrictions on trade. The colonists were not allowed to exchange goods with any country except Spain. Often they could not even trade with people in other Spanish colonies. Spain expected her colonies to buy the goods that she produced. Therefore, the colonists were usually not allowed to manufacture or export any products that could be bought from Spain. Furthermore, they were forced to pay heavy taxes on their imports and exports.

These restrictions made it very difficult for the Spanish colonies to become prosperous. Farmers in the colonies could export only those crops that Spain wanted to buy. Manufactured goods from Spain were scarce and very expensive. The colonists usually received low prices for their exports, but they had to pay high prices for the goods they imported.

Many Spanish colonists were unhappy about the restrictions on trade. They often broke the law by trading secretly with people from other countries. In Chapter 5, you will learn how restrictions imposed by Spain affected the later history of the Spanish colonies.

Facts To Review

1. Why did Europeans want to find an all-water route to the Indies when they already had a land route?
2. What part of the Caribbean Lands did the Spaniards settle first? Give at least one reason why the first settlements were established in this area. Why did these settlements decline in importance in the 1500's?
3. Where did most of the Spaniards who came to Central America settle? Why did they settle in these areas? State two or more reasons.
4. Why was the Isthmus of Panama important to the Spaniards in the 1500's?
5. Why did Havana, Cuba, become an important city during the colonial period?
6. Why were the British and French colonies in the West Indies important to their mother countries?

A Map Project

Using a piece of poster board, make a large map showing the Caribbean Lands region about 1790. (See top map on page 72.) Indicate the European territories in this region by painting them different colors. Your map should have a key box to show what the colors represent. Territories of the following countries should be shown: Spain, Great Britain, France, the Netherlands, and Denmark. You will need to use information given in the country chapters in making this map. You may also need to use outside sources.

A religious procession in Panama

Cubans take up arms under communism

The people of the Caribbean Lands have a growing desire for a better way of life. However, communism is a threat to the future of this region. In Cuba, which has the largest population of any Caribbean country, the Communists have already succeeded in gaining power.

5   The Caribbean Lands in Modern Times

Problems To Solve

Since the latter part of the 1800's, the United States has played an important role in the history of the Caribbean Lands. **Why has the United States taken such an interest in this region?** In order to solve this problem, you will need to make several hypotheses. The following questions suggest hypotheses:

a. What facts about the location of the Caribbean Lands help to solve this problem?

b. What facts about the interest of European countries in the Caribbean Lands help to solve it?

c. What facts about political unrest and problems of government in various Caribbean countries help to solve it?

d. What facts about Communist activity in the Caribbean Lands help to solve it?

Pages 8 through 13 and Chapter 21 give additional information that will be helpful in solving this problem.

See TO THE STUDENT, pages 6-7.

Spain loses most of its empire. For about three hundred years, the kings of Spain ruled over a vast area in the New World. The Spanish empire included the colonies of Cuba, Santo Domingo,* Puerto Rico, and Trinidad, and most of Central America. (See map at top of page 72.) It also included

CARIBBEAN LANDS ABOUT 1790

Spanish Territory
British Territory
French Territory
Netherlands Territory
Independent

UNITED STATES

BAHAMA ISLANDS

VICEROYALTY

BELIZE (British Honduras)

SAINT DOMINGUE

JAMAICA

OF NEW SPAIN

Held by Various European Countries

VICEROYALTY OF NEW GRANADA

CARIBBEAN LANDS ABOUT 1825

Spanish Territory
British Territory
Independent

UNITED STATES

BAHAMA ISLANDS

CUBA

MEXICO

BELIZE (British Honduras)

JAMAICA

HAITI

PUERTO RICO

Held by Various European Countries

CENTRAL

AMERICAN

FEDERATION

TRINIDAD

GREAT COLOMBIA

CARIBBEAN LANDS ABOUT 1900

British Territory
United States Territory
Independent

UNITED STATES

BAHAMA ISLANDS

CUBA

MEXICO

BRITISH HONDURAS

GUATE-MALA

HONDURAS

EL SALVADOR

JAMAICA

HAITI

DOMINICAN REPUBLIC

PUERTO RICO

Held by Various European Countries

NICARAGUA

COSTA RICA

TRINIDAD

VENEZUELA

COLOMBIA

72

Near the end of the 1700's, all of the Caribbean region was under the control of European nations. Spain ruled over much of this territory. The colonies of Cuba, Santo Domingo,* Puerto Rico, and most of Central America were part of the Viceroyalty of New Spain. Panama and Trinidad were included in the Viceroyalty of New Granada. (See page 69.) Great Britain ruled Belize, Jamaica, and the Bahama Islands. St. Domingue was a French colony. Various islands in the Lesser Antilles were owned by Great Britain, France, the Netherlands, and Denmark. The ownership of some of these islands changed frequently as the result of wars between European nations.

By 1825, several European colonies in the Caribbean region had gained their independence. The people of St. Domingue revolted against the French and set up an independent country, called Haiti, in 1804. Later, the Haitians conquered the former Spanish colony of Santo Domingo and brought the whole island of Hispaniola under their rule. In 1821, the Spanish colonies in Central America gained their independence. All except Panama joined together to form the Central American Federation. Panama became a part of Great Colombia. This new nation included what are now Colombia, Venezuela, and Ecuador. The Spanish island of Trinidad had been captured by Great Britain in 1797. Cuba and Puerto Rico were Spain's only remaining Caribbean colonies.

After 1825, other changes took place in the Caribbean region. The Central American Federation dissolved into five separate countries. In 1844, the Dominican Republic was established on Hispaniola. Spain lost Puerto Rico and Cuba, as a result of the Spanish-American War. Puerto Rico became a territory of the United States, and Cuba eventually gained its independence.

Since 1900, three more Caribbean countries have become independent. They are Panama, Jamaica, and Trinidad and Tobago. (Compare map at left with map on pages 14 and 15.) Some of the remaining foreign possessions in the Caribbean Lands have been granted more self-government.

Mexico, other parts of North America, and parts of South America.

As the years passed, many colonists became dissatisfied with Spanish rule. The colonists did not like the many restrictions the Spanish government placed on their trade and industry. Also, Spain did not allow the colonists to choose their own officials. All important government officers were appointed by the king. Usually the best positions went to people born in Spain, who knew little about the needs of the settlers. Few important positions were given to people of Spanish descent who had been born in the colonies. These people, known as Creoles, were jealous of the Spanish-born officials.

Near the end of the 1700's, people in the colonies began to think seriously about independence. They heard about the thirteen colonies in North America that had won their freedom from Great Britain. From Europe came the news that the people of France had revolted against their king. Some of the wealthy Creoles sent their sons to Europe for an education. When these students returned home, they helped to spread ideas of freedom and self-government.

In 1808, Napoleon, the emperor of France, conquered Spain and made his brother Joseph king. Now the ruler of the colonies was not even Spanish. Many colonists felt that they no longer owed any loyalty to Spain.

One by one, the Spanish colonies in America began a long, hard struggle for independence. By 1826, all of the South American colonies had broken away from Spanish rule. Meanwhile, in 1821 the people of Mexico had won their fight for independence.

A Spanish officer. The king of Spain appointed all important officials in the Spanish colonies. The best jobs usually went to people born in Spain.

The Central Americans gain their independence peacefully. When the colonists in Central America learned about events in Mexico, they, too, wanted independence. On September 15, 1821, a group of Creole leaders met in Guatemala City and issued a declaration of independence. As a result, all of the provinces in the *audiencia** of Guatemala became free of Spanish rule. In the same year, Panama also broke away from Spain, and became part of Great Colombia. (See page 218.)

Unlike many other Spanish colonists, the people of Central America did not have to fight for their independence. This area was not so rich or so heavily populated as Mexico, Peru, and some other Spanish colonies. The Spanish were busy trying to stop revolts in other places and paid little attention to events in Central America.

Central America After Independence

A new nation is born. For a short time, the provinces of the former *audiencia* of Guatemala were united with Mexico. However, this union proved unsatisfactory. In 1823, the provinces of Guatemala, El Salvador, Honduras, Nicaragua, and Costa Rica regained their independence. They joined together to form a single country called the United Provinces of Central America. This new nation was also known as the Central American Federation.

The Central American leaders adopted a constitution much like that of the United States. Each province in the federation had its own governor and lawmaking body. The country as a whole was governed by a president and a congress. In 1824, the federation became one of the first countries in the Western Hemisphere to abolish slavery.

The Central American Federation collapses. Many problems faced the new nation. The main cities and farming areas in the federation were separated from each other by rugged mountains and dense forests. Because transportation was poor, the people of the different provinces had little opportunity to get to know one another. Often they were distrustful of the people in other provinces.

The federation was also weakened by a bitter conflict between two political groups, the Conservatives and the Liberals. The Conservatives included many rich landowners and merchants, as well as high officials in the Roman Catholic Church. These people wanted things to remain much as they had been during colonial days. For example, the Catholic Church had always been very powerful in Central America. The Conservatives thought that the Church should be allowed to remain as strong as before. In the Liberal group were many professional people, as well as owners of small businesses and farms. The Liberals wanted to reduce the power of the Catholic Church. They also wanted to make the government more democratic than it had been in the past.

In 1830, a Liberal leader named Francisco Morazán became president of the federation. Morazán and his followers tried to bring about a number of changes in Central America. They encouraged public education and worked to improve farming and transportation. The government seized many buildings that had been owned by the Catholic Church. It even forced a number of Catholic priests to leave the country. These measures angered the Conservatives, who started a revolt against Morazán's government. In 1840, Morazán was defeated and driven out of Central America.

Meanwhile, the federation was falling apart. There was fighting not only between Conservatives and Liberals but also between groups in the different provinces. In 1838, the national congress declared that any province

74

A battle in Nicaragua in 1848. During much of the 19th century, there was great unrest in most parts of Central America. Wars and revolutions were frequent. Often, ambitious military leaders seized power and ruled as dictators.

could leave the federation whenever it chose to do so. By 1841, all the provinces in the federation had become independent countries.

Dictators gain power in most of the Central American countries. The new nations of Central America were not prepared for independence. The great majority of the people were poor, uneducated Indians or mestizos who took little interest in political affairs. Independence did not have much effect on their way of life. In each country, most of the land was owned by a few Creole families or by the Roman Catholic Church. Usually the government was controlled by the wealthy landowners. Under Spanish rule, these people had gained almost no experience in government.

For many years, there was great unrest in Central America. In some countries, the Conservatives and Liberals continued to struggle for power. Wars and revolutions were frequent. Often, ambitious military men seized power and ruled as dictators, killing or throwing into prison the people who opposed them. During the 1800's, Costa Rica was the only Central American country

Words To Think With

Good Neighbor policy   West Indies Federation   communism

Central American Federation   Conservatives   Liberals   Creole

dictator   Monroe Doctrine   Spanish-American War   Panama Canal

that made any progress toward democracy. (See page 208.)

Coffee and bananas become the main exports of Central America. When the Central American countries gained their independence, they were very poor. Unlike some colonies in the West Indies, they did not export large amounts of sugar or other valuable crops. The governments of these countries lacked money for roads, schools, and other projects. Central American leaders realized that ways must be found to raise more money.

Early in the 1800's, some farmers in Costa Rica began to grow coffee. They discovered that the fertile soil and mild climate of the highlands produced coffee of excellent quality. Bags of coffee beans were carried on muleback down twisting mountain trails to seaports, where they were shipped abroad. Taxes on coffee exports helped to provide money to run the government. The growing of coffee soon spread to neighboring countries. By the end of the 1800's, coffee was a leading export crop in the highlands of Central America.

During the late 1800's bananas became an important export of Central America. Businessmen from the United States established large banana plantations on the Caribbean Lowland.* The hot, moist climate of this region was very good for growing bananas. Because most Central Americans did not care to live on the Caribbean Lowland, the American companies brought Negroes from the West Indies to work on the plantations. Railroads were built to carry the fruit to nearby seaports. The bananas were exported mainly to the United States.

Businessmen from the United States and Europe helped the Central American countries in other ways as well. They provided money for railroads, electric power plants, and telephone systems. They also started banks and steamship companies. Because the Central American countries had little money of their own, they often invited foreign companies to invest money in important projects. As a result, foreigners came to own much valuable property in Central America.

The West Indies During the 1800's

The people of Hispaniola win their struggle for independence. The first colony in the West Indies to break away from its mother country was St. Domingue, on the island of Hispaniola. By the late 1700's, there were almost 500,000 Negro slaves in St. Domingue. Most of them worked on huge plantations owned by a small number of Frenchmen. In 1791, the slaves revolted against their masters. Most of the Frenchmen were killed or driven out of the colony. In 1804, after years of bitter fighting, St. Domingue became an independent country and took the name of Haiti.

The people of Santo Domingo, a Spanish colony in the eastern part of Hispaniola, also wanted independence. In 1821, they broke away from Spanish rule. However, they were soon conquered by the Haitians, who greatly outnumbered them. In 1844, the people

The slaves in St. Domingue revolted against their French masters in 1791. After years of bitter fighting, St. Domingue became an independent country and took the name of Haiti. It was the first colony in the West Indies to break away from its mother country.

of Santo Domingo revolted and set up an independent nation called the Dominican Republic.

Like the Central Americans, the people of Haiti and the Dominican Republic were not prepared for self-government. During the rest of the 1800's, these countries were ruled by many dictators. Changes in the government were usually made by force rather than through free elections.

Slavery is ended in the West Indian colonies. During most of the 1800's, the other islands in the West Indies remained under colonial rule. Cuba and Puerto Rico were the only Spanish colonies in the Western Hemisphere that had not won their independence. On

Jamaica and the islands of the Lesser Antilles, there were no important movements for independence during the 1800's. Most of the people on these islands were Negro slaves who were more interested in winning their freedom than in setting up independent countries.

For Negroes in the West Indies, the most important change during the 1800's was the ending of slavery. The Negroes in Haiti had won their freedom by force. In other places, slavery was abolished peacefully. Many people in Europe had come to believe that slavery was wrong. The British freed the slaves in their colonies between 1833 and 1838. Later, France and other European countries followed Britain's example. By 1890, slavery had been abolished throughout the Caribbean Lands.

Cuba becomes the leading sugar producer in the West Indies. At one time, St. Domingue produced more sugar than any other colony. However, most of the plantations in St. Domingue were destroyed during the long war for independence. The former slaves took over small plots of land on which they raised just enough crops to feed their families. During the 1800's, Haiti produced very little sugar for export.

On Jamaica and most of the islands in the Lesser Antilles, the production of sugar declined for other reasons. When the slaves became free, they did not want to work on plantations any longer. Hiring workers to replace the slaves was very costly. Also, the land had been used so long for growing sugarcane that it had become less fertile. To raise good crops, the planters had to use expensive fertilizers. Meanwhile, some European countries had begun to produce sugar from beets. They no longer bought so much cane sugar from the West Indies. As a result, the price of sugar dropped sharply. Many planters could no longer make a profit by raising sugarcane, so they went out of business.

During this same period, the islands of Cuba, Puerto Rico, and Trinidad were producing more sugar than ever before. Much of the land on these islands had not been used for growing crops, so the soil was still fertile. Early in the 1800's, Spain began to encourage the growing of sugarcane and other export crops on Cuba and Puerto Rico. The British did the same on their island of Trinidad.

The greatest increase in sugar production was on Cuba. This island had vast areas of fertile soil and an excellent climate for growing sugarcane. Along the coast were many fine harbors from which the sugar could be shipped to other countries. As the years passed, Cuba became the leading exporter of sugar in the West Indies.

The United States in the Caribbean

The Caribbean region becomes important to the United States. Near the end of the 1800's, the people of the United States began to take greater interest in the Caribbean Lands. Our country had grown until it extended all the way from the Atlantic Ocean to the Pacific. Many American leaders saw the need for a short sea route between our eastern and western coasts. It would be possible to obtain such a route by building a canal across Central America. As you learned earlier, American businessmen were investing large sums of money in Caribbean countries. Factory owners in the United States wanted to buy raw materials from these countries and sell them manufactured goods in return.

Because of its location, the Caribbean region was important to our country's defense. A powerful nation with bases in this region could easily attack the United States. Partly for this reason, the American people did not want any European country to extend its influence in the Caribbean Lands. Many years earlier, in 1823, the United States had set forth the Monroe Doctrine. This was a warning to outside countries not to meddle in the Western Hemisphere.

Cuba's fight for independence leads to the Spanish-American War. The United States was especially concerned about events in Cuba. During the 1800's, the people of this island revolted several times against Spanish rule. Each time, Spanish troops put down the revolt with great cruelty. Most Americans believed that Cuba should be given its independence.

Early in 1898, the United States sent a battleship, the *Maine,* to Cuba to help protect the lives and property of American citizens living there. One night, the *Maine* exploded in the harbor of Havana, killing 260 American seamen. Even today, no one knows for sure what caused the explosion. However, in the United States, people blamed it on the Spaniards. In April, 1898, the United States declared war on Spain.

The Spanish-American War was over in less than four months. A United States naval force destroyed a fleet of Spanish warships in the Caribbean Sea. Then American troops captured the city of Santiago de Cuba. Meanwhile, other American forces defeated the Spaniards in the Philippine Islands, ten thousand miles away. Faced with these defeats, the Spanish government asked for peace.

As a result of the Spanish-American War, Spain lost Cuba and Puerto Rico. In 1902, Cuba became an independent country. However, the United States retained the right to intervene on the island whenever it was considered necessary to maintain order or to preserve Cuba's independence. Puerto Rico became a territory of the United States.

During the Spanish-American War, Theodore Roosevelt led a group of volunteers called the "Rough Riders" against the Spanish army in Cuba. As a result of the war, Spain lost Cuba and Puerto Rico. Cuba became independent, and Puerto Rico became a United States territory.

A canal is built across Panama. Ever since the 1500's, people had dreamed of building a canal across the Isthmus of Panama. A French company had tried to build such a canal during the late 1800's, but it had failed. Shortly after the Spanish-American War, President Theodore Roosevelt and other American leaders decided that the United States should undertake this task.

The people of Panama knew that a canal would bring them many benefits. At that time, however, Panama was part of Colombia. (See page 218.) Colombia's government failed to give the United States permission to build the canal. The Panamanians were afraid that the United States might decide to build a canal across Nicaragua instead. In 1903, they revolted and set up an independent country. The United States government sent a warship to prevent Colombian troops from stopping the revolt. Then the United States quickly recognized Panama's independence.

The new government of Panama signed a treaty allowing the United States to build a canal across the isthmus. In return, the United States agreed to pay Panama 10 million dollars, as well as a certain sum of money each year. The United States was given the right to intervene in Panama if necessary to maintain order. It was also given control of a strip of land about ten miles wide along the route of the canal. This territory became known as the Canal Zone.

The United States found it very difficult to build a canal across the Isthmus of Panama. Huge quantities of earth and rock had to be moved in order to build the canal. Also, the canal workers had to be protected from malaria and other deadly diseases carried by insects that lived in the hot, swampy lowlands. The canal was finally opened to shipping in 1914.

A few days before the first ship traveled through the Panama Canal, World War I started in Europe. The United States wanted bases to guard shipping routes across the Caribbean Sea to the canal. The Danish Virgin Islands were considered valuable for this purpose because they were located near one of the main entrances to the Caribbean. In 1917, the United States bought these islands from Denmark for 25 million dollars.

The United States intervenes in other parts of the Caribbean region. During the early 1900's, the United States became concerned about conditions in Nicaragua, Haiti, and the Dominican Republic. These countries were often shaken by violent uprisings. The government of each country was too weak to protect the lives and property of United States citizens and other foreigners living there. Also, the three countries owed large sums of money to businessmen in Europe. Some European nations were threatening to use force to collect these debts.

To restore order and prevent European interference, the United States decided to intervene in the affairs of the three countries. American marines were sent to Nicaragua in 1912, to Haiti in 1915, and to the Dominican Republic in 1916. Marines were on duty in each country for a number of years. The taxes on each country's imports and exports were collected by United States officials. Part of the money was used to pay off the country's debts. The rest of the money was used for building roads, schools, and hospitals, and for other useful projects.

The United States adopts the "Good Neighbor" policy. Although United States intervention brought peace and order to some countries, it was bitterly resented throughout the Caribbean Lands. The people of this region argued that no country had the right to interfere in another country's affairs.

In the 1930's, the United States changed its policy toward the Caribbean countries. It promised not to interfere in the affairs of any Western Hemisphere nation. Instead, it would act as a "good neighbor" who respects the rights of others. By 1935, all of the marines had been withdrawn from Caribbean countries. The "Good Neighbor" policy helped to bring about friendlier relations between the United States and the countries of the Caribbean region.

United States companies play an important role in the Caribbean Lands. During the early years of this century, businessmen from the United States continued to invest large sums of money in the Caribbean countries. The United Fruit Company, founded in 1899, operated banana plantations in all of the Central American republics except El Salvador. United States businessmen owned plantations, sugar mills, and cattle ranches on Cuba. A number of railroads, mines, and electric power companies in the Caribbean region were also owned by people from the United States.

United States companies brought many benefits to the people of the Caribbean Lands. They employed thousands of workers, often paying them much higher wages than they could have received from local employers. Some companies built houses, schools, and hospitals for their workers. They carried on programs to eliminate malaria and other diseases. Taxes paid by the United States companies provided the national governments with much-needed income.

In spite of these accomplishments, many people in the Caribbean region disliked the United States companies. They resented the fact that foreigners were making large profits in their countries. In some places, the American companies were accused of trying to control the government.

A railroad in Costa Rica built by a United States company. Businessmen from the United States have invested large sums of money in Caribbean countries.

The Caribbean Lands Today

Several colonies gain independence or self-government. About the time World War II ended, important changes began to take place in the Caribbean region. The people of Jamaica and other colonial possessions grew more and more dissatisfied with foreign rule. They wanted independence, or at least the chance to elect their own officials.

Great Britain agreed that the people in its colonies should have more self-government. In 1958, the West Indies Federation was established. This federation included Jamaica, Trinidad and Tobago, and several smaller British colonies. It was expected that the West Indies Federation would someday become an independent country.

Many people in Jamaica were opposed to the federation, however. They feared that Jamaica, as the largest colony in the federation, would have to support the smaller members. In 1961, Jamaica decided to withdraw from the federation. Trinidad and Tobago soon followed. Both Jamaica and Trinidad and Tobago became fully independent countries within the British Commonwealth in 1962. The other members of the federation remained colonies of Britain. Late in 1964, seven of these colonies made plans to form a new federation. (See page 313.)

Meanwhile, the people of other foreign-owned territories were also being granted a larger voice in their government. Since 1952, Puerto Rico has been a self-governing commonwealth associated with the United States. The former French colonies of Guadeloupe and Martinique are now overseas* departments of France. The Dutch colony known as the Netherlands Antilles has become an equal partner with its mother country and Surinam in the Kingdom of the Netherlands.

The people of the Caribbean Lands seek a better way of life. In recent years, many people throughout the Caribbean Lands have grown tired of living in poverty and poor health. They know that people in the United States and other prosperous countries enjoy many comforts and conveniences that they lack. The people of the Caribbean Lands want to develop their agriculture and industry so that they, too, can have a better way of life.

Some Caribbean countries are making a great effort to raise their standard of living. They are taking steps to improve health and education. They have built dams to store water for irrigation and for producing electric power. Roads have been built to connect cities with remote rural areas. Some countries have passed land reform laws to help their farmers. New industries have been established, providing jobs for thousands of workers.

People from other parts of the world are helping the Caribbean countries. The United States government has loaned money to countries in this region for roads and for other important projects. It has also sent farm experts, engineers, and other trained people to this region to teach necessary skills. The United Nations is providing assistance

EDUCATION

Millions of people in the Caribbean Lands cannot read and write. In Haiti, only about one out of every ten people has these important skills. In several other countries, fewer than half of the people can read and write. There are too few schools for all of the children to attend. Many teachers are not well trained, and educational standards are often low.

Another problem is that many students leave school after the first few grades. Only a small number graduate from high school each year, and even fewer go on to study at a college or a university. There are not many universities in the Caribbean Lands, and most of them are poorly equipped.

Many countries in the Caribbean Lands are working hard to provide their people with a better education. The Costa Rican government considers schools so important that more than one fourth of the money it spends each year goes for education. In Puerto Rico, many adults attend special classes to learn how to read and write. Nearly nine out of every ten Puerto Ricans have now learned these important skills. The Cuban government is also carrying out a program to provide better education.

Outside countries and such organizations as the United Nations Educational, Scientific, and Cultural Organization (UNESCO) are trying to help the Caribbean countries solve their educational problems. The American Council on Education, which is composed of many educational associations and institutions in the United States, helps to provide schools in several Central American cities. In Nicaragua, Puerto Rico, and other Caribbean countries, missionaries have established fine schools.

An elementary school in the West Indies.

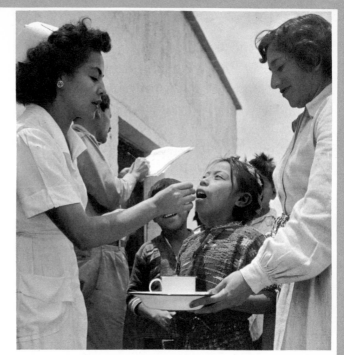

An Indian child in Guatemala receiving medicine.

HEALTH

Poor health is a serious problem in the Caribbean Lands. Among the diseases common in this region are malaria, yellow fever, and yaws.* Millions of people here suffer from diseases that result from lack of proper food.

One reason for so much sickness in the Caribbean Lands is that many of the people have poor health habits. They drink impure water and do not practice proper sanitation. Many of them do not know that flies and mosquitoes may carry disease. Their main foods are corn, other cereals, and beans, which do not provide them with all the vitamins, minerals, and proteins needed for good health.

The governments of the Caribbean countries are trying to improve the health of their people. They are being helped by other governments and by international organizations such as the Pan American Health Organization (PAHO) and the World Health Organization (WHO). Most of the countries have begun programs to eliminate malaria and yellow fever. Malaria has already been eliminated in Puerto Rico, Barbados, and Martinique. Programs for the control of other diseases are also under way. In Haiti, more than one million people have been cured of yaws. PAHO is working with many countries to provide better water supplies and more sanitary methods of waste disposal. The Caribbean countries need more doctors, nurses, and other health workers to help them carry out their health improvement programs.

In Guatemala City, Guatemala, the Institute of Nutrition of Central America and Panama (INCAP) was established to study nutrition problems. INCAP has developed a nourishing food supplement called Incaparina, which prevents malnutrition. Incaparina is sold for a low price so that poor families can afford to buy it.

83

through such agencies as the World Bank. Private businessmen are investing money in factories and other enterprises in this region.

In recent years, new efforts have been made to form a union of the Central American countries. Many people in Central America realize that a single large nation would be stronger and more prosperous than several small, weak nations. In 1951, all of the Central American republics except Panama joined together to form the Organization of Central American States. The main purposes of this organization are to work for closer cooperation among the member countries and to settle disputes that may arise between them. The same five countries have also formed a "common market."*

Many problems remain to be solved. The Caribbean countries still face a number of serious problems. Most of the countries in this region do not have truly democratic governments. Some are ruled by harsh dictators. Others are controlled by small groups of military men who came to power by force. In most countries, there is still a great gap between the few people who are wealthy, and the many who are very poor.

Communists are trying to gain control of the Caribbean Lands. Throughout the world today, a great struggle is going on between the Communist nations, led by the Soviet Union and China, and the democratic nations, led by the United States. The Caribbean region is playing an important part in this struggle. Here, as in other parts of the world, the Communists are trying to bring everyone under their rule. To attract followers, they promise to raise standards of living and to distribute wealth more evenly.

In Cuba, which has the largest population of any Caribbean country, the Communists have succeeded in gaining power. Since 1959, the island has been ruled by a Communist dictator, Fidel Castro. (See Chapter 21.)

To prevent the spread of communism in the Caribbean Lands, several things must be done. The people must be given a chance to obtain more education, better health, and a higher standard of living. Jobs must be provided for workers who have none. Dictators and military governments must be replaced by democratically elected officials. If these tasks are accomplished, the people of the Caribbean Lands can look forward to a better future.

Reviewing What You Have Learned
1. List three reasons why people in the Spanish colonies began to struggle for independence.
2. During the 1800's, what was the most important change for Negroes in the West Indies? How did this change come about on Hispaniola? on other islands?
3. Why did sugar production decline on Jamaica and most of the islands in the Lesser Antilles during the 1800's? List three reasons.

4. State three ways in which foreign businessmen have aided the development of Caribbean countries since the late 1800's.
5. Why is there so much sickness in the Caribbean Lands? State two reasons.

Defining Terms
State the meaning of the following terms as they apply to the Caribbean Lands:

Central American Federation	Creole
Spanish-American War	Liberals
Good Neighbor policy	Conservatives

People of several different racial groups live in the Caribbean Lands. Among them are Negroes, Indians, and people of European descent. Through the years, many people of different races have intermarried. As a result, there are millions of people of mixed descent in this region.

6 People

Problems To Solve

In most Caribbean countries, the yearly per capita income is less than $400. **Why do you think incomes are generally so low in this region?** Make several hypotheses to help solve this problem. The following questions suggest some hypotheses:

a. What facts about the number of jobs available help to solve this problem?

b. What facts about population growth in the Caribbean Lands help to solve it?

c. What facts about education in this region help to solve it?

Chapters 8 and 9 contain additional information that will be helpful in solving this problem.

See TO THE STUDENT, pages 6-7.

The Caribbean Lands region is a "melting pot" of peoples. People of several different racial groups live in the Caribbean Lands. Some are Indians whose ancestors lived in this region long ago. Others are descendants of European set-tlers or of Negro slaves who were brought from Africa. There are also some people from India and other Asian countries. Through the years, many people of different races have intermarried. As a result, millions of people of mixed

85

descent live in the Caribbean Lands today.

Indians. About one tenth of all the people living in the Caribbean Lands are Indians. They are descendants of the Maya and other Indian peoples who lived in this region hundreds of years ago. (See Chapter 3.) Most of them make their homes in the highlands of Central America, especially in Guatemala and western Honduras.

The highland Indians live and work in much the same way as their ancestors. Instead of living in cities, most of them live in small villages. Like their ancestors, they make a living by raising corn and other food crops. Some are skilled in handicrafts, such as weaving and making pottery. They generally wear colorful handwoven costumes. Each group of Indians speaks one of many Indian languages.

Some tribes of Indians in Central America live in the rainforests of the Caribbean Lowland and in the Pacific Lowland of Panama. Most of these people live a simple way of life that has changed little since the time of Columbus. In addition to raising a few crops, many of them obtain food by hunting or fishing. They usually live in one-room huts, and some wear very little clothing.

Negroes. About one fourth of the people in the Caribbean Lands are Negroes. On most of the islands in the West Indies, Negroes make up a large part of the population. (Compare map on page 16 with bottom map on page 91.) In some countries, such as Haiti, nearly all of the people are Negroes.

There are fewer Negroes living in Central America than in the West Indies. However, in the Caribbean Lowland of Central America, many of the people

Indians at a marketplace in Guatemala. About one tenth of the people of the Caribbean Lands are Indians. Most of them live in the highlands of Central America, especially in Guatemala and western Honduras. These people live and work in much the same way as their ancestors.

are Negroes. Most of them are descendants of free workers who moved here from the West Indies during the 1800's and early 1900's, after slavery had been abolished. (See page 77.) Some of the Negroes in Central America are descended from slaves brought here during colonial days.

Unlike the Indians, the Negroes in the Caribbean Lands do not have a way of life all their own. They have generally adopted the language, religion, and customs of the white people living in the Caribbean Lands. However, in some places, practices brought from Africa, such as voodoo, still influence the Negroes' way of life.

People of European descent. In the Caribbean Lands, there are about ten million people whose ancestors came from Spain, England, France, or other European countries. However, in most Caribbean countries, people of European descent make up only a small part of the population. Cuba, Puerto Rico, and Costa Rica are the only countries in which white people outnumber people of other racial groups. (Compare map on pages 14 and 15 with bottom map on page 91.)

Many of the white people living in the Caribbean Lands are descended from early settlers of this region. (See Chapter 4.) Others have come during the 1900's from a number of countries in Europe and from the United States. Because the white people in the Caribbean Lands

Negroes make up a large part of the population on most of the islands in the West Indies. More Negroes live on these islands than in Central America.

are descended from people of several different nationalities, they do not all have the same customs and beliefs. Most of them follow the traditions of their ancestors. For example, in Puerto Rico, which was ruled by Spain for nearly four hundred years, the official language is Spanish. Many Puerto Ricans have Spanish names. Buildings are often in a Spanish style of architecture. Also, Spanish customs are followed for festivals and family reunions.

People of Asian descent. During the 1800's and early 1900's, many people from India were brought to Trinidad to work on plantations. Today, their descendants make up more than one third of Trinidad's population. On Trinidad, these people are called "East Indians."

In several Caribbean countries, there are small groups of people whose ancestors came from China. Like the people

Words To Think With

Indian	Negro	East Indian	mestizo	mulatto	Creole
Papiamento	Roman Catholic		Protestant	voodoo	Hindu
Moslem	birthrate	emigration	slums	per capita income	

from India, many of the Chinese came to the Caribbean Lands as plantation workers. Today, most of the people of Chinese descent run shops or other businesses. They generally live in large cities, such as Panama City, Panama, and Havana, Cuba.

People of mixed descent. About one third of the people of the Caribbean Lands are of mixed descent. Those who have both Indian and European ancestors are known as mestizos. There are few mestizos in the West Indies, because nearly all of the Indians here died soon after the Spaniards came. (See pages 61 and 67.) However, mestizos make up a large part of the population in most Central American countries. Costa Rica is the only country in Central America where there are very few mestizos.

People of mixed white and Negro ancestry are called mulattoes. Most of the mulattoes live in the West Indies and in parts of the Caribbean Lowland of Central America. The Dominican Republic is the only Caribbean country where most of the people are mulattoes.

Several languages are spoken in the Caribbean Lands. The people of the Caribbean Lands do not all speak the same language. In most of the countries that were ruled by Spain, the official language is Spanish. French is the official language in Haiti, which was once a French colony, and on the French islands of Guadeloupe and Martinique. English is spoken in lands that are now, or were formerly, ruled by Great Britain. The official language of the Netherlands Antilles is Dutch.

Many people in the Caribbean Lands speak a language other than the official language of their country. On Trinidad, for example, some people of Asian descent speak Asian languages instead of English. In Guatemala, most of the

A group of Nicaraguans. People of mixed European and Indian descent, or mestizos, make up a large part of the population in Nicaragua and most other Central American countries. Many mulattoes, who are of mixed white and Negro ancestry, live in the West Indies.

A Roman Catholic church in Honduras. More than three fourths of the people who live in the Caribbean Lands are Roman Catholic.

Indians speak Mayan languages rather than Spanish. Some people speak a language that is a mixture of two or more other languages. Most Haitians, for example, speak Creole, which includes French, English, Spanish, and African words. In the Netherlands Antilles, many people speak Papiamento, a mixture of Spanish, Dutch, English, and other languages.

Most of the people in the Caribbean Lands are Roman Catholic. More than three fourths of the people in the Caribbean Lands are members of the Roman Catholic Church. Nearly all of them live in countries that were settled by Spain or France. Many years ago, Spanish and French settlers brought the Catholic religion to the Caribbean Lands. Today, there are beautiful churches and shrines in the Catholic countries of this region. Many festivals are connected with religious celebrations of the Roman Catholic Church. (See Chapter 13.)

On some British and Dutch islands, many people are Protestant. This is because Great Britain and the Netherlands are both Protestant countries. When British and Dutch settlers came to the Caribbean Lands, they brought with them the religion they had followed in their homelands. In Jamaica, which was formerly a British colony, most of the people are members of Protestant churches.

Some people in the Caribbean Lands follow other religions in addition to Christianity. The Indians in Guatemala, for example, combine Christianity with their ancient Mayan religion. Although they belong to the Roman Catholic Church, they also worship Mayan gods. In Haiti, many people practice voodoo, a religion brought from Africa by Negro slaves. Many of these people are also Catholic. (See page 269.) Religious rites brought from Africa are also practiced on some of the other islands in the West Indies.

On Trinidad, many people of Asian descent are Hindu or Moslem. These people worship in beautiful Hindu temples or Moslem mosques.

A Protestant church on Jamaica. On some islands in the West Indies, many people are Protestant.

The population of the Caribbean Lands is not evenly distributed. More than 34 million people make their homes in the Caribbean Lands. Only about 13 million of them live in Central America. Although the islands of the West Indies cover an area less than one half as large as Central America, they have nearly 9 million more people. (See table on page 19.)

The history of the settlement of this region helps to explain why the population of the West Indies is much larger than the population of Central America. During the 1600's and 1700's, thousands of Negro slaves were brought to the West Indies to work on plantations. In Central America, however, most of the settlers did not raise crops for export. Fewer workers were needed, so slaves generally were not imported. Partly for this reason, the growth of population was not as great in Central America as in the West Indies.

Very few people live in some parts of the Caribbean Lands, while other parts of this region are densely populated. (See top map on opposite page.) Several islands in the West Indies have more than five hundred people for each square mile of land. On Barbados, there are about 1,400 people for each square mile. Some areas of Central America, such as northern Guatemala and eastern Nicaragua, are almost uninhabited.

In Central America, most of the people live in the highlands. Here the climate is mild, and there are many basins and plateaus with fertile soil. Most of the first Spanish settlements in Central America were in the highlands, where the Spaniards found large numbers of Indians to work for them.

In the West Indies, most of the people live in the lowlands. Unlike the lowlands of Central America, the lowlands of the West Indies have a pleasant climate. (See Chapter 2.) Along the coasts, there are many good harbors for ships. Large cities have grown up along some of these harbors. In the highlands of the West Indies, there are few large areas of level land and fertile soil. On some crowded islands, such as Puerto Rico, there is not enough good farmland for everyone. Many people are forced to live on steep mountainsides, struggling to cultivate the rugged land.

The population of the Caribbean Lands is growing rapidly. In most Caribbean countries, the population is increasing rapidly. The birthrate is much higher in these countries than in the United States. Also, as a result of better medical care in recent years, people in the Caribbean Lands are living longer than ever before. The population is increasing more rapidly in Costa Rica than in any other Caribbean country. Costa Rica's rate of increase is possibly greater than that of any other country in the world.

In the past, emigration to Great Britain helped slow down the population growth on some islands in the West Indies. However, in 1962 the British parliament passed a new law to control immigration. Usually an immigrant must now have a job in Britain before he can move there. Therefore, fewer people are able to move from the West Indies to Britain.

Rapid population growth is creating problems for the Caribbean countries. Many of the countries do not have enough good farmland. Compared to the

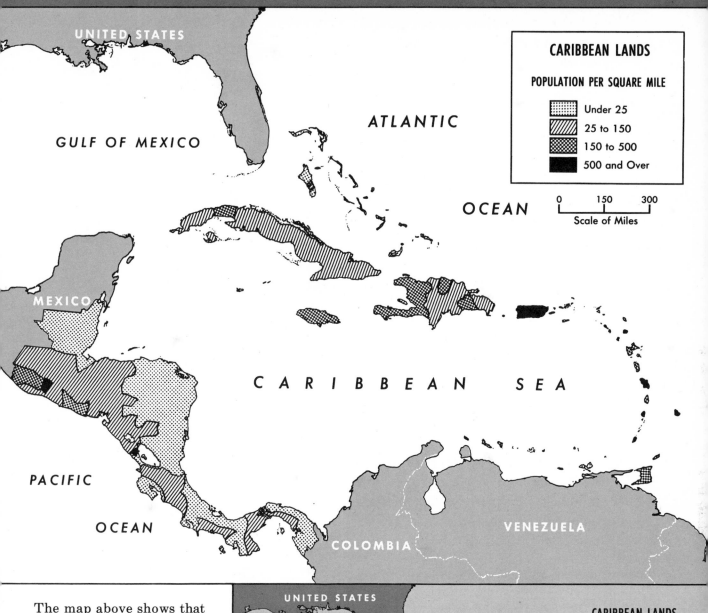

CARIBBEAN LANDS

POPULATION PER SQUARE MILE

Under 25
25 to 150
150 to 500
500 and Over

0   150   300
Scale of Miles

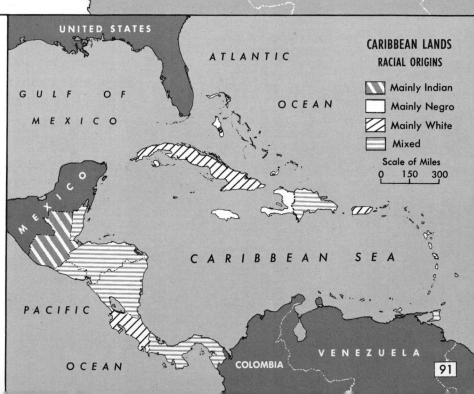

The map above shows that few people live in some parts of the Caribbean Lands, and that other parts of this region are heavily populated. Compare this map with the map on pages 14 and 15. Notice that some large lowland areas in Central America are thinly populated. Crowded areas include Puerto Rico and several islands in the Lesser Antilles.

The map on the right shows that people of different racial origins live in the Caribbean Lands. In some of the countries shown as "mixed," the people are mainly mestizo* or mainly mulatto.* In other "mixed" countries, no single racial group makes up a majority of the population. (See fact tables on pages 180 and 301.)

CARIBBEAN LANDS
RACIAL ORIGINS

Mainly Indian
Mainly Negro
Mainly White
Mixed

Scale of Miles
0   150   300

United States, the Caribbean Lands region has few factories. (See Chapter 9.) Therefore, there are not enough jobs in farming and industry for everyone. Also, more schools, more housing, and more hospitals are needed for the growing number of people. Most Caribbean countries lack the money to pay for these things.

People are moving to the cities. Many people in the Caribbean Lands have been moving from the country to cities and large towns. They hope to find a better way of life. There is a great difference between life in the cities and life in rural areas. In the country, many people live a backward way of life, with no modern conveniences. On their small farms, many rural families raise barely enough to eat. Their homes are often unpainted shacks, without electricity or running water. In the cities, many families live much as most people do in the United States. They have refrigerators, automobiles, and many other modern conveniences. Their homes are attractive and well furnished.

A slum in San Juan, Puerto Rico. Most people in the Caribbean Lands are very poor. In the cities, many people are forced to live in crowded slums.

Not all people in the cities live in this way, however. Many of the newcomers to the cities cannot find jobs. Because they have little or no income, they are forced to live in crowded slums. For these people, city life may be no better than life in rural areas.

Some people are very rich, but most are very poor. In most Caribbean countries, there is a small but powerful group of wealthy people. These people are mainly of European descent. Some are merchants or owners of large estates. Others hold important government offices. In many countries, the wealthy people control the government.

Most of the people in the Caribbean Lands are extremely poor. Nearly all of these people are Indian, Negro, or of mixed descent. Some are tenant farmers or workers on huge estates. Others own plots of land that are too small to provide them with a good living. An increasing number live in city slums, performing odd jobs because they cannot find regular work. The poor people

A backward way of life is common in rural areas of the Caribbean Lands. Many people have been moving from the country to the cities.

Cities of the Caribbean Lands

Although most of the people in the Caribbean Lands live in rural areas, the cities in this region are growing rapidly. Today, there are twenty-one cities with populations of 100,000 or more. The largest of these is Havana, Cuba, which has a population of about 900,000. San Juan, Puerto Rico, is the second largest city in the Caribbean Lands. Its population is more than 430,000.

Some parts of the Caribbean Lands have more large cities than others. Compare the map above with the map on page 16. Notice that there are more large cities in the West Indies than in Central America. Most of the main cities in the West Indies are situated on the seacoast. They are important seaports to which products from nearby farms and forests are brought for export. Cuba, the largest island in the West Indies, has more large cities than any other Caribbean country. In Central America, most of the large cities are in the highlands. The largest is Guatemala City, Guatemala, which has a population of more than 400,000.

In all of the independent Caribbean countries, the capital is the largest city. Besides being the seat of the government, the capital is usually also the most important trading and manufacturing city in each country. In some countries, such as Jamaica and Costa Rica, the capital is the only large city.

Today, many large cities in the Caribbean Lands resemble cities in the United States. Modern office buildings and stores line some of their downtown streets. In outlying sections of the cities, there are many attractive houses. In other sections of Caribbean cities, old buildings border narrow, cobbled streets. Among the oldest buildings are beautiful churches built by Spanish colonists.

generally do not know how to read and write and have no voice in their government.

In most Caribbean countries, the yearly per capita income is less than $400. This is only about one sixth as much as the yearly per capita income in the United States. People in the Caribbean Lands are able to live on such a small amount of money because they grow or make many of the things they need.

Some steps are being taken to lessen poverty in the Caribbean Lands. Most countries are trying to encourage the growth of industry. Farmers are learning to use modern methods to increase production. In many parts of the Caribbean region, efforts are being made to provide better education and medical care. (See page 83.) However, it is difficult to make improvements fast enough to keep up with the growing population. This helps to explain why the number of poor people in most Caribbean countries is not decreasing.

Today, there is a growing number of people in the Caribbean Lands who are neither very rich nor very poor. Because they are in the "middle" between rich and poor, they are often called the "middle class." Some are teachers or doctors. Many work in stores, offices, or banks. Others are skilled factory workers. These people generally earn enough money to buy all the food and clothing they need. Most of them have a good education and take an interest in the government of their country. Some are being elected to important offices. With a larger number of middle class people in the governments of more Caribbean countries, these governments may become more democratic.

Reviewing What You Have Learned
Choose five of the statements listed below. Use each as the topic sentence of a short paragraph. In each paragraph, explain why the idea stated in the topic sentence is true.
1. Most of the people of Central America live in the highlands.
2. Most of the people of the West Indies live in the lowlands.
3. The population is increasing rapidly in most Caribbean countries.
4. In the Caribbean Lands, many people are moving from rural areas to the cities.
5. More Negroes live in the West Indies than in Central America.
6. Most of the Indians of the Caribbean Lands live in Central America.
7. In the Caribbean Lands, the people do not all speak the same language.

Learning More About Caribbean Peoples
To learn more about how some of the people in the Caribbean Lands live, divide your class into two groups. One group should study the way of life of a peasant family in Haiti. (See Chapter 23.) The other should study the way of life of an Indian family in the highlands of Guatemala. (See Chapter 14.) Each group should use at least two sources in addition to this textbook. When the study is completed, each group should draw pictures or a mural showing the following:

a. the members of the family dressed in their everyday clothes
b. the house in which the family would probably live
c. the members of the family at work
d. a religious activity in which the family might participate

Hold a class discussion based on these questions:
1. How are these two families alike?
2. How are the families different?

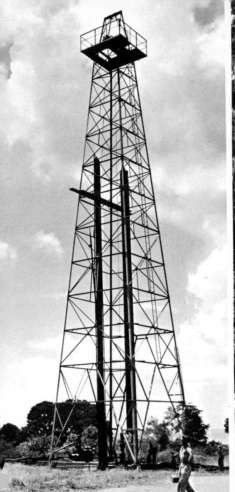

Natural resources of the Caribbean Lands include mineral deposits, forests, and fisheries. There is also waterpower that can be used to produce hydroelectricity. However, the resources that are most important to the people of this region are soil and climate.

7 Natural Resources

Problems To Solve

1. **How do the natural resources of the Caribbean Lands affect the ways in which the people of this region earn their living?** You will need to make several hypotheses in order to solve this problem. In forming your hypotheses, consider how the natural resources of this region affect each of the following:
   a. farming
   b. manufacturing

Chapters 8 and 9 contain additional information that will be helpful in solving this problem.

2. The countries of the Caribbean Lands region have not fully developed their natural resources. **Why is this so?** To solve this problem, you will need to make hypotheses about how the development of resources in the Caribbean Lands has been affected by each of the following:
   a. transportation
   b. the amount of money available

See TO THE STUDENT, pages 6-7.

Soil and climate are the most important natural resources of the Caribbean Lands. This is because more than half of the workers in this region earn their living by farming. (See Chapter 2 for more information about climate.) Other natural resources of the Caribbean region include mineral deposits, forests, and fisheries. There are also many rivers that can be used to produce hydro-electric power. At present, however, these other resources are not of great importance to most people in the Caribbean Lands.

Soil

Some parts of the Caribbean Lands have fertile soil. To learn more about soil in the Caribbean Lands, imagine that you are visiting a farm near Lake Managua in Nicaragua. (See map on page 195.) All around you are fields of corn, cotton, and other crops. In the distance is a tall volcano with smoke rising from its cone.

The dark-brown soil beneath your feet is thinly coated with ashes, which came from the distant volcano. They were blown here by the wind. Volcanic ashes help to enrich the soil.

Some of the most fertile soil in the Caribbean Lands is found near volcanoes. (See page 19.) Most of the areas of fertile volcanic soil in the Caribbean Lands are located in the highlands of Central America.

Many valleys in the Caribbean Lands also have soil that is good for growing

A fertile valley in El Salvador. Soil is an important resource of the Caribbean Lands because more than half of the workers in this region earn their living by farming. Some of the most fertile farmland is found near volcanoes, where ashes and lava have helped to enrich the soil.

crops. Among these areas are the Cibao in the Dominican Republic and the valley of the Ulúa River in Honduras. (See maps on pages 250 and 184.) Much of the land in the valleys is covered with deep layers of rich topsoil that rainwater and streams have washed down from the highlands.

Some lowland areas on Cuba and Jamaica have a red clay soil that is good for growing sugarcane. Long ago, these areas were covered with limestone. Through the centuries, wind and rain have broken up some of the limestone to form soil. This process is known as weathering.

In many parts of the Caribbean Lands, the soil is not fertile. Not all of the soil in this region is good for farming. In highlands where there are no volcanoes, the soil may lack some of the minerals needed by crops. On many mountain slopes, rainwater has carried away most of the topsoil. The soil that remains is shallow and stony.

In the Caribbean Lowland of Central America, much of the soil is poor for growing crops. The heavy rains that fall in this area have dissolved most of the mineral plant foods in the soil. Rainwater has carried the dissolved minerals deep under the ground, where the roots of plants cannot reach them.

On the Bahamas and many low islands in the Lesser Antilles, most of the soil is formed from coral. This soil is shallow and does not hold water well.

Eroded land in Haiti. In many parts of the Caribbean Lands, the soil is not fertile. Rainwater has carried away the topsoil in some places.

Rainwater drains through the soil so quickly that little of the moisture can be used by plants.

Soil conservation is needed in the Caribbean Lands. Many farmers in the Caribbean Lands have not taken good care of their soil. Often the same crop is planted on the same land year after year. As a result, the soil has become less fertile.

On many hills and mountains, trees have been cut down in order to plant crops. Trees help to prevent erosion on steep slopes because their roots hold the soil in place. When trees are cut down, the loose topsoil is easily carried away by wind and rainwater. In some countries, such as Haiti, much of the land is so badly eroded that it no longer yields good crops.

Words To Think With

hydroelectricity volcanic soil climate soil conservation

erosion bauxite petroleum asphalt raw materials

mahogany fisheries export charcoal natural gas

A power shovel scooping up bauxite on Jamaica. Bauxite, an ore from which aluminum is made, is the most important mineral resource of the Caribbean Lands. Jamaica is the world's leading producer of this mineral. Some bauxite is also mined in the Dominican Republic and Haiti.

Mineral Resources

Large amounts of bauxite are mined in the Caribbean Lands. The most important mineral resource of the Caribbean Lands is bauxite, the ore that is the chief source of aluminum. Jamaica is the world's leading producer of this mineral. Smaller amounts of bauxite are mined in the Dominican Republic and Haiti.

One way to learn more about this important resource would be to visit a bauxite mine on Jamaica. Here you would see a pit several hundred feet wide and about forty feet deep. The bottom of the pit is covered with a dark-red, claylike substance. This is bauxite. Huge power shovels scoop up the bauxite and dump it into trucks.

There are no factories on Jamaica that can produce finished aluminum from bauxite. The mine just described is owned by a company that operates large aluminum plants in the United States. Ore from this mine is taken to a seaport nearby, where it is dried in large ovens. Then it is loaded onto ships that carry it to the state of Louisiana where it is processed to make aluminum. Chapter 24 gives more information about bauxite mining on Jamaica.

Cuba has many important mineral resources. The island of Cuba has rich deposits of manganese, chromium, nickel, iron, and copper ores. These ores can be processed to make metals that are used by industry. Chapter 21 tells more about the mineral resources of Cuba.

There are many oil wells on the island of Trinidad. If you were to travel through the southern part of Trinidad, you would see the tall derricks of many oil wells. Petroleum, or crude oil, pumped from these wells is sent to refineries nearby. There it is changed into gasoline, fuel oil, and many other useful products. Trinidad is the leading petroleum producer in the Caribbean Lands. Some natural gas also comes from wells on this island.

Asphalt comes from Trinidad's Pitch Lake. Near the oil fields on Trinidad is Pitch Lake. (See map on page 300.) This lake is not a body of water. Instead, it is made up of a black, gummy substance called pitch, or asphalt. Most of it is hard enough for a man to walk on. Formerly, asphalt was dug up by workers with picks and shovels. Today, however, large digging machines are generally used. (See picture below.) Most of the asphalt is taken to a seaport and loaded onto oceangoing ships. Many roads in Great Britain and other countries as well as on Trinidad have been paved with asphalt from Pitch Lake.

Mineral resources are scarce in most parts of the Caribbean Lands. Except for Trinidad and Tobago, Jamaica, and Cuba, no countries in the Caribbean region have important deposits of mineral resources. On most islands in the West Indies, the leading mineral resources are clay, stone, sand, and gravel. They provide materials for constructing roads and buildings. Puerto Rico uses large amounts of limestone to manufacture cement.

Digging asphalt from Trinidad's Pitch Lake. Many roads in Great Britain and other countries have been paved with asphalt from Pitch Lake. Trinidad and Tobago, Jamaica, and Cuba are the only countries in the Caribbean Lands that have important deposits of mineral resources.

Central America is very poor in mineral resources. In several countries there are deposits of gold and silver. However, Nicaragua is the only Central American country that mines much gold.

The Caribbean countries lack oil, natural gas, and coal. Little oil or natural gas is produced in the Caribbean region except on Trinidad. No important coal deposits have been found in this region. Without oil, natural gas, or coal, it is difficult to establish modern industry. These mineral fuels are used to produce electricity for operating machines. Coal is also used in steelmaking. Gasoline and other petroleum products are needed to run automobiles and airplanes. The Caribbean countries must import most of their petroleum.

Forests

The forests of the Caribbean Lands supply many useful products. Forests cover almost half of the land in the Caribbean region. The largest areas of forest lands are in Central America. At one time, there were also large forests in the West Indies. However, much of this forest land has been cleared to provide land for farming.

From the forests, people obtain fuel, lumber, and other useful products. Some forest products are sent to countries outside the Caribbean Lands, but most of them are used within this region.

Floating logs to a sawmill, in British Honduras. Forests cover almost half of the land in the Caribbean region. From the forests, people obtain lumber, fuel, and other useful products. In British Honduras and northern Guatemala, lumbering is the most important industry.

Not all of the forests in the Caribbean Lands are used as fully as they could be. Some forests are located far from roads, rivers, and other means of transportation. There is no easy way to carry logs from these forests to places where they can be used. Often many different kinds of trees grow in one area. It is difficult to locate the valuable trees and remove them from the forests.

Tropical rainforests. In parts of the Caribbean Lands where the weather is hot and moist throughout the year, there are tropical rainforests. Most of the trees that grow in these dense forests are tall, and their broad leaves stay green all year round. The largest rainforest is in the Caribbean Lowland of Central America.

Many kinds of trees grow in the rainforests. Among the most valuable are mahogany, rosewood, and Spanish cedar. Because rosewood and mahogany are beautiful woods, they are highly prized for making furniture. People use Spanish cedar in making pencils, cigar boxes, and other articles.

In British Honduras and northern Guatemala, lumbering is the most important industry. Groups of lumbermen travel through the rainforests in search of mahogany trees. When they find one, they cut it down and saw it into logs. Often the logs are dragged by oxen to a river and floated downstream to a lumber mill. Where there are roads, the logs are carried to the lumber mill on trucks. Much of the lumber is sent to furniture factories in the United States or Britain.

Another valuable product of the rainforests is chicle. This is a sticky substance used in making chewing gum.

A mangrove thicket on Cuba. Mangrove trees grow in swampy places where the tide washes in and out. Their wood is used mainly for firewood.

Page 159 tells about chicle gathering in Guatemala.

Coastal forests. Along the shores of the Caribbean Sea, there are many mangrove thickets. Mangrove trees grow in swampy places where the tide washes in and out. Their wood is used mainly for firewood.

Tall, graceful coconut palms grow in sandy, well-drained places along the seacoast. Palm leaves are used to thatch roofs and to make baskets and other articles. Many people enjoy drinking coconut milk or eating the white meat of the coconuts. On Trinidad, coconut meat is dried to make copra. Oil that is squeezed from the copra is used in making soap, margarine, and other products.

Highland forests. In areas that are high above sea level, there are pines, oaks, and other trees like those found in the United States. Forests of pine trees cover the slopes of many mountains in Central America and on the islands of Hispaniola and Cuba. Pine

Fishing boats in Panama. Although many people in the Caribbean Lands are fishermen, the size of their catch is not large. Most fishermen do not have large boats or modern refrigerating equipment, so they cannot travel far from shore in search of fish.

lumber is an important product in several countries, including Honduras and the Dominican Republic.

Charcoal is made from many kinds of wood. Some of the wood taken from Caribbean forests is used in making charcoal. This is the most important cooking fuel in the Caribbean Lands. People in this region make charcoal by setting fire to a pile of green wood and then partially covering the fire with earth. In this way, very little air is allowed to reach the fire. The wood burns slowly, turning to charcoal.

Fisheries

A fishing trip on the Caribbean Sea. Early one morning, three fishermen board a small sailboat at a fishing village in Haiti. A strong breeze fills the sail and carries the boat about a mile out to sea. Here the fishermen lower a small, homemade net into the water.

A few minutes later, the men pull up the net. It is filled with many kinds of fish. The men throw most of the fish back into the water. Only a few kinds, such as red snapper and Spanish mackerel, are kept. After a few hours, the men return to shore with about forty pounds of fish. They hurry to the marketplace and sell their catch to housewives waiting there. Because the weather is very warm and refrigeration is lacking, the fish will spoil if they are not eaten right away.

The Caribbean is not an important fishing area. Although thousands of people in the Caribbean Lands are fishermen, the size of their catch is not large. There are several reasons why this is true.

Hundreds of kinds of fish live in the warm waters of the Caribbean region, but it is difficult to catch large numbers of any one kind. Some kinds of tropical fish are not edible. Among the fish that can be eaten, only shrimp are caught in large numbers. Most fishermen do not have large boats or modern refrigerating equipment, so they cannot travel far from shore in search of fish. There are few factories to can or freeze seafood.

Where there is no refrigeration, the fish must be eaten soon after they are caught. Without refrigeration, they cannot be shipped long distances.

A few Caribbean countries are now beginning to develop fishing industries. In Puerto Rico and El Salvador, for example, there are fleets of modern fishing boats. Canneries and freezing plants have been built for processing fish.

Waterpower

Much of the waterpower in the Caribbean Lands is not being used. Although the Caribbean countries lack the coal and oil needed to produce much electricity, they are fairly well supplied with waterpower. In this region, many short rivers flow swiftly from the mountains to the sea. Some of these rivers can be used to produce hydroelectricity.

Most Caribbean countries have been slow to make use of their waterpower. In many areas, electricity is produced in power plants that use imported coal or oil. Partly for this reason, electric power is scarce and expensive. Most homes do not have electricity. In Honduras, for example, more than half of all the houses are lighted with pine torches.

Building a dam in El Salvador. Although the Caribbean countries lack the coal and oil needed to produce much electricity, they are fairly well supplied with waterpower. However, most of these countries need to make better use of this resource.

Today, some Caribbean countries are developing their waterpower. Several dams and power plants have been built on rivers in Puerto Rico. The force of the moving water is used to run huge machines called generators, which produce electricity for homes and factories. Large hydroelectric plants have also been built in Costa Rica, El Salvador, and a few other countries.

The Caribbean countries need to make better use of the resources they have. You have learned that the Caribbean Lands region is not rich in natural resources. It lacks coal, oil, and other minerals needed by industry. Many of the forests in this region have been destroyed, and much of the timber that remains is far from places where it can be used. The waters bordering the Caribbean Lands region do not yield large catches of food fish.

The people of the Caribbean Lands have not made full use of the resources they have. There are several reasons for this. Roads must be built so that raw materials can be transported from mines and forests to factories. Dams and power plants are needed to make use of waterpower. The Caribbean countries do not have enough money to build all the roads, dams, and power plants they need. They also lack industries to make use of their raw materials. Therefore, they sell large amounts of bauxite, mahogany, and other raw materials to countries in other parts of the world.

People from other countries are now helping the Caribbean Lands region to make greater use of its resources. The United States has loaned millions of dollars to countries in this region. Some of this money is being used to build roads, dams, and factories. Money also has been provided by the World Bank and agencies related to it. Businessmen from the United States and other countries have established mines and factories in the Caribbean Lands. With outside help and with strong effort on the part of the people of the Caribbean Lands, the resources of this region can eventually be used more fully.

Reviewing What You Have Learned

1. What are the two most important natural resources of the Caribbean Lands? State one reason for their importance.
2. Why is soil conservation needed in the Caribbean Lands? State two reasons.
3. Why are the forests of the Caribbean Lands not used as fully as they could be? List two reasons.
4. Fishing is generally not an important industry in the Caribbean Lands. State three reasons why this is true.
5. What three mineral fuels are generally lacking in the Caribbean Lands? Why does this lack of these fuels make it difficult to establish modern industry? Give two reasons.

6. What three countries in the Caribbean region have important deposits of mineral resources? Name these resources.

Yes or No

Write the number of each of the following sentences on a sheet of paper. If the statement is true, write **yes** after the number. If it is not true, write **no,** and correct the statement.

1. The largest areas of forest lands in the Caribbean region are in the West Indies.
2. The most important cooking fuel in the Caribbean Lands is natural gas.
3. Most Caribbean countries have not made full use of their waterpower.
4. The most important mineral resource of the Caribbean Lands is iron ore.

Farming is the main occupation in the Caribbean Lands. Most farmers have small plots of land on which they grow crops for their own use. Some of the workers who make a living from agriculture are employed on large farms where bananas and other crops are grown for export.

8 Farming

Problems To Solve

Many farmers in the Caribbean Lands grow hardly enough food for their own families. **Why is this true?** To solve this problem, you will need to make several hypotheses. The following questions suggest some hypotheses:

a. What facts about the land features and soil in various parts of the Caribbean Lands help to solve this problem?

b. What facts about land ownership help to solve it?

c. What facts about the density of population in some areas help to solve it?

d. What facts about the methods of farming used in the Caribbean Lands help to solve it?

See TO THE STUDENT, pages 6-7.

Farming is the main occupation in the Caribbean Lands. More than half of the people in this region make their living from agriculture. Some of them work on large farms where coffee, bananas, and other crops are grown for sale to foreign countries. However, most farmers have small plots of land on which they grow crops for their own use.

Crops for Domestic Use

A farm in El Salvador. To learn more about one type of agriculture in the Caribbean Lands, let us visit a small farm in the highlands of El Salvador. This farm is located on steeply sloping land at the foot of a mountain. Compared with most farms in the United States, it is very small. The whole farm covers only six acres.

In the middle of the farm is a small adobe house with a thatched roof. Here the farmer lives with his wife and their eight children. The house is shaded by tall banana plants. Near the doorway are several scrawny pigs and chickens.

It is a warm, sunny morning in early spring, and the farmer is plowing his land in order to plant corn. He is using a crude wooden plow pulled by a pair

of oxen. The farmer does not own a tractor or other modern farm implements. They are too expensive for him to buy and operate.

In addition to corn, the farmer grows beans and red chili peppers. These are the main foods eaten by the farmer and his family all year round. Sometimes the farmer's wife carries a sack of corn or a basket of peppers to the marketplace in the nearest town. She trades these things for cotton cloth, cooking pans, or other articles that she needs.

The farmer wishes that he could afford to buy fertilizer to improve his soil. Years ago, his land was very fertile. However, it has been used so long for growing the same crops that it no longer yields a good harvest. Although

A farm in El Salvador. Thousands of farms in the Caribbean Lands are very small, mainly because there is a shortage of good farmland. The people who work on these farms earn little money, but they can survive on a small income because they grow or make nearly everything they use.

the farmer works very hard, he can hardly raise enough food for his own family.

To earn money for food and other necessities, the farmer works two months each year picking coffee berries on a large farm nearby. Even so, he cannot afford to buy all the things that his family needs. His children have no shoes, and their clothing is shabby. They are thin and always tired, because they do not get enough of the right foods.

Most farmers grow crops mainly for their own use. In the Caribbean Lands, there are thousands of small farms much like the one described here. The people who work on these farms grow crops mainly for their own use rather than for sale. They earn very little money, but they can survive on a small income because they grow or make nearly everything that they use. Occasionally they may take some of their crops to market to sell or to trade for articles that they cannot make themselves. The kind of farming that is done by these people is known as subsistence farming.

Corn, beans, rice, and manioc are important food crops. Many kinds of crops are grown for food in the Caribbean Lands. Because of differences in climate, the same crops are not grown in all places. For example, some crops thrive in the hot, humid lowlands, while others grow best in the cooler highlands.

Drying rice on a small farm in the Dominican Republic. Corn, beans, rice, and manioc are important food crops in the Caribbean Lands.

Corn is grown in almost all parts of the Caribbean Lands. (See map on page 113.) This crop was the main food of the Maya and other Indian groups who lived in Central America long ago. Today it is still especially important in the highlands of Guatemala, Honduras, and El Salvador, where many people are of Indian descent. Most of the corn is ground into meal, which is often used in making thin, flat cakes called *tortillas*.

Beans and rice are also leading food crops in the Caribbean Lands. The people of this region do not eat very much meat. Beans are an important food because they provide some of the proteins that people in the United States get from eating meat. Large amounts of rice are grown in Cuba, the Dominican Republic, and Panama. Rice plants need much moisture in order to grow. Therefore, rice is usually grown in places that

Words To Think With

subsistence farming   tropical crops   fertilizer   irrigation

export   tenant farmer   livestock   one-crop economy

are low and easily flooded. Some Caribbean countries do not produce enough rice for all of their people. They must import rice from the United States and other countries.

In parts of the West Indies and on the lowlands of Central America, farmers grow large amounts of manioc, yams, and sweet potatoes. These crops are better suited to the hot climate of the lowlands than corn is. The large, fleshy roots of the manioc plant can be cooked like potatoes, or they can be ground into a kind of flour that is used in making bread.

People who live on the hot, humid lowlands grow many different kinds of fruit. Among the most important are bananas and plantains. The plantain is a type of banana, but is larger and not so sweet. It is usually cooked before being eaten. Other fruits that grow in the Caribbean region include mangoes, pineapples, and papayas.

High in the mountains of Central America, the climate is too cool for tropical crops. Here, farmers raise wheat and potatoes. These crops grow well in a cool climate.

Farmers in the Caribbean Lands face many problems. Most farms that produce subsistence crops in the Caribbean region are very small. Some of them cover less than three acres in area. The main reason for this is a shortage of good farmland.

At the present time, only about one fourth of all the land in the Caribbean region is being used for farming. In some parts of this region, the land is too mountainous for growing crops. Other areas are covered with dense rainforest, which is hard to clear away for farming. The soil in many places is not fertile. (See page 97.) In some areas, the climate is so dry that crops cannot be grown without irrigation.

Some parts of Central America are not being used for farming, even though they have fertile soil and a good climate. One reason is that they lack roads and railroads. It is difficult for people wishing to start new farms to reach these areas.

Because the population of the Caribbean region is growing very rapidly, there is not enough land for everyone. "Land hunger" is especially great in El Salvador and on some of the islands in the West Indies. Here the population is very dense, and there are no large areas of empty land that can be used for farming.

Farmers who grow subsistence crops in the Caribbean Lands have other problems as well. In many places, the best farmland is used for growing sugarcane or other export crops. Often the only areas that are available for subsistence farming either have poor soil or are located on steep mountainsides.

Most farmers in the Caribbean Lands do not know much about scientific farming methods. Often they plant the same crops on the same land year after year. This causes the soil to become less fertile. In many mountainous areas, wind and rainwater have eroded much fertile topsoil. Many farmers do not know how to use fertilizer, or they cannot afford to buy it. As a result, they are unable to produce good crops.

Because their farms are small and their harvests are poor, many farmers cannot raise enough food for their own families. To earn money for things they need, they have to work part of the time at other jobs. They are often sick, because they do not eat enough of the foods needed for good health.

Many farmers in the Caribbean region do not own the land they cultivate. Instead, much of the land belongs to wealthy individuals or to foreign companies. Some farmers pay rent for the use of the land. Others work for the landowner or give him part of the crops that they produce. Many farmers are constantly in debt to landlords or storekeepers who supply them with tools, clothing, and other necessities.

Efforts are being made to help the farmers. The governments of some Caribbean countries are trying to provide a better way of life for their farmers. Several countries have adopted land reform programs. Special lending agencies have been started to make it easier for farmers to borrow money for tools, fertilizer, and other necessities. In many areas, roads have been built to open up new land for farming. The new roads will also help farmers transport their products to market. Dams and canals

Cubans clearing a plot of land to grow food in the city of Havana. The Communists have had little success in solving the problems of farmers in Cuba.

Modern equipment helps Costa Rican farmers to grow more crops. The governments of some Caribbean countries are working to improve agriculture.

have been built to provide water for irrigating dry areas.

Outside countries are also helping to improve agriculture in the Caribbean Lands. The United States has sent farm experts to this region to teach people better ways of raising crops and livestock. Under the Alliance for Progress (see page 13), the United States is lending money to countries that have started land reform programs. It is also providing money for agricultural schools. A United Nations agency called the Food and Agriculture Organization is assisting in this work. The Interamerican Institute of Agricultural Sciences, located in Costa Rica, carries on research and trains people in modern farming methods.

Much remains to be done to assist the farmers of the Caribbean Lands. Many farmers still live on the edge of starvation. If these people are not helped in the near future, they may turn to communism as a way of meeting their needs. One country in this region, Cuba, is now ruled by a Communist government. However, the Communists have had little success in solving the problems of Cuban farmers. (See page 244.)

Some farmers raise crops to be sold in cities and towns. Not all farmers in the Caribbean region grow crops mainly for their own use. There are many farms on which corn, rice, sugarcane, cotton, tobacco, and other crops are grown for sale in nearby cities and towns. These farms are usually larger than the ones that produce subsistence crops. Some of them cover thousands of acres. In Spanish-speaking countries, farms that are very large are called haciendas. On these farms, most of the work is done by tenant farmers or hired laborers.

Many farmers in the Caribbean Lands raise livestock for sale. Land that is too dry, too swampy, or too rugged for growing crops is often used for pasturing cattle. There are huge cattle ranches in the highlands and on the Pacific Lowland* of Central America. Large numbers of cattle are also raised in Cuba, the Dominican Republic, Puerto Rico, and Jamaica. Most of the cattle hides and meat are used locally. However, some countries export beef to the United States. Hogs are raised throughout the Caribbean Lands. In the highlands of Guatemala, Indian farmers raise sheep.

Export Crops

The Caribbean Lands region exports large quantities of tropical farm products. Several crops are grown for export in the Caribbean Lands. These crops are either sold directly to foreign countries or used in the Caribbean countries to make other products for export. Each

Loading bananas in the West Indies. Large amounts of tropical farm products are exported from the Caribbean Lands to other parts of the world.

year, large amounts of such farm products as sugar, bananas, and coffee are shipped from the Caribbean Lands to other parts of the world.

Because most parts of the Caribbean Lands are warm the year around, this region is well suited to growing bananas, sugarcane, and other tropical crops. These crops grow best where the weather is always warm or hot. They cannot be grown very well in most parts of the United States or in other areas outside the tropics.

The Caribbean countries have an important advantage for exporting tropical farm products. They are very close to the United States. Each year, the people of the United States buy large amounts of coffee and other farm products from the Caribbean Lands. Many of the plantations that produce export crops in the Caribbean region were started by people from the United States.

110

Harvesting sugarcane on St. Croix. The most important export crop in the West Indies is sugarcane. Because most parts of the Caribbean Lands are warm the year around, this region is well suited to growing sugarcane, bananas, and other tropical crops.

For example, American businessmen were the first to export bananas from Central America. Most of the tools, machinery, and other equipment used on the plantations were made in American factories.

If you study the map on pages 14 and 15, you will learn another reason why the Caribbean region is well suited to exporting farm products. No place in this region is very far from the seacoast. Farm products do not have to be transported long distances by land. It is much cheaper to send bulky products by sea than by land or air.

Sugarcane. In the West Indies, the most important export crop is sugarcane. The juice of this plant is used in making sugar, molasses, and other valuable products. Cuba exports more sugar than any other country in the world. Large amounts of sugar are also exported from the Dominican Republic, Puerto Rico, Jamaica, and several islands in the Lesser Antilles.

Sugarcane grows best in a constantly warm climate with moderate rainfall. Where the yearly rainfall is less than forty-five inches, the cane fields must be irrigated. If there is too much rain, especially at harvesttime, the cane juice will not contain much sugar. Therefore, cane is usually harvested during the drier months of the year.

Most sugarcane is grown on level lowlands near the seacoast. There are several reasons for this. In the highlands, the climate may be too cool for sugarcane. Also, the best soils for growing this crop are usually found in the lowlands. The cane must be taken to a sugar mill for processing within two

111

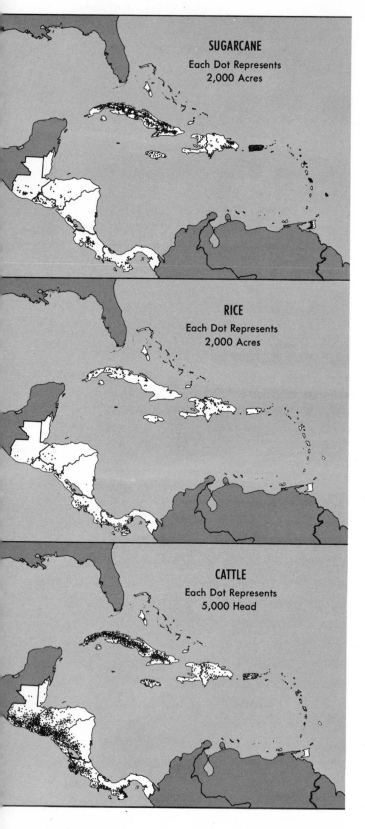

SUGARCANE
Each Dot Represents
2,000 Acres

RICE
Each Dot Represents
2,000 Acres

CATTLE
Each Dot Represents
5,000 Head

days after it is cut, or the juice will turn sour. It is quicker and easier to transport the cane on level land than it would be in mountainous areas. The sugar mills are usually located near seaports, from which the sugar is shipped to foreign countries.

To learn more about this crop, let us visit a large sugar plantation on the southern coast of the Dominican Republic. We arrive during the *zafra,* or harvest season. Bright-green fields of ripe sugarcane stretch across the level coastal plain in every direction. Rows of perspiring workers are cutting the tall cane stalks with large knives called machetes. The cane is hauled on ox-carts to a nearby railroad track. There it is loaded onto railroad cars that carry it to a sugar mill several miles away.

The plantation that we are visiting covers many thousands of acres. Only about one third of this land is used for growing sugarcane at any one time. Some of the remaining land is used to pasture oxen and other work animals. A small part is used to grow food crops for the plantation workers. The rest of the land is allowed to remain idle, or fallow, for several years. This helps to restore plant foods that sugarcane has taken from the soil.

In the West Indies, there are many large sugar plantations like this one. Some of them are owned by companies in foreign countries. In many cases, the same companies own the mills where the cane is processed. In Cuba today, all of the large sugar plantations are owned by the government.

Sugarcane is grown in every country of Central America. However, these countries export very little sugar. The Caribbean Lowland* is too wet for growing sugarcane. On the Pacific Lowland, this crop must be irrigated during the dry season. Sugarcane can be raised in some parts of the highlands, but here coffee is easier to grow and to transport. For these and other reasons, the Central American countries generally produce only enough sugar for their own needs.

Bananas. On the lowlands of Central America, bananas are a leading export crop. Banana plants grow best where the climate is hot and moist the year around.

During the late 1800's, United States companies started large banana plantations on the Caribbean Lowland. Here, the climate was just right for growing bananas. Near the rivers, the soil was very fertile. The Caribbean coast of Central America was close to New Orleans and other seaports in the southern part of the United States. Location was very important, because the bananas had to be transported rapidly to customers. Otherwise, the bananas would spoil.

For a time, the plantations on the Caribbean Lowland were very productive. Then the banana plants were attacked by disease. The fruit companies abandoned some of their plantations and started new ones on the Pacific Lowland. Here, the banana plants are irrigated during the dry season. The plants are also sprayed with chemicals to protect them from disease.

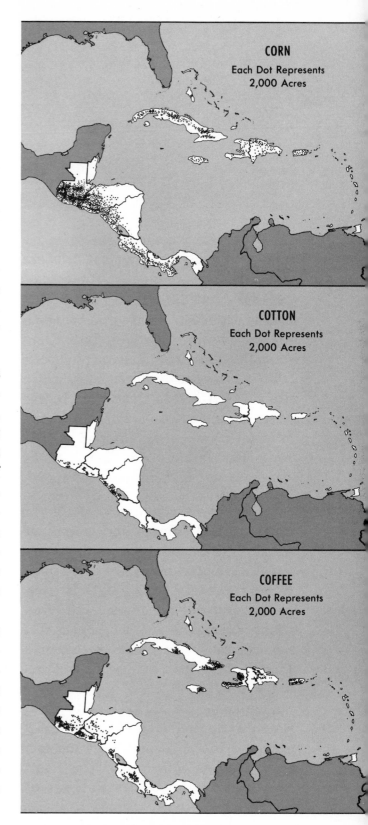

CORN
Each Dot Represents
2,000 Acres

COTTON
Each Dot Represents
2,000 Acres

COFFEE
Each Dot Represents
2,000 Acres

113

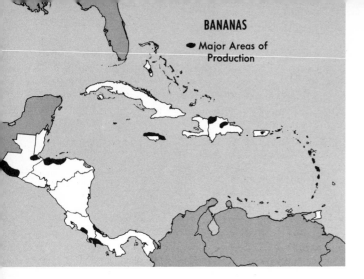

The map above shows the main banana-producing areas in the Caribbean Lands. Honduras, Panama, Guatemala, and Costa Rica rank among the world's leading exporters of this crop. Bananas are also grown in the West Indies, but in smaller quantities. Banana plants are easily destroyed by hurricanes, which often sweep across this area. In the West Indies, bananas are usually grown on small farms rather than on plantations. The farmers sell their banana crops to large fruit companies for export.

Coffee. In the highlands of Central America, the leading export crop is coffee. It is grown mainly in valleys and on mountain slopes near the Pacific coast. Here, the weather is mild the year around. Rainfall is moderate and comes mainly during the summer months. The volcanic soil is rich and well drained. These conditions are ideal for growing coffee.

Guatemala, El Salvador, and Costa Rica are the leading producers of coffee in the Caribbean Lands. Together they grow far less coffee than the South American country of Brazil. However, their coffee usually brings a higher price because of its excellent flavor. In the United States, Central American

114

coffee is blended with cheaper Brazilian coffee to produce many of the brands that are sold in grocery stores.

Coffee farms, or *fincas,* as they are called in Central America, are different from the sugar and banana plantations described earlier. Usually they are much smaller in area. Also, most of them are owned locally rather than by foreign companies.

One of the best ways to learn about the growing of coffee would be to visit a typical *finca* in the highlands of Guatemala. Here you would see rows and rows of small, dark-green coffee trees. They are planted between taller trees that shade them from the sun. Coffee trees grow best when they are protected from bright sunlight.

It is February, and the coffee trees are covered with clusters of large red and green berries. Men, women, and children are picking the red berries and dropping them into baskets. The green berries are not ripe yet. They will be picked later

Coffee farms in Costa Rica. Coffee is the leading export crop in the highlands of Central America. It is also grown in parts of the West Indies.

Bagging coffee beans at a coffee-processing plant in El Salvador. Guatemala, El Salvador, and Costa Rica are the leading producers of coffee in the Caribbean Lands. The coffee exported from these countries has an excellent flavor.

when they, too, have turned red. The ripe berries are taken to a building nearby. There they are soaked in water and put through machines that remove their soft outer covering. Inside each berry are two bluish-green coffee beans. The beans are washed and then spread out on concrete platforms to dry in the sun. Workers rake the beans frequently to make sure that they dry evenly. Several days later, the beans are taken to machines that remove their thin, tight-fitting skins. Finally they are sorted and poured into bags. The bags are carried in trucks to a seaport where they are loaded onto ships bound for Europe and the United States.

Coffee is also grown in mountainous sections of the West Indies. It is a leading export of Haiti and the Dominican Republic. Most of the coffee grown in Cuba, Jamaica, and Puerto Rico is used locally. Only a small amount is exported.

Cacao. In several Caribbean countries, cacao is an important export. The cacao tree grows best in lowlands where the climate is hot and humid. It produces many large, bright-colored pods. Each pod contains a number of purple seeds, or beans. The seeds are placed in piles and covered with banana leaves. They are allowed to stand for several days until the seeds turn brown. Then the seeds are spread out to dry in the sun. Most of the dried seeds are shipped to foreign countries, where they are used in making chocolate and cocoa.

Tobacco. Many farmers in Cuba, the Dominican Republic, and Puerto Rico grow tobacco for export. Tobacco is a crop that needs much care, so it is usually grown on small farms with the help of many workers. The tobacco grown in Cuba is especially noted for its quality. "Havana" cigars, made from Cuban tobacco, are considered to be the finest in the world.

Cotton. In recent years, cotton has become a leading export crop in Central America. The Pacific Lowland is well suited to raising this crop, which needs a hot, humid growing season and a dry harvest season. Some of the cotton grown in Central America is used locally, but much of it is exported to Japan and other countries.

Many Caribbean countries depend heavily on a single export crop. Earlier in this chapter, you learned that most farmers in the Caribbean Lands grow subsistence crops. Nevertheless, export crops are also very important to this region. Many people earn their living by

A Cuban worker pruning tobacco. Many farmers in Cuba, the Dominican Republic, and Puerto Rico grow tobacco. Cuban tobacco is noted for its fine quality.

Picking cotton in Nicaragua. In recent years, cotton has become a leading export crop on the Pacific Lowland of Central America.

growing export crops or processing them for market. Taxes on exports help provide money to operate the government. By exporting farm products, the Caribbean countries earn money to buy manufactured goods and other needed items from foreign countries.

In most Caribbean countries, a single farm product brings in more than one third of all the money earned from exports. In Cuba and the Dominican Republic, the main export is sugar. (See the graph on page 128.) Coffee is the leading export of Guatemala, El Salvador, Costa Rica, and Haiti. Any country that depends heavily on a single crop for income is said to have a one-crop economy.

There are many disadvantages to a one-crop economy. In some countries, so much farmland is used for growing the main export crop that the people do not raise enough food for themselves.

Food must be imported from other countries, often at high prices. Sometimes a country's main export crop is ruined by disease, hurricane, or other disaster. When this happens, the people of that country have little to export.

Countries with a one-crop economy do not have a steady income. The price that customers are willing to pay for a particular export crop varies greatly from time to time. When the price is high, the people who grow this crop are prosperous. When the price is low, farmers receive less money for the goods they produce. Owners of large plantations may not find it profitable to harvest all of their crop. As a result, many plantation workers may be without jobs.

Even in times of high prices, unemployment is a serious problem for countries with a one-crop economy. Most farms that produce export crops need large numbers of workers only when the crop is being harvested. During the rest of the year, many people are out of work. If other kinds of crops were produced within the country, there would be harvests at different times of the year. Then there would be less unemployment.

Today, the governments of some Caribbean countries are encouraging farmers to raise a variety of crops. In Puerto Rico, some land that was once used to grow sugarcane is now used for growing pineapples or for pasturing livestock. An increasing amount of farmland in Cuba and Central America is being used to grow rice for food. However, most parts of the Caribbean Lands still have a one-crop economy.

Reviewing What You Have Learned

Choose five of the following statements. Use each as the topic sentence of a short paragraph. In each paragraph, explain why the idea stated in the topic sentence is true.

1. Farmers who grow subsistence crops can live on a very small income.
2. Only about one fourth of all the land in the Caribbean region is being used for farming.
3. The Caribbean Lowland of Central America is well suited to the growing of bananas for export.
4. Coffee is grown in valleys and on mountain slopes near the Pacific coast of Central America.
5. Export crops are very important to most Caribbean countries.
6. The governments of some Caribbean countries are encouraging farmers to raise a variety of crops, rather than a single crop for export.

Exploring Relationships

1. How does climate help determine what food crops are grown in various parts of the Caribbean Lands?
2. What is being done by (a) local governments and (b) outside countries to help farmers in the Caribbean Lands?
3. Compare the Sugarcane map on page 112 with the map on page 16. Is more sugarcane grown in Central America or in the West Indies? State three reasons why this is true.
4. Compare the Cotton map on page 113 with the two small maps at the bottom of page 35 and the map on page 16. Why do you think cotton is grown near the Pacific coast of Central America rather than the Caribbean coast?

Defining Terms

In two or more sentences, state the meaning and significance of the following terms as they apply to the Caribbean Lands:

subsistence farming   "land hunger"
one-crop economy   export crops
tenant farmer   *finca*

Packaging butter in a Puerto Rican dairy. Puerto Rico is one of the few Caribbean countries that have made considerable progress in developing industry. Most of the factories in the Caribbean Lands are very small and employ fewer than one hundred people.

9 Industry

Problems To Solve

The Caribbean Lands region has been slow to develop industry. **Why is this true?**

To solve this problem, you will need to make several hypotheses. The following questions suggest some hypotheses:

a. What facts about the natural resources of the Caribbean Lands help to solve this problem?

b. What facts about the labor force of this region help to solve it?

c. What facts about the amount of money available for industrial development in this region help to solve it?

See TO THE STUDENT, pages 6-7.

There is very little industry in the Caribbean Lands. Compared to the United States, the Caribbean Lands region has few factories. Most of the factories in Caribbean countries are very small and employ fewer than one hundred people. Only about one out of every ten workers in this region earns his living by factory work.

At present, most of the people in the Caribbean Lands are too poor to buy many manufactured goods. However, industries here do not even produce all of the goods that the people can afford to buy. Many products must be imported from the United States and other industrial nations.

Why there is little manufacturing. There are many reasons for the lack of industry in the Caribbean Lands. Few people in this region have the technical skills needed to do factory work. Even fewer have been trained as engineers and managers. Most of the people are poor, uneducated farmers who scratch out a bare living from the soil in much the same way their ancestors did one hundred years ago.

Even if enough skilled labor were available in the Caribbean Lands, it would still be difficult to start new factories here. Most countries in this region lack the mineral resources and power needed by industry. For example, there is a lack of iron ore and coal, which are needed to make steel. The water-power of the Caribbean Lands is generally not being used to produce electricity. In most countries there is a lack of fuels, such as oil, which could be used to produce the electricity needed for running machines.

Money is needed if new industries are to be established in the Caribbean Lands. Raw materials and equipment must be bought, and sources of power must be developed. Most of the money in the Caribbean Lands is in the hands of a few wealthy people. Many of these people are unwilling to invest their money in industries in their own countries because they fear revolutions or dictatorship. Instead, their wealth is kept in banks abroad. For the same reasons, some foreign businessmen are also uneasy about investing their money in this region.

Processing farm products is the most important industry. The most important industry in the Caribbean Lands is preparing the region's farm products for market. These include not only major export products such as sugar, coffee, and tobacco, but also many farm products for use within the region. Some of the factories that process farm products are large, but most of them are very small.

The sugar industry. Some of the largest factories in the Caribbean Lands are sugar mills, or centrals.* These mills process sugarcane into raw sugar. Most of the centrals are located in the West Indies.

One large central is situated in a rich sugarcane-growing area on the southeastern coast of the Dominican Republic. The picture on page 120 shows the sugar mill with its tall smoke stacks. The company that owns this factory also owns many thousands of acres of land on which sugarcane is grown. The central has its own railroad system. Locomotives haul long lines of railroad cars loaded with sugarcane from the cane fields to the mill. The cane is then dumped on

Words To Think With

central	raw sugar	oil refineries	petrochemical
alumina	raw materials	standard of living	common market
tariff	World Bank	textiles	skilled labor

A sugar mill in the Dominican Republic. The most important industry in the Caribbean Lands is preparing the region's farm products for market. Some of the largest factories are sugar mills, or centrals,* where sugarcane is processed.

conveyor belts to be carried into the mill. Here it is crushed by a series of huge rollers which squeeze out the cane juice. By a complicated process, modern machinery then changes the juice into yellowish-brown sugar crystals. This product is called raw sugar.

Raw sugar must be further processed to make the sugar we buy in stores. Most of the centrals in the Caribbean Lands ship raw sugar to other countries for refining. However, the large factory described above is equipped to produce both raw and refined sugar. It also produces molasses and furfural, a substance used in the manufacture of synthetic fibers and in the refining of petroleum.

Almost all of the products made at this factory are sold to other countries. Like many others in the Caribbean Lands, this factory is owned by a United States company. However, much of the

money this company receives from the sale of its products is spent in the Dominican Republic. It is spent to pay Dominican taxes, to buy Dominican goods needed for operating the factory, and to pay the wages of the workers.

The company that owns this central employs thousands of workers. However, most of them are employed only during the harvest season, when they cut cane or do other agricultural work. During this time, the sugar mill grinds cane twenty-four hours a day. The rest of the year, the mill is shut down, and many of the workers are unemployed.

Other food-processing industries. Factories that process farm products other than sugarcane are found in every country in the Caribbean region. Dairies, soft-drink plants, fruit canneries, meat-packing plants, and other factories in each country produce food items for the people. Most of these plants are small and employ only a few workers. Many countries in the region also have breweries, and plants that produce rum and other liquors. Rum is made by distilling molasses, which is a by-product of sugar production. In some countries, such as Jamaica and Puerto Rico, rum is an important export. In recent years, new food-processing factories have been established in Guatemala, El Salvador, British Honduras, and other countries. Some of these factories make food products mainly for export, such as instant coffee and frozen orange juice.

Tobacco products. Another important industry in the Caribbean Lands is the manufacture of tobacco products. Many countries in this region produce cigars and cigarettes for domestic use. Cuba, Puerto Rico, and the Dominican Republic are important exporters of tobacco and tobacco products. Cuba has long been famous for the quality of its cigars. The best cigars are made by hand in small factories. Cuba formerly exported large quantities of cigars and cigar tobacco to the United States. However, in 1962, the United States stopped imports from Cuba. Today, most Cuban cigars are exported to countries in Europe.

Textiles and clothing. In Central America and on some islands in the West Indies, small factories produce textiles and clothing. Some of these factories use cotton grown in the Caribbean region. Since the weather is generally warm all year round, most people wear only light cotton clothing. Many countries manufacture much of the yarn and cloth needed by their people. However, all the countries of the Caribbean Lands import some textiles and clothing.

An instant-coffee factory in El Salvador. Factories that process farm products are found in every country in the Caribbean region. Among the most important industries are food processing, the manufacture of tobacco products, and the production of cotton textiles.

A large oil refinery on Trinidad. In a few Caribbean countries, factories have been built to process minerals. Oil refineries on Aruba, Curaçao, and Trinidad are among the world's largest. These giant refineries are owned by oil companies in countries outside the Caribbean region.

Some factories in the Caribbean Lands process minerals. In a few Caribbean countries, large factories have been built to process minerals. Oil refineries on the islands of Aruba, Curaçao, and Trinidad are among the largest in the world. These giant refineries are owned by oil companies in the United States and other countries outside the Caribbean region. Most of the oil processed by these refineries is brought in oil tankers from the nearby country of Venezuela, in South America, or from other oil-producing countries. However, some of the oil processed on Trinidad comes from wells on the island. In the refineries, crude oil is made into gasoline, fuel oil, and other valuable petroleum products. Almost all of these products are exported to other parts of the world.

In recent years, small refineries have been built in some Central American countries to process petroleum products for their own use. These refineries use imported crude oil.

Petroleum and natural gas provide the raw materials for making many valuable chemicals called petrochemicals. Large plants on Trinidad and Aruba produce fertilizers and other important products from petrochemicals.

A few countries in the Caribbean Lands have mills that process ores to make metals. On the island of Jamaica, a Canadian aluminum company operates two large factories that process bauxite. In these plants, the bauxite is refined into a substance called alumina. The alumina is then shipped to Canada and other countries, where it is made into aluminum.

Processing ores is becoming an important industry in Cuba. There are large deposits of iron, copper, nickel, and other valuable minerals on this island. Cuba is planning to build a huge steel mill and other large plants to process ores. The money and equipment needed for these plants will be supplied by the Soviet Union and other Communist countries.

Materials for construction are produced in many countries. Building materials, such as cement, glass, tile, and lumber, are manufactured in many Caribbean countries. These materials are needed for the construction of roads and buildings. The raw materials used in making these important products are generally available in the countries of the Caribbean region. There are large deposits of sand, limestone, and clay, which are used in making cement. The forests of the Caribbean Lands provide the raw material for lumber. Sawmills, cement plants, and brick kilns are found throughout the region. These factories are important to the Caribbean Lands because building materials are heavy and would be very costly if they had to be transported from other countries.

Other industries. There are many other small manufacturing plants in the Caribbean Lands. Some of these factories produce household goods, such as matches, soap, and candles. Others manufacture fertilizers, insecticides, and other products needed by farmers. Some countries, such as Puerto Rico, make products requiring highly skilled labor. Automobile tires, machinery, chemicals, and electronic equipment are among the goods produced in Puerto Rico. However, there are few factories in the Caribbean Lands that make products like these. Most factories are small and employ unskilled workers.

In a tile factory on Barbados. In many Caribbean countries, there are factories that make construction materials, such as cement, glass, tile, and lumber. These factories are important to the Caribbean Lands because building materials are heavy and would be costly to import.

The growth of industry is important to the Caribbean Lands. The countries of the Caribbean Lands are faced with an urgent need for more industry. Their people want a better way of life. However, they cannot raise their standard of living if they must depend on subsistence farming or the raising of one or two export crops, such as bananas or sugar. (See Chapter 8.)

Today, many people are leaving farm work and moving to the cities. In the cities, they often cannot find jobs and are forced to live in crowded slums. New industries are needed to provide jobs for these people.

New industries will help to solve many of the problems of the Caribbean Lands. People who work in factories will earn more money to spend on manufactured goods than they did as farmers. By selling more goods, factories will earn money that will help them to grow.

Governments in the Caribbean Lands are encouraging new industries. The governments of many Caribbean countries are trying to encourage the growth of manufacturing. Special government agencies have been formed to assist people who wish to start new businesses. Some governments offer lower taxes and other benefits to companies opening new factories.

In Central America, all of the countries except Panama and British Honduras have joined together in a "common market."* These countries are gradually removing tariffs, or taxes, on products shipped from one common-market country to another. They hope that the common market will help increase trade and encourage industry.

Outsiders are also encouraging the growth of industry. People in countries outside the Caribbean Lands are also helping to develop industry in this region. Businesses from abroad have established factories in several Caribbean countries, including Puerto Rico, Jamaica, and Costa Rica. These companies not only provide jobs for many people but also train workers and managers in skills needed for industry. Money for new industries is also provided by the World Bank. The United States government has made loans and grants to countries of the Caribbean Lands. Great Britain, France, and the Netherlands are providing assistance to their possessions and former colonies in the Caribbean region.

Industry is growing in some parts of the Caribbean Lands. Puerto Rico and Cuba are examples of countries that have made considerable progress in developing industries. Before World War II, Puerto Rico depended almost entirely on farming and had very little industry. Most Puerto Ricans lived in extreme poverty. Today, Puerto Rican factories employ thousands of workers and produce a wide variety of goods, from soap to electronic equipment. Chapter 25 explains how industry is being developed here through a program called "Operation Bootstrap."

Cuba is also one of the leading manufacturing countries in the Caribbean Lands. Factories on this island produce steel and machinery as well as clothing and household goods. The Communist government of Cuba controls most of the industries. Chapter 21 describes the difficulties the Communists are facing as they try to expand industry in Cuba.

In a large textile mill in Cuba, one of the leading manufacturing countries in the Caribbean Lands. Factories on this island produce steel and machinery as well as clothing and household goods. The governments of many Caribbean countries are trying to develop more industry.

Yes or No

Write the number of each of the following sentences on a sheet of paper. If the statement is true, write **yes** after the number. If it is not true, write **no**, and correct the statement.

1. Most of the factories in the Caribbean Lands employ several hundred persons.
2. About one out of every four workers in the Caribbean Lands earns his living by factory work.
3. Most Caribbean countries have the mineral resources and power needed by industry.
4. The most important industry in the Caribbean Lands is processing minerals.
5. Some of the largest factories in the Caribbean Lands are centrals.
6. Most centrals in the Caribbean Lands produce refined sugar.
7. There are food-processing plants in every Caribbean country.

8. Most oil refineries in the Caribbean Lands use petroleum produced within the region.

Ideas To Review

1. Why are many wealthy people uneasy about investing money in industries in the Caribbean Lands? Give one reason.

2. State two ways in which governments of Caribbean countries are encouraging the development of industry.

3. How are outsiders encouraging the development of industry in the Caribbean Lands? List two ways.

4. What is a common market? In what part of the Caribbean Lands has a common market been formed? What are its aims? The information under "common market" in the Glossary will help you answer these questions.

The harbor of Kingston, Jamaica, where many ships stop to load and unload goods. Countries in the Caribbean Lands region must buy many products from outside nations. Most Caribbean countries sell farm products and other raw materials to help pay for the goods they import.

10 Trade and Tourists

Problems To Solve

Most Caribbean countries depend heavily on trade with nations outside their region. **Why is this true?** In solving this problem, you will need to make hypotheses about how trade in the Caribbean Lands is affected by the following:

a. manufacturing in this region
b. farming in this region
c. transportation within the region and to other parts of the world
d. the relationship between each colony and its mother country during colonial days

Chapters 8, 9, and 11 contain information that will be helpful in solving this problem.

See TO THE STUDENT, pages 6-7.

A large ocean liner moves slowly into the harbor of Kingston, Jamaica. Its decks are crowded with tourists who have come to enjoy Jamaica's warm, sunny climate and beautiful scenery.

The tourists are watching other ships entering or leaving the harbor. Their vessel passes within a few hundred feet of a Dutch oil tanker loaded with fuel oil from the Netherlands Antilles.

As the passenger liner prepares to dock, the tourists see several large cargo ships anchored alongside the wharves. Dock workers are loading some of the ships with bags of raw sugar and others with stems of green bananas. Cargoes of flour and rice are being unloaded from other ships. At one end of the waterfront, huge cranes are unloading crates of heavy machinery from a British ship.

Trade

Foreign trade is very important to the Caribbean Lands. The Caribbean countries must buy many products from other nations. As you learned in Chapter 9, most Caribbean countries have very little industry. Therefore, they must import large quantities of textiles, machinery, and other factory-made goods. Most of them also need to buy petroleum products, such as fuel oil, from other nations.

The Caribbean countries also import some of the food that their people eat. Food imports are especially large in the West Indies. Many West Indian islands have little land that is suitable for farming. On others, most of the farmland is used for raising export crops. As a result, some islands do not produce enough food for their own needs. They must import rice, flour, and other food items.

To help pay for the goods they import, most Caribbean countries sell farm products and other raw materials to other nations. The main exports of Central America are bananas and coffee. Sugar is the main export of the West Indies. A few countries in the West Indies export large amounts of valuable minerals. Puerto Rico is the only Caribbean country that exports large amounts of factory-made goods.

There are other reasons why foreign trade is important to the Caribbean Lands. By taxing exports and imports, the governments of many Caribbean countries raise part of the money they need for roads, schools, and other projects. Also, a large number of people earn a living by raising crops or producing other raw materials for export. If other countries did not buy these products, many people in the Caribbean Lands would be without jobs.

The map on page 16 shows that the Caribbean countries have another advantage for foreign trade. They are very near the United States, which imports

Unloading a tractor. Because most Caribbean countries have little industry, they must import machinery, textiles, and many other factory-made goods.

MAIN EXPORTS OF ELEVEN CARIBBEAN COUNTRIES

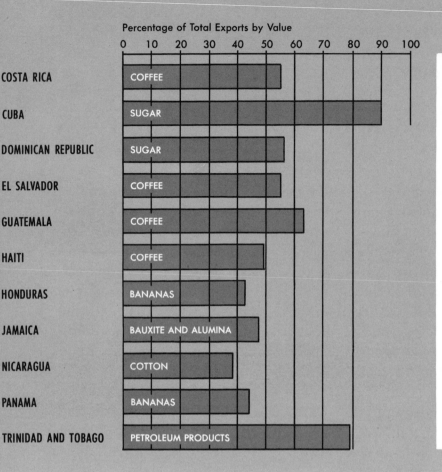

Percentage of Total Exports by Value

COSTA RICA	COFFEE
CUBA	SUGAR
DOMINICAN REPUBLIC	SUGAR
EL SALVADOR	COFFEE
GUATEMALA	COFFEE
HAITI	COFFEE
HONDURAS	BANANAS
JAMAICA	BAUXITE AND ALUMINA
NICARAGUA	COTTON
PANAMA	BANANAS
TRINIDAD AND TOBAGO	PETROLEUM PRODUCTS

The graph at the left shows the main exports of all the independent countries in the Caribbean Lands. Each country depends heavily on a single export product. Several countries make more money from their leading export than from all their other exports combined.

In nearly every country listed, the main export is a farm product, such as coffee or sugar. Mineral products are the leading exports of the countries of Jamaica and Trinidad and Tobago. Because most of the Caribbean countries produce the same crops as other countries in the region, they have little need to trade with one another.

(Based on 1962 figures, except for Guatemala, for which 1961 figures were used.)

and exports more goods than any other country in the world. From the Caribbean Lands, the United States obtains large amounts of such products as sugar, coffee, bananas, and bauxite. In return, it supplies the Caribbean countries with machinery, metals, and other products they need.

The location of the Caribbean Lands is favorable to foreign trade. Shipping their products to other parts of the world is easy for the Caribbean countries because they border on important waterways. The Caribbean Lands region lies between the world's two largest oceans, the Atlantic and the Pacific. These oceans are connected by the Panama Canal. Each year, thousands of ships

from all parts of the world pass through the Caribbean Sea on their way to or from the canal. These ships can easily stop at ports in the Caribbean Lands to load and unload goods.

The Caribbean countries trade mainly with nations outside their region. The Caribbean countries have never traded very much with one another. During the 1600's and 1700's, each European colony in the region traded mainly with its mother country. It sent the mother country farm products and bought manufactured goods in return. Most of the colonies produced the same crops for export. Today, most of the Caribbean countries still produce the same crops as other countries in the region.

128

Therefore, they have little reason to trade among themselves. Because these countries have not developed large industries, they still buy most of the manufactured goods they need from countries outside the region.

Many Caribbean countries trade mainly with the United States. This nation is the chief buyer of exports and the chief supplier of imports for each of the six Central American republics. Puerto Rico and the Virgin Islands trade almost entirely with the United States. Trade with our country is also important to Haiti, the Dominican Republic, and the Bahamas.

Some Caribbean countries trade mainly with nations other than the United States. Great Britain is the chief buyer of exports and supplier of imports for nearly all of its colonies in the West Indies. The independent nation of Trinidad and Tobago, which was formerly a British colony, also trades mainly with Britain. The French islands of Guadeloupe and Martinique trade almost entirely with France.

Cuba is the only Caribbean country that trades mainly with Communist countries. Formerly, about three fourths of Cuba's trade was with the United States. Today, the United States and some other countries have stopped trading with Cuba. They do not wish to aid its Communist government. The United States government allows no products from this country to be sold to Cuba except medicine and some foods. Cuba now exports thousands of tons of sugar each year to the Soviet Union, China, and other Communist countries. In return, Cuba receives food, fuel oil, machinery, and many other products from these countries.

A Russian oil tanker in the harbor of Havana, Cuba. The Caribbean countries trade mainly with nations outside their region. Many of them buy most of the manufactured goods they need from the United States. Cuba is the only Caribbean nation that trades mainly with Communist countries.

Some of the Caribbean countries are trying to increase trade with each other. All of the Central American republics except Panama have joined together to form a "common market."* They are reducing or eliminating taxes on many goods shipped between them. Since the common market was formed, trade among the member countries has nearly tripled.

Tourists

In recent years, the tourist industry has become important to several Caribbean countries. Many people have jobs in stores, hotels, and restaurants that serve tourists. Also, money that each country receives from its tourist industry helps to pay for the goods it must import.

Many islands in the West Indies have a large tourist industry. Each year, more than one and one-half million tourists visit the West Indies. About half of them come from the United States. Large numbers of visitors also come from Great Britain and Canada.

The islands of the West Indies have many attractions for tourists. The climate here is pleasantly warm. This area has beautiful scenery, including tropical forests, towering volcanoes, and fine, sandy beaches. The people of the islands are interesting to visitors from other countries because they have different customs and ways of life. Many luxurious hotels built in the West Indies in

Tourists enjoy the warm climate and beautiful scenery in the Virgin Islands of the United States, one of the leading tourist areas in the West Indies. Each year, more than one and one-half million tourists visit the West Indies. About half of them come from the United States.

recent years have also helped to attract tourists.

The leading tourist areas in the West Indies are Puerto Rico, the Bahamas, the Virgin Islands of the United States, and Jamaica. More tourists visit Puerto Rico than any other island in the West Indies. Under "Operation Bootstrap," many new hotels have been built, and a profitable tourist industry has been developed on the island. At one time, more tourists went to Cuba than to any other country in the Caribbean Lands. Today, hardly any people from the United States visit Cuba.

In Central America, the tourist industry has just begun to develop. Not nearly so many tourists visit Central America as the West Indies. Central America has some disadvantages for vacationers. The climate of the lowlands in Central America is hotter and more humid than the climate of the West Indies. In the highlands of Central America, the climate is mild and generally pleasant. However, lack of transportation makes travel difficult in many parts of this region.

Most of the Central American countries are trying to develop a large tourist industry. In recent years, several

A modern hotel in Panama City, Panama. Most of the Central American countries are trying to develop a large tourist industry.

modern hotels have been built in Central America. Tourists who come here can enjoy viewing the beautiful mountain scenery, giant volcanic cones, and lovely lakes. In some parts of Central America, the interesting customs of the Indians are also an attraction for tourists. The Inter-American Highway, which has recently been completed, is expected to increase the number of tourists who visit Central America. (See page 134.)

Taking a Trip

Guatemala has many attractions for tourists. Pretend you are going to travel there by car from your hometown. Draw a map showing the route you would follow from your home to Guatemala City. (The maps on pages 133, 134, and 157 will be helpful. You will also need to use a road map of the United States.) Read about Guatemala in at least two sources in addition to this textbook. Then write a report telling what you would like to see and do there. Locate places of interest on your map, and describe the proposed trip to your classmates.

Ideas To Review

1. Why do some Caribbean countries trade mainly with Great Britain? Why does Cuba trade mainly with the Soviet Union and other Communist countries?

2. How is the Central American common market affecting trade between its members?

3. Why do more tourists visit the West Indies than Central America?

Walking to market

A railroad in Guatemala

At an airport in Puerto Rico

It is difficult to travel and to transport goods overland in most Caribbean countries because of the lack of roads and railroads. Many people must carry their goods to market themselves.

11   Transportation and Communication

Problems To Solve

Inadequate land transportation is one of the handicaps holding back industrial development in the Caribbean Lands. **Why is it difficult for the people of the Caribbean Lands to improve their transportation facilities?** In solving this problem, you will need to make hypotheses about how efforts to improve land transportation in this region are affected by the following:

a. the land features of the Caribbean Lands

b. the climate of the Caribbean region

Chapters 1 and 2 contain information that will be helpful in solving this problem.

See TO THE STUDENT, pages 6-7.

Land transportation is poor in most Caribbean countries. It is difficult to build roads and railroads in the Caribbean Lands region. In both Central America and the West Indies, much of the land is rugged and mountainous.

Some areas, such as the Caribbean Lowland of Central America, are covered with dense rainforest. Most Caribbean countries cannot afford the cost of building and maintaining roads and railroads in mountainous or densely forested areas.

132

The lack of roads and railroads makes it difficult to travel and to transport goods in most Caribbean countries. Many people live in small communities that are not connected with other parts of the country by good roads or railroads. If they have products to sell, they have difficulty getting them to market. Goods must be transported on the backs of animals or in carts, or by the people themselves. Also, it is difficult for manufacturers to distribute their products in areas that lack roads and railroads. In many forested areas, there is no way to get valuable logs out of the forests.

Some deposits of valuable ores are not mined, partly because of the lack of good land transportation.

Roads. In the Caribbean Lands region, there are about 70,000 miles of roads. However, only about 16,000 miles are paved. Most roads are dirt or gravel. During times of heavy rainfall, the dirt roads often become too muddy for cars and trucks to travel on them. In some places, there are no roads except narrow trails.

Most Caribbean countries are trying to develop a better network of roads.

Main roads in the Caribbean Lands. There are about 70,000 miles of roads in this region. However, only about 16,000 miles are paved. In some areas, there are no roads at all. Most Caribbean countries are trying to develop a better network of roads.

133

ATLANTIC OCEAN

Mexico City

PACIFIC

Caracas

Panama City

Bogotá

Quito

OCEAN

Lima

La Paz

Rio de Janeiro

Santiago

Buenos Aires

ATLANTIC

OCEAN

—— Pan American Highway
∿∿ Country Boundaries
Scale of Miles
0   500 1000 1500

PAN AMERICAN HIGHWAY

The Pan American Highway is a system of roads extending through Mexico, Central America, and much of South America. Its total length is more than 21,000 miles.

Nearly all of the Pan American Highway is completed. The only gap is a section about 450 miles long in Panama and Colombia. This section will not be finished until about 1970. Rugged mountains and dense forests along much of the route have made it very difficult to construct the highway.

No Pan American Highway routes have been established in the United States or Canada. However, the Pan American Highway system connects with United States highways at the Mexican border. When the Pan American Highway is finished, it will be possible to drive all the way from the southernmost countries of South America to Alaska.

One purpose of the Pan American Highway is to help maintain friendly relations among the American nations. The highway is also expected to increase trade among the countries that it connects, by making shipment of goods faster and easier.

They realize that good roads for transporting raw materials and finished products are necessary for the growth of industry. During recent years, new roads have been built in many parts of the Caribbean Lands, and many old roads have been widened and improved. In some countries, such as Jamaica and Puerto Rico, no city or town is far from an all-weather highway. One of the aims of the Alliance for Progress is to build more roads in Latin-American countries. (See page 13.)

The longest road in the Caribbean Lands is the Inter-American Highway. It begins in the United States, in Laredo, Texas, and extends through Mexico and Central America as far as Panama City, Panama. The part of the highway in Central America is more than 1,500 miles long. It links all of the Central American countries except British Honduras. (Compare map on page 133 with map on pages 14 and 15.) Although sections in Guatemala, Costa Rica, and Panama are not yet paved, it is possible to drive from the United States to Panama City on the Inter-American Highway.

The Inter-American Highway is part of a huge highway system that is planned to connect Mexico and all the independent countries of Central and South America. This system is called the Pan American Highway. (See map at left.)

Railroads. There are few miles of railroads in any Caribbean country except Cuba. This island has more than 11,000 miles of railroad tracks. All of the other railroads in the West Indies total less than 1,500 miles. In Central America,

Main railroads in the Caribbean Lands. There are few miles of railroads in any Caribbean country except Cuba. In many countries, trains and railroad tracks are old and in poor condition. An important use of railroads is transporting products from farm areas to seaports.

there are only about three thousand miles of railways. (Compare map above with map on pages 14 and 15.) In many Caribbean countries, most of the trains and railroad tracks are old and in poor condition.

Many of the railroads in the Caribbean Lands were built to transport products from farming areas to seaports. In Cuba, most of the railways are used to carry sugarcane from the fields to nearby mills, and to take raw sugar from the mills to seaports. Some of the railways in

Central America are used to haul coffee from the highlands to cities on the coasts. In the lowlands of Central America, there are several railroad lines that connect banana plantations with nearby harbors. Some railways in the Caribbean Lands also provide passenger service.

Airways. Air transportation is especially useful in a region where land transportation is usually poor, such as the Caribbean Lands. Airplanes can fly over rugged mountains and dense forests where it is difficult to build roads and

135

railroads. Although air transportation is very costly, even bulky products, such as coffee and chicle, are sometimes carried by airplane. However, most people who live in the Caribbean Lands cannot afford to travel by plane.

As the map below shows, many international airlines serve the Caribbean Lands. Planes from South America, Mexico, the United States, Europe, and other parts of the world make regular flights to Caribbean countries. Several cities in the Caribbean Lands, such as Panama City, Panama, and San Juan,

Puerto Rico, have large, modern airports. Many Caribbean countries have their own airlines, which connect most of the important cities and towns in each country.

Water transportation. Sugar, bananas, coffee, and other leading exports of the Caribbean Lands are carried mainly by ship. Because these cargoes are bulky and must be transported for long distances, it is usually cheaper to send them by sea than by air or by land. The Caribbean countries border on important waterways. Ships from all over the

Main airways of the Caribbean Lands. Planes from South America, the United States, Europe, and other parts of the world make regular flights to Caribbean countries. Air transportation is especially useful in the Caribbean Lands because land transportation here is usually poor.

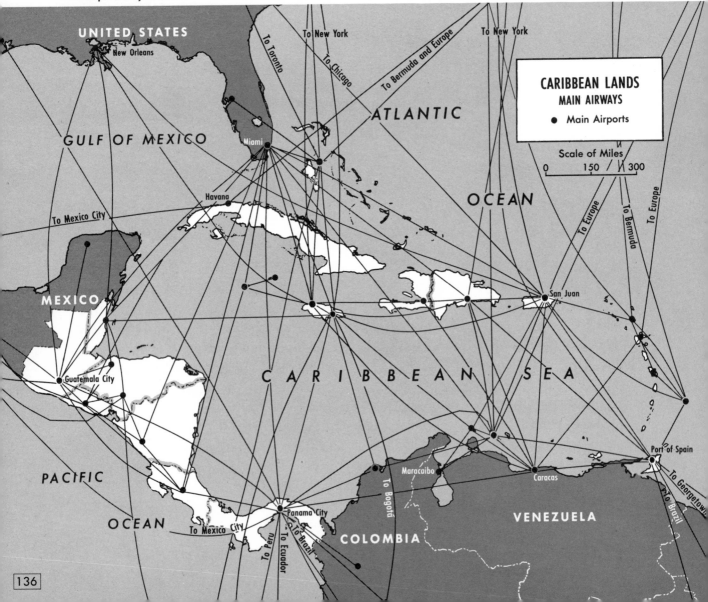

The Gatun Locks, one of three sets of locks that raise or lower ships on their way through the Panama Canal. This canal is one of the world's most important waterways. Each year, thousands of ships from all over the world pass through it.

world pass through the Caribbean Sea on their way to or from the Panama Canal. These ships can easily stop at ports in the Caribbean Lands to load or unload goods.

Ships bring to Caribbean countries fuel oil and many other goods that must be imported. Also, many tourists come to the Caribbean Lands by ship. The tourist industry provides an important source of income for many countries in this region. (See Chapter 10.)

The Panama Canal. Stretching across the Isthmus of Panama is one of the world's most important waterways, the Panama Canal. It provides a shortcut of several thousand miles for ships sailing between the Atlantic and Pacific oceans. If these ships did not use the canal, they would have to travel all the way around the tip of South America. Each year, thousands of ships from many different

nations pass through the Panama Canal. They carry fuel oil, metals, lumber, and many other products. (Pages 220 and 221 tell about the building of the Panama Canal. Additional information can be found in the special feature on page 139.)

A trip through the Panama Canal. One of the best ways to learn about the Panama Canal would be to take a trip through it. A ship entering the canal from the Pacific Ocean passes the city of Balboa. For several miles, the canal resembles a slow-moving river. Then the ship approaches the Miraflores Locks, the first of three sets of locks that raise or lower ships on their way through the canal. From the air, the Miraflores Locks look like giant stairsteps.

Before the ship enters the Miraflores Locks, a canal pilot who has come aboard gives an order to stop the ship's engines. Then towing cables are tossed aboard the ship. The cables are attached to small electric locomotives that run on tracks alongside the canal. These locomotives pull ships through the locks.

Two steel gates swing open, and the ship is towed into a huge concrete chamber that is partly filled with water. Then the gates are closed behind the ship. Because the walls of the chamber are so high, the ship seems to be at the bottom of a huge tub. Canal workers operate valves that allow water to rush into the chamber from openings in its floor. As the water level in the chamber slowly rises, the ship also rises. It takes about fifteen minutes to raise the ship to the level of the water in the second lock. Then the gates between the two chambers are opened, and the ship is towed into the second one. Here it is "lifted" to the level of Miraflores Lake. (See map on opposite page.)

The ship moves under its own power across Miraflores Lake. On the other side of the lake, it enters the Pedro Miguel

The Gaillard Cut, which is the narrowest and most hazardous part of the Panama Canal, looks like an enormous, water-filled ditch.

Locks. Here it is lifted to the level of the water in the Gaillard Cut. This section of the canal looks like an enormous, water-filled ditch, with steep hills rising on both sides. It was dug through solid rock for almost its entire length of about eight miles. Because the Gaillard Cut is so narrow, it is the most hazardous part of the canal.

After winding its way through the narrow Gaillard Cut, the ship enters Gatun Lake. This is one of the largest man-made lakes in the world. The ship sails about twenty-four miles across the lake, passing between several islands.

Before the ship reaches the Caribbean end of the canal, it must be brought down to sea level again. After leaving Gatun Lake, it enters the Gatun Locks. Here it must pass through three chambers. Each chamber is already filled with water when the ship enters. As the water is slowly let out, the ship is lowered to the next level. When the ship leaves the Gatun Locks, it goes through a short channel into Limon Bay, an inlet of the Caribbean Sea. The trip through the canal, a distance of nearly fifty-one miles, has taken about eight hours.

Another canal may be built across Central America. Many people feel that there is need for another canal linking the Atlantic and Pacific oceans. In recent years, there has been such an increase in ship traffic through the Panama Canal that vessels often have to wait in line for several hours to enter. Also, the Panama Canal is too small to be used by some of the larger ships built today. A new canal would be deeper and wider.

The United States government is considering several possible routes for another canal. Two of the routes pass

138

The Panama Canal

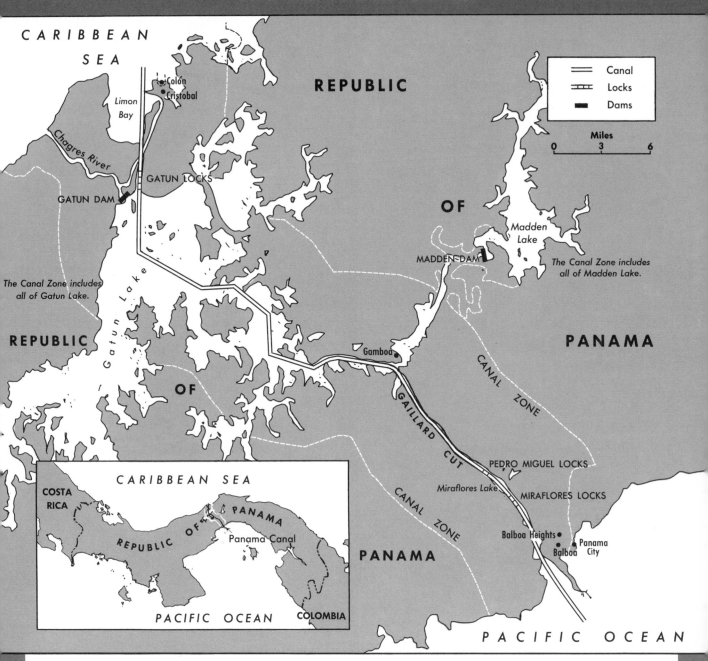

The Panama Canal connects two great bodies of water, the Pacific Ocean and the Caribbean Sea, an arm of the Atlantic Ocean. It extends from northwest to southeast across the narrowest part of the Isthmus of Panama. The United States operates the canal and governs the Canal Zone, a strip of land about ten miles wide along the route of the canal.

Because much of the land on the Isthmus of Panama does not lie at the same level as the oceans, constructing a canal here presented many problems. In order to build a canal at sea level, workmen would have had to dig through many miles of almost solid rock and remove thousands of tons of earth.

This type of canal would have been very costly and would have taken many years to complete. Therefore, it was decided to build most of the canal at a level higher than the oceans.

The Chagres River was dammed to form Gatun Lake at about eighty-five feet above sea level. With great difficulty, the Gaillard Cut was dug at the same level. (See page 221.) On the Caribbean side of Gatun Lake and at the Pacific end of Gaillard Cut, locks were built to raise or lower ships. Each lock consists of a huge concrete chamber with gates at both ends. Pages 137 and 138 tell how the locks are used to raise or lower ships on their way through the canal.

In a marketplace. Many small towns and rural areas do not have modern means of communication. News is often spread by people talking in the marketplace.

through the eastern part of Panama. Another crosses Nicaragua. Canal routes through Mexico and across the northwestern part of Colombia have also been studied. It is possible that nuclear explosives could be used to blast out a new canal route. This would greatly reduce the cost of constructing the waterway.

Communications. In all the large cities of the Caribbean Lands, and in many smaller ones, there are radios, telephones, and telegraph offices. A few cities have television stations. Postal service is available throughout the Caribbean Lands region, although mail delivery is often much slower here than in the United States.

Many small towns and rural areas do not have modern means of communication. Most people in these areas cannot afford television sets, telephones, or even radios. In some places, stores or village meeting places have radios to which people may listen, or television sets for them to watch. On special occasions, such as election days, the government may set up radio loudspeakers to broadcast the news in small towns.

In most Caribbean countries, several daily newspapers are published. However, not nearly so large a part of the population reads newspapers in the Caribbean Lands as in the United States. Many people in Caribbean countries cannot read and write. News is often spread by people talking to each other in the marketplace.

Facts To Review
1. For what purpose were most of the railroads in the Caribbean Lands built?
2. Why is air transportation especially useful in the Caribbean Lands?
3. Why are export goods such as bananas and sugar usually transported by ship?
4. Only a small part of the population in the Caribbean Lands reads newspapers. State one reason why this is true. List three ways by which news is spread in this region.
5. State two reasons for the importance of the Pan American Highway.

A Discussion Topic
The United States may build another canal across Central America. Where do you think this canal might be built? What factors do you think the United States would have to consider in selecting a site? Discuss these questions with your classmates. Then locate possible sites for another canal on the map on pages 14 and 15. Choose the site you think would be best, and state your reasons for selecting this site. Knowledge of the problems faced in building the Panama Canal may be helpful in making your decision.

Weaving is an important craft among the Indians of Guatemala, who are some of the best craftsmen in the Caribbean Lands. Since people of many nationalities have settled in the Caribbean Lands, the arts and crafts of this region reflect a variety of cultures.

12 Arts and Crafts

Problems To Solve

How do the arts and crafts of the Caribbean Lands reflect the different backgrounds of the peoples of this region? To solve this problem, you will need to find information about the backgrounds of the peoples who live in the Caribbean Lands. Then you will need to make several hypotheses about how their backgrounds are reflected in the arts and crafts of this region. The following questions suggest some hypotheses:

a. What facts about music and dancing in the Caribbean Lands help to solve this problem?

b. What facts about the architecture of this region help to solve it?

c. What facts about handicrafts help to solve it?

See TO THE STUDENT, pages 6-7.

In any civilization, the arts express the beliefs, the feelings, and the goals of the people. Because people of many nationalities have settled in the Caribbean Lands, the arts of this region reflect a variety of cultures. For instance, the stately homes built in the Spanish colonial style of architecture reflect the

141

influence of people from a highly developed European civilization. Rhythmic folk songs and dances show the influence of the many people in the Caribbean Lands whose ancestors came from African Negro or American Indian civilizations. Slowly, however, these influences are beginning to merge into new styles of art. This reflects the boldness and adventurousness of a people struggling to develop a civilization of their own.

Music and dancing. Music and dancing are perhaps the forms of art most enjoyed by both the people of the Caribbean Lands and visitors in this region. People in the Caribbean countries make music an important part of their daily lives. On farms in Costa Rica, the coffee pickers may chant folk songs as they work. Calypso singers on Trinidad may beat on steel drums as they sing about the events of the day.

The music of the West Indies is famous for its strong, exciting rhythms. Most of these rhythms originated in Africa. Negro slaves who were brought to the West Indies to work on plantations brought their music and dances with them. As time passed, the African rhythms blended with Spanish and French melodies to create a new kind of folk music.

The rumba. On a warm summer night, people are gathered at a sugar plantation in Cuba for an outdoor dance. The small orchestra is made up of three musicians. One man strums a guitar. Another pounds on a drum made from a small, hollow log covered at one end with animal hide. The third musician is shaking maracas. These are dry gourds

Dancing at a fiesta. The music of the West Indies is famous for its strong, exciting rhythms. Most of these rhythms originated in Africa. Music and dancing are perhaps the forms of art most enjoyed by both the people of the Caribbean Lands and visitors in this region.

A steel band on Antigua. The instruments in a steel band are made from large oil barrels cut in various lengths to produce different tones. Each player strikes the end of his steel drum with rubber-tipped sticks. Steel bands are popular on many islands in the West Indies.

filled with seeds that rattle when the maracas are shaken. The dancers are performing the rumba, a fast, lively dance with an unusual African rhythm.

Other West Indian dances. The rumba is not the only dance that comes from the West Indies. Perhaps you have heard of the conga and the cha-cha. These dances originated in Cuba. The merengue is a popular dance in Haiti and the Dominican Republic. People on Jamaica and Trinidad often perform the limbo for visitors. Dances from the West Indies are enjoyed in the United States and many other countries.

Steel bands. It is a festival day in San Fernando, a city on Trinidad. People gathered at a street corner are clapping their hands to the music of a steel band. The instruments in this band are very unusual. They are made from large oil barrels cut in various lengths to produce

different tones. Each player strikes the end of his steel drum with rubber-tipped sticks. No written music is used. The musicians play "by ear." However, a good steel band can play anything from hymns to popular dance tunes. There are steel bands on many islands in the West Indies.

Calypso. An important part of the festival celebration in San Fernando is calypso. Throughout the city, calypso singers accompanied by guitars, steel drums, or other instruments perform songs they have composed themselves. These songs are usually about important happenings in the news, and they are often humorous. Calpyso songs are heard in many parts of the West Indies, but Trinidad is especially noted for this kind of music.

Calypso began with the "chantwells," Negro slaves who entertained plantation

143

owners in colonial times. The chantwells made up songs about the people they knew and the things that happened to them. Since most of the islanders could not read or write, they began using calypso songs as a way of spreading news and gossip.

Central American music and dancing.

In Central America, people enjoy listening to the music of the marimba. This is an instrument that somewhat resembles a xylophone. (See picture below.) It is played by striking wooden keys with small, cloth-covered hammers. Under each key is a wooden tube or a gourd that gives the marimba music its distinctive sound.

Other musical instruments are also popular in Central America. In Costa Rica and Guatemala, some people play the ocarina. This instrument was popular long ago among some of the early Indian tribes in Central America. In Panama, the music of the *rabel*, a three-stringed violin, is frequently heard. People in many parts of Central America enjoy hearing and dancing to guitar music.

Playing the marimba. In Central America, people enjoy listening to the music of the marimba. This instrument somewhat resembles a xylophone.

One of the most interesting Central American dances is the *tamborito*, the national dance of Panama. It is a graceful, happy dance performed by a group of people in colorful costumes. The *danza* is enjoyed in Costa Rica and some other parts of Central America. Negroes who live in the Caribbean Lowland sometimes perform dances of African origin like those enjoyed in the West Indies.

Classical music. There are only a few noted composers or performers of classical music in the Caribbean Lands. Ernesto Lecuona, a Cuban composer who died in 1963, wrote "Malagueña" and other well-known compositions. Jesús María Sanromá, a Puerto Rican pianist, has given many concerts in the United States. The famous Spanish cellist Pablo Casals now makes his home in Puerto Rico. Each year, leading musicians from many parts of the world come to Puerto Rico to perform in the Casals Festival.

Architecture. Some of the oldest buildings in the Caribbean Lands were constructed by the Maya Indians long ago. The ancient city of Tikal, in northern Guatemala, has many fine examples of Mayan architecture. This city, the largest built by the ancient Maya, covers more than six square miles. Different sections of the city are connected by stone causeways. In the central part of Tikal are several high, flat-topped pyramids made of stone. Some are more than 150 feet high. On the top of each pyramid is a small temple with thick walls and no windows. (See picture on page 51.) Here the Mayan priests made sacrifices to their gods. Another interesting sight in Tikal is the Palace of Nobles. It consists of several large buildings and courtyards on a platform eighty

144

feet above the ground. Many of the outside walls of Mayan buildings were decorated with beautiful sculptures and carvings. Inside some of the temples and palaces were bold, colorful paintings, which often showed scenes from the daily life of the Maya. (See picture on page 50.)

The architecture of the Caribbean Lands today shows the influence of European civilization. Many buildings in Central America and the Greater Antilles resemble Spanish dwellings. They have tile roofs and thick walls made of stone or adobe. Usually they are built around a central courtyard, or patio.

Many churches in the Caribbean Lands were built when this region was ruled by Spain. An excellent example of Spanish colonial architecture is the cathedral at Santo Domingo, in the Dominican Republic. Completed in 1540, it is the oldest church in the Western Hemisphere. Inside the cathedral are many beautiful paintings, sculptures, and wood carvings. The high altar is richly carved and is decorated with silver obtained from mines nearby.

Other European countries have also influenced the architecture of the Caribbean Lands. For example, in Jamaica, which was formerly a British colony, some of the houses and churches are similar to those found in Great Britain. Willemstad, on the Dutch island of Curaçao, resembles a city in the Netherlands. Some of the buildings in Willemstad are made of brick and have steeply slanted tile roofs. Fort-de-France, the capital of the French island of Martinique, looks much like a town in France.

Today there are many buildings of modern design in the cities of the Caribbean Lands. These buildings are usually

The cathedral at Santo Domingo, in the Dominican Republic. Completed in 1540, this cathedral is an excellent example of Spanish colonial architecture.

made of steel, concrete, and glass. They have a very plain, "streamlined" appearance. San Juan, Puerto Rico, is noted for its modern hotels and apartment buildings. Some of the factories, schools, and office buildings in San Juan are also designed in contemporary styles.

Painting. For a long time after Europeans came to the Caribbean Lands, the painters of this region imitated artists in Europe. They painted mostly portraits and religious pictures. The paintings of this early period tell us little about the Caribbean countries and the people living there.

In recent years, the artists of Central America and the West Indies have begun to develop their own styles. Such painters as Carlos Mérida of Guatemala use vivid colors and bold, strong designs to paint scenes of everyday life. Their paintings tell us much about the joys and sorrows of people in the Caribbean Lands.

Among the best-known works of art of the Caribbean Lands today are the

145

At the art center in Port-au-Prince, Haiti, a Haitian painter, Castera Bazile, talks with the director of the center. Bazile's colorful paintings of Haitian life are admired by many people. The "primitive" paintings of Haiti are among the best-known works of art of the Caribbean Lands.

"primitive" paintings of Haiti. To encourage Haitian painters, an art center was founded at Port-au-Prince in 1944. Two of the "primitive" painters whose works have been displayed in the art center are Hector Hyppolite and Castera Bazile. Their simple, colorful paintings of Haitian life are admired by many people.

Literature. Folktales were the earliest form of literature in the Caribbean Lands. The Indians of this region knew many stories which were told by parents to their children. African slaves brought many folktales with them to the West Indies.

During colonial times, most Caribbean authors were influenced by European styles of writing. They wrote many religious poems, and stories about the conquest of the Indians. None of them are remembered as important authors, since they copied European ways of writing instead of writing in a style of their own.

Near the end of the 1800's, a young Nicaraguan poet named Rubén Darío helped to change this situation. Instead of imitating European writers, Darío developed his own style and influenced other authors to write in this simple, musical style. Darío traveled to many countries in Latin America. In some of his poems, he tells about his love for Latin America and his hopes for the future of this area. Rubén Darío is now recognized as one of the greatest poets ever to write in the Spanish language.

Since Darío's time, many Caribbean authors have written in a direct, clear

146

style about the people of their own countries. Their works tell about the hard life of the peasants and about the struggle that many people have in trying to get an education. The well-known Puerto Rican poet Luis Palés Matos wrote with deep feeling about the needs and hopes of the Negro people in Puerto Rico. One of the leading authors in the Caribbean region today is V. S. Naipaul of Trinidad. He writes vivid novels about the East Indians who live on this island.

Crafts. The crafts of the Caribbean Lands show the influence of Indian and Negro cultures. The skills of the people who came from these civilizations have been handed down from generation to generation.

Some of the best craftsmen in the Caribbean Lands are the Indians of Guatemala. They have carefully preserved the crafts handed down to them from their ancestors. The Indian craftsmen take pleasure in creating things that are beautiful. They believe that even useful items should be attractive.

Some Indian handicrafts, such as weaving, have remained almost unchanged since before the time of Columbus. Long ago, some of the Indians in Central America learned to spin cotton into yarn and to weave the yarn into cloth on handlooms. Then they colored the cloth with animal and vegetable dyes and made it into clothing.

Weaving is still an important craft among the Indians of Guatemala. Indian weavers are able to create beautiful designs without following a pattern. The women of each village weave cloth that is different in texture and design from the cloth of any other village. It is possible to tell where an Indian comes from by the design in the clothing he wears.

The Indians of Guatemala are skilled in many other handicrafts. Some of them weave bags, rugs, and hammocks from the strong fibers of the henequen plant. Others are known for their pottery work. Bowls and vases decorated with designs in bright colors are offered for sale in village markets.

People in other parts of the Caribbean Lands are also skilled craftsmen. Some weave baskets, mats, and rugs from palm fibers. Others make beautiful vases and jewelry from such metals as silver and copper. The craftsmen of Haiti and the Dominican Republic are noted for their wood carving. From valuable woods, such as mahogany, they carve boxes, religious statues, and other objects. Many Central American craftsmen are skilled in leather work. They make fine purses, wallets, and shoes from cowhide or from alligator skin. Handicraft articles made in the Caribbean Lands are very popular with tourists.

Facts To Review

1. Describe the folk music of the West Indies. How did this music originate?
2. Name three places in the Caribbean Lands where you would find buildings designed in European styles of architecture.
3. Who was Rubén Darío? Why was he important?
4. What is meant by the term "primitive" painting? (The picture on page 146, and the information under "primitive" painting in the Glossary will help you answer this question.)
5. Describe three kinds of handicrafts made by the Indians of Guatemala.

Holy Week in Chichicastenango, an Indian village in Guatemala. Here the Indians of the surrounding area observe Holy Week with a combination of Christian and Mayan ceremonies. This festival is only one of many celebrations held each year in the Caribbean Lands.

13 Festivals and Recreation

Problems To Solve

Why are there so many festivals in the Caribbean Lands? In order to solve this problem, you will need to make several hypotheses. The following questions suggest two hypotheses:

a. What facts about religion in the Caribbean Lands help to solve this problem?
b. What facts about the importance of festivals to the people of this region help to solve it?

See TO THE STUDENT, pages 6-7.

Holy Week in Chichicastenango. It is the Sunday before Easter in Chichicastenango, an ancient Indian village high in the mountains of Guatemala. Here the Indians of the surrounding area observe Holy Week with a combination of Christian and Mayan ceremonies. They celebrate not only the resurrection of Christ but also the coming of springtime, when they can plant their crops.

148

Since daybreak, throngs of Indians have been coming to the village. Some of them have walked many miles to take part in the Holy Week festival. The marketplace in the center of the village is crowded with men and women wearing bright-colored clothing. There are rows of booths where people are selling pottery, baskets, and other goods.

In the marketplace, the noise is almost deafening. The air is filled with the sound of drums, flutes, and marimbas. People are shouting and laughing. Every now and then, a skyrocket shoots into the air with a loud hiss and a puff of smoke. The Indians believe that these skyrockets will carry their prayers to heaven.

In some parts of the marketplace, groups of Indians are performing dances that have been handed down from their ancestors. One of their favorites is called *La Conquista*, which means "The Conquest." In this dance, the performers wear wooden masks and act out the conquest of Guatemala by the Spaniards long ago. Some of the dancers are dressed to represent Indian warriors. The dancers who represent the Spaniards wear red wigs because the Spanish leader, Pedro de Alvarado, is said to have had red hair.

Indian dancers dressed as Spanish soldiers. During Holy Week, Indians in Guatemala perform dances that have been handed down from their ancestors. One of their favorites is "La Conquista," in which the performers act out the conquest of Guatemala by the Spaniards long ago.

Indians burn incense on the steps of the church of Santo Tomás as part of the Holy Week celebration. They are praying to their ancient Mayan gods.

Now a procession enters the marketplace. Several men dressed in long, purple robes are carrying a richly decorated platform. On the platform is a life-size statue of Christ wearing a crown of thorns.

At one end of the marketplace is the church of Santo Tomás. Several Indian men on the steps of the church are swinging pots of sweet-smelling incense. They are praying to their ancient Mayan gods. Inside the church, a Roman Catholic priest is saying a Mass. The stone floor of the church is covered with hundreds of flickering candles. All day long, men and women will come to the church to light more candles and to pray for good crops.

The people of the Caribbean Lands celebrate many festivals. The Holy Week festival at Chichicastenango is only one of many celebrations held each year in the Caribbean Lands. Nearly every city and town has certain days that are set aside for merrymaking. In countries that once belonged to Spain, these celebrations are usually known as fiestas.

Many festivals in the Caribbean Lands are connected with religious ceremonies of the Roman Catholic Church. In countries where most of the people are Catholic, every village holds a festival on its "Saint's Day." This is the birthday of the saint who is believed to watch over the village. People also celebrate many days honoring Mary, the Mother of Christ. Another religious festival is Carnival, which comes just before Lent.

Carnival time on Trinidad. The most colorful of all the Carnival celebrations in the Caribbean Lands is the one held on Trinidad. Each year, thousands of visitors from the United States and other countries come to Trinidad for this famous celebration.

For months before Carnival, the calypso singers of Trinidad are busy composing new songs. (To learn more about calypso music, see Chapter 12.) Each night, these songs are performed before large audiences in tents that have been set up along the streets of Port of Spain. The listeners show by their applause how well they like each song. When Carnival finally arrives, the most popular new calypso song is heard everywhere in the city. Its composer becomes

Words To Think With

jai alai	cricket	*beisbol*	Chichicastenango
Holy Week	*La Conquista*	fiestas	"Saint's Day"
Carnival	calypso	*fútbol*	cockfighting

Calypso King for the year. The contest gives every calypso singer on Trinidad a chance to have his song heard by thousands of people and to win fame throughout the island.

Carnival is a very exciting time for the people of Trinidad. Steel bands parade through Port of Spain, playing lively calypso tunes. They are followed by groups of dancers in colorful costumes. Some of the dancers may be dressed as pirates, Roman soldiers, or cowboys. Others may represent storybook characters, such as goblins and dragons. The costumes glisten in the sunlight as the dancers sway in time to the gay calypso music. Before Carnival ends, prizes are given to the best steel bands and to the people wearing the most unusual costumes. Many people on Trinidad work on their costumes for a whole year before Carnival.

Festivals are held on national holidays. The people of the Caribbean Lands also celebrate important dates in history. September 15 is the day set aside by most Central American nations to celebrate their independence from Spain. On this day, people sing, dance, and parade through the streets in costume. Another national holiday is Columbus Day, October 12, which commemorates the discovery of America by Christopher Columbus.

Why festivals are important. Festivals are important to the people of the Caribbean Lands. In this region, many families do not have radios or television sets for entertainment. They look forward eagerly to the gaiety and excitement of the festivals. At festival time, people living in rural areas have a chance to go to the villages to meet their friends and hear the latest news.

Carnival on Trinidad. During this religious festival, steel bands parade through the streets of Port of Spain. They are followed by groups of dancers in colorful costumes. Festivals play an important part in the lives of the people of the Caribbean Lands.

Festivals are enjoyed by rich and poor alike. Even the poorest peasant may win praise for his skillful dancing or his unusual costume.

Family celebrations. Public festivals are not the only celebrations held in the Caribbean Lands. In most countries of this region, family life is very important. All the members of a family gather for special occasions, such as baptisms and weddings. At these times, there are usually gay parties with singing and dancing. Grandparents, cousins, aunts, and uncles gather to see each other and to take part in the celebrations.

Several sports are popular in the Caribbean Lands. During their leisure time, the people of the Caribbean Lands enjoy watching or taking part in various sports. Most of these sports did not originate within the region. They were brought here from Europe or the United States.

Beisbol. In Spanish-speaking countries, baseball is known as *beisbol*. Our national game has become the leading sport in several Caribbean countries where United States influence has been especially strong. Puerto Rico, Cuba, the Dominican Republic, Panama, and Nicaragua now have many baseball teams. Some of these countries have organized a baseball league, whose teams play during the winter months. United States teams have obtained many good players from this league.

Fútbol. In spite of its name, *fútbol* is not the United States game of football. It is actually soccer, a European sport that has become very popular in many Caribbean countries. Nearly every weekend, thousands of spectators flock to huge stadiums to watch their favorite *fútbol* teams in action. *Fútbol* is played on a field that resembles a football field. There are eleven men on each team. The players move the ball toward their goal by kicking it or by batting it with the head. Only the goalkeepers may touch the ball with their hands.

Cockfighting. It is a Saturday afternoon in Port-au-Prince, the capital of Haiti. People are gathering at an outdoor stadium to watch a cockfight. In the center of the stadium is a large pit enclosed by a fence. At opposite ends of the pit, two men are holding birds called gamecocks. A gamecock is a special kind of rooster that has been bred for fighting. The gamecocks have bright-colored feathers, and a sharp spur, like a claw, on each leg.

When a signal is given, the birds are released. They fly at each other

A baseball game in Panama. Baseball, or "beisbol," is the leading sport in several Caribbean countries where United States influence has been strong.

152

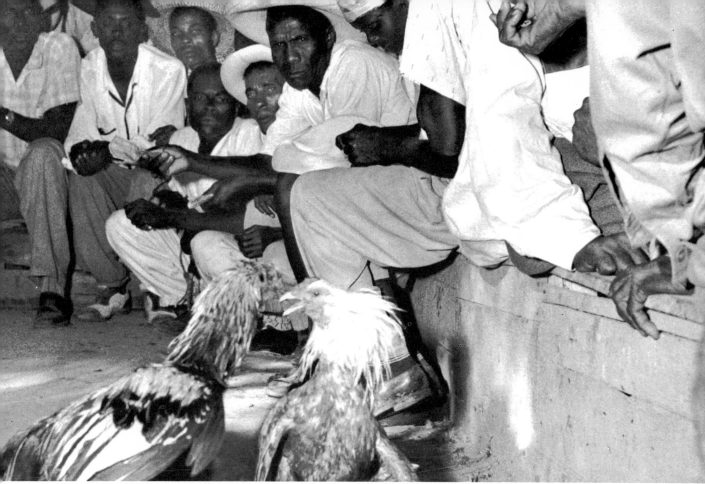

A cockfight in Haiti. In the cruel sport of cockfighting, two birds called gamecocks fight each other until one of them is dead. Cockfighting is also popular in Puerto Rico and other Spanish-speaking countries. This sport is illegal in the United States.

and strike fiercely with their spurs. The fight continues until one of the brave birds is dead.

Cockfighting is also a popular sport in Puerto Rico and other Spanish-speaking countries. Spectators often bet large sums of money on their favorite gamecocks.

Jai alai. Jai alai, like cockfighting, was brought to the Caribbean Lands from Spain. Many people, especially in Cuba, enjoy watching this fast, vigorous game. Jai alai is played on an oblong court. One side of the court is open except for a wire fence. The spectators sit here. On the other three sides of the court are high walls.

In jai alai, there are two opposing sides, with one to three players on each side. Each player wears a narrow, curved wicker scoop strapped to one wrist. This scoop is called a *cesta*. The ball used in jai alai is about the size of a baseball, and very hard. The server hurls the ball with his *cesta* against one wall of the court. One of his opponents catches the ball in his *cesta* and hurls it back. Each player tries to place the ball so that his opponent will miss it. Sometimes the ball travels as fast as 150 miles an hour. Jai alai is said to be the fastest game in the world.

Cricket. The game of cricket was brought to the Caribbean Lands by British settlers. This game is very popular

Playing cricket in Jamaica. The game of cricket was brought to the Caribbean Lands by British settlers. It is somewhat like baseball.

in British colonies and in countries formerly ruled by Great Britain. Cricket teams from Jamaica, Trinidad, Barbados, and other islands compete against each other. Sometimes teams from Britain come to the islands to play.

Cricket is somewhat like baseball. The pitcher is called the "bowler." Batters use a paddle-shaped bat, and the points scored are called "runs." There are eleven players on a cricket team, instead of nine as in baseball. A cricket game has only two "innings." Each inning lasts until ten men on each team are "out."

Water sports. The Caribbean countries have many miles of seacoast, so water sports are very popular. The mild climate makes it possible to go swimming and skin diving all year round. Many people in the Caribbean Lands go fishing or sailing in their leisure time. Water sports are also enjoyed by thousands of vacationers who come to the Caribbean Lands during the winter months.

Think and Write

1. Why do you think the Holy Week celebration in Chichicastenango is a combination of Christian and Mayan ceremonies? Information on pages 89 and 163 will help you answer this question.
2. Which celebrations in the Caribbean Lands are not public? Why are these private celebrations important to the people?
3. Name two types of recreation that attract tourists to the Caribbean Lands.

Making Comparisons

1. Cricket is a popular sport in the Caribbean Lands. What United States sport does it resemble? How are the two sports alike? How are they different? A comparison of the pictures on pages 152 and 154 will help you answer these questions. You may also need to do research in an encyclopedia.
2. How do festivals and celebrations in the Caribbean Lands compare with the holidays and special events you celebrate? Make a list of the celebrations you observe and describe each one briefly. Then compare them to the ones discussed in this chapter. You may wish to have a class discussion on this subject.
3. Carnival on Trinidad is similar to Mardi Gras in New Orleans, Louisiana. Read about Mardi Gras in an encyclopedia or some other source. How are Mardi Gras and Carnival alike? How are they different? Write a brief report comparing the two.

Central

America

14   Guatemala

Problems To Solve

Guatemala gained its independence from Spain in 1821. Since then, it has had a history of political unrest and dictatorships. **Why do you think this is true?** To solve this problem, you will need to make hypotheses about how each of the following has affected Guatemala's political history:

a. Spanish rule in Guatemala
b. the way of life followed by the Indians in Guatemala
c. Communist activity in Guatemala

See TO THE STUDENT, pages 6-7.

GEOGRAPHY

Land. Guatemala is the northernmost of the six Central American republics. As the map on the opposite page shows, it is bordered on the north and west by Mexico. Guatemala, which is smaller than Tennessee, is the third largest country in Central America.

More than half of Guatemala is made up of highlands. In the western part of the highland region are high, rugged mountains and plateaus. In many places, they are cut by deep canyons. Farther

Lake Atitlán, in southern Guatemala. More than half of Guatemala is made up of highlands. In the southern part of the highlands, there are many lofty volcanoes. Through the centuries, ashes and lava from the volcanoes have enriched the soil of farmland nearby.

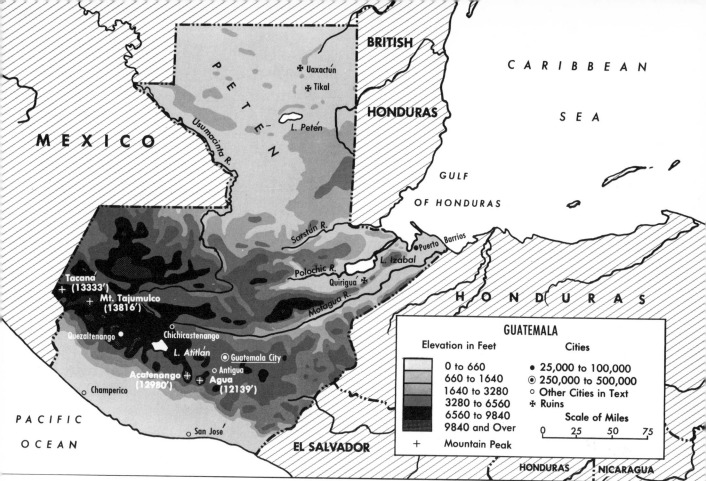

Guatemala. In the western part of Guatemala's highland region are high, rugged mountains and plateaus. Farther eastward, the highlands are lower and less rugged. Mount Tajumulco, a volcanic peak in western Guatemala, is the highest mountain in the Caribbean Lands.

eastward, the highlands are lower and less rugged. The northeastern part of the highland region consists of long mountain ranges that extend toward the Caribbean Sea. (See map above.)

Many lofty, cone-shaped volcanoes are located in the southern part of the highlands. They are part of a long chain of volcanoes that stretches from southern Mexico into western Panama. Several of the volcanic peaks in Guatemala are more than twelve thousand feet high. One of them, Mount Tajumulco, is the highest mountain in the Caribbean Lands. It rises nearly fourteen thousand feet above sea level.

Although most of the volcanoes in Guatemala have not erupted for many

years, a few are still active. At times, a volcano may pour out smoke or shower the surrounding countryside with ashes. Through the centuries, weathered ashes and lava from volcanoes have enriched the soil of much of southern Guatemala. The same forces within the earth that cause these volcanoes to erupt also produce earthquakes in Guatemala. Earthquakes have sometimes destroyed Guatemalan cities and killed thousands of people.

There are small basins between some of the volcanic mountains in Guatemala. These basins lie between 3,500 and 8,000 feet above sea level. They are covered with a deep layer of fertile volcanic soil. Most of Guatemala's people live in these

157

Facts About Guatemala

Area: 42,042 square miles.

Population: About 4,100,000.

Density of Population: 98 people per square mile; 663 people per square mile of arable* land.

Capital and Largest City: Guatemala City (population about 407,000).

Racial Composition: More than half of all Guatemalans are Indian. Most of the rest are of mixed Spanish and Indian descent. Only about five out of every one hundred Guatemalans are white.

Literacy: About three out of every ten people in Guatemala can read and write.

Main Language: Spanish. However, many Indians speak only Indian languages.

Main Religion: Roman Catholicism.

Main Occupation: Nearly seven out of every ten workers in Guatemala are farmers.

Income: Yearly per capita income is about $150. Most Guatemalans grow or make many of the things they need, so they are able to live on a very small income.

Important Farm Products: Coffee, bananas, and cotton are the most important export crops of Guatemala. Leading domestic crops are food crops, such as corn and beans.

Natural Resources: Forests, lead, zinc, and nickel.

Manufacturing: Among Guatemala's industries are food processing and oil refining. Many Indians earn their living by making handicrafts.

Currency: Guatemala's unit of money is the *quetzal*, which is officially worth $1.00.

basins. Guatemala City, the capital, is located in one of them. In a few of the basins, there are beautiful lakes. The largest of these is Lake Atitlán.

A narrow lowland extends along the entire Pacific coast of Guatemala. In most places, it is less than thirty miles wide. This is part of the Pacific Lowland of Central America. Most of it is a savanna, on which herds of cattle are grazed. The part of this lowland that borders Guatemala's highland region is an area of gently sloping, forest-covered hills.

Two areas of Guatemala lie in the Caribbean Lowland of Central America. One of them, called the Petén, is in northern Guatemala. (See map on page 157.) The Petén, which makes up about one third of Guatemala, is a low, gently rolling limestone plateau. Through the centuries, rainwater has eroded much of the limestone, forming many deep sinkholes. Dense, jungle-like rainforest covers most of the Petén. This part of Guatemala is thinly populated.

Three long valleys in eastern Guatemala are also part of the Caribbean Lowland. These valleys have been formed by rivers that flow from the highlands into the Caribbean Sea. The Motagua Valley is the largest of the three. Bananas are grown on large plantations in this area.

Climate. The climate of Guatemala varies greatly from place to place. In the lowlands, the weather is generally

The Motagua River. Three long valleys in eastern Guatemala are part of the Caribbean Lowland. The Motagua Valley is the largest of the three.

hot and humid. The average annual temperature here is about eighty degrees. In some of the highland basins and on the lower mountain slopes, days are usually warm and nights are cool. The pleasant climate helps to explain why the highland basins are the most densely populated areas of Guatemala. On the higher mountain slopes, the weather is always cool. Here the temperature sometimes drops below freezing during the winter, and some snow may fall on the highest peaks.

Most of Guatemala receives more than sixty inches of rain a year. Rainfall is especially heavy in the Caribbean Lowland and in the northeastern part of the highlands. These areas lie in the path of moist trade winds that blow southwestward toward Guatemala all year long. On the Pacific Lowland, rainfall is heavy only during the summer and early fall. At this time of year, moist winds from the Pacific Ocean are blowing toward Guatemala. During the rest of the year, the weather here is very dry, and farmers must irrigate their fields to grow most crops.

Natural resources. Forests cover more than three fifths of Guatemala. The most valuable forest area is the Petén, where mahogany and Spanish cedar trees grow in the dense rainforest. Some of these trees are cut and made into lumber for export. However, Guatemala does not produce much lumber. Lumbering is difficult, because few roads lead into the Petén.

Another forest product from Guatemala is chicle, a substance used in making chewing gum. It is obtained from sapodilla trees, which grow in the rainforest of the Petén. Chicle gatherers tap

Boiling sap to make chicle, a substance used to make chewing gum. Chicle is an important product obtained from forests in northern Guatemala.

trees by cutting long, zigzag gashes in their trunks. They place a container at the bottom of each tree to collect the milky sap that drains from it. Later, the sap is boiled in huge kettles until a soft, sticky substance remains. The men mold this substance into large blocks. Because of the lack of roads, most of the blocks of chicle are taken out of the Petén by airplane. Much of the chicle is exported to the United States.

Deposits of lead, zinc, nickel, and a few other minerals have been found in Guatemala. However, none of these minerals is mined in large amounts. Some of the deposits are located in rugged areas where transportation is difficult.

There are many rivers in Guatemala that could be used to produce hydro-electric power. In recent years, hydro-electric plants have been built on some of these rivers. However, there is still a shortage of electric power in many parts of Guatemala.

HISTORY

Spaniards settle in the highlands of Guatemala. In 1523, the Spanish in Mexico sent an army southeastward into the territory that is now Guatemala.

This army was led by Pedro de Alvarado. (See page 63.) Like most other Spaniards who explored parts of the New World, Alvarado hoped to find gold, silver, and other riches. In the highlands of Guatemala, Alvarado's army came upon several warlike tribes of Maya Indians. Most of these tribes were conquered by Alvarado and his men.

During the 1500's, a few Spanish settlements were founded in Guatemala. They were located in highland valleys and basins where settlers found fertile soil and a pleasant climate. Nearby, there were small deposits of gold and silver. Also, most of the Indians in Guatemala lived in highland areas. The Spaniards divided much of their land into large estates and forced Indians to

Mayan sculpture. Several tribes of Maya Indians were living in the highlands of what is now Guatemala when Spaniards came to this territory. During the 1520's most of these Indian tribes were conquered by a Spaniard named Pedro de Alvarado.

work for them. In addition to food crops for their own use, some of the Spaniards raised cacao, indigo, and other crops for export to Spain. Others had large cattle ranches.

Although the Indians of Guatemala were treated cruelly and many died from diseases brought by the Spaniards, more of the Indians here survived colonial days than in any other Central American country. One reason was that there were more Indians in Guatemala when the Spaniards came. Also, some of the Indians lived in isolated parts of the highlands, where the Spaniards did not settle. These Indians continued to follow their old customs and did not change their way of life much under Spanish rule.

Shortly after 1540, Spaniards founded the settlement of Santiago in the southern part of the Guatemalan highlands. For more than two hundred years, Santiago was the capital of the *audiencia** of Guatemala. This *audiencia* included most of Central America, as well as a small part of what is now Mexico. Santiago, with its many fine buildings, became the most splendid city in Central America. In 1773, however, it was almost completely destroyed by an earthquake. A new capital, known as Guatemala City, was founded nearby.

Guatemala becomes an independent nation. Like most other Central American countries, Guatemala gained its independence in the early 1800's. In 1821, the provinces in the *audiencia* of Guatemala broke away from Spanish rule. Two years later, Guatemala and four other provinces formed a nation called the Central American Federation. (See page 74.) Its first capital was Guatemala City. This federation broke up in

Ruins of Santiago. For more than two hundred years, Santiago was the capital of the "audiencia"* of Guatemala, which included most of Central America.

1838, and shortly afterward Guatemala became an independent nation.

Dictators control Guatemala for many years. When Guatemala became independent, its people were not prepared for democratic government. Most of them were Indians who lived in remote mountain valleys or on plateaus. These people were poor and lacked education. They had little experience in governing themselves. Therefore, dictators were able to control the government. They usually stayed in office until new leaders became powerful enough to overthrow them.

The first dictator to rule Guatemala was a leader named Rafael Carrera. He came to power at the time the Central American Federation broke up. The Indians supported Carrera because they believed he would help them gain more rights. Members of the Conservative party in Guatemala thought they could control the government themselves by pretending to support Carrera. After

161

Carrera gained control, however, he generally ignored his supporters and ruled as he pleased until his death in 1865.

During the 1870's and early 1880's, Justo Rufino Barrios, another dictator, brought many changes to Guatemala. For this reason, he was called the "Reformer." Barrios improved education and allowed freedom of religion. He promoted the construction of roads, telegraph lines, and the nation's first railway. Barrios also encouraged the production of coffee and bananas.

After the rule of Barrios, other dictators ruled Guatemala. Two of them, Manuel Estrada Cabrera and Jorge Ubico, remained in office for long periods of time. Like Carrera and Barrios, they completely controlled the government. Free elections were not allowed under their rule.

Shortly after 1900, during the time that Estrada Cabrera was in office, bananas became one of Guatemala's important crops. They were produced mainly on large plantations established by a large United States firm called the United Fruit Company. Many Guatemalans resented the fact that these plantations were owned by foreigners.

Communists try to take over the Guatemalan government. During the 1940's, some changes began to take place in Guatemala. The people revolted, and the dictator Ubico was forced to resign. Shortly afterward, a constitution was adopted that provided for many reforms. Unused land on large estates was to be taken over and given to peasants who had no land. Workers were given the right to organize labor unions, and minimum wage laws were established.

About 1950, Communists began to interfere in the Guatemalan government. They pretended to support the new, democratic policies and tried to take credit for them. Some Communists held key positions in powerful labor unions. A few were appointed to government offices. Communist propaganda was spread throughout Guatemala. In 1954, a group of Guatemalan military officers opposed to communism organized a small army in neighboring Honduras. This army, with the support of the United States, marched into Guatemala and overthrew the Communist-backed government.

Since then, political unrest has continued in Guatemala. One president was assassinated. Another was overthrown by members of the armed forces. In 1963, Colonel Enrique Peralta Azurdia, a military leader, became head of the government. He dismissed the lawmaking body and declared the constitution no longer in effect. However, he promised to hold free elections sometime in the future.

The Tower of the Reformer, built to honor Justo Rufino Barrios, one of many Guatemalan dictators. Guatemala's government is still not democratic.

162

In Guatemala, more than one half of all the people are Indian. The rest of the people are mainly of mixed Indian and Spanish descent. Most of them have a higher standard of living than the Indians, who generally earn a living by farming small plots of land on high plateaus.

THE PEOPLE AND HOW THEY LIVE

People. Guatemala has a larger population than any other Central American country. The most heavily populated areas of the country are the fertile basins in the southern part of the highlands. Much of Guatemala is thinly populated. Few people live in the densely forested Petén or on the highest mountain slopes.

Indians make up a greater part of the population in Guatemala than in any other Caribbean country. More than one half of all Guatemalans are Indian. They are descendants of the Maya Indians who were living in Guatemala when the Spaniards came. Most of the rest of the people are of mixed Indian and Spanish descent. They are called Ladinos in Guatemala. Any pureblood Indian who does not follow the Indian way of life is also called a Ladino. Only about five out of every one hundred Guatemalans are white.

Indians and Ladinos lead very different ways of life. The Ladinos speak Spanish and generally live in cities or large towns. Most of them earn more money than the Indians and have a higher standard of living. Together with the people of Spanish descent, Ladinos control Guatemala's government. The Indians generally live on high plateaus and earn their living by farming small plots of land. They take little interest in the government of the country. Most Indians speak Indian languages, although some of them also speak Spanish.

About nine out of every ten Guatemalans belong to the Roman Catholic Church. However, most of the Indians also worship ancient Mayan gods.

163

Earning a living. Nearly seven tenths of all Guatemalan workers earn their living by farming. Export crops are generally produced on large estates. Crops for use within the country are usually grown on farms only a few acres in size.

Most of the land on small farms is used to grow corn and other food crops. Corn is produced on more than two fifths of the farmland in the country. Beans, wheat, and rice are other important food crops.

Coffee is Guatemala's main export crop. (See graph on page 128.) Most of the coffee orchards are on the lower mountain slopes in the southern part of the highlands. Here the soil is fertile, and the climate is mild. Rainfall is heavy during part of the year, and the weather is dry the rest of the year. Coffee grows well under these conditions. Most of the coffee beans produced in Guatemala are exported, mainly to the United States. Some of them are used in Guatemala to make instant coffee. Guatemala exports instant coffee to the United States, Germany, and other countries.

For many years, bananas have also been one of Guatemala's important exports. The country's first banana plantations were located on the hot, humid Caribbean Lowland, along the Motagua River. (See map on page 157.) During the 1930's, however, disease killed many of the banana plants. As a result, the United Fruit Company established new plantations on the Pacific Lowland. This is now Guatemala's main banana-producing area. Most of the bananas are sent by railroad to Puerto Barrios, on

An Indian woman picking coffee, Guatemala's main export. Most coffee orchards are on the lower mountain slopes in the southern part of the highlands, where the soil is fertile and the climate is mild. Nearly seven tenths of all Guatemalan workers earn their living by farming.

A banana plantation on the Caribbean Lowland. For many years, bananas have been one of Guatemala's important export crops. Large amounts of cotton have also been produced in Guatemala in recent years. Cotton is expected to become a more important export than bananas.

the Caribbean coast. From here, they are shipped to the United States and other countries.

In recent years, large amounts of cotton have been produced on the Pacific Lowland. Some of the cotton is processed by textile mills in Guatemala, but most of it is exported to Japan and to European countries. Cotton is expected to become a more important export than bananas.

Raising livestock is a fairly important way of earning a living in Guatemala. Cattle are raised mainly on a few large estates on the Pacific Lowland. Some beef is exported.

Only about one out of every eight Guatemalan workers is employed in manufacturing. However, the number is increasing. In recent years, many new factories have been built in Guatemala.

In a textile mill. Only about one out of every eight Guatemalan workers is employed in manufacturing. However, the number of factory workers is increasing.

The Inter-American Highway has been completed through Guatemala, although in some places it is not yet paved. Guatemala has a larger network of roads than any other Central American country except Costa Rica. Most of the roads are located in the southern part of the country.

These include a steel plant, a factory that produces automobile tires and parts, and an oil refinery. The refinery imports crude oil and changes it into fuel oil and other useful products. Other goods manufactured in Guatemala include glass, fertilizer, paper, furniture, and cement. There are also food-processing plants, such as canning factories and breweries. A large number of Indians in Guatemala earn their living by making pottery, handwoven textiles, and other handicrafts.

Transportation and communication. Guatemala has a larger network of roads than any other Central American country except Costa Rica. There are more than seven thousand miles of roads in Guatemala, but only about eight hundred miles are paved. Most of the roads are located in the southern part of the country. (Compare map on page 133

with map on pages 14 and 15.) The Inter-American Highway has been completed through Guatemala, although in some places it is not yet paved.

Guatemala has more than seven hundred miles of railroads. The largest railroad system is controlled by the United Fruit Company. The main line of this system connects Guatemala City with Puerto Barrios to the northeast on the Caribbean coast, and with a Mexican railway to the west.

Seven international airlines connect Guatemala with other countries. One of these, called Aviateca, is operated by the Guatemalan government. This airline also provides service between Guatemala City and many other cities and towns in Guatemala.

Ships from many foreign nations load and unload goods at Guatemala's ports. Government-owned ships carry goods between Guatemala and ports in other parts of North America and in Europe. Guatemala's main seaport is Puerto Barrios.

Government-owned telephone and telegraph lines connect Guatemala's main cities. However, there are fewer than 25,000 telephones in the country, most of them in Guatemala City. Guatemala has more than fifty radio stations. The country's two television stations, as well as most of the radio stations, are also located in Guatemala City.

Education. Guatemala's literacy rate is one of the lowest in the Caribbean Lands. Only about three out of every ten Guatemalans know how to read and write. There are fewer than four thousand elementary schools and only about one hundred high schools in Guatemala. Many communities have no school at all. Some of the Indians either refuse to send their children to school or allow them to attend for only a short time. In recent years, special classes have been held to educate adults who cannot read and

Guatemala City, the capital of Guatemala, is the largest city in Central America. It is Guatemala's main trading and manufacturing city.

write. Guatemala's University of San Carlos, which was founded in 1676, is located in Guatemala City.

Cities. About three fourths of all Guatemalans make their homes in rural areas. Guatemala's capital is its only large city.

Guatemala City (population about 407,000) is the capital of Guatemala and the largest city in Central America. The city lies in a highland basin nearly five thousand feet above sea level. (See map on page 157.) In recent years, Guatemala City has grown rapidly. Today, about one out of every ten persons in Guatemala lives here.

Guatemala City is the nation's main trading and manufacturing city. Most of Guatemala's factories and businesses are located here. Among the goods these factories produce are textiles, clothing, tobacco products, and cement. Guatemala City is connected with most other parts of the country by roads, railroads, and airways. The main international airport in Guatemala is located here.

Indian boys in school. Many Guatemalan communities have no school at all. Guatemala's literacy rate is one of the lowest in the Caribbean Lands.

167

Indian women washing clothes near Quezaltenango, Guatemala's second largest city. Most of the people who live in Quezaltenango are Indian.

In 1917 and 1918, Guatemala City was severely damaged by earthquakes, and much of it had to be rebuilt. Today, it is a very clean and attractive city. Its broad avenues are lined with one-story houses as well as tall hotels and modern office buildings. Not far from the city, at Antigua, are the ruins of the former capital, Santiago.

Quezaltenango (population about 40,000) is Guatemala's second largest city. It lies in a fertile basin in the western part of the highlands. (See map on page 157.) Most of the people who live here are Indian. On market day, large numbers of Indians from the surrounding highland area bring goods to Quezaltenango to sell.

Reviewing What You Have Learned

1. Why did the first Spaniards who came to Guatemala settle in highland valleys and basins? List four reasons.
2. What areas of Guatemala are most densely populated today?
3. Why were the Guatemalan people not prepared for democratic government when their country became independent? State two reasons.
4. State four ways in which the Indians' way of life in Guatemala today is different from the Ladinos' way of life.
5. What product from Guatemala's forests is used to make chewing gum? Briefly describe how this forest product is gathered and processed for export.
6. Guatemala has not made full use of its mineral resources. State one reason why this is true.
7. Where is Guatemala's main coffee-growing area? State three reasons why coffee grows well here.

Drawing Conclusions

Why do you think there is little industry in Guatemala? Discuss this question with your classmates. Consider the availability of each of the following in Guatemala: mineral resources and other raw materials, electric power, money, workers, transportation. How does each of these affect the development of industry in Guatemala?

Names To Know

Identify the following persons and places and tell why each is significant:

Petén	Puerto Barrios
Lake Atitlán	Justo Rufino Barrios
Guatemala City	Pedro de Alvarado

Making Comparisons

In Guatemala, only about three out of every ten persons know how to read and write. State two reasons why this is true. Then study the bottom picture on page 167. In what ways is the classroom in this picture like the one in which you study? In what ways is it different? Judging from this picture, what advantages do you think your classroom has? Why do you think there is such a difference between the two classrooms? Discuss these questions with your classmates.

15 El Salvador

Facts About El Salvador

Area: 8,260 square miles.

Population: About 2,700,000.

Density of Population: 327 people per square mile; 1,191 people per square mile of arable* land.

Capital and Largest City: San Salvador (population about 263,000).

Racial Composition: More than nine tenths of all Salvadorans are of mixed European and Indian descent. Most of the rest of the people are either white or Indian.

Literacy: About half of the people of El Salvador can read and write.

Main Language: Spanish.

Main Religion: Roman Catholicism.

Main Occupation: About six out of every ten Salvadoran workers earn their living in agriculture.

Income: Yearly per capita income is about $175. Most Salvadorans can live on a very small income, because they grow or make many of the things they need.

Important Farm Products: Coffee is El Salvador's leading export crop. Corn, beans, sorghum, rice, and fruit are important domestic food crops.

Natural Resources: Forest products, such as balsam of Peru and rubber, and shrimp.

Manufacturing: Textile manufacturing is the most important industry in El Salvador. Other products manufactured here are food products, leather goods, cigarettes, and beverages.

Currency: El Salvador's unit of money is the *colón,* which is officially worth about 40 cents.

GEOGRAPHY

Land. El Salvador is the smallest country in Central America. It is about the size of the state of Massachusetts. This small country lies along the Pacific

coast of Central America and is bordered by Guatemala and Honduras. (See map on pages 14 and 15.) El Salvador is the only Central American country without a coastline on the Caribbean Sea.

El Salvador may be divided into two main regions. Extending along the Pacific Ocean is a narrow plain which is part of the Pacific Lowland of Central America. The rest of El Salvador is made up of highlands.

The highland region of El Salvador consists of two chains of mountains separated by plateaus and valleys. Both mountain ranges extend generally from east to west across the country. One range is in the south, close to the coast, and the other is in the extreme north.

There are about twenty volcanoes in the highlands of El Salvador. Several of them are still active. The highest mountain in the country is a volcano called Santa Ana, which is located in

A volcano in El Salvador. Much of the land in El Salvador is covered with fertile volcanic soil.

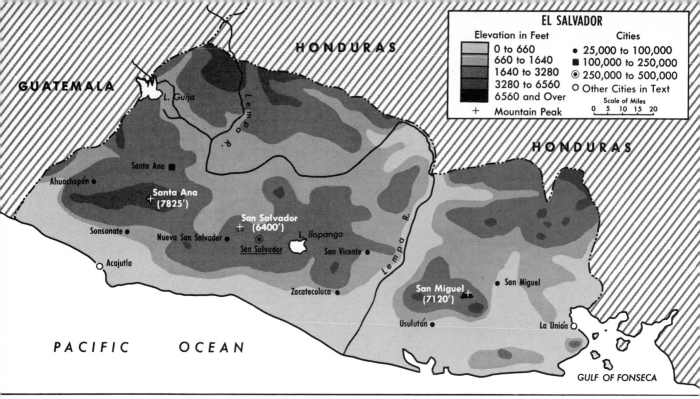

El Salvador is the only Central American country without a coastline on the Caribbean Sea. Extending along the Pacific coast of El Salvador is a narrow plain which is part of the Pacific Lowland of Central America. The rest of the country is made up of highlands.

the southern mountain range. This volcano reaches a height of nearly eight thousand feet above sea level. Weathered lava and ashes from volcanoes have enriched the soil in the southern mountains. The best farmland and most of the cities and large towns of El Salvador are located in this area.

Between the northern and southern mountain ranges are many small plateaus. Most of them lie about two thousand feet above sea level. Many rivers flow across the plateaus through fertile valleys. The longest of these rivers is the Lempa.

The Pacific Lowland in El Salvador makes up only about one tenth of the country's area. It extends the entire length of El Salvador's coast, but is only ten to fifteen miles wide. The fertile soil and hot climate here make this an important cotton-growing region.

Like other countries where there are active volcanoes, El Salvador is frequently shaken by earthquakes. Most of the earthquakes here are mild, but some have caused severe damage and loss of life.

Climate. Although El Salvador is located in the tropics, most of the country has a mild, pleasant climate. In the highlands, the days are usually warm and the nights are cool. The capital city, San Salvador, is located in the highlands. It has an average yearly temperature of about 75 degrees. The mild climate in the highlands helps make El Salvador an important coffee-growing country. The Pacific Lowland is the only part of the country that is hot all year round.

El Salvador has a rainy season and a dry season. The dry season usually lasts from November through March. During

170

these months, the Pacific Lowland receives almost no rain, and very little falls on the rest of the country. During the remainder of the year, rainfall is heavy in most places.

Natural resources. The most important natural resource of El Salvador is the volcanic soil that covers much of its land. This rich soil is well suited to growing coffee, which is the country's leading export crop. However, El Salvador faces a serious problem of soil erosion. In the highlands, most of the forests have been cut down for fuel or to clear the land for farming. On mountain slopes where trees have been cut down, rainwater has washed away much of the topsoil. The soil that remains is often stony.

The lack of forests in El Salvador today is a problem in other ways as well. Most of the people depend on wood or charcoal for fuel. In many areas of the country there is a shortage of firewood and charcoal. El Salvador is also faced with a shortage of lumber for building and for other industries. Almost all of its lumber must be imported from Honduras and other nearby countries.

There are still some forests in the Pacific Lowland. Important products from these forests are balsam of Peru and rubber. Balsam of Peru is a syrupy substance that comes from a tropical tree that grows in El Salvador. This valuable substance is used in making medicines and perfume.

In recent years, fishing has become an important industry in El Salvador. Hundreds of tons of shrimp are caught in its coastal waters each year. Most of these shrimp are frozen for export to other countries. Today, shrimp is El Salvador's third most important export item, after coffee and cotton.

Some of the waterpower of El Salvador is being used to produce hydroelectricity. The government's Lempa River project is the largest of its kind in all of Central America. The project's power plants supply electricity to many new factories in El Salvador.

A dam on the Lempa River. Some of El Salvador's waterpower is being used to produce hydroelectricity. The Lempa River project is the largest of its kind in Central America. Since it began operating, in 1954, many new factories have been built in El Salvador.

Pedro de Alvarado, a Spanish conqueror, led an army into what is now El Salvador in 1524. The Pipil Indians, the largest and most advanced of many Indian groups living here, fought fiercely against the invaders. However, within three years, the Spanish conquered all of El Salvador.

HISTORY

Indian days. Before the coming of the white man, what is now El Salvador was the home of many Indian groups. The largest and most advanced group were the Pipil Indians. The Pipil called their homeland Cuscatlán, which means "land of jewels." These Indians built several large towns, including a capital, which was also named Cuscatlán. Although some of the Pipil were weavers, potters, carpenters, and builders, most of them were farmers.

Under Spanish rule. In 1524, Pedro de Alvarado, a Spanish conqueror, led an army into El Salvador. This army had just conquered most of the Indians of southern Guatemala. The Pipil fought fiercely against the invaders, but within three years, all of El Salvador was conquered by the Spaniards.

El Salvador remained under Spanish rule for nearly three hundred years. During this time it was part of the *audiencia* of Guatemala. (See page 69.) Few Spaniards settled in El Salvador because it was difficult to reach the Pacific coast of Central America. Also, the country had little mineral wealth to attract settlers.

During their long rule over El Salvador, many Spaniards married Indian women. In time, much of the population became a mixture of Spanish and Indian.

172

These people of mixed descent adopted the customs, language, and religion of the Spaniards. They became known as Ladinos.

El Salvador joins the Central American Federation. In 1821, El Salvador, together with the other provinces in the *audiencia* of Guatemala, declared its independence from Spain. Two years later, five of these provinces formed the Central American Federation. (See Chapter 5.) El Salvador played an important part in this federation. A priest named José Matías Delgado, who helped to organize the federation, became El Salvador's national hero.

The Central American Federation lasted for less than twenty years. From the very beginning, two political groups fought for control of the federation. One of these groups was called the Liberal party, and the other was called the Conservative party. The federation broke up in 1838. After a period of civil war, El Salvador became an independent nation.

Conservatives and Liberals struggle for power in El Salvador. After independence, El Salvador had few periods of peace and order. The Liberals and the Conservatives in El Salvador fought each other for control of the country, and revolutions were frequent. For many years, the countries of Central America interfered in each other's affairs. Before 1900, El Salvador fought wars with Guatemala, Nicaragua, and Honduras.

El Salvador begins to make progress. After 1900, El Salvador slowly began to make progress. The Salvadoran army became strong enough to prevent frequent revolutions. For the first time

since independence, there were long periods of peace and order. Coffee, a crop which had been introduced from Brazil in 1840, became an important export. The sale of coffee to other countries brought badly needed money to El Salvador. Roads and railroads were built, as well as some schools, and low-cost housing for Salvadoran workers.

Military leaders rule El Salvador. The progress that has been made in El Salvador has not benefited many of its people. The majority of the people are very poor farmers who have little or no voice in their government. Dictators have frequently ruled El Salvador. Since 1931, the government has been under the control of military leaders. In 1960, and again in 1961, groups of army officers seized control of the government. An army colonel, Julio Adalberto Rivera, was chosen president in 1962 in an election controlled by the army. Under Rivera, El Salvador's government has been more stable.

The National Palace in San Salvador. Dictators have often ruled El Salvador. The government has been under the control of military leaders since 1931.

173

Coffee drying in the sun. El Salvador is one of the world's leading coffee-exporting countries. Its best farmland is used to raise crops for export.

THE PEOPLE AND HOW THEY LIVE

People. Fewer than three million people live in El Salvador. However, its land area is so small that it is the most densely populated country in Central America. There are no large areas of rainforest and few of the rugged mountains found in other Central American countries. For this reason, there are people living in nearly all parts of El Salvador.

Because the population of El Salvador is increasing rapidly, overcrowding is becoming a serious problem. Almost all of the land available for farming is already being cultivated. The best farmland is not used to raise domestic food crops. Instead, export crops, such as coffee and cotton, are raised on this land. As a result, the country does not grow enough food for its people, and food products must be imported.

Earning a living. Nearly three fourths of the land in El Salvador is used for farming. The country is so densely populated that farmers grow crops even in the craters of extinct volcanoes. Although many farmers own or rent small plots of ground, most of them work on large farms where coffee and other export crops are grown.

El Salvador is one of the world's leading coffee-exporting countries. This single crop brings in more than one half of the money Salvadorans make from selling products to other countries. Coffee is raised in most parts of the country. The highland plateaus and lower mountain slopes are the best coffee-growing areas.

Cotton is El Salvador's second most important export crop. It is grown mainly on plantations in the Pacific Lowland,

174

In a textile mill. Textile manufacturing is the most important industry in El Salvador. Most of the factories here make goods used by the people of the country. Only about one out of every ten workers in El Salvador is employed in manufacturing.

where the climate is well suited to growing this crop. Since the end of World War II, the government of El Salvador has encouraged the growing of cotton and other export crops, such as sesame, sugarcane, and cacao. It has done this because the country has been too dependent upon its coffee exports. El Salvador faces real hardship whenever world coffee prices fall.

Although export crops are important, many farmers in El Salvador earn their living by raising food crops for domestic use. The principal food crop is corn. Other important crops grown mainly for use at home are beans, sorghum, rice, and fruit. Livestock are raised mainly on the coastal lowland. The number of cattle and hogs raised does not provide

enough meat for the people of El Salvador. Beef and pork are imported.

Only about one out of every ten workers in El Salvador is employed in manufacturing. Textile manufacturing is the country's most important industry. El Salvador has more cotton mills than any other country in Central America. Cotton yarn and fabrics are used to make clothing, and some textiles are exported. Most of the factories in El Salvador make goods used by the people of the country. Besides textiles and clothing, these include food products, leather goods, cigarettes, and beverages.

Since the Lempa River project began to generate electricity, many new factories have been built in El Salvador. The country's first oil refinery began operations in 1963 at the Pacific port of Acajutla. A large fertilizer plant is being built in the same area. The first steel mill in Central America was constructed in El Salvador, and a plant for assembling Volkswagen automobiles is planned.

Transportation and communication. El Salvador has the best system of roads in all of Central America. Two modern highways extend across the country from east to west. The Inter-American Highway crosses the central part of El Salvador and connects most of the important cities and towns. Coffee and other products of the highlands can be shipped by truck to the country's chief port, La Unión. (Compare maps on pages 133 and 170.) The second cross-country highway, called the Coastal Highway, was recently built across the Pacific Lowland. Much of the forested land in this area has been opened to settlement by the highway. Unused land here is now being cleared for farming.

Railroads in El Salvador are not as important to the country as its roads. Two railroads connect the important inland cities of El Salvador with ports on the Pacific coast. In addition, one of them connects with a Guatemalan railroad that runs to Puerto Barrios, an important Guatemalan port on the Caribbean Sea. The new highways that have been built in El Salvador generally follow the same routes as the railroads. As a result, cargo and passengers previously carried by the railroads can now be transported over the new roads.

Distances are so short in El Salvador that air travel is not an important means of transportation within the country. However, most people entering or leaving the country travel by air. Flights of several foreign airlines land at

Building the Coastal Highway across the Pacific Lowland of El Salvador. The Coastal Highway has made it possible for more people to settle in this area. It is one of two modern highways that cross El Salvador. This country has the best system of roads in all of Central America.

A school in San Salvador. The government of El Salvador has spent large sums of money on teacher training and schools. However, many children still receive little or no schooling. Only about half of the people of El Salvador can read and write.

Ilopango International Airport, which is located just outside San Salvador.

El Salvador has poor communications. Few people have telephones or radios in their homes, even in the cities. There are two television stations in San Salvador. However, very few people can afford television sets.

Education. Public education is free in El Salvador, and all children between the ages of seven and thirteen are required by law to attend school. However, only about half of the people of El Salvador can read and write. Although the government has spent large sums of money on teacher training and schools, many children, especially those in rural areas, still receive little or no schooling. In 1960, there were about 2,500 elementary schools in the country but only about 160 high schools.

The University of El Salvador, which was founded in 1841, is located in the capital city. About 2,000 students attend this university, which offers courses in law, medicine, engineering, and other fields.

Cities. San Salvador (population about 263,000) is the capital and largest city of El Salvador. It is located in the central part of the highland region, about twenty-five miles from the Pacific coast. (See map on page 170.) The city lies at the foot of a volcano called San Salvador, in a fertile valley about 2,200 feet above sea level.

San Salvador is the chief manufacturing city of El Salvador. Many workers here are employed in mills that make cotton textiles. Other factories produce coffee bags, clothing, beverages, and food products. San Salvador ships

A street in San Salvador, the capital and largest city of El Salvador. San Salvador is more modern than many other cities in the Caribbean Lands.

San Salvador is more modern than many other cities in the Caribbean Lands. Most of the old colonial buildings in the capital were destroyed by an earthquake in 1854. Since then, the city has twice been severely damaged by earthquakes. Today, buildings in El Salvador are generally low and solidly built as a protection against earthquakes. For example, the National Palace in San Salvador is only two stories high.

Santa Ana (population about 146,000) is the second largest city in El Salvador. It is located about forty miles northwest of the capital. The city is situated about 2,100 feet above sea level, near Santa Ana Volcano.

Santa Ana is sometimes called El Salvador's coffee capital. It is surrounded by the nation's richest coffee-growing area. One of the largest coffee mills in the world is located in this city.

some of its manufactured goods to other parts of the country. The city is located on the Inter-American Highway and is connected by road and railroad with most other important cities and towns in El Salvador.

Think and Write

1. What three major problems does El Salvador face due to lack of forests?
2. Why did El Salvador have few periods of peace and order after it became independent from Spain? State two reasons.
3. List three ways in which El Salvador began to make progress after 1900.
4. Why is El Salvador unable to produce enough food for its people? State two reasons.
5. Give one reason why the number of new factories in El Salvador has increased since 1954.
6. Why are buildings in El Salvador generally low and solidly built?
7. Much of the forested land in the Pacific Lowland of El Salvador is now being cleared for farming. What has made it possible to open up this area for settlement?

How Geography Affects People

List two facts about the geography of El Salvador that make it different from other Central American countries. Name at least one way in which each of these geographical differences affects the people of El Salvador.

Learning More About Coffee

As you learned in this chapter, coffee is El Salvador's most important crop. Read about coffee in at least one outside source. Then write a report on coffee production. You may wish to draw pictures or cut some from magazines to illustrate your report. Chapter 8 contains additional information that will be helpful. Your report should include the following general topics:

a. how coffee grows
b. how coffee is harvested
c. how coffee is prepared for market
d. how instant coffee is made

16 British Honduras

GEOGRAPHY

Land. British Honduras, sometimes called Belize, occupies a narrow strip of land on the Caribbean coast of Central America. (Compare map at right with map on pages 14 and 15.) It is about the size of Massachusetts, and is smaller than any other Central American country except El Salvador.

Most of British Honduras consists of a lowland covered with dense rainforest. This area is part of the Caribbean Lowland of Central America. (See map on page 20.) Along the coast of British Honduras, the land is generally swampy. In the southwestern part of the country are the Maya Mountains, which rise to about three thousand feet above sea level. Many small rivers wind through British Honduras. Because there are few good roads, these rivers are the chief means of travel within the country.

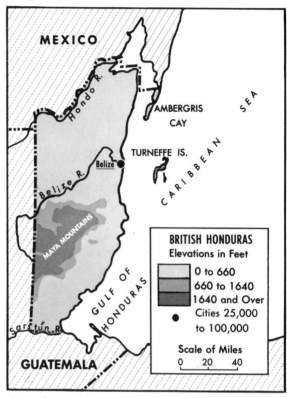

British Honduras occupies a strip of land on the Caribbean coast of Central America.

In British Honduras, the land along the coast is generally swampy. Most of the country consists of a lowland covered with dense rainforest.

Climate. The climate throughout British Honduras is hot and humid. Rainfall is heaviest in the southern part of the country. Here the average rainfall is more than one hundred inches a year, compared to about sixty inches in the northern part of the country.

HISTORY

In the early 1500's, Spanish explorers sailed along the coast of what is now British Honduras. However, they did not consider this swampy lowland suitable for settlement. More than one hundred years later, British settlers moved into the area at the mouth of the

179

Facts About British Honduras

Area: 8,866 square miles.

Population: About 93,000.

Density of Population: 11 people per square mile; 44 people per square mile of arable* land.

Capital and Largest City: Belize (population about 33,000).

Racial Composition: More than one third of the people of British Honduras are Negro. About one third are mulatto or mestizo. Most of the rest are Indian.

Literacy: More than nine tenths of the people can read and write.

Main Language: English.

Main Religion: Roman Catholicism.

Main Occupation: Most workers are employed in the lumbering industry or on sugar or citrus plantations.

Income: Figures are not available.

Important Farm Products: Citrus fruits and sugarcane are the leading export crops.

Natural Resources: Forests.

Manufacturing: Processing products from forests and farms is the leading industry in British Honduras.

Currency: The British Honduras dollar is officially worth about 70 cents in United States money.

Belize River to cut logwood trees. The wood from these trees was shipped to Europe, where it was in great demand for use in making a dye. The first British settlement was on the site of Belize, the present capital of British Honduras.

Although no Spaniards had settled in the area near Belize, this territory was considered a possession of Spain. Spaniards attacked the settlement at Belize many times, but they were unable to drive out the British settlers.

After Mexico and Guatemala had gained their independence from Spain, in the early 1800's, each of them claimed part of British Honduras. However, these countries later signed treaties recognizing British claims to the territory. In 1862, British Honduras officially became a colony of Great Britain. In recent years, Guatemala has renewed its claims to British Honduras. These claims have been rejected by Great Britain.

In January, 1964, the colony of British Honduras became internally self-governing. Laws for the colony are made by an assembly whose members are elected by the people. Great Britain continues to be responsible for the colony's defense and foreign affairs.

THE PEOPLE AND HOW THEY LIVE

People. British Honduras has fewer people per square mile of land than any other Caribbean country. Large parts of its forested lowland are almost uninhabited. About half of the people live in the capital city, Belize, and a few towns. The rest live in many scattered settlements. Many British Hondurans are descended from Negro slaves who

Reviewing troops in Belize. British Honduras is a colony of Great Britain. It is self-governing except for matters of defense and foreign affairs.

Lumber is one of the main exports of British Honduras. Forests cover about nine tenths of the land.

were brought from the West Indies during the early days of the colony to work in logging camps.

Earning a living. Lumbering has always been an important occupation in British Honduras. Forests cover about nine tenths of the land. Mahogany and Spanish cedar trees are found in the rain-forest, and pine trees grow on the slopes of the Maya Mountains. Many people in Belize work in sawmills where logs are cut into lumber for export. Some of the best trees have already been cut down, and lumber production has declined in recent years.

In 1962, a United States company opened a plant in British Honduras to extract resins from the stumps of pine trees. Resins are used in making paint, varnish, and other useful products.

Chicle is another forest product of British Honduras. This sticky substance, which is obtained from the sapodilla tree, is used in making chewing gum. (See page 159 for information about gathering chicle.)

An increasing number of people in British Honduras work on sugar and citrus plantations. A sugar mill and a plant for processing grapefruit and oranges have been built in the colony. Citrus products and sugar are now among the country's most important exports.

Except for the sugar and citrus plantations, only a small amount of land in British Honduras is used for farming. The people do not raise enough food for their own needs. Food items, such as meat and canned milk, make up about one third of the country's imports.

In addition to food, British Honduras imports clothing, machinery, petroleum products, and many other items. It pays more money for these imports than it receives from the lumber and other products that it exports. British Honduras depends on financial aid from Great Britain to make up some of the difference between the amount received for exports and the cost of imports.

Tapping a sapodilla tree to obtain chicle, a substance used in making chewing gum. Not much land is used for farming in British Honduras.

A street in Belize, the capital and main port of British Honduras. Houses in Belize have large containers to collect rainwater for drinking.

Cities. Belize (population about 33,000) is the capital of British Honduras, and the only city in the country with a population of more than 10,000. It is built on swampy land at the mouth of the Belize River.

Belize is the main port of British Honduras. However, the harbor is not deep enough for large ships to enter. These ships must stop about a mile offshore and transfer their freight to smaller vessels, which carry it to the shore. Some of the people in Belize have jobs loading and unloading cargo on the waterfront. Others work in the warehouses and offices of companies that import and export goods.

Most of the houses in Belize are made of wood and have roofs of galvanized iron. There are no underground sewers in Belize, and most homes have no running water. Each house has a container to collect rainwater for drinking. Unsanitary conditions are the cause of much sickness in Belize.

In 1961, Belize was badly damaged by a hurricane. Plans are being made to build a new capital city about fifty miles inland.

Education. More than nine out of every ten people in British Honduras can read and write. Children between the ages of six and fourteen are required to attend school. Very few students go on to high school, however. There are no universities in British Honduras.

Think and Write

1. Who were the first settlers of British Honduras? Why did they come here?

2. What is the most important natural resource of British Honduras? State two reasons for its importance.

3. Explain why British Honduras depends on financial aid from Great Britain. Facts about farming and manufacturing in this colony should be included in your answer.

4. Why are rivers the chief means of transportation in British Honduras?

Using Your Imagination

Imagine that you have recently moved to Belize, British Honduras. How does life in this city compare to life in your hometown? Write a letter describing the differences to a former classmate. In your letter, tell him about the following:

a. the kind of house in which you live
b. the problems involved in living here
c. the weather
d. what you have seen on trips to other parts of the country

17　Honduras

GEOGRAPHY

Land. Honduras, the second largest country in Central America, is about the size of Tennessee. It is shaped roughly like a triangle. (See map on page 184.) The northern coast of Honduras stretches along the Caribbean Sea for about four hundred miles. The country has only a short coastline on the Pacific Ocean. This coastline, which is about fifty miles long, borders an inlet called the Gulf of Fonseca.

Honduras is the most mountainous country in Central America. About four fifths of the country consists of highlands. Here there are many jagged mountain ranges. The highest peaks, which lie in the southwestern part of the country, are more than nine thousand feet above sea level. There are many basins and valleys in the highlands. Most of the people of Honduras live in these valleys and basins where the climate is mild and the soil is generally fertile. Tegucigalpa, the capital of Honduras, lies in a valley about 3,200 feet above sea level.

A plain extends along the northern coast of Honduras. This plain is part of the Caribbean Lowland of Central America. (Compare map on page 20 with map on pages 14 and 15.) In Honduras, much of this lowland is narrow.

Mountainous land in Honduras. About four fifths of Honduras consists of highlands. It is the most mountainous country in Central America. Most of the people of Honduras live in highland basins and valleys where the climate is mild and the soil is generally fertile.

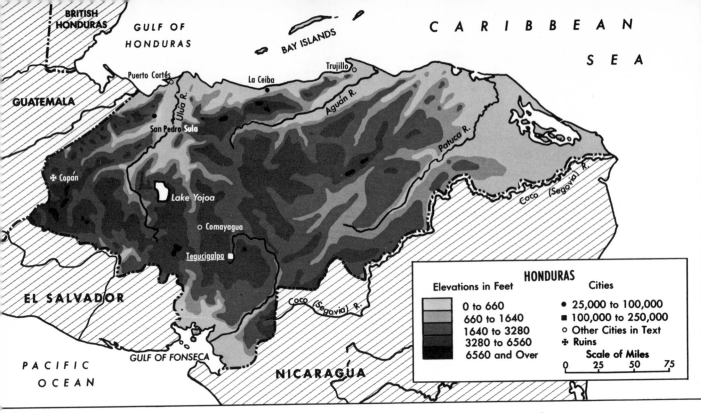

Honduras is the second largest country in Central America. The northern coast of Honduras stretches along the Caribbean Sea for about four hundred miles.

In some places, broad river valleys extend many miles inland from the coast. The largest of these is the fertile valley of the Ulúa River. There are many banana plantations in this part of the Caribbean Lowland. The coastal plain is widest in the northeastern part of Honduras. Here the land is covered with dense tropical rainforest. Parts of this area have never been explored. Lying off the northern coast is a group of islands that belong to Honduras. These are called the Bay Islands.

On the Pacific coast of Honduras is a narrow, fertile plain that is part of the Pacific Lowland. Most of the cotton produced in Honduras is grown here.

Climate. In the lowlands of Honduras, the weather is hot and humid the year around. It is cooler in the highlands. Tegucigalpa has an average daytime temperature of about seventy-five degrees.

Rainfall is heavier in the northern part of Honduras than in the southern part. On the Caribbean Lowland and the northern mountain slopes, the yearly rainfall ranges from seventy to more than one hundred inches. The Pacific Lowland and most areas in the highlands have a rainy season that lasts from May to November. During the rest of the year, little rain falls on these areas.

Natural resources. Among the important natural resources of Honduras are the fertile soil and hot climate in the western part of the Caribbean Lowland. These resources have made this part of the lowland an important banana-growing area.

More than two fifths of Honduras is covered with forests. Mahogany and

Spanish cedar trees grow in the rainforest of the Caribbean Lowland. There are large pine forests in the cooler highlands. Although lumbering is important to Honduras, the country has not been able to make full use of its forest resources. It is costly to build roads into the rugged highland areas and dense rainforest. Forest fires are another serious problem in Honduras. Farmers often start fires to clear the land for raising crops. These fires sometimes get out of control and burn valuable forests. In recent years, the Honduran government has been carrying out a program to prevent forest fires and to plant young trees in areas where forests have been destroyed.

Honduras is believed to be richer in mineral resources than any other Central American country. However, the lack of good transportation has hindered mining as well as lumbering. At the present time, the main minerals being produced in Honduras are silver, lead, and zinc.

There are many rivers in Honduras that could be used to produce hydroelectric power. In the past, however, the country's water resources have not been used. Honduras has less electric power than any other country in Central America except British Honduras. The shortage of power is one reason why the country has little industry. In 1960, Honduras received loans from the World Bank and other sources to build its first large hydroelectric power plant. This plant will use water from Lake Yojoa and the Lindo River to produce electricity for homes and factories in the main cities of Honduras.

Until a few years ago, fishing was not important to Honduras. Recently, a

Pouring molten silver into molds. Honduras is believed to be richer in mineral resources than any other Central American country. Silver, lead, and zinc are the main minerals produced here, but even these are not mined in large amounts. Lack of transportation has hindered mining.

Facts About Honduras

Area: 43,277 square miles.

Population: About 1,950,000.

Density of Population: 45 people per square mile; 492 people per square mile of arable* land.

Capital and Largest City: Tegucigalpa (population about 133,000).

Racial Composition: About nine tenths of all Hondurans are mestizo. Most of the rest are Indian.

Literacy: About four tenths of the people of Honduras can read and write.

Main Language: Spanish.

Main Religion: Roman Catholicism.

Main Occupation: More than eight tenths of all Honduran workers earn their living by farming.

Income: Yearly per capita income is about $180. Most Hondurans can live on a very small income, because they grow or make many of the things they need.

Important Farm Products: Bananas and coffee are Honduras' leading export crops. Corn, rice, and beans are the most important domestic food crops.

Natural Resources: Forests, fisheries, silver, lead, and zinc.

Manufacturing: The leading industry in Honduras is the manufacture of beverages. Other products manufactured here are soap, vegetable oil, sugar, cigarettes, textiles, and furniture.

Currency: Honduras' unit of money is the *lempira,* which is officially worth about 50 cents.

small shrimp-fishing industry has been developed, mainly on the Caribbean coast. There are three shrimp-freezing plants in Honduras. Most of the frozen shrimp are shipped to the United States.

HISTORY

Early peoples. Long before Europeans came to the New World, several groups of Indians were living in what is now Honduras. The most civilized of these Indians were the Maya. They built the great city of Copán. (See lower right-hand map on page 53.) Sometime after A.D. 800, this Mayan civilization began to decline, and the city of Copán was abandoned.

Honduras becomes a Spanish possession. Christopher Columbus landed on the Caribbean coast of Honduras in 1502 and claimed the land for Spain. About twenty years later, Spanish explorers began coming to Honduras. Among these explorers was the conqueror of Mexico, Hernán Cortés. He stayed for about a year and then returned to Mexico.

The Spanish explorers found it very difficult to conquer Honduras. They had to cut their way through dense forests and climb rugged mountains. The Spaniards fought hostile Indians, and they also quarreled among themselves. Pedro de Alvarado came from Guatemala to restore order among the men. In 1536, Alvarado founded the town of San Pedro Sula. (See map on page 184.) A year later, the town of Comayagua was founded in the highlands. This town became the first capital of Honduras.

Very few Spaniards settled in Honduras until the 1570's. At that time, rich deposits of silver were found in the southern part of the highlands. Many Spaniards moved into this area, and the mining town of Tegucigalpa was founded.

During colonial days, Honduras was in the *audiencia** of Guatemala. However, part of Honduras was not actually under Spanish control. English pirates and logwood cutters founded settlements along the Caribbean coast of Honduras and on the Bay Islands. It was not until 1859 that the British completely gave up control of these settlements.

Honduras joins the Central American Federation. In 1821, Honduras and the other provinces in the *audiencia* of Guatemala declared their independence from Spain. Two years later, the Central American Federation was formed. Francisco Morazán, a Honduran leader, became the second president of this federation, in 1830. (For more information, see page 74.)

Morazán, a leader of the Liberals, tried to bring about many reforms in Central America. Under Morazán, the Liberals worked to improve agriculture and transportation. They introduced trial by jury and other legal reforms. The government took over many buildings that had been owned by the Roman Catholic Church, and used them for schools or hospitals.

The Conservatives strongly opposed Morazán's policies. Conservative leaders stirred up the people against the Liberals. Morazán tried to hold the Central American Federation together, but he was not successful. In 1838, the federation broke up, and Honduras became an independent nation.

A struggle for power develops in Honduras. After Honduras gained its independence, Liberals and Conservatives often fought each other for control of the government. Honduras was one of the weakest of the Central American republics. Therefore, neighboring countries found it easy to interfere in Honduran affairs. The government of Honduras was often overthrown, either by foreign troops or by revolts within the country.

187

A statue of Francisco Morazán, national hero of Honduras. As president of the Central American Federation, Morazán worked to bring about reforms.

Honduras becomes a leading producer of bananas. Early in the 1900's, United States fruit companies began to grow bananas in the Caribbean Lowland of Honduras. These companies cleared the land and drained the swamps in order to establish banana plantations. They built homes, schools, and hospitals for their workers. Efforts were made by the fruit companies to eliminate malaria and other tropical diseases. During the 1920's, Honduras became the largest exporter of bananas in the world. Taxes on banana exports provided the government of Honduras with an important source of income.

A dictator rules the country. In 1933, after almost a century of political unrest, an army general named Tiburcio Carías Andino became president of Honduras. Carías Andino ruled the country for sixteen years, keeping himself in power by military force. During his rule, Honduras made little progress.

Changes come to Honduras. In 1949, the rule of Carías Andino came to an end. Since that time, some progress has been made in Honduras. Schools and roads have been built. In 1954, workers for a large fruit company went on a long strike. As a result, the government recognized the right of the workers to join labor unions.

The election of 1957 was fairer than those previously held in Honduras. Ramón Villeda Morales was elected president. A short time later, a new democratic constitution was adopted. Under Villeda Morales, Honduras continued to make progress. In 1963, however, Villeda Morales was overthrown by a group of military leaders who opposed his policies. The United States at first refused to recognize this military junta.* However, after the new government promised to hold elections before the end of 1965, the United States resumed diplomatic relations with Honduras.

A banana worker's home. Early in the 1900's, United States fruit companies established large banana plantations in the Caribbean Lowland of Honduras. These companies built homes, schools, and hospitals for the workers on the plantations.

In the marketplace of a Honduran town. Most of the people of Honduras are mestizo. They are descended from Indians and early Spanish settlers.

THE PEOPLE AND HOW THEY LIVE

People. Most of the people of Honduras are mestizo. They are descended from Indians and early Spanish settlers. About six out of every hundred Hondurans are of pure Indian descent. Some of the Indians live in the dense forests that cover the northeastern part of Honduras. Small numbers of Negroes live along the Caribbean coast. They were brought here from Jamaica and Costa Rica to work on banana plantations. Very few Hondurans are white. Most of the white people are of Spanish descent. On the Bay Islands, however, many of the people are descended from British settlers. They speak English instead of Spanish.

Most Hondurans are Roman Catholic, but there are Protestant missions throughout the country. Many of the people on the Bay Islands are Protestant.

Earning a living. Farming is the most important occupation in Honduras. More than eight tenths of all Honduran workers earn their living on small farms or on plantations. Bananas, cotton, sugarcane, and other crops needing a hot climate are grown in the lowlands. In the highlands, where the climate is cooler, farmers grow such crops as coffee and vegetables. Most farmers throughout the country grow corn on small plots of land. Corn, rice, and beans are the main foods eaten by Hondurans.

Bananas are grown on large plantations in the Caribbean Lowland. Most of these plantations are owned by two United States fruit companies. In recent years, plant disease has caused a decrease in banana production. However, Honduras is still one of the world's leading banana producers.

On the banana plantations, there are villages of neat homes, which the fruit companies have built for their employees. The plantation workers shop in stores owned by the fruit companies.

A potato field. Farming is the most important occupation in Honduras. In the highlands, farmers grow such crops as coffee and vegetables.

Their children attend company schools. The plantation workers live much better than most farmers in other parts of Honduras. However, some Hondurans resent the fact that the fruit companies are owned by foreigners.

In recent years, coffee has become an important export of Honduras. This crop is grown mainly on the lower slopes of mountains. Coffee farms in Honduras are generally small. Unlike the banana plantations, most of these farms are owned by Hondurans. Therefore, coffee exports are especially important to the people of Honduras.

Some Hondurans raise livestock on pastures in the highlands. Honduras exports beef cattle and hogs, mainly to the neighboring countries of Guatemala and El Salvador. However, some dairy products must be imported from other countries. The government of Honduras has started a program to improve the quality of dairy cattle.

Few workers in Honduras are employed in industry. Most of the manufacturing plants make products that are used by the people of Honduras. The leading industry is the manufacture of beverages, such as beer, rum, and soft drinks. Other products made in Honduras include soap, vegetable oil, sugar, cigarettes, and cotton textiles.

Honduras has about seventy sawmills, where logs from the country's forests are made into lumber. Some of the lumber is used within Honduras for construction and in the manufacture of furniture. Lumber is also one of the country's leading exports.

Bananas are dipped to protect them from insects and disease and to keep them from spoiling during shipment. Honduras is one of the world's leading banana exporters. Coffee and lumber are also important export products. Few Honduran workers are employed in manufacturing.

Air transportation is important to Honduras, because the country lacks railroads and good highways. Even bulky cargo is sometimes carried by airplane. In many places, airplanes are the only means of transportation other than oxcarts or mules.

Transportation and communication. A lack of good transportation has always been one of the major problems of Honduras. Settlements in the rugged highlands are isolated from towns in the coastal lowlands. Because there are few good roads, products from the highlands are often carried to seaports in two-wheeled oxcarts or on the backs of mules.

In recent years, the government of Honduras has been building new roads and improving the ones that already exist. However, Honduras still has only about two thousand miles of roads, most of which are unpaved. The most important road is the Inter-Oceanic Highway. It connects Puerto Cortés on the northern coast with the Inter-American Highway, close to the southern coast. The Inter-American Highway passes through a small part of southern Honduras. (Compare maps on pages 133 and 184.)

Honduras has three railroads, with a total of about eight hundred miles of tracks. One of these railroads is owned by the government. It connects towns in the northern part of the country. The other two railroads are owned by United States fruit companies. They are used mainly to transport bananas from plantations to ports on the Caribbean Sea. There are no railroads in the southern part of the country, where many of the people live.

Because of the lack of highways and railroads, air transportation is important to Honduras. In many places, airplanes are the only means of transportation other than oxcarts or mules. There are more than one hundred small airfields in Honduras. Even bulky cargo, such as coffee, is sometimes carried by airplane.

The telephone system of Honduras is owned by the government. There are only about six thousand telephones, and most of them are in Tegucigalpa and San Pedro Sula. Honduras has one television station and fewer than twenty radio stations.

Education. Only about four tenths of the people of Honduras can read and write. Children between the ages of seven and fifteen are required by law to attend school. However, there are not enough schools for everyone. Only about six tenths of the children attend classes. In recent years, the government of Honduras has been trying to make education available to more of its people. In 1962, the United States government agreed to provide Honduras with more than one million dollars for the construction of ninety-six school buildings.

Honduras today has more than three thousand elementary schools and about sixty-five high schools. The National University of Honduras is located in Tegucigalpa, with a branch at San Pedro Sula. This university offers courses in medicine, law, engineering, and other fields. Courses in tropical farming are given at the Pan American Agricultural School, near Tegucigalpa.

Cities. Tegucigalpa (population about 133,000) is the capital and largest city of Honduras. It is situated in a highland valley about 3,200 feet above sea level. Part of the city is built on a hillside. Tegucigalpa has not changed greatly in appearance since colonial days. Much of the city resembles an old Spanish town. However, there are modern homes in a residential section north of the city.

The most important products manufactured in Tegucigalpa are construction materials, such as bricks and lumber.

At the Pan American Agricultural School, near Tegucigalpa, students learn modern methods of tropical farming. In recent years, the government of Honduras has been trying to make it possible for more people to gain an education.

Some factories process farm products raised in the highlands and on the Pacific Lowland. Among the products of these factories are cotton fabrics and beverages.

Tegucigalpa is one of the few capital cities in the world that is not served by a railroad. However, planes of several local and international airlines land here. There are roads connecting Tegucigalpa with San Pedro Sula and other Honduran cities.

San Pedro Sula (population about 79,000) is the second largest city in Honduras. It is located in the northwestern part of the country, on the Caribbean Lowland. Near the city are large plantations where bananas and sugarcane are grown. San Pedro Sula is the most modern and fastest-growing city in Honduras. It has sawmills, a sugar refinery, a cigarette factory, a cement plant, and a flour mill. The city

Tegucigalpa, the capital and largest city of Honduras, is situated in a highland valley. Much of the city resembles an old Spanish town.

is connected by road and railroad with ports on the Caribbean coast of Honduras. Goods that enter the country through these ports are brought to San Pedro Sula for distribution to other parts of the country.

Exploring Relationships

1. Why has Honduras been unable to make full use of its forest resources? State two reasons.

2. List four kinds of goods manufactured in Honduras that are made with raw materials produced in this country.

3. Why is air transportation especially important to Honduras?

4. Bananas are an important product of Honduras. List three things that companies operating banana plantations have done for their workers.

5. Where do most of the people of Honduras live? State two reasons for this.

6. Most of the people of Honduras are mestizo. From what Indian groups do you think they may be descended? A comparison of the map on pages 14 and 15 with the right-hand maps on page 53 will help you answer this question.

7. Why do many of the people on the Bay Islands speak English instead of Spanish? Relate your answer to the history of these islands.

Studying the History of Honduras

1. Why did the Spaniards find it difficult to conquer Honduras? State two reasons.

2. List three ways in which Francisco Morazán and his followers tried to help the people of Central America. Why do you think Morazán is the national hero of Honduras?

3. Why has Honduras had unstable government since 1838, when it became independent?

4. Since 1948, some changes have been made that have benefited the people of Honduras. List two of these changes.

193

18 Nicaragua

The Caribbean Lowland in Nicaragua. This broad, level plain is mostly covered with dense rainforest. Trade winds bring heavy rainfall to this area.

Facts About Nicaragua

Area: 57,143 square miles.

Population: About 1,550,000.

Density of Population: 27 people per square mile; 433 people per square mile of arable* land.

Capital and Largest City: Managua (population about 226,000).

Racial Composition: About seven tenths of the Nicaraguan people are mestizo. Fewer than two tenths are of pure Spanish descent. Most of the rest of the people are either Negro or Indian.

Literacy: About one third of the people of Nicaragua can read and write.

Main Language: Spanish.

Main Religion: Roman Catholicism.

Main Occupation: More than two thirds of all Nicaraguan workers are farmers.

Income: Yearly per capita income is about $235. Most Nicaraguans can live on a very small income, because they grow or make many of the things they need.

Important Farm Products: Cotton and coffee are Nicaragua's leading export crops. Corn, rice, and beans are the most important domestic food crops.

Natural Resources: Forests, gold, silver, and copper.

Manufacturing: Among the leading products of Nicaraguan factories are lumber, refined sugar, processed meat, cigarettes, alcoholic beverages, and textiles.

Currency: Nicaragua's unit of money is the *cordoba,* which is officially worth about 14 cents.

GEOGRAPHY

Land. The Central American country of Nicaragua is smaller than the state of Michigan. Yet it is the largest country in the Caribbean Lands. (See map on pages 14 and 15.)

About one third of Nicaragua is made up of highlands. A rugged, mountainous area extends southward through the central part of the country almost to the border of Costa Rica. The steep-sided mountains of the central highlands are not very high. None of them rises more than seven thousand feet above sea level. Several mountain ridges extend eastward from the central highlands like crooked fingers pointing toward the Caribbean Sea. Between these ridges are deep valleys, which have been cut by rivers flowing into the Caribbean. In the southwestern part of Nicaragua are low mountains that extend into Costa Rica.

More than half of Nicaragua is made up of lowlands. The largest lowland is a broad, flat plain along the Caribbean Sea. This plain is part of the Caribbean Lowland of Central America. (Compare map on page 20 with map on pages

14 and 15.) In Nicaragua, most of this area is forested. Much of the northern part of the lowland is a savanna dotted with pine trees. Throughout the Caribbean Lowland, the soil lacks some of the plant foods needed for growing crops. Another lowland extends along part of Nicaragua's Pacific coast. This is part of the Pacific Lowland. In most places, it is only about ten miles wide. Both the Caribbean and Pacific lowlands of Nicaragua are thinly populated.

The most densely populated region of Nicaragua is a level plain that lies west and south of the central highlands. This is the Nicaraguan Lowland. (Compare map below with map on page 20.) The largest lakes in Central America, Lake Nicaragua and Lake Managua, lie in this lowland.

More than twenty volcanic cones rise from the Nicaraguan Lowland. An irregular row of volcanoes extends northwestward from Lake Managua almost to the Pacific Ocean. Other volcanoes are located on islands in the two lakes. Some of the volcanoes send up smoke or shower the countryside with ashes from time to time. Volcanic eruptions and earthquakes have sometimes caused great damage to cities in Nicaragua. However, weathered lava and ashes from the volcanoes have enriched the soil of the Nicaraguan Lowland. The fertile soil is one reason why many people live in this part of Nicaragua.

Climate. The eastern part of Nicaragua has a very rainy climate. The northeast trade winds that blow toward Nicaragua bring heavy rainfall to the

Nicaragua is the largest country in the Caribbean Lands. More than one half of Nicaragua is made up of lowlands. In the central part of the country there is a rugged, mountainous area.

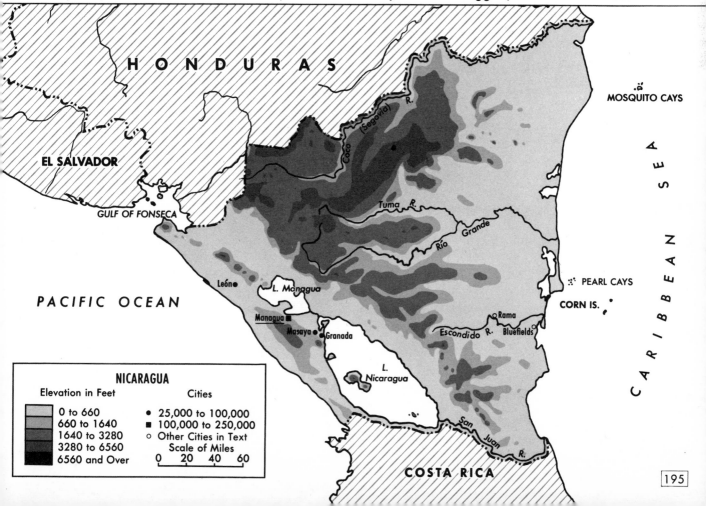

NICARAGUA

Elevation in Feet

0 to 660
660 to 1640
1640 to 3280
3280 to 6560
6560 and Over

Cities

● 25,000 to 100,000
■ 100,000 to 250,000
○ Other Cities in Text

Scale of Miles
0 20 40 60

Caribbean Lowland and to the eastern slopes of the highlands. Most of this area receives more than eighty inches of rain a year. It is one of the rainiest parts of Central America.

Rainfall is lighter in the western part of Nicaragua than in the eastern part. In western Nicaragua, there is a dry season from December through April when little or no rain falls. Much of the land northeast of Lake Managua and Lake Nicaragua lies in the rain* shadow of the central highlands. This area receives so little rain that most crops cannot be grown without irrigation.

The weather is very warm throughout the year in most parts of Nicaragua. The average annual temperature in the lowlands ranges from about eighty to eighty-six degrees. The highlands are cooler.

Natural resources. Gold is the only important mineral resource of Nicaragua.

There are three gold mines in operation in this country. One of them is located near the city of León. The others are in the northeastern part of the central highlands, where small amounts of silver and copper are also mined. Nearly all of the copper and much of the gold and silver are exported to the United States.

Forests cover nearly half of Nicaragua. The most important lumbering area is in the Caribbean Lowland, where large amounts of pine, mahogany, and Spanish cedar are cut. Nearly three fourths of the logs are made into lumber. This is one of Nicaragua's most important exports. Some logs are cut into thin sheets, which are glued together to make plywood.

There are many rivers in Nicaragua that could be used to produce hydroelectricity. However, most of the country's waterpower is not being used at the

Making lumber by hand. Lumber is one of Nicaragua's most important exports. Forests cover nearly half of the country. The most important lumbering area is in the Caribbean Lowland, where large amounts of pine, mahogany, and Spanish cedar are cut.

The Cathedral in León. This Spanish colonial building is the largest cathedral in Central America. The first Spanish settlements in Nicaragua were León and Granada.

present time. In 1960, Nicaragua borrowed money from the World Bank to help develop a power project. This project will use the waterpower of the Tuma River to produce hydroelectricity for cities and towns in western Nicaragua.

HISTORY

Early explorations. In 1502, during his fourth voyage to the New World, Christopher Columbus sailed southward along the Caribbean coast of what is now Nicaragua. He claimed the land for Spain. Twenty years later, a Spaniard named Gil González led an expedition from Panama to the shores of Lake Nicaragua. (See page 63.) Here he found large numbers of peaceful Indians. González converted thousands of these Indians to Christianity. Later, some fierce

Indians attacked González and his men, and the expedition returned to Panama.

Spain and Great Britain take over parts of Nicaragua. In 1524, Spaniards established two settlements in Nicaragua. Both were in the Nicaraguan Lowland, where there were many Indians who could be forced to work for the Spaniards. One settlement was Granada, on the western shore of Lake Nicaragua. Granada became very prosperous. Indigo, cacao, and sugarcane were raised on large farms in the area. Other valuable goods, such as silver and hides, were brought here from many parts of Central America. From Granada, these goods were shipped across Lake Nicaragua and down the San Juan River. (See map on page 195.) When the ships reached the Caribbean Sea, they sailed to ports in other parts of Central America, where their cargoes were traded for products from Spain.

The other settlement established by the Spaniards in 1524 was León, which lies between Lake Managua and the Pacific Ocean. The soil here was not so rich as the soil near Granada. On small farms near León, people grew corn, rice, and beans to provide food for themselves.

The first settlements on the Caribbean Lowland in Nicaragua were established by English pirates about 1625. Spaniards had not settled in this area because there were no large groups of Indians to work for them. The pirates used these settlements as bases from which they attacked Spanish ships. In 1740, the British brought Negroes from Jamaica to help settle the Caribbean Lowland. Because of these settlements, Great Britain claimed the eastern part of Nicaragua. However, Spain still considered this area to be part of its territory. Eventually, the British gave up their claims to land in Nicaragua, but they did not withdraw completely until the end of the 1800's.

Nicaragua remained under Spanish control until 1821, when the provinces in the *audiencia** of Guatemala declared their independence from Spain. Five of these provinces later formed the Central American Federation. In 1838, the federation broke up, and Nicaragua became an independent country.

Political parties fight for power. The cities of León and Granada each wanted to control Nicaragua's new government. Most of the people in León were Liberals. The wealthy merchants and landowners in Granada were Conservatives. (To learn more about the Liberals and Conservatives, see pages 74 and 75.) For many years, the two groups fought bitterly. When the Liberals controlled the government, the capital of Nicaragua was at León. When the Conservatives were in power, they moved the capital to Granada.

In 1855, an American adventurer named William Walker came to Nicaragua with a band of fewer than sixty men. He joined forces with the Liberals and helped them gain control of the government. Soon Walker made himself dictator. Other Central American countries were afraid that he wanted to control them also. They sent troops to help the people of Nicaragua overthrow their dictator. In 1857, Walker was forced to leave the country.

After Walker's defeat, Nicaragua remained peaceful for about thirty years. The Liberals and Conservatives agreed to move the government to Managua, a city located between León and Granada. This compromise helped to keep peace in Nicaragua.

Political unrest causes the United States to intervene. In 1893, another dictator came into power. He was a leader of the Liberals, and the Conservatives revolted against his rule. For several years, the country was in constant turmoil.

Political unrest in Nicaragua caused concern in the United States. The Nicaraguan government owed large amounts of money to European bankers, and it was feared that some European country might take over Nicaragua to collect these debts. The Monroe Doctrine* opposed interference in the affairs of the Western Hemisphere by European countries. Therefore, the United States decided to intervene to restore order in

Anastasio Somoza, inspecting a project to obtain salt by evaporating seawater. Somoza ruled Nicaragua as a military dictator for almost twenty years, until his death in 1956. He helped develop new industries in Nicaragua, but many of them were owned by members of the Somoza family.

Nicaragua. United States marines were stationed in Nicaragua for most of the period between 1912 and 1933. In 1933, as a result of the "Good Neighbor" policy, the United States withdrew its forces from the country.

The Somoza family rules Nicaragua. In 1937, an army general named Anastasio Somoza took over the government of Nicaragua by force. He ruled the country as a military dictator for almost twenty years. While Somoza was in power, he made some improvements in agriculture, education, health, and transportation. He also helped to develop new industries. However, many of these industries were owned by Somoza or members of his family. In 1956, Somoza was assassinated, and his son Luis became president. Like his father, Luis Somoza ruled as a dictator.

An election was held in 1963, but it made little change in Nicaragua's government. The new president of Nicaragua, René Schick Gutiérrez, continued the policies of the Somoza government.

THE PEOPLE AND HOW THEY LIVE

People. Nicaragua is not a very densely populated country. Large areas of land are very thinly settled. Few people live on the Caribbean and Pacific lowlands or on the rainy eastern slopes of the highlands. Most of the people live on the Nicaraguan Lowland or in the western part of the central highlands. These areas have fertile volcanic soil and are important for farming.

Most of the people of Nicaragua are mestizo. They are descendants of Spanish settlers, and Indians who were living in Nicaragua when the Spaniards came. Fewer than two tenths of the people are of pure Spanish descent. Negroes, who live mainly along the Caribbean coast, make up about one tenth of the population. There are some pureblood Indians living in remote areas of Nicaragua.

Earning a living. More than two thirds of all Nicaraguan workers earn their living by farming. Many operate their own small farms. Others work as tenant farmers on haciendas.

The most important food crops in Nicaragua are corn, rice, and beans. These are grown mainly on the flat, fertile Nicaraguan Lowland. More land is used to grow corn than to grow any other crop.

Cotton and coffee are Nicaragua's leading export crops. The main cotton-producing areas are on the Nicaraguan Lowland, near León and Managua. Here there are high temperatures, plenty of sunshine, and a long growing season with little rainfall. Cotton grows well under these conditions. Coffee is grown in the cooler highlands west of Lake Nicaragua and northeast of Lake Managua.

Nicaraguan farmers also grow sugarcane, sesame, and tobacco. Much of the sugarcane is made into an alcoholic beverage called *aguardiente*. Small amounts of sesame seeds and raw sugar are exported. All of the tobacco grown in Nicaragua is used within the country.

Picking cotton on the Nicaraguan Lowland. Cotton and coffee are Nicaragua's leading export crops. More than two thirds of all Nicaraguan workers earn their living by farming. Although new industries have been established in recent years, few workers are employed in factories.

Cattle raising is an important industry in Nicaragua. Farmers in the western part of the country raise many thousands of cattle. Some live cattle are exported, mainly to Panama and Peru. Processed beef is shipped to the United States.

Although new industries have been established in recent years, few Nicaraguan workers are employed in factories. Most factories in this country are small. Among Nicaragua's leading manufactured products are lumber, refined sugar, processed meat, cigarettes, alcoholic beverages, and textiles. All of these goods are made from raw materials produced within the country.

Transportation and communication. Nicaragua has less than four thousand miles of roads. Only about five hundred miles are paved. Nearly all of the paved roads are in western Nicaragua, where most of the people live. One of the main roads in this area is Nicaragua's section of the Inter-American Highway. (See page 134.)

The only road connecting the western and eastern parts of Nicaragua is the Rama Road, which is nearly completed. It begins northeast of Managua at a point on the Inter-American Highway, and extends 155 miles eastward to the town of Rama, on the Escondido River. (Compare map on page 195 with map on page 133.) Goods unloaded at the Caribbean port of Bluefields can be shipped up the river to Rama. When the road is finished, it will be possible to transport goods from the Caribbean coast to cities in the western part of Nicaragua.

Almost all of Nicaragua's railroads are part of a government-owned sys-

Cattle on their way to a slaughterhouse. Cattle raising is an important industry in Nicaragua. Processed beef and live cattle are exported.

tem. This system, which is only 216 miles long, connects Managua, León, and other cities and towns in the western part of the country.

Planes of eleven foreign airlines land at Nicaragua's international airport, near Managua. A Nicaraguan airline provides service between Managua and Miami, Florida, as well as between cities and towns within the country.

The western part of Nicaragua has a better communications network than the eastern part. Only Managua and neighboring cities have good telephone service. Nearly half of the country's thirty-five radio stations and its only television station are in Managua. The eastern and western parts of the country are connected by radiotelephone and telegraph.

Education. Only about one third of the Nicaraguan people know how to read and write. Many children of school age do not go to school. Although the number of schools in Nicaragua is increasing, there are not enough schools for all children to attend. Also, more teachers are needed. Nicaragua has more than four thousand elementary and secondary schools, and several teacher-training and trade schools. There are two universities, the National University of Nicaragua, located in León, and the Central American Catholic University, in Managua.

Cities. The largest cities of Nicaragua are in the western part of the country, where the Spaniards first settled. Al-

Workers in Managua preparing to install a new telephone system. The western part of Nicaragua has a better communications network than the eastern part.

though some cities are growing rapidly, about six out of every ten Nicaraguans still live in rural areas.

Managua (population about 226,000) is the capital and largest city of Nicaragua. The city began to grow rapidly after it became the capital. It is located on the Nicaraguan Lowland, on the southern shore of Lake Managua. (See map on page 195.)

Managua is Nicaragua's most important city for manufacturing and trade. Factories here make soap, textiles, and other products that are used by Nicaraguans. A large meat-packing plant processes beef. Raw materials for some of the industries are produced near Managua. There are cattle-raising areas nearby. Some of the cotton used in the textile mills is grown on the Nicaraguan Lowland.

Most of the buildings in Managua are modern. In 1931, a large part of the city was destroyed by an earthquake and fire, and it had to be rebuilt. Today, Managua has modern apartment buildings, stores, and hotels.

León (population about 53,000) is Nicaragua's second largest city. It is located west of Lake Managua, on the Nicaraguan Lowland. Near León is a rich farming area. Cotton, rice, and other crops grown here are brought to the city to be sold. Leather goods, wine, cheese, and other products are made in León.

With its many cobbled streets and adobe houses, León looks like a Spanish colonial city. In León is the largest cathedral in Central America. It contains the tomb of Rubén Darío, a famous Nicaraguan poet. (For more information about Darío, see page146.)

202

Managua, on the southern shore of Lake Managua, is the capital and largest city of Nicaragua. It is also the country's most important city for manufacturing and trade. Although some cities in Nicaragua are growing rapidly, about six out of every ten people still live in rural areas.

Think and Write

1. Give one reason why Spaniards did not settle on the Caribbean Lowland of Nicaragua during the 1500's. Who were the first people to settle here, and why did they establish settlements?
2. For many years after Nicaragua became independent from Spain, the country had no permanent capital. Why?
3. Why did the United States intervene in the affairs of Nicaragua in the early 1900's?
4. Why do you think most Nicaraguans live on the Nicaraguan Lowland or on the western slopes of the central highlands? List at least two reasons.
5. How will the Rama Road, when finished, affect transportation in Nicaragua?
6. Who were William Walker and Anastasio Somoza?

Using Map Skills

Make a relief map of Nicaragua, using plaster of paris. Before you begin your map, study carefully the Land section in this chapter, and the maps on pages 14, 15, 16, 20, and 195. You may also wish to do outside research on the land features of Nicaragua. When you have molded your map, paint it to indicate differences in elevation and to show special features, such as lakes and rivers.

A Question for Discussion

Discuss the following with your classmates: Lake Nicaragua and the San Juan River could be used as part of a canal route across Central America. If a canal were built using this route, in what ways might it affect the Nicaraguan people and their way of life? Information in Chapter 20 may be helpful.

Facts About Costa Rica

Area: 19,575 square miles.

Population: About 1,350,000.

Density of Population: 69 people per square mile; 1,080 people per square mile of arable* land.

Capital and Largest City: San José (population about 134,000).

Racial Composition: Nearly four out of every five Costa Ricans are white people of Spanish descent.

Literacy: About eight out of every ten of the people can read and write.

Main Language: Spanish.

Main Religion: Roman Catholicism.

Main Occupation: About half of the workers of Costa Rica are farmers.

Income: Yearly per capita income is about $290.

Important Farm Products: Coffee and bananas are the most important export crops. Other important farm products are cacao, abaca, sugarcane, and livestock.

Natural Resources: Costa Rica's most valuable resource is waterpower.

Manufacturing: Processing farm products is Costa Rica's most important industry. Textile manufacturing and printing are also important.

Currency: Costa Rica's unit of money is the *colón*, which is officially worth about 15 cents.

GEOGRAPHY

Land. Costa Rica is slightly smaller than the state of West Virginia. It is bordered by the Pacific Ocean, the Caribbean Sea, and the countries of Nicaragua and Panama. (See map at right.)

Most of Costa Rica consists of a mountainous highland region that extends through the country from north-

west to southeast. In the southern part of the country, the highlands reach almost from coast to coast. The mountains here are higher than those in the northern part of the country. The highest peaks are more than eleven thousand feet above sea level. Throughout the highlands, rivers have cut deep, narrow canyons. In some places, there are small basins surrounded by steep mountains.

In the central part of the highlands is a basin called the Meseta Central. San José, the capital of Costa Rica, is

Costa Rica consists mainly of mountainous highlands, with lowlands along both coasts.

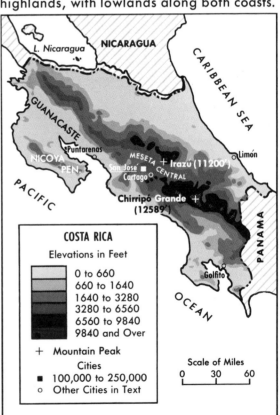

COSTA RICA
Elevations in Feet

0 to 660
660 to 1640
1640 to 3280
3280 to 6560
6560 to 9840
9840 and Over

+ Mountain Peak
   Cities
■ 100,000 to 250,000
○ Other Cities in Text

Scale of Miles
0   30   60

located here. This area is the most densely populated part of Costa Rica. The Meseta Central lies between three and four thousand feet above sea level. The land is generally flat, with some gently rolling hills. Northeast of the basin, four huge volcanic cones tower into the sky. Weathered ashes and lava from the volcanoes have made the soil of the Meseta Central very fertile. However, one of these volcanoes, Irazú, has been so active since early in 1963 that the great quantity of ashes settling to earth is threatening the fertility of farmland in a large area around the volcano.

Along both coasts of Costa Rica are level lowland areas. Much of the lowland on the Caribbean coast is swampy, and nearly all of it is covered with dense rainforest. This area is part of the Caribbean Lowland of Central America. (Compare map on pages 14 and 15 with map on page 20.) In northern Costa Rica, this lowland joins the Nicaraguan Lowland.

The land along the Pacific coast of Costa Rica is part of the Pacific Lowland. In two places, boot-shaped peninsulas jut into the ocean. The Nicoya Peninsula is the larger of the two. On this peninsula is a range of low mountains. Between these mountains and the highlands of central Costa Rica is a broad plain called the lowland of Guanacaste.

Climate. The weather in the lowlands of Costa Rica is hot throughout the year. In the Caribbean Lowland, the average yearly rainfall is more than eighty inches. Trade winds blowing from the northeast help bring heavy rainfall to this area at all seasons. The Pacific Lowland receives heavy rainfall only from May through November. During

Farmland in the Meseta Central, a fertile basin in the Costa Rican highlands. This basin is the most densely populated part of the country.

these months, winds from the Pacific Ocean bring moisture to the western part of Costa Rica. During the rest of the year, the weather here is dry. The lowland of Guanacaste lies in the rain* shadow of the mountains on the Nicoya Peninsula. Most crops cannot be grown here without irrigation.

The weather is cooler in the highland region of Costa Rica than on the lowlands. The weather in the highland basins and on the lower slopes of the mountains is always mild. This part of the country lies in the *tierra templada.** Only the highest peaks, which lie in the *tierra fría,** receive any snow. Throughout the year, trade winds bring heavy rainfall to the eastern part of the highlands. The rest of the highland region, including the Meseta Central, has a dry season during the winter and early spring.

Steam and ashes are sent high into the air from Irazú, a volcano in central Costa Rica. Since early in 1963, Irazú has been so active that the great quantity of ashes settling to earth is threatening the fertility of farmland in a large area around the volcano.

Natural resources. About four fifths of the land in Costa Rica is covered with forests. However, Costa Rica does not produce much lumber. Lumbering is difficult in this country, partly because roads into forested areas are lacking. Also, the most valuable trees, such as mahogany, are often scattered throughout a forest. It is too expensive to find these trees and remove them from the forest. Only small amounts of mahogany, Spanish cedar, cativo, and other tropical woods are exported.

Costa Rica is poor in mineral resources. Gold, limestone, and calcium carbonate are among the leading minerals, but even these are produced in small quantities. The calcium carbonate is used mainly as a fertilizer on coffee plantations.

Water resources are very important to Costa Rica. The country lacks coal, oil, and natural gas to use for generating power. Waterpower is used to produce most of Costa Rica's electricity. Large dams and power plants have been built on swift rivers that flow out of the highlands.

HISTORY

Spaniards come to the Meseta Central. For many years after Spanish settlements had been founded in other parts of Central America, the land that we now call Costa Rica was still unsettled. Although Columbus sailed along the Caribbean coast and claimed the land for Spain in 1502, few Spaniards were attracted to Costa Rica. Explorers found no gold or other precious metals here.

Also, Costa Rica did not have large numbers of Indians to work for the Spaniards. Some hostile Indians attacked Spaniards who tried to start settlements along the coasts.

Shortly after 1560, the first governor of Costa Rica brought about fifty families from Spain to Costa Rica's fertile Meseta Central. The settlement of Cartago was founded here. These settlers were poor but hardworking farmers. They were seeking a pleasant land where they could establish farms of their own. These people grew wheat, corn, and beans to provide food for themselves. They also raised cattle, horses, and pigs.

For about three hundred years, Costa Rica remained under Spanish control. During the early 1700's, some people from Cartago moved to another part of the Meseta Central and founded the town of San José. Later, two other settlements were founded nearby. The small towns in the Meseta Central were far from the colonial capital of Central America, which was located in Guatemala. Therefore, the Costa Ricans were generally allowed to manage their own affairs.

A Spanish mission in Cartago. The Spanish settlers who founded Cartago, in Costa Rica's fertile Meseta Central, were poor but hardworking farmers. When Costa Rica became independent, its people were better prepared for self-government than those in many other parts of Central America.

Costa Rica gains its independence. The people of Costa Rica won their freedom from Spain without any fighting. In 1821, Costa Rica broke away from Spanish rule. (See page 73.) Two years later, it joined the Central American Federation. When the Central American Federation broke up, in 1838, Costa Rica became an independent country.

Coffee and bananas bring prosperity to Costa Rica. Costa Rica was the first Central American country to produce coffee. In 1808, coffee trees were brought here from Cuba. The fertile Meseta Central provided ideal conditions for growing coffee. When Costa Rica became independent, money was needed to run the government. The government could make money by taxing exports of a valuable product such as coffee. Therefore, it encouraged coffee production by offering free land to anyone who would plant coffee trees. By 1850, large amounts of flavorful Costa Rican coffee were being shipped to Europe.

About 1870, the Costa Rican government decided that a railroad was needed to connect the Meseta Central with the Caribbean port of Limón. (See map on page 204.) This would make it easier to export coffee. A United States company was asked to undertake the job of building a railroad. Since few Costa Ricans lived in the Caribbean Lowland, the company hired large numbers of Negro workers from Jamaica. The swamps, dense forests, and heavy rainfall of the Caribbean Lowland made it very difficult to build the railroad. Thousands of workers died of tropical diseases. The railroad was not completed until 1890, about twenty years after construction had begun.

One of the railroad builders, Minor C. Keith, started banana plantations near Limón. The hot sunshine and heavy rainfall of this area helped the bananas to grow well. Soon large amounts of bananas were being exported from Costa Rica to the United States. In 1899, Keith and other businessmen formed the United Fruit Company.* This became the largest banana company in the Caribbean Lands.

Costa Rica's political history is peaceful. When Costa Rica became independent, in 1838, its people were better prepared for self-government than those in many other parts of Central America. Most of the Costa Ricans lived fairly close together, in the Meseta Central. They were mainly hardworking, law-abiding farmers. Few of them were very rich or very poor. These people believed in equality and took a deep interest in the government of their country.

Although some of the early presidents of Costa Rica were dictators, this country was the first in Central America to make any progress toward democratic government. In 1889, Costa Rica held the first free elections in Central America. Since that time, presidents and other important officials have usually been chosen by a vote of the people.

Unlike most Central American countries, Costa Rica has seldom been divided by political conflicts. Revolutions have taken place only twice since 1889. The first was in 1917. Another revolution took place following the presidential election of 1948. The men who had controlled the government before the 1948 election refused to let the new president, Otilio Ulate, take office. These men were opposed by José Figueres, a supporter of Ulate. Figueres led a successful revolt and established a temporary government to restore order. In late 1949, Ulate was allowed to take office as president.

In 1953, José Figueres was elected president of Costa Rica for a term of five years. He and the presidents who have followed him have maintained an orderly, democratic government.

THE PEOPLE AND HOW THEY LIVE

People. In Costa Rica, people of European descent make up a greater part of the population than in any other Caribbean country. About four out of every five Costa Ricans are of Spanish descent. Most of these people live in the Meseta Central. Mestizos make up most of the rest of Costa Rica's population. Many of the mestizos live in the Pacific Lowland. More than half of the people living in the Caribbean Lowland are Negroes. They are descended mainly from Jamaicans who were brought here to work on the railroad (see opposite page) or on banana plantations. Few Negroes live in other parts of Costa Rica.

About two thirds of all Costa Ricans live in the Meseta Central. The population of this area is increasing rapidly, and some people are moving to other areas where more land is available for farming. However, there are still large areas in Costa Rica where few people live. Among these areas are the hot, humid lowlands in northeastern Costa Rica, and some parts of the highlands.

A Costa Rican farmer and his family. About two thirds of all the people of Costa Rica live in the Meseta Central. Most of the farmers in the Meseta Central have their own small plots of land, on which they grow coffee and other crops.

A banana plantation on Costa Rica's Pacific Lowland. Costa Rica is one of the world's largest exporters of bananas. The main banana-growing region is in the Pacific Lowland. Overhead sprays are used to water the plants and to spread chemicals that protect them from disease.

Earning a living. About half of all Costa Rican workers are employed in agriculture. Most farmers in the Meseta Central have their own small plots of land. Large plantations are found mostly in the coastal lowlands.

Coffee is Costa Rica's leading export crop. It accounts for about half of the money that people in Costa Rica make by selling products to other countries. Most of the coffee is exported to West Germany and the United States.

Ever since the early 1800's, the fertile Meseta Central has been an important coffee-growing region. About half of the coffee planters have farms of less than two acres. These small farms do not produce as much coffee per acre as larger farms, partly because the owners of small farms cannot afford to fertilize their land.

Costa Rica's second most important export crop is bananas. During the 1930's, disease killed many banana plants on the Caribbean Lowland. As a result, new banana plantations were established in the southern part of the Pacific Lowland. This is now the main banana-growing region of Costa Rica. Types of bananas that are better able to resist disease have been developed. Overhead sprays are used to irrigate large banana plantations and to spread chemicals that protect the plants from disease. Costa Rica now produces more bananas than ever before. This country is one of the world's largest exporters of bananas. Most of the bananas are shipped to the United States.

Several other crops grow well in certain parts of Costa Rica. Cacao and abaca are raised in some parts of the

Caribbean Lowland where bananas were formerly grown. The abaca plant has tough fibers that are used in making rope. Both cacao and abaca are exported, mainly to the United States. Sugarcane is grown in the Meseta Central for use within the country. Irrigation has made it possible to grow cotton, as well as rice and other food crops, on the lowland of Guanacaste.

Cattle raising is important in Costa Rica. Most of the beef cattle are raised on ranches on the lowland of Guanacaste. This area is good for grazing because much of it is covered with tall grass. Both live cattle and frozen beef are exported.

Most of the industries in Costa Rica produce goods needed by the people of the country. The main industries are food processing, textile manufacturing, and printing. Many products, such as textiles, beverages, and furniture, are made from raw materials available in Costa Rica. One reason for the importance of the printing industry here may

A worker in a candy factory. The most important industries in Costa Rica are food processing, textile manufacturing, and printing.

be that most Costa Ricans know how to read and write. (See page 212.)

Transportation and communication. Costa Rica has a larger network of roads than any other Central American country. There are more than 11,000 miles of roads in Costa Rica, but only about 650 miles are paved. The Costa Rican portion of the Inter-American Highway was recently completed. (See page 134.) Most of the good roads in Costa Rica are located in or near the Meseta Central. There are very few roads in other parts of the highland region or in the dense rainforest of the Caribbean Lowland.

There are three main railroad lines in Costa Rica. Their total length is about seven hundred miles. One line connects San José with the Caribbean port of Limón. Another extends from San José to Puntarenas, a port on the Pacific coast. The third line is located in the southern part of the Pacific Lowland. The United Fruit Company owns this line and uses it mainly to carry bananas to the port of Golfito for export.

Workers on a coffee farm move coffee beans through a canal. Coffee, which is grown mainly in the Meseta Central, is Costa Rica's leading export.

Water and air transportation are important to Costa Rica. Ships from many foreign countries load and unload goods at Limón, Puntarenas, and Golfito. Also, goods are often transported by ship from one part of the Pacific Lowland to another because there are few good roads in this area. Planes of five foreign airlines land at El Coco International Airport, near San José. This is one of the largest and most modern airports in Central America. Several local airlines serve the main towns in Costa Rica. One of these airlines also has flights to the United States and other foreign countries.

Most cities and towns in Costa Rica are connected by telegraph, but only the largest have telephone service. There are thirty-nine radio stations and one television station in Costa Rica.

Education. Costa Rica has one of the highest rates of literacy in the Caribbean Lands. About four fifths of the people know how to read and write. The Costa Rican government has spent large amounts of money on education. There are now more than 1,500 elementary schools and about 60 high schools in the country. Costa Rica also has 23 job-training schools and a teacher-training school. There is a national university in San José. Courses in law, pharmacy, engineering, and other fields of study are offered here.

Costa Rican schoolchildren. About four fifths of the people in Costa Rica know how to read and write. This country has one of the highest literacy rates in the Caribbean Lands. Its government has spent large amounts of money on education.

Cities. About one third of all Costa Ricans live in cities and towns. Most of the larger towns are located in the Meseta Central. Costa Rica's largest city by far is the capital, San José.

San José (population about 134,000) is located in the Meseta Central, about four thousand feet above sea level. (See map on page 204.) The city was founded in 1736 and became the capital of Costa Rica in 1823. Since that time, the population of San José has increased rapidly.

Trade and manufacturing have helped San José to grow. The city is located in a rich coffee-growing region. It is connected with the Caribbean and Pacific coasts by railroad and is on the Inter-American Highway. There are two airports near the city. Many factories have been built in San José in recent years. Some of the products manufactured here are textiles, leather goods, candles, furniture, and beverages.

A modern building in San José, Costa Rica's capital. Trade and manufacturing have helped San José to grow. The city has many factories.

Think and Write

1. Why do you think the Meseta Central is the most densely populated part of Costa Rica? List at least three reasons.
2. Although most of Costa Rica's land is covered with forests, this country does not produce much lumber. State two reasons for this.
3. All of the countries in Central America that were in the Central American Federation became independent republics by 1841. Compare the history of Costa Rica since that time with the histories of the other countries that were in the Central American Federation. (See Chapters 14, 15, 17, and 18.) In what major way has Costa Rica's history been different from that of the others? How do you explain this difference?
4. How did the government of Costa Rica encourage the development of coffee growing in this country?
5. How and where was banana growing started in Costa Rica? Where is the country's main banana-growing region today?
6. Costa Rica is the only Central American country in which the printing industry is important. State one possible reason for this.

Finding More Information

Since March, 1963, the volcano Irazú has been extremely active. People living near Irazú face many problems as a result of the great quantity of ashes settling to earth. Locate recent information about this volcano by using the Readers' Guide in your library. Then write a short report about how the activity of Irazú is affecting each of the following:

a. agriculture
b. health
c. the daily life of the people living nearby

20   Panama

Problems To Solve

Panama has been one of the most important countries in the Caribbean Lands region since colonial days. **Why is this so?** To solve this problem, you will need to make several hypotheses. Remember to consider Panama's importance in both colonial and modern times. The following questions suggest some hypotheses:

a. What facts about the location of Panama help to solve this problem?

b. What facts about Panama's land features help to solve it?

Information in Chapters 1, 4, and 11, and the map on pages 14 and 15 will be helpful in solving this problem.

See TO THE STUDENT, pages 6-7.

GEOGRAPHY

Land. Panama is the southernmost country of Central America. It occupies the long, narrow Isthmus of Panama, which lies between Costa Rica and Colombia. (See map below.) At its narrowest point, the isthmus is less than forty miles wide. The border between Panama and Colombia is the dividing

The country of Panama occupies the long, narrow Isthmus of Panama. It is divided into two nearly equal parts by the Panama Canal, which crosses the lowest and narrowest part of the isthmus. Along both coasts of Panama are level lowlands.

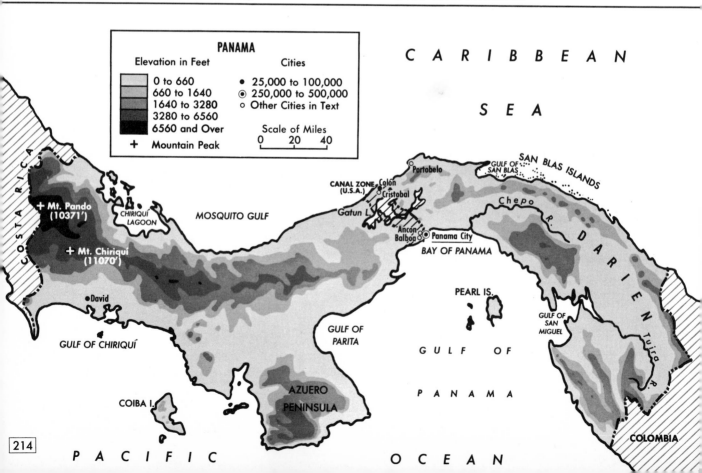

Mountains in western Panama. About three fifths of the land in Panama is hilly or mountainous. The highest peaks are located in the western part of the country. Although the high mountains have a cool climate, most places in Panama are hot and humid.

line between the continents of North America and South America.

Because of its location, Panama has often been called the "Crossroads of the World." The isthmus not only connects the American continents but also separates the two largest oceans of the world, the Atlantic and the Pacific. The location of Panama has affected its entire history. The history section of this chapter will help you understand why this has been so.

The Panama Canal divides the country into two nearly equal parts. It extends through the lowest and narrowest part of Panama. The canal lies in a belt of valleys and low, rolling hills. The United States operates the Panama Canal and governs a strip of land about five miles wide on each side of the canal. This area is called the Canal Zone. The Panama Canal is described more fully in Chapter 11.

Although three fifths of Panama is hilly or mountainous, most of the land is less than 2,300 feet above sea level. The highest peaks in Panama are located west of the Canal Zone. These mountains include several volcanic peaks. The highest is Mount Chiriquí, which rises more than 11,000 feet above sea level.

Along both coasts of Panama are level lowlands. The lowland on the northern coast is only about five to twenty miles wide. It is part of the Caribbean Lowland. Here, the weather is hot and rainy all year round, and the land is covered with dense rainforest. Few people live on the Caribbean Lowland of Panama. The land on the southern side is part of the Pacific Lowland. In Panama, part of this lowland consists of tropical savannas. Much of it is covered by rainforest. Some of the densest jungle in Central America is found in the

Darien, a region east of the Canal Zone. (See map on page 214.)

Climate. Most places in Panama have a hot, humid climate. On the lowlands, daytime temperatures are sometimes more than 90 degrees. A drop in temperature in the evening makes the nights comfortably cool. In the high mountains, the climate is much cooler, with temperatures averaging between 50 and 66 degrees.

Panama has a rainy season and a dry season. The rainy season generally lasts from April to December. During this period, rainfall is very heavy, particularly on the Caribbean Lowland and in the mountains. In some places, as much as 180 inches of rain fall in a single year. Much of the Pacific side of the isthmus lies in the rain* shadow of the mountains. Here, rainfall is not so heavy, with a yearly average of about 70 inches.

Natural resources. Forests cover almost three fourths of the land in Panama. They provide the country with almost all of the lumber used for building houses. Lumber produced here is also used to manufacture such products as

A river in eastern Panama. During the rainy season, which lasts from April to December, much of Panama receives very heavy rainfall.

Facts About Panama
Area: 28,753 square miles.
Population: About 1,180,000.
Density of Population: 41 people per square mile; 606 people per square mile of arable* land.
Capital and Largest City: Panama City (population about 285,000).
Racial Composition: About two thirds of the people of Panama are of mixed ancestry. Most of the rest are white, Indian, or Negro.
Literacy: About seven out of every ten Panamanians can read and write.
Main Language: Spanish.
Main Religion: Roman Catholicism.
Main Occupation: About half of all the workers in Panama earn their living on farms or plantations.
Income: Yearly per capita income is about $365.
Important Farm Products: Bananas are the leading export crop. Some cacao and coffee are also exported. Corn, rice, and livestock are among the farm products raised for domestic use.
Natural Resources: Forests, manganese, limestone, and shrimp.
Manufacturing: Petroleum products, cement, lumber, and beverages are among the most important products manufactured in Panama.
Currency: Panama's unit of money is the *balboa,* which is officially worth $1.00.

furniture and plywood. Most of the forest areas in Panama cannot be reached easily because there are few roads. As a result, lumbermen usually cut down trees that grow close to rivers. The logs are then floated down the rivers to sawmills.

Many different minerals have been found in Panama. Because of the transportation problem, few of them are being mined today. Manganese, which is used in making steel, is mined in the western part of the country. A good

216

A netful of fish being hauled aboard a fishing boat. Fishing has recently become an important occupation in Panama. In addition to fisheries, Panama also has valuable forests and mineral deposits. A lack of roads and railroads has hindered development of these resources.

grade of limestone is found in Panama. The country manufactures enough cement from this limestone to supply its own needs and to export some to nearby countries.

Many different kinds of fish are found in the waters off the coasts of Panama. The name Panama comes from an Indian word meaning "abundance of fish." Fishing has recently become an important occupation. Today, shrimp is among Panama's leading exports.

HISTORY

Spaniards come to Panama. A Spanish explorer named Rodrigo de Bastidas discovered the Isthmus of Panama in 1501. A year later, Columbus sailed along the northern coast of the isthmus in search of a route to the Indies. Columbus found gold in northern Panama. He attempted to establish a settlement here, but was driven off by hostile Indians. Columbus' reports of gold in Panama reached Spain and made other Spaniards anxious to explore the isthmus.

The Spaniards found it extremely difficult to explore the interior of Panama. The first explorers came from Santo Domingo in 1509. They found a land covered with dense jungle. Crocodiles, poisonous snakes, and swarms of disease-carrying insects infested the swamps. There was little food to be found in the jungle, and savage Indians frequently attacked the Spaniards.

217

Balboa discovers the Pacific Ocean. The first governor of Spanish settlements in Panama was an adventurer named Vasco Núñez de Balboa. Unlike most other Spanish conquerors, Balboa treated the Indians fairly and tried to make peace with them. One of the Indians told Balboa of a vast ocean to the south and of rich lands bordering on this ocean. In 1513, Balboa led a small band of men through the dense forests of the isthmus in search of this ocean. After a difficult journey, Balboa stood one day on a mountaintop in the Darien and became the first European to look upon the Pacific Ocean. He claimed this ocean and all lands bordering it for Spain.

Panama becomes part of an important trade route. After Balboa discovered the Pacific Ocean, the Isthmus of Panama became the most important trading center in the New World. A town named Panama was founded on the Pacific coast in 1519. In the 1530's, Francisco Pizarro sailed from Panama to conquer

Ruins in the old town of Panama. In 1671, an English pirate named Henry Morgan captured and destroyed the town of Panama.

Peru, in South America. There Pizarro found immense riches of gold and silver. A steady stream of wealth began to flow across the Isthmus of Panama. Gold and silver were brought from Peru in ships and unloaded at the town of Panama. From here the treasure was carried on muleback to Portobelo, a settlement on the Caribbean coast. Spanish ships brought supplies for the explorers to Portobelo and carried the gold and silver back to Spain.

Panama is attacked by pirates. The treasure transported across the Isthmus of Panama attracted many English pirates. One of the most famous of these was Sir Francis Drake. During the late 1500's, Drake attacked ships and towns along both coasts of the isthmus. Although he captured several other towns and seized much treasure, he was unable to take Panama. Another English pirate, Henry Morgan, succeeded in capturing it in 1671. The town was blown up and completely destroyed by fire. Two years later, a new town was built six miles away on the site of the present capital, Panama City.

In the 1700's, Panama began to decline as a trading center. Most traders preferred to go around the tip of South America rather than to make the difficult and dangerous journey across the Isthmus of Panama. Treasure ships no longer stopped at Portobelo, and even Panama City lost much of its former importance.

Panama breaks away from Spain. Panama declared its independence from Spain on November 28, 1821. It gained its freedom without fighting and joined the nation of Great Colombia. Besides Panama, Great Colombia included what

The Panama Railroad, which extends across the Isthmus of Panama, began operating in 1855. Before this railroad was built, travelers between the Caribbean and the Pacific Ocean had to cross the isthmus on foot or muleback, or make the long ocean trip around the tip of South America.

are now Venezuela, Ecuador, and Colombia. This union broke up in 1830, but Panama remained united with Colombia.

Panama again becomes part of an important trade route. In the middle of the 1800's, Panama suddenly gained new importance. Gold was discovered in California in 1848. Thousands of people hurried to the California goldfields from the eastern part of the United States and from other countries. Many of the gold seekers preferred to journey to California by way of Panama rather than cross the United States or make the long ocean trip around South America. These travelers came by ship to the Caribbean coast of Panama. From here, they journeyed across the isthmus to Panama City on muleback or on foot. Often they had to wait months in Panama City for vessels to carry them to California.

In 1855, a railroad began operating between the Caribbean and Pacific coasts of Panama. This reduced the hardships of traveling across the isthmus. For some years, the railroad was very successful. However, in 1869 a railroad was completed across the United States. Travelers began using this new route to California, and traffic on the Panamanian railroad came almost to a halt.

A canal across the isthmus is planned.
Since the time of Balboa, men had dreamed of building a canal across Central America to connect the Atlantic and Pacific oceans. In 1879, a French company was formed to build a canal across the Isthmus of Panama. The French tried for about twenty years to complete the canal, but they were unsuccessful. Disease, bad planning, and lack of money forced them to abandon the project.

The United States took over the job of building the canal. The property and rights of the French company were purchased for 40 million dollars. In 1903, a treaty with Colombia was signed granting the United States permanent control of the land needed for a canal. However, the Colombian senate refused to approve this treaty.

The people of Panama were anxious for a canal to be built across their territory. They felt that it would bring them prosperity. In November, 1903, Panama revolted against Colombia and declared its independence. The United States supported Panama in its revolt.

After gaining its independence, Panama quickly signed a treaty with the United States. This treaty gave the United States permanent control of a strip of land about ten miles wide, which became known as the Canal Zone. The United States was also given the right to intervene in Panama if it became necessary to maintain order. In return, this country paid Panama 10 million dollars, and agreed to pay $250,000 yearly, beginning in 1913.

The United States has to solve many problems before the canal can be built.
Before construction could be started on the Panama Canal, many problems had to be solved. It was necessary to assemble an army of workers as well as a great deal of equipment. Most of the workers were Negroes from the West Indies, who had to be transported to Panama in ships. Roads, houses, and schools were needed, and food and other supplies had to be provided for the workers.

The most serious difficulty was the problem of disease. The hot, swampy lowlands of Panama were among the most unhealthy areas in the world. The marshes swarmed with disease-carrying mosquitoes and other insects. An American medical officer, Colonel William C. Gorgas, was placed in charge of a program to rid the Canal Zone of tropical diseases. Colonel Gorgas set his army of workers to clearing jungle, draining swamps, and spreading oil on marshes and other breeding places for mosquitoes. Within two years, the Canal Zone was free from yellow fever, and malaria was brought under control.

Colonel William C. Gorgas, an American medical officer, helped bring tropical diseases under control in the Panama Canal Zone.

Constructing the Panama Canal was very difficult. Part of the canal had to be built across land that is many feet above sea level. Most of one section had to be cut through solid rock. When the canal was finally completed, it provided many jobs and brought prosperity to Panama.

The construction of the canal proves to be very difficult. The construction of the canal was also a difficult task. The project would have been easier if all the land across the isthmus were at the same level as the oceans. Instead, the path of the canal lies at sea level for only about fifteen miles of its length. Much of the remainder of the canal had to be built across land that is many feet above sea level. A large dam was built across the Chagres River. (See map on page 139.) This dam held back the waters of the river to form a large lake. This is Gatun Lake, one of the largest man-made lakes in the world. To raise ships to the level of Gatun Lake, locks were built at both ends of the canal. For a description of how these locks work, see page 138.

The section of the canal that was most difficult to build was a channel about eight miles long, called the Gaillard Cut. Almost all of this channel had to be cut through solid rock. Landslides from hills on either side of the Gaillard Cut frequently undid the work of weeks of digging.

In spite of these difficulties, the canal was finally completed in 1914. The first ship sailed through the canal in August of that year.

The canal brings prosperity and problems to Panama. The Panama Canal brought prosperity to the new nation of Panama. It gave work to thousands of Panamanians. New businesses were started in the cities. Farmers were able to sell their crops in the Canal Zone and to ships passing through the canal.

However, most of the wealth that came to Panama because of the canal was owned by a few powerful families. These families usually controlled the government, which was often corrupt and undemocratic. This caused much dissatisfaction and unrest in Panama. The United States sent troops to preserve order here in 1908, 1912, and 1918.

Panama opposes the treaty of 1903. The people of Panama were dissatisfied with many provisions of the treaty of 1903. They objected to United States intervention in their country. They did not think the yearly sum of $250,000 was sufficient payment. They also resented the fact that American citizens working in the Canal Zone were paid higher wages than Panamanians performing the same jobs in the zone.

The United States tried to satisfy Panama's objections. In 1936, it gave up its right to intervene in Panama. It also increased the yearly payment to $430,000. In 1955, this was raised again, to $1,930,000. At that time, Panamanians were promised equal pay for equal work in the Canal Zone.

American students raising the United States flag in the Canal Zone. A crisis resulted because the students did not also display the Panamanian flag.

Despite these measures, many people in Panama continued to resent the United States. Some workers claimed that they were still receiving lower wages than Americans in the Canal Zone. There were objections to United States control over the zone and the canal, which many Panamanians regarded as the property of their country. Twice during 1959, mobs tried to enter the Canal Zone to raise the Panamanian flag. An agreement made in 1962 between Panama and the United States authorized the flag of Panama to be flown in the Canal Zone beside the Stars and Stripes. Many Americans in the zone were opposed to this agreement.

Resentment toward the United States leads to violence. In January, 1964, rioting and violence broke out in Panama. American students at a high school in the city of Balboa, in the Canal Zone, provoked the incident. They raised the American flag without also displaying the flag of Panama. Riots quickly broke out, and United States troops and Panamanians fired on one another. Twenty-six persons were killed, and about four hundred were wounded, most of them Panamanians.

Following these riots, the government of Panama broke off diplomatic relations with the United States. Later in 1964, the two countries agreed to discuss the problems that led to the crisis in Panama.

THE PEOPLE AND HOW THEY LIVE

People. Panama has a population of slightly more than one million. This is less than the population of any other country in Central America except British Honduras. Nearly half of the

A Panamanian family. Panamanians are descended from many different races and nationalities. Most are of mixed white, Negro, and Indian descent.

people of Panama live in cities near the Panama Canal or on farmland near the canal. Most of the Panamanians outside the Canal Zone area live in a farming region on the Pacific side of the isthmus west of the canal. The densely forested areas of the country are very thinly populated.

People have come to Panama from many parts of the world, and today Panamanians are descended from many different races and nationalities. About six out of every ten people are of mixed white, Negro, and Indian descent. About one tenth of the people are white, and there is a slightly larger number of Negroes. Most of the Negroes are English-speaking descendants of laborers brought from the West Indies to build the Panama Canal. Tribes of Indians live in the western mountains, in the Darien region, and on the San Blas Islands in the Caribbean Sea. (See map on page 214.) Some of these Indians are still uncivilized and live much as their ancestors did. Small groups of people of

Asian descent live in the cities and towns near the Canal Zone. About 36,000 United States citizens live in the zone.

Spanish is the official language of Panama. However, English is also spoken by many people, particularly in the Canal Zone area. Because people from many lands have come to Panama, French, Italian, Chinese, and other languages are often heard in the larger cities. Indian languages are spoken by various tribal groups.

Earning a living. About half of all the workers in Panama earn their living by farming. The most fertile farming areas are on the Pacific Lowland between the Costa Rican border and the Panama Canal. Most farmers grow rice, corn, and other food crops for their own use. Many of them also raise cattle and other livestock on the excellent pastureland found in this area.

Most farming in Panama is carried on by very backward methods. Farmers generally work on small plots of land with very simple tools. Nine tenths of

Indians on the San Blas Islands squeezing juice from sugarcane. Tribes of Indians in some parts of Panama live much as their ancestors did.

223

the farmers in Panama do not own the land they work on. These farmers are known as "squatters," because they settle on public land without paying rent. Since the farmers do not own their farms, they do not take good care of the land. Panama is unable to grow enough food for all of its people, and food products must be imported from other countries.

Many Panamanians work on large banana plantations. The most important banana-growing region is on the Pacific Lowland near the Costa Rican border. Panama is among the world's leading exporters of bananas.

Other crops raised in Panama include cacao, sugarcane, and coffee. Some cacao and coffee are exported. Much of the sugarcane is used in Panama to make rum.

In recent years, fishing for shrimp in the coastal waters off Panama has become an important industry. Today, many Panamanians earn their living by catching shrimp or by preparing them for export.

Very few Panamanians work in manufacturing. Most of Panama's factories are located in the cities and towns near the Canal Zone. Clothing, beverages, cement, and lumber are among the products manufactured in this country.

A large oil refinery began operating near the city of Colón in 1962. This plant refines crude oil imported from Venezuela and other countries. Most of the oil refined here is exported. Until recently, bananas were Panama's leading export. (See graph on page 128.) Since the completion of this refinery, refined petroleum products have taken

Transporting bananas. Panama is among the world's leading exporters of bananas. Other crops raised in Panama include rice, cacao, sugarcane, and coffee. About half of Panama's workers earn their living by farming. Very few Panamanians are employed in factories.

Towing a ship through the Panama Canal. Many Panamanians are employed by the Panama Canal Company, which operates the canal.

the lead as the country's most valuable export.

Many Panamanians depend on the Canal Zone for their living. The Panama Canal Company, which operates the canal, employs many workers from Panama. Other Panamanians provide goods and services to cargo and passenger ships that pass through the canal. Many tourists visit Panama each year. Some of the people of Panama earn their living by working in restaurants, shops, and hotels that serve these tourists.

Many United States citizens work in the Canal Zone for the Panama Canal Company and for the Canal Zone government. Members of the United States Army, Navy, and Air Force and their families are also stationed in the Canal Zone.

Transportation and communication. Panama has only about 2,500 miles of roads. The mountains and jungles of the isthmus have made road building very difficult. The lack of roads in Panama is a serious problem, since there is

almost no other means of transportation. Many farmers have no way to ship their products to markets in the towns and cities. This is one reason why they grow only enough crops to feed themselves and leave much land uncultivated.

There are two important highways in Panama. The Trans-Isthmian Highway connects Panama City and the city of Colón. The Panamanian section of the Inter-American Highway extends from the Costa Rican border to Panama City. (Compare maps on pages 15 and 133.)

There are very few railroads in Panama. The most important one is the Panama Railroad, which was completed in 1855. It extends from Colón to Panama City. This railroad is owned by the United States government and lies within the Canal Zone.

Panama City is an important center of air transportation. Many flights between North and South America land at Tocumen International Airport, near Panama City. Local airlines connect the capital with smaller towns in Panama.

Building a road in Panama. The lack of roads in Panama is a serious problem. Many farmers have no way to ship their products to market.

Panama has more telephones than any other Central American country. Most telephones are located in the cities in the Canal Zone area. Panama also has more radio sets than any other country in Central America. Television was recently introduced into Panama, and the number of people owning television sets is increasing.

Education. Panama has a higher literacy rate than most other Central American countries. About seven out of every ten Panamanians can read and write. A law requires all children in Panama to attend school through the sixth grade. However, there are not enough schools in Panama. About one fourth of all city children of school age do not go to school. In rural areas, almost half of all school-age boys and girls do not attend classes. In recent years, the government of Panama has spent large amounts of money to improve education. The Canal Zone government operates a school system separate from that of Panama for children who live in the zone.

Panama has one university, which was opened in 1935. About 4,500 students attend the University of Panama.

Cities. The most important cities in Panama are located near the two entrances to the Panama Canal. The only large town outside the Canal Zone area is David, which is located in a fertile farming region in western Panama.

The University of Panama, in Panama City. Panama has a higher literacy rate than most other Central American countries. In recent years, its government has spent large amounts of money to improve education. However, there are still not enough schools.

Panama City is the capital and largest city of Panama. Because of its location near the Pacific entrance to the Panama Canal, it is an important trading city. It is also noted for its shops, theaters, hotels, and nightclubs. Thousands of tourists visit Panama City each year.

Panama City (population about 285,-000) is the capital and largest city of Panama. It lies near the Pacific entrance to the Panama Canal. (See map on page 139.) Although Panama City is located within five miles of the canal, the city is not included in the Canal Zone.

Because of its location, Panama City is an important trading center. A large part of Panama's exports and imports passes through this port city. However, its harbor is too shallow for large ships to enter. Cargo is loaded and unloaded at the port of Balboa.

Many tourists visit Panama City each year. A great many of these visitors are passengers on ships using the canal, who stop off for only a short time to see the city. Panama City is noted for its shops, theaters, hotels, and nightclubs.

Panama City is a mixture of the old and the new. A few miles away from the capital are the ruins of the old town of Panama, which was destroyed by English pirates in 1671. In Panama City today, many of the buildings are built in old Spanish style. Wrought-iron balconies overhang narrow streets. Not far from these old sections of town are modern apartment houses and skyscrapers.

Many sections of Panama City are hot, crowded slums. Most homes in the slums are wooden shacks with tin roofs. Here, the streets are usually unpaved, and there is no running water.

Two suburbs of the capital, Balboa and Ancon, are located within the Canal

Attractive homes in Ancon, a suburb of Panama City where many Canal Zone employees live. Many sections of Panama City are hot, crowded slums.

Zone and are governed by the United States. Balboa is the headquarters of the Canal Zone government. Ancon is a small residential section where many Canal Zone employees make their homes. In Ancon, there are attractive houses such as you might find in a suburb in the United States.

Colón (population about 63,000) is the second largest city of Panama. It lies near the Caribbean entrance to the Panama Canal, and is almost surrounded by the Canal Zone. (See map on page 139.) The city occupies a small island, together with the town of Cristobal. Cristobal is part of the Canal Zone.

Large ships cannot dock at Colón, so cargo is unloaded at the port of Cristobal. Thousands of ships dock at Cristobal each year on their way to or from the Panama Canal. Recently, plans have been made to construct docks in the harbor at Colón.

Reviewing Panama's History

1. Why did Spaniards find it difficult to explore Panama in the early 1500's? State three reasons.
2. Why was Panama important in the middle of the 1800's? Why did it decline in importance after 1869?
3. State three problems that had to be solved before and during the construction of the Panama Canal.

Exploring Relationships

1. People of many different races and nationalities live in Panama. State at least two reasons for this.
2. How does the lack of roads affect farming in Panama? How does it affect the development of forest and mineral resources?
3. Locate on the map on page 214 the cities in Panama that have populations of 25,000 or more. Then state your opinion as to the reasons for each city's location.

Facts To Remember

State at least two important facts about each of the following:

Darien	Vasco Núñez de Balboa
Portobelo	Henry Morgan
Gatun Lake	William C. Gorgas

A Discussion Topic

The United States control of the Canal Zone and the Panama Canal has been the source of much unrest in Panama. Do you think Panamanians are justified in opposing United States control? Why, or why not? Discuss this with your classmates. Before you begin your discussion, you may wish to learn more about the situation in Panama by reading recent newspaper and magazine articles on this subject.

Greater Antilles

21 Cuba

Problems To Solve

1. In 1959, Fidel Castro came to power in Cuba as a result of a revolution. **Why did this revolution take place?** In order to solve this problem, you will need to make several hypotheses. In forming your hypotheses, consider the following:

    a. the way in which Fulgencio Batista ruled the country
    b. the promises made by Castro

    You may wish to do some outside research to solve this problem.

2. Since Castro's rise to power, there have been many changes in Cuba. **Why have these changes taken place?** The following questions suggest some hypotheses that will help to solve this problem:
    a. What facts about industry in Cuba help to solve the problem?
    b. What facts about farming help to solve it?
    c. What facts about education help to solve it?
    d. What facts about transportation help to solve the problem?

See TO THE STUDENT, pages 6-7.

Cuba is a Communist nation. Among the countries of the Caribbean Lands region, Cuba has special importance today. It is the only country in the Western Hemisphere that is controlled by a Communist government. Cuba became a Communist nation after revolutionary forces led by a young Cuban lawyer named Fidel Castro seized control of the country in 1959. In Cuba today, almost all of the agriculture and industry are controlled by the government, just as in the Soviet Union and other Communist countries.

The United States is extremely concerned about the situation in Cuba. This island is located only about ninety miles south of the state of Florida. Our government is firmly opposed to having a Communist country so close to our shores. It particularly objects to the fact that Cuba is attempting to spread revolution throughout the Caribbean Lands and the rest of Latin America.

The other Latin-American nations are watching events in Cuba with the keenest interest. They are aware that the Cuban Communists are attempting to solve the problems of the island. These problems are the same as those faced by other countries of the Caribbean Lands and the rest of Latin America. They include poverty, illiteracy, lack of industry, and dependence on one or two export crops. To try to solve Cuba's problems, Castro's government is using the means of Communist dictatorship rather than the democratic methods favored by the United States. If the Communists in Cuba should succeed in solving problems that other Latin-American countries have not yet solved, the people of these countries may follow the same path as Cuba.

GEOGRAPHY

Land. Cuba is the largest island in the West Indies. Although it is smaller than the state of Pennsylvania, Cuba is almost as large as all of the other islands in the West Indies combined. As the map on page 232 shows, the island is shaped like a huge fish. It extends for more than 750 miles from northwest to southeast and averages about 50 miles in width.

Almost three fourths of Cuba's land is level or gently rolling. Much of this land was once covered with limestone. Through the centuries, the limestone has been weathered into a deep layer of a red soil called Matanzas clay. This is one of the best soils in the world for growing sugarcane. Large areas of Matanzas clay are found in central and western Cuba. Some other types of soil found in Cuba are also well suited for growing sugarcane, as well as other crops. The sandy soil found in the Vuelta Abajo region of western Cuba produces some of the finest cigar tobacco in the world. More than one half of the island of Cuba is level and fertile enough for farming.

There are three main highland areas on Cuba. The highest mountains are in the Sierra Maestra, in the southeastern part of the island. Some of the steep slopes here rise more than 6,000 feet above sea level. Valuable minerals have been found in the Sierra Maestra. The mountains of the Sierra de Trinidad are in the south central part of the country. The highest peak here is more than 3,500 feet above sea level. In the western part of the island is a low range called the Sierra de los Órganos.

Farmland on Cuba. Almost three fourths of the land on Cuba is level or gently rolling. Much of this land is covered with a deep layer of a red soil called Matanzas clay, which is one of the best soils in the world for growing sugarcane.

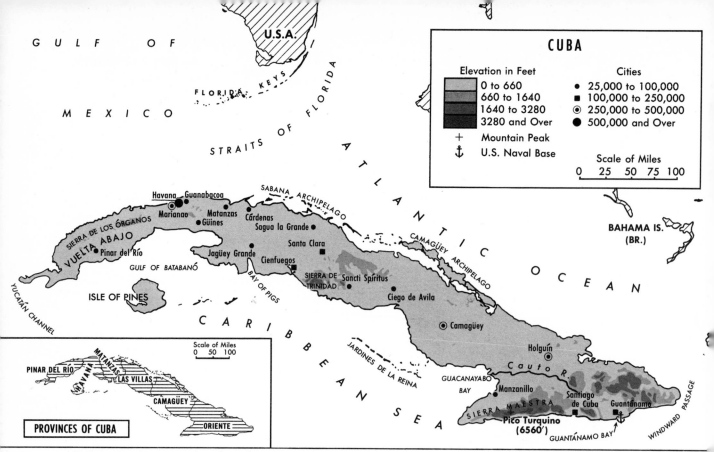

Cuba, the largest island in the West Indies, extends for more than 750 miles from northwest to southeast and averages about 50 miles in width. Some of Cuba's largest cities are seaports. They are located on excellent harbors provided by sheltered bays along the coast.

Along the coastline of Cuba are many sheltered bays, which provide excellent natural harbors. Large cities such as Havana, the capital, have grown up along some of these fine harbors.

The country of Cuba includes more than one thousand islands lying off the coasts of the main island. Most of these islands are very small. The Isle of Pines, off the southwestern coast, is the largest. It has an area of more than one thousand square miles.

Climate. The weather in Cuba is pleasantly warm all year round. In Havana, the average temperature is about 70 degrees in January and 80 degrees in July and August. Cuba lies farther north than the other large islands of the West Indies. Cold air masses from the mainland of the United States sometimes send winter temperatures as low as 40 degrees. However, Cuba never experiences freezing weather except in the mountains.

Rainfall does not vary greatly from place to place on Cuba as it does on many other islands in the Caribbean region. Although trade winds blow across the island, there are few mountains to produce orographic rainfall. (See page 39.) The average yearly rainfall on Cuba is about fifty inches. Rainfall is heaviest from May to November. During the rest of the year, the island receives much less rain. This pattern of rainfall is very favorable for growing and harvesting sugarcane. The cane receives ample rainfall while it is growing, and it can be harvested during the drier months.

Cuba lies in the hurricane belt. Violent storms have frequently caused damage on Cuba, usually on the western end of the island. In October, 1963, a hurricane battered the island for five days. This was one of the worst storms ever to hit Cuba. About one thousand people were killed, and more than half of all crops were destroyed.

Natural resources. Cuba is richer in natural resources than most Caribbean countries. The fertile soil, warm climate, and adequate rainfall on Cuba provide excellent conditions for growing a variety of crops. Before Castro's revolution, the production of crops such as sugarcane helped to make Cuba the richest country in the Caribbean Lands.

Cuba has rich deposits of several valuable minerals. The mining and processing of minerals are being given priority by the Cuban government. Like other Communist nations, Cuba is trying to become an important manufacturing country very rapidly. To do this, it needs machinery and other equipment made from metals.

Iron ore. Cuba's deposits of iron ore are among the largest in the world. These deposits are located mainly in Oriente Province. Before the revolution, little of Cuba's iron ore was mined. Almost all of it was owned by United States companies who held it in reserve for future use. Today, the Cuban government is trying to increase production of iron ore so that it can develop a large steel industry. Plans have been made to build a steel mill that will cost 150 million dollars. The money and equipment for this plant will come from other Communist countries. Cuban authorities claim that the steel mill will be in

operation by 1967. However, such claims cannot always be trusted. Many of the goals set by planners in Cuba are unrealistic and are not being fulfilled.

Nickel. Cuba is one of the world's largest producers of nickel ore. This valuable mineral has several important uses. Its chief use is in making alloy* steel, which is needed for manufacturing many types of machinery.

Nickel-processing plants in Cuba were owned by Americans until 1960, when these plants were taken over by Castro's government. Without the aid of American technicians, production of nickel almost came to a halt. Cuba has since received technical help from the Soviet Union and is planning to build the world's largest nickel plant.

Other minerals. Cuba has deposits of other important minerals. Manganese, copper, cobalt, and chromium ores are found mainly in the highlands near the eastern end of the island.

Cuba is the only Caribbean country besides Trinidad and Tobago where

A nickel-processing plant. Cuba has rich deposits of several important minerals. The government of Cuba is working hard to develop these resources.

Facts About Cuba

Area: 44,218 square miles.

Population: About 7,203,000.

Density of Population: 163 people per square mile; 911 people per square mile of arable* land.

Capital and Largest City: Havana (population about 897,000).

Racial Composition: About three out of every four Cubans are white. Most of the rest are Negro or mulatto.

Literacy: According to the Cuban government, almost all of the people in Cuba can read and write.

Main Language: Spanish.

Main Religion: Roman Catholicism.

Main Occupation: About four out of every ten Cuban workers are farmers. About two out of every ten are employed in factories or mines.

Income: Yearly per capita income was about $340 in 1958. Later figures are not available.

Important Farm Products: Sugarcane is Cuba's most important export crop. Tobacco is also grown for export. Rice and beans are the most important domestic food crops.

Natural Resources: Iron, nickel, chromium, copper, manganese, and cobalt ores, and petroleum.

Manufacturing: Sugar processing is Cuba's most important kind of manufacturing. Some Cuban factories make tobacco products, textiles, clothing, cement, chemicals, or light machinery.

Currency: Cuba's unit of money is the *peso,* which is officially worth $1.00.

Spaniards settle on Cuba. Cuba was discovered by Christopher Columbus in 1492, on his first voyage to the New World. Columbus landed on the northern coast of the island. Two years later, on his second voyage, he explored the southern coast. Because of Cuba's great length, Columbus at first believed that he had discovered the mainland of China.

The conquest of Cuba began in 1511. A Spaniard, Diego Velásquez, led an expedition of about three hundred men from the nearby colony of Santo Domingo. This expedition quickly conquered the peaceful Arawak Indians who lived on Cuba. Within a few years, Havana, Santiago, and other settlements were founded. Cuba was a Spanish colony for about four hundred years.

Cuba becomes an important Spanish base. During the 1500's and 1600's, Cuba was important mainly as a base for further Spanish exploration in the New World. There was little gold or silver on Cuba, and many of the early explorers left the island to search for riches on the mainland. Cortés, the conqueror of the Aztecs of Mexico, was the most famous of the conquistadors who sailed on expeditions from the island of Cuba. The city of Havana became one of Spain's principal ports in the New World. (See map on page 65.) Ships coming from Spain sometimes made Havana their first stop. Vessels returning to Spain from the mainland assembled in Havana Harbor. From here, they proceeded across the Atlantic in convoys* for protection against pirates.

The few Spaniards who settled on Cuba engaged mainly in cattle raising

petroleum has been found. Thus far, the amount of oil produced has been very small. Cuba's oil comes from more than one hundred wells, which are located mainly in the central part of the main island and on islands off the northern coast. Exploration and drilling for oil were carried on by United States companies until 1960, when the Cuban government seized the equipment owned by these companies.

and other kinds of farming. They supplied food to the ships stopping at the island. Indians were forced to do the hard labor in the fields. Most of them soon died from overwork and from harsh treatment by the Spaniards. Small numbers of Negro slaves were brought from Africa to replace them.

Because of Cuba's strategic location, the island was frequently attacked by the English, Dutch, and French. In 1762, a British fleet captured Havana. The city was returned to Spain by a treaty signed the following year.

After the British occupation, Spain began to devote more attention to Cuba. Trade between the colony and the mother country grew, and a large sugar industry was started on the island. Many Spaniards settled on Cuba and imported large numbers of slaves from Africa to work on sugar plantations. Near the end of the 1700's, French and Spanish colonists fleeing uprisings on the nearby island of Hispaniola also settled on Cuba.

The Cuban people fight for independence. In the 1800's, the people of Cuba became dissatisfied with Spanish rule. Spanish officials who governed the island did not permit freedom of speech. The Cubans were forced to pay heavy taxes, and they were not permitted to trade freely with other countries. Many Cuban patriots conspired against their Spanish rulers. Some of these patriots fled to the United States, where they organized revolutionary groups dedicated to freeing Cuba. In the mid-1800's, Cuban expeditions from the United States invaded their homeland. These attacks were easily crushed by the Spaniards, and many of the Cuban rebels were shot.

A fortress built by the Spaniards in Havana, Cuba. During the 1500's and 1600's, Cuba was an important base for Spanish exploration in the New World.

Between 1868 and 1878, a full-scale war was fought in Cuba. More than 200,000 Cubans and Spaniards perished in this long conflict, known as the Ten Years' War. The revolt came to an end when Spain promised reforms on the island. The Negro slaves were freed in 1886, but little else was done to help the people of Cuba.

A new revolt broke out in 1895. This revolt was organized by a famous Cuban writer and orator, José Martí, who became Cuba's national hero. Spain was determined to crush the rebellion. More than 100,000 troops were sent from Spain. The Spaniards rounded up Cuban civilians and herded them into concentration camps, where thousands of them died. The Spaniards also laid waste much of the farmland of Cuba to deprive the rebels of food.

The struggle between Cuba and Spain leads to the Spanish-American War. In 1898, an American battleship, the *Maine,* was sent to Cuba to help protect the lives and property of United States citizens living on the island. On the night of February 15, 1898, the

The "Maine," an American battleship, blew up in Havana Harbor in 1898. The United States blamed the Spanish for this and declared war on Spain.

Maine blew up in Havana Harbor, and 260 members of its crew were killed. The people of the United States, who strongly favored the Cuban rebels, blamed this disaster on the Spaniards. The United States declared war on Spain in April, 1898.

The Spanish-American War lasted only a few months. The United States Navy blockaded Cuban ports and succeeded in destroying a Spanish fleet just outside the harbor of Santiago de Cuba. After Santiago was captured by American troops, the Spaniards surrendered. All Spanish troops were soon withdrawn from the island.

The United States helps the Cubans rebuild their country. American military forces occupied Cuba from 1899 to 1902. Although the United States had promised Cuba its independence after the Spanish-American War, the island was not ready for self-rule. There was no organized government, and much of the land had been laid waste. Thousands of Cubans were dying from starvation and disease.

The United States helped Cuba to recover. The occupation forces assisted Cubans to organize their own government. A modern highway system was started. New schools were built to educate the Cubans, most of whom could not read and write.

One of the most important achievements was the control of yellow fever. This dread disease had killed many hundreds of Cubans every year. American doctors proved the theory of a Cuban, Carlos Finlay, who believed that yellow fever was spread by the bite of a mosquito. Swamps and other breeding places for mosquitoes were drained, and in a short time Cuba was freed of yellow fever.

In 1901, the Cubans adopted a constitution modeled after the Constitution of the United States. One section of the Cuban constitution was known as the Platt Amendment. It permitted the United States to intervene in Cuba whenever it was considered necessary to preserve Cuban independence or to maintain orderly government on the

American doctors helped free Cuba of yellow fever after the Spanish-American War. The United States aided Cubans in many ways.

island. It also gave the United States the right to build naval bases on Cuba. Following the adoption of this constitution, the new nation held its first democratic elections. A short time later, United States troops were withdrawn from the island.

Cuba began to prosper under the honest administration of its first president, Tomás Estrada Palma. American businessmen were eager to invest money in Cuba's sugar industry. Large quantities of Cuban sugar could be sold in the United States. The businessmen felt that the island would be free from unrest and revolution because the United States had the right to intervene in Cuban affairs. In the years that followed, American businessmen invested more than one billion dollars in Cuba, most of it in the sugar industry. Many large centrals* were built. They were equipped with the most modern machinery for processing sugarcane.

Cuba's lack of experience in self-government leads to dictatorship. Although Cuba had a democratic constitution, its people had no experience in governing themselves. Most of them were poor, uneducated farmers. Government leaders were often corrupt and undemocratic. Frequently, elections were dishonest, and Cuban leaders were more interested in getting rich in office than in governing well. As a result, there were many revolts during the early years of the new nation. On several occasions, the United States intervened in Cuba to preserve order. United States marines occupied the island from 1906 to 1909 and landed again during World War I.

In 1924, Gerardo Machado was elected president of Cuba. Machado promised many reforms but failed to carry out most of them. When opposition to his rule developed, Machado began a reign of terror. He became Cuba's first dictator. Machado killed many of his opponents, closed the University of Havana and many other schools, and used other harsh measures to stay in power. A general strike by the workers of Cuba forced Machado to resign from office and flee the country in 1933. A new government was formed with the help of the United States.

Another dictator came to power in Cuba almost immediately. An army sergeant, Fulgencio Batista, led a revolt that overthrew the new government. Batista promoted himself to commander in chief of the army and soon became the most powerful man in Cuba. He ruled the country from 1933 to 1944, and again from 1952 to 1959.

During the first period he held power in Cuba, Batista did some good things for his country. An agreement with the United States set aside the Platt Amendment, which was very unpopular in Cuba. In 1940, a new democratic constitution was drawn up for the country. Batista built many roads and schools, and improved the wages and working conditions of Cuba's laborers. He permitted free elections in 1944. When the candidate he supported for president was defeated, Batista left Cuba for a time.

In 1952, Batista again seized power by overthrowing a democratically elected government. This time he proved to be a much harsher dictator than before. Batista suspended the constitution of 1940, controlled the press, and shut down all public universities. Opposition to his rule soon began.

Castro's revolution begins. On July 26, 1953, a band of young rebels led by Fidel Castro attacked an army post at Santiago. Most of the rebels were killed, and Castro and his brother Raúl were imprisoned for almost a year on the Isle of Pines. This attack marked the beginning of Castro's campaign to take over Cuba.

After Castro was released from prison, the rebel leader continued his efforts to overthrow Batista's dictatorship. He went to Mexico and began to organize a guerrilla force to invade his homeland. Castro obtained money from Cuban exiles in the United States. At this time, he was joined by Ernesto (Ché) Guevara, an experienced revolutionary from Argentina. Together they trained a force of about eighty men and sailed for Cuba.

The invasion took place in Oriente Province on December 2, 1956. It was nearly a complete failure. The small force was almost wiped out by Batista's modern planes and well-equipped army. Only one small group of twelve men, including the Castro brothers and Guevara, escaped into the mountains of the Sierra Maestra.

For the next two years, Castro and his followers carried on guerrilla warfare against the Batista government. They were gradually joined by other rebels. In April, 1958, Castro proclaimed a general strike in an effort to overthrow the government. This strike was unsuccessful. Most of the workers of Cuba did not support it, and the Cuban Communist Party, which had not been consulted, worked against the strike.

Batista's cruelty causes people to revolt. Following the failure of Castro's general strike, Batista struck back through his army and secret police. Anyone even suspected of being against the government was arrested and often cruelly tortured. Young students were the chief victims, because many of them sided with Castro.

Batista's reign of terror led to his downfall. Thousands of Cubans flocked to the support of Castro. Many young men felt that it was safer to join the rebels in the mountains than to be picked up by Batista's secret police in the cities. Even members of the army and secret police were shocked at the atrocities being carried on to suppress the revolution. Army units sent against Castro often refused to fire on the rebels. By late 1958, almost all of Cuba supported the revolutionary forces. Only Havana Province was still held by troops loyal to Batista. On January 1, 1959, Batista gathered his family and a few aides and fled to the Dominican Republic.

Fidel Castro and two of his followers. In the 1950's, Castro led a revolution against a dictator named Batista. Almost all of Cuba supported Castro.

Castro's victory parade. In January, 1959, Fidel Castro rode into Havana in triumph. The people celebrated what they believed would be freedom from dictatorship. However, all political parties except the Communist Party were dissolved, and Castro quickly established a new dictatorship.

Castro comes to power. In January, 1959, Fidel Castro rode into Havana in triumph. Thousands of Cubans cheered and showered him with flowers. They were celebrating what they believed would be freedom from dictatorship. Other countries also welcomed his victory. The United States was among the first to recognize the new government.

The people of Cuba had good reason to expect the new government to be democratic. Castro had often promised that, after Batista was overthrown, free elections would be held in Cuba. He had also pledged freedom of speech and freedom of the press. Because of Castro's promises, the Cuban people expected that the democratic constitution of 1940 would once again be put into effect.

Cuba becomes a Communist dictatorship. Instead of carrying out his promises, Castro quickly established a new dictatorship over the Cuban people. His government dissolved all political parties in Cuba except the Communist Party. Raúl Castro and Ché Guevara, who were supporters of communism, were given high positions in the new government. Despite Castro's many promises, no plans were made to hold elections.

Under communism, the government controls all means of production and decides what goods are to be produced. The Cuban government began to take over the land, factories, and other property owned by businesses and private citizens. By the end of 1960, much of the privately owned property in Cuba had been seized. Most of the owners were not paid for the land and businesses they lost. Many business firms in the United States and other countries had their land and factories in Cuba taken from them. Oil refineries, sugar mills, hotels, and electric power and telephone companies were among the properties seized from United States owners. American businessmen lost more than one billion dollars' worth of investments in Cuba.

Castro's government began to crush all opposition. In 1959, hundreds of former Batista supporters were shot by firing squads, sometimes without trial. In the next few years, more than 200,000 Cubans fled the island. Many of them were wealthy or middle-class Cubans whose property had been taken over by the Castro government. As the dictator began to turn his country into a Communist police state, many of the men who had fought side by side with him in the Sierra Maestra turned against him. Some members of his own government who were not Communists also opposed him and were jailed or exiled. Many Cuban exiles in the United States formed opposition groups dedicated to fighting Castro.

The United States opposes Castro's dictatorship. The United States watched the events in Cuba anxiously. When Cuba seized American oil refineries, the United States reduced the amount of sugar it purchased from Cuba. Later, this country stopped all of its trade with Cuba except for exports of food and medicine to the island.

Cuba began to trade with the Soviet Union and other Communist countries soon after the revolution. In return for sugar, these countries shipped crude oil, machinery, food, and other badly needed items to Cuba. They also provided the island with military supplies. Near the end of 1960, the United States Department of State reported that large

quantities of military equipment, including rockets and jet fighter planes, had been delivered to Cuba by the Russians.

The United States opposed the government of Castro for two main reasons. This country had been engaged in the Cold War* against Communist nations since shortly after World War II. The United States did not want Cuba, located only about ninety miles from its shores, to be used as communism's first base in the Western Hemisphere.

There was another reason for American opposition. Like other Communists, the Cuban leaders were not satisfied with building a Communist society in their own country. They were spreading propaganda throughout Latin America. Young students from other countries were brought to Cuba for training. They then returned to their own countries to stir up revolution.

Cuban exiles attempt to overthrow Castro. In 1961, a brigade of about 1,500 Cuban exiles was formed to invade Cuba and overthrow the Castro government. This force was trained in Central America by United States advisors. It sailed toward Cuba in five ships on the morning of April 13, 1961. The brigade landed on Cuba at the Bay of Pigs. (See map on page 232.) During a three-day battle, the brigade was defeated, and more than one thousand prisoners were taken by Castro's forces. Most of these prisoners were later released in exchange for 53 million dollars' worth of medical supplies and other goods from the United States.

Russian missiles on Cuba threaten the world with atomic war. Following the Bay of Pigs invasion, Cuba began to receive larger quantities of military equipment from the Soviet Union. The Communists claimed that these weapons were needed to defend the island against United States aggression. In September, 1962, the president of the United States, John F. Kennedy, reported that there was a military buildup on Cuba. He ordered American planes to take photographs of the island and of Soviet ships approaching Cuban ports.

On October 22, 1962, President Kennedy reported by radio and television to the American people. He announced that United States planes had taken pictures of missile sites on Cuba. Missiles fired from these sites would be capable of reaching and destroying many major cities in the Western Hemisphere. The President ordered a "quarantine," or partial blockade, of Cuba. All ships approaching the island were to be searched. They were to be turned back if they were found to be carrying offensive* weapons. In addition, President Kennedy appealed directly to Premier Nikita Khrushchev, the leader of the Soviet Union. He called upon him to withdraw the offensive weapons already on Cuba or face further action by the United States.

For several days, the world was faced with the possibility of atomic war. During this time, the missile crisis was debated in the United Nations, and messages were exchanged between Premier Khrushchev and President Kennedy. Finally, the Soviet leader agreed to withdraw the missiles. In return, the United States promised not to invade Cuba if Castro would permit a United Nations team to supervise the removal of Soviet missiles from the island. However, the Cuban dictator refused to allow inspection teams to enter his country.

Communists continue to rule Cuba. Since the missile crisis, Cuba has remained under Communist control. It has also continued close ties with the Soviet Union, China, and other Communist

A United States ship approaches a large Russian ship removing missiles from Cuba. In October, 1962, President Kennedy called for the withdrawal of Russian missiles from Cuba. For a time, the world faced the threat of atomic war. Finally, the Soviet Union agreed to United States demands.

countries. Followers of Castro have increased their efforts to overthrow other governments in the Western Hemisphere. Almost all of the Latin-American republics have broken relations with Cuba.

THE PEOPLE AND HOW THEY LIVE

People. Cuba has the largest population of any Caribbean country. More than seven million people live on this island. However, this is fewer people than live in the city of New York. Because of its size, Cuba is not so densely populated as many other islands in the West Indies.

About three out of every four Cubans are white. Most of the others are Negro or mulatto. Before the wars for independence in the 1800's, there were more Negroes than white people in Cuba. However, Negroes made up a large part of the rebel armies, and many of them were killed or died of disease. Many died in concentration camps. After independence, almost 800,000 white people settled on Cuba. Most of them came

from Spain. There are small groups of Chinese in Havana and other large cities.

Most Cubans are Roman Catholic. Some are members of Protestant churches. The Communist philosophy does not recognize the existence of God. Some priests and ministers have been forced to leave Cuba. Private schools that were formerly operated by religious groups have been taken over by the government or closed. However, there is more religious freedom in Cuba than in most other Communist countries. Because so many Cubans are Catholic, the Communist leaders are careful not to attack religion openly.

Sugarcane is Cuba's main crop. Most Cuban farm workers earn their living on farms that produce sugarcane. It is grown on more than half of the land farmed in Cuba. The cane is made into raw sugar in about 160 sugar mills, which provide jobs for about one fourth of Cuba's factory workers. For many years, Cuba has been the world's leading exporter of raw sugar. Because producing sugar has been so important, Cuba is said to have a one-crop economy.

The best soil in Cuba for growing sugarcane is the Matanzas clay found in the central and western parts of the island. However, exporting sugar has been so profitable that cane is also grown in many less fertile areas. Much of the eastern part of Cuba, which was formerly used for grazing livestock, is now used for raising sugarcane.

Some farmers produce other crops. Although sugarcane is by far Cuba's most valuable crop, some Cuban farmers raise other crops. Tobacco is the most important of these. It is grown in many parts of the island, but the best tobacco comes

Young Cubans gathered on a beach. About three out of every four Cubans are white. Most of the others are either Negro or mulatto.

242

Harvesting sugarcane, Cuba's most valuable crop. Cuba is one of the world's largest producers of sugarcane. Because so much of the island's farmland is planted in cane, there is little room left to grow other food crops needed by the Cuban people.

from the Vuelta Abajo region in western Cuba. (See map on page 232.) Tobacco is generally grown on small plots of land, on which many workers are employed. More than 100,000 Cubans are engaged in growing and processing tobacco. Both tobacco and tobacco products are exported.

Because so much of Cuba's farmland is planted in sugarcane, there is little room left to grow the food crops most needed by its people. Rice and beans are the two main foods eaten by Cubans. Only about half the quantity needed is grown on the island. The rest must be imported. Large quantities of meat, dairy products, and eggs must also be purchased from other countries.

A one-crop economy presents problems in Cuba. Before Castro's revolution, Cuba depended so much on the one crop, sugarcane, that the country was faced with serious problems. Land that could have been used to grow rice, cotton, and other crops was planted in sugarcane. Each year, Cuba was obliged to import more than 100 million dollars' worth of foodstuffs, as well as large quantities of cotton and textiles.

Unemployment was another problem resulting from the dependence on sugar. Cuban workers who cut sugarcane for a living worked only during the harvest season. After the cane was harvested, thousands of cane cutters and men who worked in the sugar mills were without work. For several months of each year, about one fifth of all workers in Cuba were unemployed.

The price of sugar exported by Cuba often varied from one year to the next. A sudden drop in the price of sugar brought real hardship to the island. When this happened, there was less money available to buy goods from other countries. Sugarcane was grown mainly on land that was owned or rented by centrals. Many of these centrals were the property of United States companies. In the years when the price of sugar was low, the large sugar companies did not harvest all of the cane that was planted. This left thousands of Cuban cane cutters without work. Because the cane fields were not harvested, this also meant that some of the best farmland of the country was being wasted.

Under communism, farming in Cuba has changed. After Castro seized power in Cuba, many changes were made that affected farming. In 1959, many large estates were taken over by the government. Some of the land was distributed to poor farmers. However, much of the farmland was kept by the government and divided into cooperatives* and "people's farms"* similar to farms in the Soviet Union and other Communist countries. The government promised to pay the owners for the land that was taken from them. However, few of them received any payment.

In December, 1960, Fidel Castro announced that the following year many different food crops, such as rice, beans,

Transporting tomatoes on a "people's farm."* Castro made plans to grow other food crops on land that had been planted in sugarcane.

and corn, would be grown on land that had been planted in sugarcane. Hundreds of thousands of acres of cane were uprooted for this purpose. Castro promised that this new program would increase total farm production and that it would provide jobs for all farm workers.

Castro's farm program is a failure. The results of Castro's program were disastrous. Some of the best sugarcane on the island was destroyed, and sugar production declined to one of the lowest levels in many years.

Castro's program also failed to increase the supply of other crops. The large government-owned farms were managed very poorly. The managers were often chosen for their loyalty to Castro rather than for their ability and experience. Also, the Communist planners in Havana made many mistakes. Frequently, equipment or fertilizer that was promised to the large farms arrived too late to be useful. Instead of increasing the supply of food crops, the Communist program produced a serious food shortage. In 1961, rationing of food items was announced, and is still in effect today.

Castro's government is trying to make Cuba an industrial nation. Although the Communists are trying hard to develop industry in Cuba, only about two out of every ten Cuban workers earn a living by working in mines and factories. Before Castro came to power, Cuba, like most other Caribbean countries, had few factories. Its main industry was the production of sugar in the large centrals located throughout the island. There were also some textile mills, cement plants, and oil refineries. Many workers were employed in factories that made

244

cigars and processed tobacco, mainly for export. However, most other factories in Cuba were small and produced goods for the use of the people of the country. In most parts of the island, there was very little manufacturing. More than half of all the factories were located in Havana.

There were several reasons for the lack of industry in Cuba. Because of its nearness to the United States, Cuba could very easily order manufactured goods from this country. Also, much of the industry in Cuba was owned by large, efficient United States companies. It was difficult for Cubans to operate businesses that could compete with these companies. Therefore, Cubans with money to invest preferred to build tourist hotels or expensive apartment houses rather than to invest in factories.

Castro has seized industries in Cuba. Shortly after the revolution, Castro's government began to take over industries in Cuba. In 1960, most of the oil refineries, sugar mills, and electric power and telephone companies were seized. Within two years, the Communist government controlled almost all of the country's industries.

The Cuban government quickly began to reorganize industry. The Communist leader Ché Guevara was placed in charge of the government department that controls industry. In 1960, a Five-Year Plan was announced. This was similar to plans followed by other Communist countries. Its purpose was to increase production of manufactured goods at a very rapid rate. Automobile factories, steel mills, chemical plants, and other factories were planned. The government claimed that by 1965, Cuba would lead all Latin-American countries in industrial output per worker.

However, Cuba is faced with serious problems in trying to expand its industry. Most of its present factory equipment was originally purchased in the United States. This equipment is wearing out, and spare parts cannot be imported from the United States to repair it. Another problem is lack of raw materials. Although Cuba has a good supply of mineral resources, they are largely undeveloped. The most serious problem Cuba faces in increasing its industry is the country's lack of skilled workers and managers. Many engineers, technicians, and factory managers fled the island after Castro seized power. Because of these problems, Cuba must depend on help from the Soviet Union and other Communist countries to develop its industry.

Transportation and communication. It has not been as difficult to build roads and railroads in Cuba as in more mountainous Caribbean countries. More than eight thousand miles of roads connect the major cities of Cuba. The most important road is called the Central Highway. It extends nearly the entire length of the island, from the city of Pinar del Río in the west to Santiago de Cuba on the southeastern coast. (Compare maps on pages 133 and 232.)

Before the revolution, Cuba had more automobiles and trucks than any other Caribbean country. Most of these vehicles were imported from the United States. Cuba can no longer buy American spare parts to repair this equipment as it wears out, nor can it buy new cars from the United States. Vehicles are being imported from other countries.

Making spare parts for textile machines. Since the revolution, Castro's government has taken over almost all of Cuba's industries. Most of the equipment in Cuban factories was produced in the United States. Now the machines are wearing out, and spare parts cannot be imported.

Today, buses that were made in Poland and Czechoslovakia carry people to work in Havana, but there is still a shortage of such equipment. The Cuban government claims that it is going to build a 90-million-dollar factory to assemble its own automobiles, trucks, and buses.

Cuba has many more miles of railroads than all of the other Caribbean countries combined. More than seven thousand miles of railroads were built by sugar companies. They were used to haul sugarcane to the mills and to transport sugar to seaports. Two companies controlled most of the public railroad system, which had a total of more than three thousand miles of track. All railroads have now been taken over by the Castro government. Much railroad equipment that was manufactured in

the United States is wearing out and lacks spare parts. In 1964, Cuba arranged to purchase twenty new diesel locomotives from France.

Because the United States has broken relations with Cuba, American-owned airlines no longer schedule flights to the island. A Cuban airline flies to Mexico City from Havana. However, few Cubans are allowed to travel outside their country, except to go to other Communist countries. Aeroflot, the Soviet airline, makes one of the world's longest regular flights, from Moscow to Havana.

The communications system in Cuba is operated by the government. Many people have radio and television sets. The government conducts classes over television to help educate the Cuban people. It also uses radio and television to spread propaganda. Newspapers are another important means of spreading Communist ideas. Telephone service in Cuba is not good. More than half of all the telephones are in the city of Havana.

Education in Cuba before Castro. Before Castro's revolution, the people of Cuba had one of the highest literacy rates in the Caribbean Lands. Nearly four out of every five Cubans fifteen years of age and older could read and write. However, most of the people were not well educated. Fewer than one fourth of all students finished elementary school, and even fewer went on to high school. Many children did not attend school at all. Although the law required children between the ages of six and fourteen to attend school, there were not enough schools for all students, particularly in rural areas.

Before the revolution, there were three public universities and one Roman Catholic university in Cuba. The University of Havana, which was founded in the early 1700's, was the largest of these. Near the end of his rule, Batista closed the public universities, because the students opposed his dictatorship. They were reopened in 1959, after the revolution.

Castro begins a program to educate all Cubans. Soon after Castro came to power, he announced a campaign to teach all Cubans how to read and write. Many new schools were built, and children who had not previously gone to school were now required to attend. The Communists began to reorganize the educational system in Cuba. All private schools were either closed or taken over by the government. Teachers who did not agree with the government lost their jobs, and many of them left the

country. Communism was taught in the schools, and it was announced that the Russian language would become a required subject. The Cuban leaders sent many students to the Soviet Union and other Communist countries for training.

The Communist leaders also wanted to educate Cuban adults who could not read and write. Fidel Castro proclaimed 1961 as the "Year of Education." Almost 300,000 Cubans, mostly young people, were organized to take part in this program. Some of them worked in the cities. Thousands of others were assembled into uniformed brigades, like an army. They were sent into rural areas to teach illiterate peasants to read and write. These student teachers often lived with the people they were teaching and helped with the farm work. During most of the Year of Education, the regular schools in Cuba were shut down.

Cuban schoolchildren. The Communist government of Cuba considers education important. It claims that Cuba has the highest literacy rate in Latin America.

The results of the Year of Education.
Near the end of 1961, the Cuban government announced that almost one million illiterate people had been located, and that seven out of every ten of them had been taught to read and write. The government claimed that Cuba had achieved the highest literacy rate in all of Latin America. Many people believe that these claims were exaggerated.

The Cuban government itself has recognized that the Year of Education was only a beginning. A program of courses for adults was begun in 1962 to provide education through the sixth-grade level. In addition, classes in technical subjects, such as carpentry and accounting, were held in factories and business offices to educate Cuban workers.

Why Castro wants Cubans to be educated. Like Communists everywhere, the Cuban leaders regard education as very important in building a Communist society. There are several reasons for this. The Castro government is trying to make Cuba an industrial nation in as short a time as possible. It is also trying to solve the agricultural problems of the country. To do these things, Cuba must have skilled workers. It must also have educated managers and technicians. The Cuban leaders know that they cannot succeed in changing Cuba if a large part of the people have little or no education.

There is another reason why Cuba's leaders are trying to educate the people of the country. In order to remain in power and achieve their goals, they need the support of most Cubans. Therefore, they are using the schools not only to teach useful skills but also to spread propaganda in support of communism.

Cities. There are more large cities in Cuba than in any other Caribbean country. Havana, which is described below, is by far the largest city in the Caribbean Lands. Greater Havana, which includes the city of Marianao and other suburbs, has a population of more than one million. In all, eight Cuban cities have more than 100,000 inhabitants. (See map on page 232.)

Some of Cuba's most important cities are located in the eastern part of the island. Holguín, which lies in a sugar-cane and cattle-raising region, is the fastest-growing city in Cuba. Its population has increased from 57,000 in 1953 to more than 300,000 today. Camagüey and Santiago de Cuba were founded in the early 1500's. Although these cities are growing in importance as industrial centers, they still look much like Spanish colonial cities. About twelve miles south of the city of Guantánamo lies the large United States naval base at Guantánamo Bay. The United States has retained this base despite Castro's repeated demands that American troops be withdrawn.

Havana (population about 897,000) is the capital and largest city of Cuba. It is located on a beautiful sheltered bay on the northwestern coast of the island. About one fifth of all the people of Cuba live in Havana and the surrounding area.

Havana has been an important seaport since the early days of Spanish exploration. More than half of all Cuba's imports and a large part of its exports pass through the city's fine, deep harbor. Tobacco, sugar, and tropical fruits are exported from Havana, while foodstuffs, petroleum, and manufactured goods such as machinery are imported. Most of this trade is with other Communist countries.

Havana is the principal manufacturing city of Cuba. When United States companies began to invest large sums of money in Cuba, Havana became their headquarters. Modern office buildings were constructed, and factories were established. Sugar refineries, textile mills, rum distilleries, and oil refineries were built. Havana's cigar factories were among the largest in the world. Today, however, the Communist planners in Cuba do not intend to build many new factories in Havana. Most of the factories will be built in Oriente Province, where many of Cuba's mineral deposits are located.

Before Castro's revolution, hundreds of thousands of American tourists came to Havana each year. They were attracted by the pleasant climate and by the city's beautiful beaches, modern hotels, and gay entertainment. Havana's wide boulevards, flowering trees, and fine residential districts made many people consider it the most beautiful city in the Caribbean Lands.

In Havana, an armed woman member of the Cuban militia stands guard on a downtown street. Havana is Cuba's capital and main manufacturing city.

Today, the once-gay city of Havana is very different. Because the United States no longer has diplomatic relations with Communist Cuba, Americans are not permitted to travel freely to the island. The luxury hotels are now almost empty of tourists. Armed members of the Cuban militia stand guard on downtown streets. In the shops, which were formerly well stocked with goods, many items are rationed.

Reviewing What You Have Learned
Choose four of the statements listed below. Use each as the topic sentence of a short paragraph. In each paragraph, explain why the idea stated in the topic sentence is true.
1. The island of Cuba is well suited to farming.
2. The United States played an important role in the development of Cuba.
3. Cuba has many of the resources needed to develop modern industries.

4. The restrictions placed on Cubans by their Spanish rulers led to the Cuban struggle for independence.
5. In 1962, the United States set up a partial blockade of Cuba.

Facts To Review
Briefly identify and give the most important facts about each of the following:

José Martí	Bay of Pigs
Fulgencio Batista	Sierra Maestra
Five-Year Plan	Year of Education

22 Dominican Republic

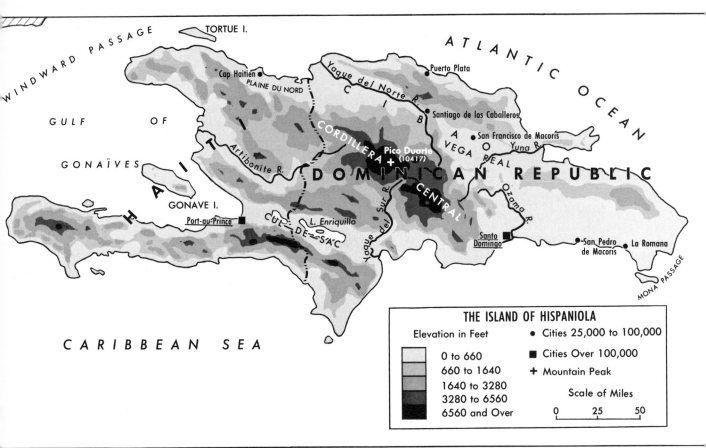

THE ISLAND OF HISPANIOLA

Elevation in Feet

	0 to 660
	660 to 1640
	1640 to 3280
	3280 to 6560
	6560 and Over

• Cities 25,000 to 100,000
■ Cities Over 100,000
+ Mountain Peak

Scale of Miles

0   25   50

Hispaniola is the second largest island of the West Indies. On this island are two independent countries, the Dominican Republic and Haiti. The Dominican Republic occupies the eastern two thirds of Hispaniola. The highest peak in the West Indies is found here.

GEOGRAPHY

Land. Almost midway between the islands of Cuba and Puerto Rico lies the island of Hispaniola. (See map on pages 14 and 15.) On this island are two independent countries, the Dominican Republic and Haiti. The Dominican Republic occupies the eastern two thirds of the island. It is about the size of Vermont and New Hampshire combined.

The Dominican Republic is a land of rugged mountains, deep valleys, and broad plains. About half of the country consists of mountains. The Cordillera Central, or "Central Range," begins near the southern coast of the Dominican Republic, west of the capital city, Santo Domingo. It curves northwestward into Haiti. The highest peak in the West Indies is found in the Cordillera Central. This is Pico Duarte, which is more than ten thousand feet above sea level. To the north, east, and southwest of the Cordillera Central are

250

Facts About the Dominican Republic

Area: 18,816 square miles.

Population: About 3,300,000.

Density of Population: About 175 people per square mile; about 1,180 people per square mile of arable* land.

Capital and Largest City: Santo Domingo (population about 367,000).

Racial Composition: Nearly seven tenths of the Dominican people are mulatto. Most of the rest are either white or Negro.

Literacy: About seven out of every ten of the people can read and write.

Main Language: Spanish.

Main Religion: Roman Catholicism.

Main Occupation: About half of the workers are farmers.

Income: Yearly per capita income is about $230. Most Dominicans can live on a very small income, because they grow or make many of the things they need. Many farmers grow more than they need and sell their surplus.

Important Farm Products: Sugarcane is the most important export crop grown in the Dominican Republic. Other export crops include coffee, cacao, and tobacco. Rice, beans, corn, sweet potatoes, and peanuts are important domestic food crops.

Natural Resources: Forests, bauxite, iron ore, and salt.

Manufacturing: Processing farm products, especially sugarcane, is the most important industry. Products besides sugar that are manufactured here include cement, lumber, cigars, cigarettes, textiles, and shoes.

Currency: The Dominican Republic's unit of money is the *peso,* which is officially worth $1.00.

the country lies a broad valley called the Cibao. The eastern part of the Cibao is called the Vega Real, or "Royal Plain." This area contains some of the most fertile farmland in the Caribbean region. Most of the farms in the Vega Real are small. However, the soil is so rich that farmers are able to grow enough crops to feed their families and still have food to sell. In the southeastern part of the Dominican Republic, a broad plain stretches eastward from Santo Domingo. Here sugarcane is grown on vast plantations, and large herds of horses and cattle graze on pasturelands.

Climate. In most of the Dominican Republic, the weather is pleasantly warm throughout the year. People can swim and play baseball even during the

A valley in the Cordillera Central, or "Central Range." The Dominican Republic is made up of valleys, broad plains, and rugged mountains.

other mountain ranges. (See map on opposite page.) These ranges extend generally from east to west and are lower than the Cordillera Central.

There are two important lowland regions in the Dominican Republic. Between the Cordillera Central and the mountains in the northern part of

251

Coconut palm trees growing along the coast of the Dominican Republic. Although this country lies in the tropics, temperatures are seldom very high. Cooling trade winds from the ocean make the weather in most places pleasant the year round.

winter months. Temperatures are seldom extremely high, because the Dominican Republic lies in the path of cooling trade winds. However, some lowlands, particularly in the southwestern part of the country, are sheltered from the trade winds by mountains. These areas are often uncomfortably hot.

The climate is cooler in the highlands than in the lowlands. Temperatures in the mountains sometimes drop below freezing.

The trade winds and the mountains also affect rainfall in the Dominican Republic. The northeastern part of the country faces the trade winds directly.

Some areas here may receive more than one hundred inches of rain a year. Most of the southern part of the country lies in the rain* shadow of the mountains. Here the land is often so dry that irrigation is necessary to grow crops.

The Dominican Republic lies in the hurricane* belt. In 1930, a violent hurricane almost completely destroyed Santo Domingo.

Natural resources. The most important natural resource of the Dominican Republic is the fertile soil of its plains and valleys. In the Vega Real, the rich, black soil provides excellent farmland.

The soil in the southeastern plains is well suited for the cultivation of sugarcane.

More than half of the land in the Dominican Republic is covered with forests. The country produces enough lumber for its own needs and exports a small surplus. Nine tenths of the lumber comes from pine trees that grow on high mountain slopes. In many places, the trees that were easiest to reach have been cut down. Lumbermen often must go high in the mountains to cut the pine trees. It is becoming a problem to transport the logs to sawmills.

Many different kinds of minerals have been found in the Dominican Republic, but few of them are mined in large quantities. Bauxite, salt, and iron ore are the most important minerals. In 1959, a United States aluminum company began mining a large deposit of bauxite in the southwestern part of the Dominican Republic. Salt is also obtained from this section of the country. High-grade iron ore is mined in the Cordillera Central. Most of the bauxite and iron ore produced in the Dominican Republic is exported to other countries for processing.

A salt mine in the southwestern part of the Dominican Republic. Many kinds of minerals have been found in this country, but few of them are mined in large quantities. Bauxite, salt, and iron ore are the most important minerals mined here.

A monument to Columbus stands in Santo Domingo, in front of the oldest cathedral in America. The cathedral contains the tomb of Columbus, who discovered Hispaniola in 1492. Santo Domingo was founded a few years later. It was the first permanent European settlement in the New World.

HISTORY

A Spanish colony is founded on Hispaniola. Columbus discovered the island of Hispaniola in 1492, during his first voyage to the New World. Four years later his brother Bartholomew founded a settlement on the southeastern coast of the island. This was the first permanent European settlement in the Western Hemisphere. It came to be known as Santo Domingo. As time passed, the entire Spanish colony on Hispaniola became known as Santo Domingo.

The colony of Santo Domingo quickly became an important base for further Spanish exploration in the New World. From Santo Domingo, expeditions were sent out to the neighboring islands and the mainland. Colonies on Puerto Rico, Cuba, and Jamaica were established by settlers from Santo Domingo. For a time, the *audiencia** of Santo Domingo had jurisdiction over all Spanish possessions in the West Indies.

Santo Domingo remained an important colony for only about fifty years. The early Spanish conquerors forced the Indians on Hispaniola to work hard in gold mines and on farms. Most of the Indians soon died from disease or overwork, or in warfare against the Spaniards. There were few Indians left to work in the fields and mines. Many of the Spaniards had come to Hispaniola in search of gold and silver, but they did not find large deposits of these precious metals on the island. When the

254

riches of Mexico and Peru were discovered, a great many of the settlers deserted Santo Domingo and went to the mainland. Soon the colony became just another sleepy outpost of Spain's empire.

Haitians occupy Santo Domingo. In 1697, Spain ceded the western third of Hispaniola to France. (See page 266.) Unlike the Spanish in Santo Domingo, the French established huge plantations in their part of the island and imported vast numbers of slaves from Africa. In 1791, the slaves began to revolt against the French, and in 1804, they established the independent Republic of Haiti. The Haitians greatly outnumbered the Spanish colonists in Santo Domingo. After Santo Domingo broke away from Spain, in 1821, the Haitians overran the eastern part of the island. They occupied it from 1822 to 1844.

The people of Santo Domingo were unhappy under Haitian rule. White persons were not permitted to own land. Many of the wealthy white people fled from the colony. Although slavery was abolished, the Haitians forced the workers in Santo Domingo to do hard labor in the fields. Secret opposition to the Haitians' rule was organized by groups of patriots led by Juan Pablo Duarte. In 1844, the people of Santo Domingo revolted and drove the Haitians from the country. The independent Dominican Republic was proclaimed.

Independence brings many problems. The new nation was faced with great obstacles from the very start. Most Dominicans had little education, and no experience in governing themselves. The Haitians continued to invade the Dominican Republic. Also, for a short time in the 1860's, Spain regained control of the country. The Dominicans again had to struggle to win back their independence.

Under these conditions, democratic government was almost impossible. The leaders of the Dominican Republic were often cruel or corrupt, and revolts were frequent. Between 1844 and 1930, there were forty-three presidents and more than seventy revolutions.

During the early 1900's, the United States considered it necessary to intervene in the affairs of the Dominican Republic. The Dominican government owed large sums of money to several European countries. These countries were threatening to use force to collect the money that was owed to them. In 1905, the United States made an agreement with the Dominican Republic to take over its customhouses and collect the country's taxes on imports and exports. With the money it collected at the customhouses, the United States began to pay off the country's large debts. However, violence and disorder continued in the Dominican Republic. In 1916, the United States landed marines at Santo Domingo and set up a military government. The United States occupation lasted eight years. Although the occupation brought peace and order to the country, the Dominicans did not like having foreign troops on their soil. In 1924, the United States withdrew its forces.

The "Era of Trujillo." In 1930, an army officer named Rafael Trujillo was elected president of the Dominican Republic. The next thirty-one years of Dominican history were known as the "Era of Trujillo."

During this era, Trujillo did some good things for his country. For the first time since independence, there was a long period of peace and order. New industry was encouraged, and many fine roads, bridges, and public buildings were constructed. Education and medical care were made available to more people than ever before.

Although he brought about some improvements, Trujillo was a brutal dictator. After his election, he took complete control of the government. By the time of the presidential election of 1938, most of his opponents had been killed or exiled, and Trujillo's political party was the only one on the ballot. In the years that followed, Trujillo ruled the country as though it were his private estate. He and his family controlled the newspapers, the army, and most of the

A statue of Trujillo, former dictator of the Dominican Republic. After his assassination in 1961, statues of Trujillo were torn down by angry mobs.

farming and industry in the country. Fear of his secret police and of his torture chambers kept the people from revolting. The assassination of Trujillo on May 30, 1961, brought an end to his cruel dictatorship.

The Dominican people still do not have a democratic government. After thirty-one years of dictatorship, the Dominican people are determined to have a better standard of living and more personal freedom. However, they have been ruled by a dictator for so long that they do not know how to proceed. After Trujillo's death, most of his followers were forced to leave the country. Many Dominicans who had opposed Trujillo returned from exile to form new political parties. Juan Bosch was elected president in 1962, in the country's first free election in almost forty years. However, Bosch's government was overthrown after only seven months in office.

Since then, the country has been governed by a three-man junta.* The United States at first refused to recognize this new government and broke off diplomatic relations with the Dominican Republic. However, when the junta promised to hold free elections, diplomatic relations were restored.

THE PEOPLE AND HOW THEY LIVE

People. The most densely populated part of the Dominican Republic is the fertile farming area between Santiago de los Caballeros and San Francisco de Macorís. (See map on page 250.) In this area, most of the people live on small farms or in farm villages. Many other Dominicans make their homes in the area near Santo Domingo and in

256

A cigar factory in Santiago de los Caballeros. The fertile farming area between Santiago and San Francisco de Macorís is the most densely populated part of the Dominican Republic. Nearly seven out of every ten Dominicans are mulatto. Most other Dominicans are white or Negro.

the sugarcane region to the east of the capital. Few people live in the mountainous areas or in the dry southwestern part of the country.

The population of the Dominican Republic has grown from about two million in 1950 to more than three million today. However, the Dominican Republic is still not so densely populated as many other parts of the West Indies. Enough food is grown on the fertile farmlands of the country to feed the growing population, and there is still plenty of land available for settlement.

Nearly seven out of every ten Dominicans are mulatto. Most other Domini-

cans are white or Negro. The mulattoes are descended from Spanish settlers and from Negroes who were brought to Santo Domingo as slaves. Today, most of the people think of themselves as Dominicans rather than as white or black, and work side by side with little thought of color.

Most Dominicans are Roman Catholic. However, there is complete freedom of religion, and Protestant churches are found even in some of the smaller towns.

Earning a living. About half of all Dominican workers earn their living by farming. Many farmers, particularly those in the Cibao, have their own small

257

Drying cacao on a farm in the Cibao. Chocolate and cocoa are made from these seeds. Cacao is an important export of the Dominican Republic.

plots of land. Because of the rich soil, many Dominican farmers grow more than enough food for their own needs and are able to send part of what they raise to market. Some people make their living by buying and selling food and other supplies in the marketplaces of the towns and villages.

Sugarcane is the leading export crop grown in the Dominican Republic. Many thousands of people work on sugarcane plantations in the southeastern part of the country. Most of them are Haitians who were brought to the Dominican Republic to help cut the cane. Most of the sugar mills and plantations in the Dominican Republic were once owned by the Trujillo family. They are now being managed by the government. One huge central* is owned by a United States company.

Dominican farmers also grow other crops for export. Cacao and tobacco are grown in the Cibao, and coffee is

258

cultivated on the lower slopes of the northern mountains. The Dominican Republic is the leading producer of cacao in the Caribbean Lands. Some of the cacao is made into chocolate in Dominican factories. Both chocolate and cacao are exported.

The number of Dominicans who work in manufacturing is growing. The largest industry is the processing of sugarcane to make sugar, molasses, and other products. Most of the sugar is exported to the United States or to Europe. The Dominican Republic is one of the world's important sugar producers. A by-product of sugar manufacturing is bagasse, the pulp of sugarcane. In the Dominican Republic, bagasse is used to make a liquid called furfural.* Most of the furfural is exported to the United States. Other important products manufactured in the Dominican Republic include cement, lumber, cigars, cigarettes, textiles, and shoes.

A furfural* plant. Furfural is made from bagasse, the pulp of sugarcane. An increasing number of Dominican workers are employed in manufacturing.

Modern buildings of the University of Santo Domingo. This university was founded in 1538. In recent years, many new public schools have been built in the Dominican Republic. However, there is still a shortage of schools and teachers, especially in the rural areas of the country.

Education. As part of Trujillo's program to improve the country, education was made available to more Dominicans than ever before. In 1935, seven out of every ten Dominicans could not read and write. A law passed in 1951 required every child between the ages of seven and fourteen to attend school. Special courses were organized for adults who had not learned to read and write. However, today about three out of every ten Dominicans are still illiterate.

Many Dominicans are still unable to obtain enough education. In spite of the education law of 1951, many children of school age do not attend classes. There are not enough schools or teachers. The Dominican Republic has about 4,500 elementary schools, but only 76 high schools. Although more Dominicans can read and write than ever before, most people need more education so that they will be able to do skilled work.

The University of Santo Domingo was founded in 1538. It has an enrollment of about four thousand students. Many Dominicans go abroad for their college training, especially to schools in the United States.

Transportation and communication. The rugged mountains of the Dominican Republic have helped to make transportation one of its major problems. Thirty years ago, there were almost no roads from the coast to the interior. Farmers in the Cibao found it difficult to get their products to market. Therefore, they raised only enough crops to feed themselves and left much of the land uncultivated. After Trujillo took over the government, he built roads connecting the capital with almost all parts of the republic. This permitted him to impose his dictatorship on remote areas of the country.

Today there are almost four thousand miles of roads in the Dominican Republic. About two thirds of the roads are paved. From Santo Domingo, three modern highways branch out to the north, east, and west. Smaller roads connect almost all the main towns and cities. However, more roads are needed, particularly in the mining areas of the southwest and in the lumber-producing regions in the mountains.

There are about 800 miles of railroads in the Dominican Republic. Almost all of the railroads are located on sugar plantations. The railroads are needed to transport cut sugarcane long distances from the fields to the sugar mills.

Flights of several international airlines land at Santo Domingo's modern new airport. The Dominican Republic

Modern roads branch out from Santo Domingo. Partly because of rugged mountains, transportation has been a major problem in the Dominican Republic. Many fine roads have been built in recent years, but more are needed. There are few railroads in this country.

Santo Domingo, the capital of the Dominican Republic, lies along the banks of the Ozama River. It is the country's most important seaport. Santo Domingo lies in the rich sugar-producing region of the Dominican Republic. Large quantities of sugar are shipped from this port.

has its own airline, *Compañía Dominicana de Aviación* (CDA). Airplanes of the CDA make flights to Miami, Florida, and to San Juan, Puerto Rico. The country also has a small fleet of merchant ships.

There are more than 21,000 telephones in the Dominican Republic. Most of them are located in the capital and a few of the larger towns. Although both television and radio stations operate on the island, most of the people are too poor to own radios or television sets.

Cities. Santo Domingo (population about 367,000) is the capital and largest city of the Dominican Republic. It is located on the southeastern coast of the island, at the mouth of the Ozama River. (See map on page 250.) From 1936 to 1961, Santo Domingo was called Ciudad Trujillo, or "Trujillo City."

Santo Domingo is also the chief manufacturing city in the Dominican Republic, and the country's most important seaport. It handles most of the goods entering the country. Santo Domingo lies in the sugar-producing region of the Dominican Republic, and large quantities of sugar and molasses are shipped from this port. Products manufactured in the city include rum, cement, alcohol, shoes, and clothing.

Santo Domingo is the oldest city settled by Europeans in the Western Hemisphere. A hurricane destroyed most of the city in 1930. However, many landmarks of the old Spanish colony were left standing. One of the most interesting of these landmarks is the Alcázar, a castle where Columbus' son Diego lived as governor of the early colony. This castle has been restored and furnished as it was in the early 1500's. Not far away is the cathedral of Santo Domingo, which contains the tomb of Christopher Columbus.

Most of the city has been rebuilt since the hurricane. Its broad avenues, fine parks and well-kept residential sections make it one of the most attractive capitals in the Caribbean Lands.

Santiago de los Caballeros (population about 84,000) is the second largest city in the Dominican Republic. It is located about eighty-five miles northwest of Santo Domingo, in the Cibao. Santiago de los Caballeros is the largest center for processing and distributing the products of this fertile region. Coffee and tobacco are raised near Santiago, and much lumber is obtained from the nearby mountains. Factories in Santiago manufacture cigars, cigarettes, furniture, and drugs.

Drawing Conclusions

Rafael Trujillo ruled the Dominican Republic as absolute dictator for thirty-one years. How was this man able to stay in power for so long? Answer this question by writing a paragraph in which you include the following information:

1. three ways in which Trujillo helped his country
2. three ways in which Trujillo oppressed the Dominican people
3. an explanation of how each of these six things helped to keep Trujillo in power

Facts To Review

Identify the following and explain the significance of each:

audiencia	Vega Real
junta	Cordillera Central
central	Santo Domingo

Studying Relationships

Study the map on page 250. In what general areas of the Dominican Republic are the largest cities (population 25,000 or more) located? Using the map and the text as a guide, write a short paragraph explaining the probable reasons why the cities are located in these areas.

Yes or No

Write the number of each of the following sentences on a sheet of paper. If the statement is true, write **yes** after the number. If it is not true, write **no,** and correct the statement.

1. Most people in the Dominican Republic live in the highlands, because the lowlands are hot and humid.
2. There is no shortage of farmland in the Dominican Republic.
3. Schools have been much improved in recent years, but most Dominicans are still not well educated.
4. The broad plains in the southern part of the Dominican Republic are the most fertile farming areas of the country.
5. Mainly because of the trade winds and mountains, the southern part of the Dominican Republic receives much more rainfall than the northern part.

23 Haiti

GEOGRAPHY

Land. Haiti is slightly larger than the state of Maryland. It occupies the western third of the island of Hispaniola. (See page 25.) To the east is the Dominican Republic. The map on page 250 shows that most of Haiti is made up of two peninsulas. These extend westward from the rest of Hispaniola like the open jaws of a crocodile. Between the peninsulas is the Gulf of Gonaïves.

About four fifths of Haiti is made up of mountains. Stretching all the way along the southern peninsula is a range of steep-sided mountains. The highest peak is almost nine thousand feet above sea level. Several parallel ranges of lower mountains extend from southeast to northwest across the rest of the country. Some of the mountains in Haiti are forest-covered, but most of them are

High, steep-sided mountains extend all the way along Haiti's southern peninsula. About four fifths of this country is made up of mountains.

bare of trees. High on many slopes are small patches of farmland. Where steep slopes have been cultivated, the land is badly eroded.

Between the mountain ranges and along the seacoast are patches of level lowland. Most of Haiti's people live in these areas. A narrow plain called the

---

Facts About Haiti

Area: 10,714 square miles.

Population: About 4,400,000.

Density of Population: 411 people per square mile; 2,453 people per square mile of arable* land.

Capital and Largest City: Port-au-Prince (population about 250,000).

Racial Composition: About 95 out of every 100 Haitians are Negro. Most of the rest are mulatto.

Literacy: About one tenth of the people of Haiti can read and write.

Main Language: The official language is French. Most Haitians speak Creole.

Main Religion: Roman Catholicism. Many people also practice voodoo.

Main Occupation: More than four fifths of all Haitian workers earn their living by farming.

Income: Yearly per capita income is about $70. Haiti has the lowest per capita income of any Caribbean country.

Important Farm Products: Coffee is the leading export crop. Sisal and sugarcane are also grown for export. Yams, plantains, and corn are among the crops grown for domestic use.

Natural Resources: Bauxite and forests.

Manufacturing: Haiti has very few factories. Products manufactured for local use include textiles, cement, flour, and shoes. Many Haitians are skilled at handicrafts.

Currency: Haiti's unit of money is the *gourde,* which is officially worth about 20 cents.

A field of sisal on a coastal lowland. Along the coast and between the mountain ranges of Haiti are areas of level lowland. Mountains shelter some of the lowlands from moist, cooling trade winds. These lowlands receive little rainfall and are often very hot.

Cul-de-Sac extends from the Gulf of Gonaïves eastward into the Dominican Republic. On the fertile Cul-de-Sac, there are vast fields of sugarcane. Farther north along the Gulf of Gonaïves is the broad Artibonite Plain. Haiti's longest river, the Artibonite, flows westward through this lowland. Much of this area is covered with fertile soil that the river has carried down from the mountains. Another important lowland is the Plaine du Nord, which extends along the seacoast in the northeastern part of Haiti. Here there are many fields of sugarcane and sisal.

Climate. Temperatures are not the same in all parts of Haiti. In the mountains, the weather is usually mild and pleasant. Some of the lowlands, such as the Cul-de-Sac and the Artibonite Plain, are sheltered from cooling trade winds by mountain ranges. As a result, these

lowlands are often very hot. Cool sea breezes often sweep across the lowlands along the northern and southern coasts.

The mountains of Haiti also affect rainfall. (See pages 38 and 39.) On mountain slopes facing the trade winds, rainfall is heavy. In sheltered lowland areas, such as the Cul-de-Sac and the Artibonite Plain, rainfall is so light that neither trees nor grass will grow. The ground is dotted with cactus plants and thorny shrubs. Farmers here must irrigate their fields to grow most crops.

Hurricanes sometimes cause great destruction in Haiti. In October, 1963, a hurricane struck Haiti's southern peninsula. About 5,000 people were killed, and at least 100,000 were left homeless. The violent winds and rain destroyed half of Haiti's coffee crop.

Natural resources. Bauxite is the only mineral produced in large quantities in

Haiti. The ore is mined on the southern peninsula by a United States company and shipped to the United States for processing. Haiti has no known deposits of coal or oil, so the country imports oil for heating and for producing electric power.

During colonial days, dense forests covered many mountains in Haiti. From these forests came large amounts of logwood, which was used in making a valuable dye. Mahogany and other woods used in making furniture were also taken from Haitian forests. Gradually most of the trees were cut down for lumber or charcoal, or to provide land for farming. Valuable trees still grow near the Dominican border and in the high mountains of the southern peninsula. It is hard to transport logs from these forests to sawmills, because there are no good roads.

In Haiti there are several rivers that could be used to produce hydroelectricity. However, the government lacks the money needed to build dams and power plants.

HISTORY

Spaniards come to Hispaniola. The first European explorer to visit the land we now call Haiti was Christopher Columbus. In 1492, one of his ships, the *Santa María*, was wrecked off the northern coast of Hispaniola. Here Columbus and his men built a fort called La Navidad, which was later destroyed by Indians. (See page 58.)

In the years that followed, the Spaniards founded Santo Domingo and other settlements in the eastern part of Hispaniola. However, they avoided the western part of the island. This area contained little gold or silver, and most

Rolling logs at a Haitian sawmill. Valuable trees grow near Haiti's eastern border and in the high mountains of the southern peninsula. However, most of the country's trees have been cut down for lumber or charcoal, or to clear the land for farming.

On the island of Tortue, off the northern coast of Hispaniola. In the early 1600's, French and English pirates began to settle on Tortue. Later some of them went to the western part of Hispaniola to live. Other settlers came to this area from France, and it became a French colony.

of the land appeared to be too rugged for farming.

The western part of Hispaniola becomes a French colony. About 1625, French and English pirates began to settle on the small island of Tortue, or Tortuga, off the northern coast of Hispaniola. (See map on page 250.) They used the island as a base from which to attack Spanish ships. Later, some of the pirates came to the western part of Hispaniola to hunt wild cattle and hogs. They killed these animals and smoked the meat over small wooden grills called *boucans*. For this reason, the pirates became known as "buccaneers."

As the years passed, other settlers came to Hispaniola from France. The Spanish government at Santo Domingo was not strong enough to drive them out. In 1697, Spain recognized France's claim to the western third of Hispaniola. This area became the French colony of St. Domingue.

Some of the French settlers established plantations on the Plaine du Nord and other fertile lowlands. They grew sugarcane, coffee, indigo, and other crops for export to Europe. Thousands of Negro slaves were brought from Africa to work on the plantations. In dry areas, such as the Cul-de-Sac, the French colonists built stone aqueducts to bring water for irrigating their fields.

By the late 1700's, St. Domingue was one of the richest colonies in the world. Some of the French planters had grown very wealthy. They lived in beautiful houses and had many servants to wait on them.

Life was not so pleasant for the great majority of people in St. Domingue. About 500,000 Negro slaves lived in the colony. The slaves had to work hard from dawn to sunset, and they were often treated very cruelly. Besides the Negroes, there were about 25,000 mulattoes. Although the mulattoes were

266

not slaves, they had few of the privileges enjoyed by the French colonists.

Haiti wins its independence. In 1791, the Negro slaves in St. Domingue revolted against their masters. Many Frenchmen were killed, and most of the others fled the colony. Slavery was abolished in 1793, but this failed to stop the bitter fighting between the Negroes and the French.

Gradually, a Negro general named Pierre Toussaint L'Ouverture gained control of St. Domingue. Toussaint was a wise and courageous leader. He restored law and order in the colony, and tried to repair the damage caused by years of warfare.

The ruler of France, Napoleon Bonaparte, did not want to lose this rich colony. In 1801, he sent a huge army to reconquer St. Domingue. Toussaint was tricked into surrendering and was sent to France, where he later died in prison.

France did not succeed in regaining control of St. Domingue. When the Negroes learned that Napoleon planned to restore slavery in the colony, they fought bravely against the invaders. Also, the French commander and thousands of his men died of yellow fever. At last the French were forced to leave the colony. In 1804, St. Domingue became an independent country. It was given the name of Haiti, from an Indian word meaning "land of mountains."

Haiti suffers from poverty and poor government. The new nation was faced with many problems. Most of the plantations and aqueducts had been destroyed during the war for independence. Haiti's land was divided into thousands of farms, which were generally too small to provide a good living for the people

who owned them. Most Haitians were poor and uneducated, and they lacked any experience in governing themselves.

During the next hundred years, Haiti made little progress. Exports of farm products decreased, because the former slaves did not want to work on plantations. The country had no money for roads, schools, and other improvements. One dictator after another came to power by force. Often these men became rich by stealing money from the national treasury.

The United States intervenes. By 1915, events in Haiti were causing serious concern in the United States. Several Haitian presidents had been murdered or overthrown. The Haitian government owed large sums of money to foreign businessmen. Germany and France were threatening to use force to collect these debts. World War I had started, and the United States did not want any European country to interfere in the Western Hemisphere.

To restore order in Haiti, the United States government sent marines into the country. The United States forces remained for nineteen years. During that time, schools and roads were built in Haiti. Hospitals were established, and efforts were made to eliminate malaria and other diseases. American officials collected taxes on Haiti's imports and exports and used the money to pay off Haiti's debts. In spite of these accomplishments, the Haitian people did not like having foreign troops in their country. The marines were finally withdrawn in 1934.

Haiti still does not have democratic government. The United States occupation did not solve all of Haiti's problems.

After 1934, the country was ruled by a series of strong leaders. While they were in office, some of these men encouraged farming and industry and brought about some much-needed reforms. However, they seldom allowed people to express any opposition to their rule.

In 1957, a doctor named François Duvalier was elected president of Haiti. Shortly afterward, he began ruling as a dictator. He dismissed the elected parliament and set up a new one with members chosen by himself. Many people who opposed him were killed or thrown into prison. In 1964, Duvalier announced that he would remain president of Haiti for the rest of his life. The United States has stopped giving money to Haiti because it does not want to aid this cruel dictator.

THE PEOPLE AND HOW THEY LIVE

People. With almost four and one-half million people living in a small area, Haiti is one of the most densely popu-

Expensive modern homes in Port-au-Prince. A very small part of Haiti's population is wealthy. These people make up a group called the "élite."

lated countries in the Western Hemisphere. Since much of the land in this mountainous country is too steep for farming, most of Haiti's people are crowded into the lowlands.

About ninety-five out of every hundred Haitians are Negro. Most of the rest are mulattoes who are descended from Negro slaves and early French settlers. Nearly all of the mulattoes belong to a small group of wealthy, well-educated people known as the *élite*.

Members of the *élite* usually live in expensive modern homes in the city of Port-au-Prince. These people speak French, the official language of Haiti. They are proud of their French ancestors and their knowledge of French culture. Most of the *élite* are Roman Catholic, but some are members of Protestant churches.

The great majority of people in Haiti are poor peasants who have had little or no education. They live on small farms or in villages dotting the countryside.

In a Haitian village. The great majority of people in Haiti are poor peasants who live on small farms or in villages dotting the countryside.

268

The peasants speak a language known as Creole, which has an interesting history. When settlers from France came to Hispaniola during the 1600's, the French that they spoke was very different from the French language of today. Their Negro slaves learned this language, which was handed down from one generation to the next. Although it is based on the language spoken by the early French settlers, Creole also contains African, English, Spanish, and Indian words.

Most Haitian peasants belong to the Roman Catholic Church, but nearly all of them also practice voodoo. This is a form of religion that was brought from Africa by Negro slaves. Followers of voodoo believe that their lives are influenced by invisible spirits. They think that they can communicate with these spirits by singing, dancing, and playing on drums.

Earning a living. More than four fifths of all workers in Haiti make their living by farming. No other country in the Western Hemisphere except Honduras has such a large part of its population working in agriculture. Some Haitians work on large plantations. However, most Haitians have small farms of their own. Because so many people are farmers and so much of the land is rugged, there is a shortage of good farmland. The average farm covers less than three acres.

A voodoo ceremony. Although most Haitian peasants belong to the Roman Catholic Church, nearly all of them also practice voodoo, a religion brought from Africa by Negro slaves. They believe that invisible spirits influence their lives and that they can communicate with these spirits.

Farming is Haiti's leading occupation. Most farms in Haiti are small and not very productive. Because most of the people are farmers and much of the land is rugged, there is a shortage of good farmland. Haitian farmers earn little money, but generally raise enough food for their families.

Most farms in Haiti are not very productive. Usually the farmer's only tools are a hoe and a large knife called a machete. He cannot afford to buy tractors and other modern farm implements. Because of the shortage of farmland in Haiti, many steep slopes must be cultivated. As a result, wind and water have eroded much of the topsoil. In addition, farmers plant the same crop over and over again on the same land. This practice wears out the soil very rapidly. Most farmers cannot afford to buy fertilizer to replace the plant foods that have been taken from the soil. In some areas, the land is too dry to produce good crops.

Efforts have been made to help the farmers of Haiti. Experts sent by the United Nations and the United States government have tried to improve farming methods. A dam has been built on the Artibonite River to store water for irrigating fields on the dry Artibonite Plain. Irrigation is also used on the Cul-de-Sac and other dry lowlands, but more is needed.

Most Haitian farmers earn very little money. The per capita income in Haiti is only about $70 a year. However, Haitian farmers generally can live on a very small income. They grow corn, yams, plantains, and other crops to feed their families. Some of them own a few chickens, pigs, or goats. If the members of a family raise more food than they need, they take the surplus to a market and sell it. Haitian women, carrying large baskets of goods on their heads, often walk many miles to a marketplace.

With the money they receive from selling their goods, the peasants buy the few manufactured items that they need. About the only things that they have to buy are clothing, oil for their lamps, and a few cooking utensils. The peasants make their own furniture and live in small houses that they have built themselves. These houses usually have walls made of boards covered with clay, and roofs made of palm leaves or straw.

Coffee trees grow on many Haitian farms. The Haitian farmers give the trees very little care, but the coffee produced is noted for its excellent flavor. Coffee is Haiti's most important export.

Other export crops include sugarcane and sisal. Sugarcane is grown on the Cul-de-Sac, the Plaine du Nord, and other fertile lowlands. There are large sisal plantations on parts of the Plaine du Nord and in dry areas near Port-au-Prince. Sisal is a desert plant that grows well with little water. Its fibers are used in making rope.

Haiti has very little industry. A few small factories make cement, flour, shoes, textiles, and other goods for local use. Haitian workers seldom have a chance to learn the skills needed in modern industry. However, many of them are very skilled at handicrafts. From mahogany and other valuable woods, Haitian craftsmen make trays and bowls that are highly prized for their beauty. Haitian women make excellent baskets from sisal and palm-leaf fibers.

Sorting coffee beans. Haiti's main export is coffee. Although the coffee trees receive little care, the coffee that they produce is noted for its excellent flavor. Sugarcane and sisal are also important export crops. There is very little manufacturing in Haiti.

271

A river in Haiti. Peasants in rural areas often get water from rivers that are unclean. Even most towns in Haiti do not have pure water supplies or good sewer systems. Health conditions in Haiti are very poor, and such diseases as malaria, tuberculosis, and hookworm are common.

Health. In Haiti, health conditions are very poor. One reason is a lack of proper sanitation. Most Haitian towns do not have good sewer systems or pure water supplies. In rural areas, people often get water from rivers that are unclean. Also, many Haitians cannot obtain the variety of foods needed for good health. Often large families are crowded together in small, unsanitary huts. It is not surprising that such diseases as malaria, tuberculosis, and hookworm are very common. Throughout Haiti, there is a serious shortage of doctors and hospitals. Clinics have been started in some rural areas, but many more are needed.

Education. About nine out of every ten people in Haiti cannot read and write. No other country in the Western Hemisphere has such a low rate of literacy. Education is free in Haiti, but there are not enough schools or teachers. Many children live too far away to walk to towns where schools are located, and they have no other means of transportation. The only school buses in Haiti are in Port-au-Prince. Some children cannot go to school because they have to help their parents with farm work. In Haiti, only one out of every five children of school age attends school regularly.

Few Haitian children receive more than an elementary-school education. There are fewer than 50 high schools in the entire country. Small numbers of students attend teacher-training or job-training schools. The University of Haiti, in Port-au-Prince, has about 1,500 students. It offers courses in law, medicine, engineering, and a few other fields.

Transportation and communication. It is difficult and costly to build roads in Haiti because the country is so mountainous. The government does not have enough money to build many roads and to keep them in good repair. There are about four hundred miles of paved roads in Haiti, but even these are in poor condition. Haiti has about 1,500 miles of unpaved roads. During the rainy season, most of these roads are too muddy to be used. Sometimes bridges and sections of road are washed away by flooding rivers. Hundreds of small villages in Haiti are connected only by footpaths and donkey trails.

There are two short railroad lines in Haiti. Both lines connect Port-au-Prince with nearby towns. They are used mainly to haul sugarcane and other kinds of freight.

Water transportation is important in Haiti. Nearly all of the large towns are seaports. Sailboats and a few motor launches carry passengers and freight from one port to another. Haiti is served by shipping lines from the United States, Panama, France, and other countries.

The planes of several foreign airlines stop at Haiti's international airport, near Port-au-Prince. A local airline run by the Haitian Air Force connects the country's main cities and towns.

Haiti lacks a good system of communications. There is only one telephone for every thousand persons. Even in Port-au-Prince, telephone service is poor. The country has fewer than twenty radio stations, and one television station. There are only a few newspapers in Haiti. They have a total circulation of about 20,000.

An unpaved road after heavy rains. During the rainy season, most of the unpaved roads in Haiti are too muddy to be used. Haiti has only about four hundred miles of paved roads, and even these are in poor condition. Many villages are connected only by footpaths and donkey trails.

Cities. About one tenth of the people of Haiti live in cities or large towns. The only large city is Port-au-Prince, the capital.

Port-au-Prince (population about 250,000) lies along the Gulf of Gonaïves at the western end of the fertile Cul-de-Sac. (See map on page 250.) The city has a fine harbor and is Haiti's leading seaport. Sugar, rum, coffee, bananas, and other products are exported from this city. There are sugar mills, rice mills, and textile factories in the area.

Port-au-Prince is an interesting city to visit. It stretches between wooded hills and the deep-blue waters of the gulf. In the downtown section are wide avenues lined with churches, shops, and government buildings. Only a few blocks away, however, there are dirty, crowded slums. Port-au-Prince has a large marketplace, called the Iron Market, where peasants come to sell their goods.

The Iron Market in Port-au-Prince is a large marketplace where peasants come to sell their goods. Port-au-Prince is Haiti's capital and only large city. It has a fine harbor and is the country's leading seaport. About one tenth of the people of Haiti live in cities or large towns.

Cap Haitien (population about 36,000) is Haiti's second largest city. It is located on the northern coast, at the edge of the Plaine du Nord. Until 1770, this city was the capital of the French colony of St. Domingue. Today, it is noted for its beautiful old houses, which are painted in bright colors and decorated with balconies.

On a mountain peak near Cap Haitien are the ruins of a huge fortress called the Citadel. (See picture at right.) The Citadel was built by King Henri Christophe, who ruled over the northern part of Haiti in the early 1800's. Thousands of laborers worked for sixteen years to construct this fortress, which has been called "the eighth wonder of the world."

Ruins of the Citadel, a huge fortress near Cap Haitien, Haiti's second largest city. The Citadel was built by King Henri Christophe.

Studying the People of Haiti
1. Why do you think such a large number of Haitians are Negro?
2. What is meant by the term *élite* in referring to some of the people of Haiti?
3. What does "Creole" mean in Haiti?

Reviewing Haiti's History
1. Why did few Spaniards settle in the western part of Hispaniola? How did the French happen to settle in this part of the island?
2. How did the French settlers make their living in the 1700's?
3. Explain how Haiti gained its independence.
4. Name at least four problems Haiti faced after gaining its independence.
5. Why did the United States intervene in the affairs of Haiti in the early 1900's?

Exploring Relationships
1. Name two ways in which the mountains of Haiti affect the weather on the Cul-de-Sac and the Artibonite Plain.

2. What does the name Haiti mean? Why is it a good name for this country?
3. Give three reasons why health conditions in Haiti are so poor.
4. Give two examples to show that the craftsmen of Haiti make use of products from the country's forests and farms.

Learning From Pictures
Farm production in Haiti is not very high, despite the fact that more than four out of every five Haitian workers are farmers. Study the pictures and captions on pages 263, 264, and 270. What do they tell you about the difficulties of farming in Haiti? Write a short paragraph telling what you have learned.

Finding More Information
The picture on page 269 illustrates a Haitian voodoo ceremony. Read about this religion in encyclopedias and other outside sources. Then report to your class what you have learned. You may wish to tell what you think the people in this picture are doing.

Facts About Jamaica

Area: 4,411 square miles.

Population: About 1,700,000.

Density of Population: 385 people per square mile; 1,914 people per square mile of arable* land.

Capital and Largest City: Kingston (population about 141,000).

Racial Composition: Almost all of the people of Jamaica are either Negro or of mixed Negro and white ancestry. Only about two out of every one hundred are white.

Literacy: About three fourths of the people can read and write.

Main Language: English.

Main Religion: Most of the people are members of Protestant churches, such as the Church of England.

Main Occupation: About half of the workers earn their living by farming. Others work in mines, factories, or businesses that provide services to tourists.

Income: Yearly per capita income is about $355. Most Jamaicans are able to live on a small income, because they grow or make many of the things they need.

Important Farm Products: Sugarcane and bananas are Jamaica's leading export crops. Rice, sweet potatoes, and coconuts are among the foods raised for domestic use.

Natural Resources: Bauxite and gypsum. Jamaica is the world's largest producer of bauxite.

Manufacturing: Processing sugarcane and other products from the island's farms is an important type of manufacturing in Jamaica.

Currency: Jamaica's unit of money is the Jamaican pound, which is officially worth about $2.80.

GEOGRAPHY

Land. About 90 miles south of Cuba lies the island of Jamaica. (See map on pages 14 and 15.) This island extends

A valley on Jamaica. About two thirds of the island of Jamaica consists of a limestone plateau which is broken by many hills and valleys.

generally from east to west for about 150 miles and at its widest point is about 50 miles from north to south. It is about the size of the state of Connecticut. Jamaica was a British colony until it gained its independence in 1962. It is a member of the British Commonwealth.

Most of Jamaica consists of highlands. A limestone plateau makes up about two thirds of the island. At its highest point, this plateau is about three thousand feet above sea level. In some places, it extends directly to the sea and forms a coastline with steep cliffs one thousand feet high.

The plateau area of Jamaica is not level. It is broken up by many hills, valleys, and sinkholes. In Jamaica these sinkholes are called cockpits. Some of them are as much as five hundred feet deep and one-half mile wide. They have been caused by underground streams that have dissolved the limestone formation and caused the surface of the plateau to cave in. A large area in the northwestern part of the island is called the Cockpit Country because of the large number of these sinkholes. This is a barren area, where few people live.

In other parts of the plateau, there are large basins. One of these, the Vale of Clarendon, is twenty-five miles wide and fifty miles long. Many people live in these basins because the rich, red soil found here makes excellent farmland.

In the eastern part of Jamaica are the Blue Mountains, which are noted for their rugged beauty. The tops of the Blue Mountains are almost always hidden in rain clouds. This gives them a misty-blue appearance. The highest mountain on Jamaica is Blue Mountain Peak, which rises 7,520 feet above sea level.

Only a small part of Jamaica is made up of lowlands. Most of the lowlands lie along the coast. The soil in these coastal plains is generally fertile, and most of the people in Jamaica make their homes here. The Liguanea Plain on the southeastern coast is one of the most important lowland areas. Kingston, the capital of Jamaica, is located on this plain.

Climate. The weather in most parts of Jamaica is pleasantly warm the year around. It attracts thousands of tourists each year. Although the coastal lowlands are hot and humid, cooling breezes from the sea bring relief from the heat. Daytime temperatures at Kingston range between 80 and 86 degrees throughout the year. In the highlands, it is much cooler, with the temperature sometimes dropping below 50 degrees.

Rainfall in Jamaica varies considerably from place to place. In the northeastern part of the island, trade winds sweep in over the Blue Mountains. Here, more than two hundred inches of rain may fall in a single year. Kingston, which lies in the rain* shadow of the

The island of Jamaica. Most of Jamaica is made up of highlands. Along the coast, there are level lowland areas. The soil in these coastal plains is generally fertile, and most of Jamaica's people make their homes here.

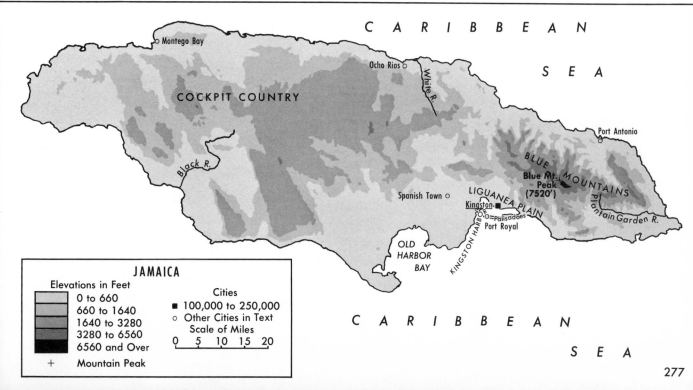

A bauxite-processing plant on Jamaica. Jamaica is the world's leading producer of bauxite, an ore from which aluminum is made. Most of the bauxite is mined by foreign companies. Gypsum is the only other mineral produced in large amounts on Jamaica.

mountains, usually receives only about thirty inches of rainfall each year. It is necessary to irrigate fields in the southern part of the island in order to grow most crops.

Jamaica lies in the hurricane belt. Violent tropical storms have sometimes damaged crops and caused loss of life on the island.

Natural resources. Jamaica is one of the few countries of the Caribbean Lands region that have any wealth in mineral resources. It is the world's leading producer of bauxite, an ore from which aluminum is made. Most of the bauxite is mined by a large Canadian aluminum company and several United States firms. The Canadian company operates plants in Jamaica that refine bauxite into a substance called alumina. This substance is then shipped to Canada and other countries for final processing into aluminum. The American companies ship bauxite to the United States for all stages of processing.

Bauxite and alumina are Jamaica's leading exports. More than half of all money received from exports comes from these valuable products.

Gypsum is the only other mineral produced in large quantities on Jamaica. It is used to make cement and plasterboard. Some of the gypsum is exported to the United States.

In many parts of Jamaica, swift streams race down from the highlands to the sea. Some of these streams have been dammed to store water for cities and towns or for irrigating farmland. Others are used to produce hydroelectric power.

HISTORY

Spaniards settle on Jamaica. Christopher Columbus discovered Jamaica in 1494 and claimed the island for Spain. The Spaniards first settled on the northern coast but later moved to the southern part of the island. Here they established a settlement that later became known as Spanish Town. (See map on page 277.) Jamaica was a Spanish colony for about 150 years. During this time, the island was used mainly as a base to supply expeditions on their way to the mainland. The peaceful Arawak Indians who lived on Jamaica were enslaved and forced to work for the Spaniards. These Indians soon died from disease and overwork. Negro slaves were imported from Africa to replace them.

The English occupy Jamaica. In 1655, an English fleet attacked Jamaica. This fleet had been sent to capture a Spanish base in the Caribbean for use by England. There were only about three thousand Spanish colonists and Negro slaves on Jamaica. The English quickly captured Spanish Town. The Spaniards were driven from the island, and most of the slaves fled into the mountains.

Jamaica becomes a base for buccaneers. After capturing Jamaica, the English established a town called Port Royal at the end of a long peninsula that separates Kingston Harbor from the sea. Soon afterward, English pirates in the West Indies made Port Royal their home port. This town soon became one of the richest and wickedest cities in the New World. From Port Royal, the buccaneers raided Spanish shipping and settlements throughout the Caribbean region. They returned to Port Royal with their rich booty and spent their days and nights in wild gambling and drinking.

In 1692, a great earthquake destroyed most of Port Royal. A large part of the town sank beneath the sea. The people who survived this disaster moved across the bay and founded Kingston, the present capital of Jamaica.

Sugar brings prosperity to Jamaica. Under British rule, Jamaica became a wealthy colony. British landowners planted sugarcane, coffee, and cacao on large estates. Many thousands of slaves were brought from Africa to do the hard work on these large farms. During the 1700's, Jamaica became one of the world's leading sugar producers.

Slavery comes to an end in Jamaica. In 1838, the British gave the slaves of Jamaica their freedom. Many of the freed slaves deserted the sugar estates and fled to the interior of the island, where they started small farms for themselves. To replace the slaves on the sugar plantations, laborers were brought to Jamaica from India and China. This greatly increased the cost of labor on the plantations. At the same time, the price paid for sugar in Europe dropped suddenly. As a result, most of the large sugar estates failed. In 1842, there were nineteen plantations on which sugarcane was grown. By 1864, only one of these plantations was still in operation.

Ruins of an old sugar mill. During the 1700's, Jamaica became one of the world's leading sugar producers. Sugar brought much wealth to the island.

After the decline in sugarcane cultivation, Jamaica became a land of small farms. The farmers were mainly freed slaves who grew barely enough to feed their families. Many Jamaicans left the island during this period to work on sugar plantations on neighboring islands or on banana plantations in Central America.

In the years after 1870, Jamaicans began to grow large quantities of bananas for export. The country began to prosper from the sale of this crop. However, just before World War II, a plant sickness called Panama disease almost completely destroyed the banana plants in Jamaica. A type of banana plant that resists Panama disease is now grown in Jamaica. In recent years, both sugar and bananas have again become important export products.

Jamaica gains its independence. Jamaica is one of the newest independent nations in the Western Hemisphere. The island became partly self-governing about twenty years ago. In 1958, Jamaica joined other British islands in the Caribbean to form the West Indies Federation. In 1961, Jamaica voted to leave this federation. The following year, Jamaica became an independent nation within the British Commonwealth. The queen of England is still considered the queen of Jamaica and appoints a governor-general as her representative on the island. However, Jamaica is a completely self-governing nation.

THE PEOPLE AND HOW THEY LIVE

People. The most densely populated parts of the island of Jamaica are the lowland plains and fertile plateau basins. Although almost half of the people live on farms and plantations, many Jamaicans have been moving to the cities in recent years. About one fourth of all the people live in or near the city of Kingston. Many Jamaicans are forced to live in slums because they cannot find jobs after they come to the cities.

More than three fourths of the people of Jamaica are Negroes whose ancestors were brought from Africa as slaves. Most other Jamaicans are of mixed Negro and white ancestry. There are also small groups of people whose ancestors came to Jamaica from China and India in the 1800's. Only about two Jamaicans out of every hundred are white.

Jamaica was a British colony for about 300 years, and today Jamaicans observe many British customs. Many of them are members of the Church of England. English is the official language. However, most Jamaicans speak English with an accent that Americans find difficult to understand.

A judge and other officials at the opening of a court session in Kingston. Jamaica is a self-governing nation within the British Commonwealth.

280

In a sugar mill. Almost one third of all Jamaican farm workers are employed in the sugar industry. Some are hired by large estates to cut cane or to do other farm work. Others grow sugarcane on their own small farms and sell it to the estates, where it is processed.

Jamaica is one of the most densely populated countries of the Caribbean Lands. There is neither enough good farmland nor enough industry to provide jobs for all of the Jamaican workers. Large numbers of Jamaicans leave the island each year to find work elsewhere. Until recently, many went to live in Great Britain. Today, a British law makes it difficult for them to move to that country.

Earning a living. About one half of the workers of Jamaica are farmers. Most farmers own small plots of land on which they grow such food crops as rice, sweet potatoes, cabbages, and coconuts. They use most of this food for themselves and their families, and sell what is left over in nearby towns and villages. Jamaica does not grow enough food for all of its people, and food products must be imported from other countries.

Almost one third of all farm workers in Jamaica are employed in the sugar

industry. Many of them grow sugarcane on their own small farms and sell it to the large sugar estates, where it is made into raw sugar. Other Jamaicans are hired by the estates to cut cane or to do other farm work. Many of these laborers work only during the harvest season, which lasts about half the year. There are about twenty sugar estates on the island. They produce almost 500,000 tons of sugar each year. Molasses and rum are also produced. Large quantities of these products are exported to other countries.

Jamaica is one of the world's important banana-producing countries. Nine tenths of all the bananas are grown on a few large estates. However, this fruit is also grown on thousands of small farms. Many of these farms cover less than five acres of land. Unlike sugarcane, bananas can be harvested all year round. They provide a steady source of income to poor farmers who may sell

281

just a stem or two of bananas each week throughout the year. Most of the bananas grown in Jamaica are exported.

Other important crops that are grown in Jamaica for export are cacao, coffee, citrus fruits, and allspice. Jamaica is one of the few countries in the world that produces allspice. This flavorful spice comes from berries of the pimento tree.

Mining and manufacturing are growing in importance in Jamaica. Bauxite is the island's most valuable product. However, bauxite mining and processing provide jobs for only a few thousand Jamaicans because most of the work is done by machines.

One of Jamaica's most important sources of income is the tourist industry. Each year, more than 200,000 tourists visit Jamaica and spend many millions of dollars. On the northern coast of the island, towns such as Montego Bay, Ocho Rios, and Port Antonio have become world-famous resorts. Many beautiful hotels have been built here to serve the tourists. Thousands of Jamaicans work in these hotels and in shops that sell Jamaican products to tourists. Others work in restaurants or as taxi drivers.

Transportation and communication. Jamaica has a better system of roads than most other countries of the Caribbean Lands region. A network of about nine thousand miles of roads connects most cities and towns on the island. Almost one third of the roads are paved, and most of the unpaved roads are usable even during the rainy season. The most

Tourists at a straw market in Kingston. Each year, more than 200,000 tourists visit Jamaica and spend millions of dollars. The tourist industry is one of the island's most important sources of income. Many Jamaicans work in shops that sell Jamaican products to tourists.

A highway on Jamaica. This island has a better system of roads than most other Caribbean countries. Almost one third of its roads are paved.

important road in Jamaica is a highway that runs along much of the coast. Several other good highways cross the highlands and connect Kingston with towns on the northern coast.

Modern international airports are located at both Kingston and Montego Bay. Flights from other parts of the Western Hemisphere and from Europe land on Jamaica. Air travel to the island has increased considerably in recent years. About 150,000 visitors come to Jamaica by plane each year.

The most important seaports in Jamaica are Kingston and Port Antonio. Most of the exports and imports of the island are shipped through Kingston. Port Antonio is an important banana port. Cruise ships dock mainly at Kingston. In 1962, more than 60,000 tourists traveling on cruise ships stopped in Jamaica.

Jamaica does not have a good system of communications. More than three fourths of the country's telephones are located in Kingston. There are several radio stations and one television station on the island.

Education. Jamaica needs many more schools. Only about one half of the children of elementary-school age are able to attend school. Few students go on to high school. The government of Jamaica is making an effort to relieve the school shortage and to train more teachers. Trade Training Centers provide one-year courses to train young Jamaicans as carpenters, electricians, plumbers, and mechanics. The United States government is cooperating in this training program.

Jamaica is the home of the first university established in the British Caribbean colonies. It is called the University College of the West Indies. This university was founded to provide higher education for students from British possessions throughout the Caribbean area. It began classes in 1948, and includes schools of science, arts, and medicine.

Cities. Kingston is the only city in Jamaica with a population of more than 15,000. Montego Bay, Port Antonio, and Ocho Rios on the northern coast of the island are important chiefly as resort towns for tourists.

Graduation night at the University College of the West Indies, in Kingston. Many more teachers and schools are needed in Jamaica.

Kingston, Jamaica's capital, spreads across a coastal plain into the foothills of the Blue Mountains. This city is the island's chief port.

Kingston (population about 141,000) is the capital and largest city of Jamaica. It is located on the southern coast and spreads across the Liguanea Plain into the foothills of the Blue Mountains.

Kingston is situated along one of the best harbors in the Caribbean Lands. The deep bay which forms Kingston Harbor is protected from the sea by a narrow, sandy peninsula called the Palisadoes. At the end of this peninsula lie the ruins of the town of Port Royal. Kingston is Jamaica's chief port. Sugar, bananas, and other products of the fertile Liguanea Plain are exported through Kingston Harbor.

The capital is also important as a manufacturing city. Clothing, furniture, drugs, cigars, and many other products are made in Kingston. A Jamaican government agency has set aside several hundred acres of land to be used for new factory sites. Many plants have already been built by the government and have been rented or sold to new industries starting operations in the capital.

Kingston was destroyed by an earthquake in 1907 and has since been rebuilt. Modern bank buildings, shops, and government offices are located near the center of town. In the suburbs, there are ranch-type homes like those found in the United States, as well as shopping centers and supermarkets. However, many of the people of Kingston live in crowded slums. Here most of the houses are unpainted shacks made of packing cases and scraps of old metal.

Think and Write

1. In what parts of Jamaica do most of the people live?
2. What was the main use the Spaniards made of Jamaica during the 150 years they controlled this island? Why was Jamaica valuable to the English from about 1655 to 1860? Give two reasons.
3. Why have large numbers of Jamaicans left the island? Where have many of them gone? Why might there be less emigration from now on? (Information on page 90 will help you answer the last question.)
4. Why is banana production especially important to the poor farmers of Jamaica?

5. Although Jamaica is the world's leading producer of bauxite, only a few thousand Jamaicans are employed in mining and processing this resource. Why is such a small part of the island's working population employed in this industry?

Finding More Information

Bauxite is Jamaica's most valuable mineral. Read about bauxite and aluminum in at least one outside source. Then write a short report based on the following topics:

a. how bauxite is mined
b. how bauxite is processed into alumina
c. how aluminum is made from alumina

25 Puerto Rico

Problems To Solve

Since 1940, the Puerto Rican government has been successfully carrying out a program, called "Operation Bootstrap," to improve living conditions on the island. **Why has Operation Bootstrap been successful?** Make several hypotheses in solving this problem. The following questions suggest some hypotheses:

a. What facts about the government of Puerto Rico help to solve this problem?

b. What facts about Puerto Rico's ties to the United States help to solve it?

c. What facts about the tourist industry help to solve it?

See TO THE STUDENT, pages 6-7.

GEOGRAPHY

Land. Puerto Rico is the easternmost island in the Greater Antilles and the smallest of the four main islands in this group. (Compare map on pages 14 and 15 with map on page 16.) This island is somewhat smaller than the state of Connecticut.

There is very little level land on Puerto Rico. Rugged mountains extend from east to west through the central part of the island. These mountains are generally steep-sided. No peak is much more than four thousand feet above sea level. In some places, small farms cling to the mountainsides. There is also a mountainous area in the northeastern part of Puerto Rico. Rainfall is very heavy in this area, and some of the mountain slopes are covered with dense tropical rainforest.

Rolling hills border the central mountains on the north and the south. At one time, the area north of the mountains was a limestone plateau. Wind and rainwater have eroded some of the limestone, forming steep cliffs, deep holes, and hills shaped like haystacks.

Except for a few small inland valleys, the only level area on Puerto Rico is a narrow coastal plain that fringes the island. Some of the island's most fertile soil is in the coastal plain. Green fields of sugarcane cover much of the land here.

Climate. Most of Puerto Rico has a warm, pleasant climate. The temperature does not change much from one

A tobacco farm in the mountains of Puerto Rico. There is very little level land on this island. In places, small farms cling to the mountainsides.

285

season to another. Along the coasts, the average temperature is about eighty degrees during the summer and about seventy-five degrees during the winter. At higher altitudes, temperatures are usually a few degrees cooler. In Puerto Rico, the sun shines for at least a short time every day.

The mountains of Puerto Rico affect rainfall on this island. Throughout the year, moist trade winds blow toward Puerto Rico from the northeast, producing orographic rainfall. (See page 39.) These winds bring more than one hundred inches of rain a year to mountain slopes in the northeastern part of the island.

Rainfall varies between forty and eighty inches a year in most of Puerto Rico. Some areas in the central mountains receive more than eighty inches. The driest area is the southwestern part of the island, which lies in the rain* shadow of the highest mountains. In this area, the yearly rainfall is only

Rainforest covers some of the mountain slopes in northeastern Puerto Rico, where rainfall is heavy. Most of the island has a warm, pleasant climate.

Facts About Puerto Rico

Area: 3,435 square miles.

Population: About 2,500,000.

Density of Population: 728 people per square mile; 1,993 people per square mile of arable* land.

Capital and Largest City: San Juan (population about 432,000).

Racial Composition: About three fourths of all Puerto Ricans are white. Most of the rest are of mixed ancestry.

Literacy: Almost nine tenths of the people can read and write.

Main Language: Spanish.

Main Religion: Roman Catholicism.

Main Occupations: About one fourth of the workers are farmers and about one fourth have jobs in businesses that provide services to other people. About one sixth work in factories. However, the number of people who earn their living in manufacturing is growing rapidly.

Income: Yearly per capita income is about $685. In the Caribbean Lands, only the Virgin Islands of the United States has a higher per capita income than Puerto Rico.

Important Farm Products: Sugarcane is Puerto Rico's most important export crop. Coffee, tobacco, fruits, vegetables, and livestock are also raised.

Natural Resources: Waterpower, clay, limestone, and salt.

Manufacturing: Food processing is the main kind of industry. Cement, textiles, tobacco products, plastics, and many other products are also manufactured.

Currency: United States money is the official currency of Puerto Rico.

about thirty inches. Farmers in this part of the island must use irrigation to grow most crops. Between June and October, hurricanes sometimes strike Puerto Rico. (See page 46.)

Natural resources. Puerto Rico is very poor in natural resources. It has no deposits of mineral fuels, such as coal and

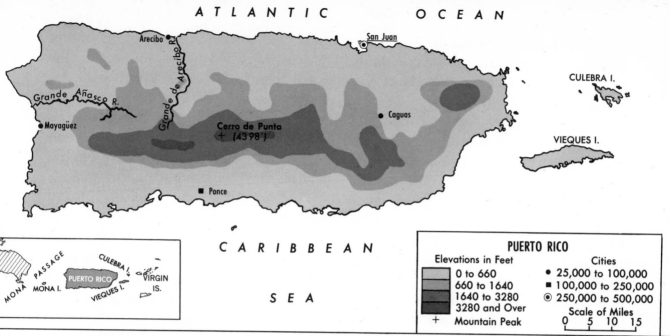

ATLANTIC OCEAN

Arecibo
San Juan
CULEBRA I.
Grande Añasco R.
Grande de Arecibo R.
Mayagüez
Cerro de Punta
+ (4398')
Caguas
VIEQUES I.
Ponce

CARIBBEAN

SEA

MONA PASSAGE
CULEBRA I.
PUERTO RICO
VIRGIN IS.
MONA I.
VIEQUES I.

PUERTO RICO

Elevations in Feet | Cities
0 to 660 | ● 25,000 to 100,000
660 to 1640 | ■ 100,000 to 250,000
1640 to 3280 | ◉ 250,000 to 500,000
3280 and Over
+ Mountain Peak | Scale of Miles
0   5   10   15

Puerto Rico is the smallest of the four main islands in the Greater Antilles. Rugged mountains extend from east to west through the central part of Puerto Rico. Rolling hills border these mountains on the north and the south.

oil. It lacks iron ore and other ores containing metals needed by industry. About the only valuable minerals produced on Puerto Rico are limestone, clay, and salt. Limestone is quarried in fairly large quantities. It is used in making cement and as a building stone. Clay found on Puerto Rico is used to make bricks, tiles, and pottery. In the southwestern part of the island, salt is obtained by evaporating seawater.

At one time, forests covered much of Puerto Rico. However, most of the trees were cut down long ago to make room for the growing population. The wood was needed for building houses and for making charcoal, which was used as a fuel. Today, there are few forests left on the island.

Puerto Rico has made good use of limited water resources. Although there are many rivers on the island, all of them are shallow. Small valleys between the steep mountains provide little space for water storage. Only high dams can

hold back enough water to produce much electric power. Every possible site for building a dam has been used. This full development of waterpower has helped to make electricity available for new industries in Puerto Rico.

Water is also used for irrigation, especially in the dry southwestern part of the island. More than sixteen thousand acres of land in this area are being irrigated with water from mountain streams. Irrigation has made it possible to grow sugarcane and other crops here.

HISTORY

Spain controls Puerto Rico for nearly four hundred years. The first Europeans to come to the island of Puerto Rico were explorers sent by Spain. Columbus discovered the island in 1493, on his second voyage to the New World. One of the men who accompanied him was a young Spaniard named Juan Ponce de León. Fifteen years later, Ponce de León founded the first Spanish settlement on

287

Puerto Rico. This settlement was located on the northern coast of the island, near the present site of the city of San Juan.

The early Spanish settlers found gold and large numbers of Indians on Puerto Rico. They forced the Indians to work in gold mines and on farms. Soon other Spaniards were coming to Puerto Rico in search of wealth. However, the Spanish settlers were disappointed. The amount of gold on Puerto Rico proved to be small. Most of the Indians died from overwork or from diseases brought by the Spaniards. To replace the Indian workers, the Spaniards began to import Negro slaves from Africa.

Puerto Rico was important to Spain because of its location. Ships from Europe could enter and leave the Caribbean Sea through Mona Passage, which

A statue of Ponce de León, who founded the first Spanish settlement on Puerto Rico. Spain controlled this island for nearly four hundred years.

lies west of the island. This is one of the main passageways connecting the Caribbean with the main part of the Atlantic Ocean. For this reason, Puerto Rico was important to the defense of other Spanish colonies in the Caribbean region. Between the early 1500's and the end of the 1700's, Puerto Rico was attacked many times by English, French, and Dutch fleets.

Puerto Rico did not become prosperous under Spanish rule. Most of the people lived in small settlements on the coastal plain, where they earned a poor living by raising sugarcane and other crops and by grazing cattle. Few Spanish trading ships came to the island. Spain had forbidden the Puerto Ricans to trade with other countries, so the colonists lacked markets for their crops. Therefore, they began to trade secretly with traders from England and other European countries. Cattle, tobacco, ginger, and other products were exchanged for slaves and cloth.

During the 1800's, changes began to take place in Puerto Rico. For the first time, Spain allowed the island to trade with other countries. This made it easier for Puerto Ricans to export their crops. Many people moved to the highlands and began to grow coffee, which became one of Puerto Rico's leading exports. Spain encouraged immigrants to come to Puerto Rico by offering them free land. People came not only from Spain but also from several other European countries and from the United States. However, the island still did not become prosperous.

Puerto Rico becomes a possession of the United States. In 1898, Spain signed a treaty that gave Puerto Rico to the

A sugar plantation. In 1898, Puerto Rico became a possession of the United States. Shortly afterward, a few American companies established huge sugar plantations on the island. By using modern farming methods, they greatly increased Puerto Rico's sugar production.

United States. This treaty was a result of the Spanish-American War, in which Spain had been defeated. (See page 79.)

At first, the United States gave the Puerto Ricans little opportunity to govern themselves. Nearly all of their government officials were appointed by the president of the United States. In 1917, the Puerto Ricans were granted United States citizenship and the right to elect their own lawmaking body. However, the governor and other high-ranking officials of Puerto Rico continued to be appointed by the president.

Many improvements were made in Puerto Rico under United States rule. Schools and roads were built on the island. Hundreds of teachers from the United States came to Puerto Rico to teach the people how to read and write. The government helped to eliminate yellow fever and other diseases. A few

American companies established huge sugar plantations on the island. By using modern farming methods, they greatly increased Puerto Rico's sugar production.

In spite of United States aid, Puerto Rico was known as the "poorhouse of the Caribbean." Because health conditions were better than before, fewer people died of disease. The population of Puerto Rico grew rapidly. Many people on this small, crowded island found it hard to make a living. Much of the good farmland was owned by the sugar companies. Although large numbers of Puerto Ricans worked on the sugar plantations, their jobs usually lasted only during the harvest season. Some people moved to the cities to find work, but there were not enough factories to provide jobs for all of them. Often they were forced to live in slums.

289

A cement plant built by the government of Puerto Rico. During the 1940's, Puerto Ricans started a program called "Operation Bootstrap" to improve living conditions on the island. As part of this program, the government built several factories to encourage the development of industry.

Puerto Ricans help themselves through "Operation Bootstrap." Some political leaders in Puerto Rico believed that reforms were needed. One of these men, Luis Muñoz Marín, was elected president of the Puerto Rican senate in 1940. He and his followers started a broad program to improve living conditions on the island. People who make a better life for themselves by their own efforts are often said to be "pulling themselves up by their bootstraps." For this reason, the program started by Muñoz Marín is called "Operation Bootstrap."

Operation Bootstrap has brought many improvements to Puerto Rico. In the early 1940's, the government began to purchase much of the farmland owned by the large sugar companies. It sold or rented small plots of land to farmers who had no land of their own. New ma-chinery and modern farming methods are helping to increase agricultural production in Puerto Rico.

The Puerto Rican government has also helped to develop new industries on the island. Government funds were used to build several factories. Later these plants were sold to a private company.

Manufacturing companies from the United States mainland have been encouraged to build factories on the island. The Puerto Rican government helps to select factory sites and to train workers for jobs in industry. Most firms that establish plants on the island do not have to pay taxes for several years. The United States government does not tax goods imported from Puerto Rico. Therefore, many manufacturers on the island sell their products on the mainland.

The growth of industry is providing more jobs for Puerto Ricans and is helping each worker to earn more money. As a result, the standard of living is rising. Today, the yearly per capita income in Puerto Rico is among the highest in the Caribbean Lands.

Other changes have taken place in Puerto Rico. Many new roads have been built, and older roads have been improved. New dams and power plants produce much of the electricity needed by industry. The government has constructed many apartment buildings and low-priced houses for Puerto Rican families. Many fine, modern hotels have been built to serve the large numbers of tourists who come to Puerto Rico each year.

Puerto Rico is a self-governing commonwealth. In 1952, the people of Puerto Rico approved a constitution written by their own representatives. The United States government also approved this constitution. Under it, Puerto Rico became a self-governing commonwealth associated with the United States. In some ways, the Commonwealth of Puerto Rico is like a state. It has a governor and a lawmaking body elected by the people. However, Puerto Rico is not like a state in every way. Although Puerto Ricans are citizens of the United States, they do not pay federal income taxes. They cannot vote for the president of the United States. There is a Puerto Rican representative in the United States Congress, but he has no vote. He can only introduce bills that he wants Congress to make into law.

Puerto Rico's form of government does not satisfy everyone. Some people think that Puerto Rico should be a state. Others want it to become an independent nation. However, most Puerto Ricans seem to want the island to keep its present form of government.

One of the world's largest housing projects, on Puerto Rico. Under Operation Bootstrap, the government has constructed many apartment buildings and low-priced houses for Puerto Rican families. The island's standard of living is rising as a result of Operation Bootstrap.

Governor Luis Muñoz Marín and President Johnson, discussing Puerto Rico's future. Puerto Rico is a self-governing commonwealth associated with the United States. Muñoz Marín was first elected governor of Puerto Rico in 1948.

Puerto Rican girls learning to sew. Most people who live in Puerto Rico are white. Only about one fourth of all Puerto Ricans are of mixed ancestry.

The people of Puerto Rico gained the right to elect their own governor in 1947. The governor chosen in the first election, in 1948, was Luis Muñoz Marín.

THE PEOPLE AND HOW THEY LIVE

People. Puerto Rico is one of the most densely populated countries in the Western Hemisphere. Almost two and one-half million people live on this small island, and the population is still growing. From the 1930's through the 1950's, thousands of Puerto Ricans moved to the United States mainland in search of jobs. This helped relieve overcrowding on the island. Today, there are more job opportunities in Puerto Rico, and fewer people are leaving.

Most Puerto Ricans are white. Their ancestors came from Spain and other European countries or from countries in

292

the Western Hemisphere, such as the United States and Venezuela. About one fourth of all Puerto Ricans are of mixed ancestry. They are descended from whites who intermarried with Negroes or Indians.

Earning a living. Manufacturing brings more money to the people of Puerto Rico than farming. The main type of industry on the island is food processing. Nearly all of the food-processing plants use raw materials grown on Puerto Rican farms. For example, there are mills where raw sugar is made from sugarcane, and plants where the raw sugar is refined. Rum is made from molasses, a by-product of sugar manufacture. Other factories freeze or can fruits and vegetables grown on the island.

Puerto Rican factories also manufacture textiles, tobacco products, cement, and many other goods. Some of these products can be manufactured from raw materials available in Puerto Rico. For example, limestone quarried on the island is used in making cement. However, many raw materials used by Puerto Rican factories must be imported.

Under Operation Bootstrap, more than nine hundred factories have been started on the island. They produce hundreds of different items, including ball-point pens, electric shavers, medicines, plastics, and radar equipment. The manufacture of many items produced in Puerto Rican factories requires skilled labor. Hardworking Puerto Ricans have quickly learned the skills needed in modern factories.

The factories started under Operation Bootstrap have been built in small towns as well as in large cities. Jobs have been created for people in all parts of the island. However, there are still not enough jobs for everyone. Unemployment is a serious problem in Puerto Rico.

Assembling telephone equipment in a factory in Puerto Rico. Factories here produce hundreds of different items. The manufacture of many of these items requires skilled labor. Although new factories have created jobs for many people, unemployment is still a problem in Puerto Rico.

Only about one out of every four Puerto Rican workers is employed in agriculture. Because much of the island is hilly or mountainous, less than half of the land is suitable for farming. Modern machines that do work formerly done by men are now being used on many Puerto Rican farms. As a result, there are fewer jobs for farm workers.

Sugarcane has long been Puerto Rico's most important export crop. In 1940, it accounted for nearly half of all the money earned by Puerto Ricans. Today, other crops are also important, and fewer people depend on sugar production for their living. Yet Puerto Rico now produces more sugar than ever before, partly because modern farming methods have increased the amount of sugarcane that can be produced on each acre of land.

Sugarcane is grown on many parts of the coastal plain, especially along the northern coast, where rainfall is plentiful. About forty mills grind the cane and produce raw sugar. Some of the raw sugar is refined in Puerto Rico, but

A small herd of cattle. Farmers in many parts of Puerto Rico raise cattle, pigs, or poultry.

much of it is exported to the United States.

Livestock raising has become nearly as important as the growing of sugarcane in Puerto Rico. Farmers in many parts of the island raise cattle, pigs, or poultry. Dairy farming is especially important.

Many farmers grow coffee or tobacco on the mountainsides of Puerto Rico. Coffee orchards are located mainly in the western part of the central mountains. The coffee trees help to prevent soil erosion on steep slopes. Tobacco is grown mostly in the eastern part of the central mountains. Much of the tobacco is made into cigars at factories in nearby towns. Tobacco is also exported to the United States mainland.

Some Puerto Rican farmers raise fruits, vegetables, and other crops. There are fields of corn throughout the island. Coconuts and pineapples are grown in a few areas. Other fruits grown on Puerto Rico include grapefruit, oranges, and bananas. Some vegetables are produced for sale on the United States mainland during the winter.

Drying coffee beans. Less than half of the land on Puerto Rico is suitable for farming. Many farmers grow coffee or tobacco on mountain slopes.

294

Transportation and communication.

Puerto Rico has one of the best highway systems in the Caribbean Lands. It has about three thousand miles of paved roads, including several modern expressways. Some of the roads in mountainous areas are narrow and winding, but these are being improved. There is no public railroad on Puerto Rico. Some sugar companies operate local railroads for their own use.

Many shipping lines and airlines serve Puerto Rico. Most of the ships stop at San Juan on the northern coast, at Ponce on the southern coast, or at Mayagüez on the western coast. These are Puerto Rico's three main ports. Planes from many parts of the world land at San Juan's modern international airport. A local airline connects San Juan, Ponce, and Mayagüez.

Highways on Puerto Rico are among the best in the Caribbean Lands. There are about three thousand miles of paved roads on the island.

At the international airport at San Juan, Puerto Rico. Planes from many parts of the world land at this large, modern airport. Puerto Rico is also served by many shipping lines.

The University of Puerto Rico is the largest university in the Caribbean Lands. Courses are offered in law, medicine, education, and many other fields of study. The governments of the United States and Puerto Rico have done much to improve education on the island.

Puerto Rico has a good communications network. There are almost 150,000 telephones on the island. An underwater telephone and telegraph cable connects Puerto Rico with the United States mainland. Puerto Rico has forty-five radio stations and nine television stations. Nearly half of all Puerto Rican families own television sets.

Education. The governments of the United States and Puerto Rico have done much to improve education on the island. When Puerto Rico became a possession of the United States, only about two out of every ten people knew how to read and write. Today, nearly nine out

of every ten Puerto Ricans have learned these important skills. The literacy rate is among the highest in the Caribbean Lands. Special classes are held to educate adults who cannot read and write.

Almost every town in Puerto Rico has at least one school. In addition to elementary schools and high schools, there are several job-training schools and three universities on the island. The University of Puerto Rico, which has more than twenty thousand students, is the largest university in the Caribbean Lands. Courses are offered in law, medicine, education, and many other fields of study.

Cities. During recent years, many Puerto Ricans have left the rural areas and moved to the cities. Today, nearly half of all the people on the island live in cities or towns. The largest cities are on the coastal plain.

San Juan (population about 432,000) is the capital and largest city of Puerto Rico. (See map on page 287.) It is the second largest city in the Caribbean Lands. San Juan was founded in 1521, on a tiny island very close to Puerto Rico's northern coast. Today, only a small part of the city, known as Old San Juan, is located on this island. Old San Juan still has buildings from the Spanish colonial days. The streets are narrow and cobblestoned. Most of the people of San Juan live on the main island of Puerto Rico. This part of the city has many modern buildings.

San Juan is Puerto Rico's chief seaport and an important trading city. It has a very fine harbor. Ships bring goods and passengers to San Juan from many

Modern buildings in San Juan, Puerto Rico, the second largest city in the Caribbean Lands. San Juan is Puerto Rico's capital and chief seaport.

parts of the world. Just outside the city is the busiest airport in the West Indies.

The effects of Operation Bootstrap are especially apparent in San Juan. Many manufacturing firms from the United States mainland have built factories in the city. Several chain stores and banks from the mainland have branches in San Juan. Housing projects are being built to provide better homes for people who live in slum areas. San Juan has a number of modern hotels to serve tourists who visit the city. Most of these hotels are on the seashore near Old San Juan.

Ponce (population about 114,000) is the second largest city in Puerto Rico. It lies on the southern coast of the island. Ponce has a large harbor and is Puerto Rico's main port on the Caribbean Sea. Sugarcane is grown on irrigated plains near the city, and sugar and rum are shipped from Ponce.

There are many factories in Ponce. West of the city is a large oil refinery.

Old San Juan. This part of San Juan is located on the tiny island where the city was founded, in 1521. Old San Juan still has buildings from colonial days.

297

A fire station in Ponce, the second largest city in Puerto Rico. Ponce has a large harbor and is the country's main port on the Caribbean Sea.

Because Puerto Rico has no petroleum deposits, the refinery processes imported crude oil.

Ponce has many old Spanish houses and business buildings. It has been called the "most Spanish" of Puerto Rican cities. A Roman Catholic university is located here.

OUTLYING PUERTO RICO

Off the coasts of the main island are several small islands that are part of the Commonwealth of Puerto Rico. The largest of these islands are Vieques, Culebra, and Mona. (See map on page 287.) They are known as Outlying Puerto Rico. Most people on Vieques and Culebra earn their living by farming or by working for the United States Navy, which has bases on both islands. Because Mona has light rainfall and poor soil, it is almost uninhabited.

Think and Write

1. Why were most of the trees on Puerto Rico cut down? Give two reasons.
2. Why has it been difficult to produce hydroelectric power on Puerto Rico?
3. Explain why the southwestern part of Puerto Rico receives less rainfall than the rest of the island. How do farmers in this area get water for their crops?
4. During colonial days, Puerto Rico was important to Spain because of the island's location. Explain the reason for this. Do you think Puerto Rico's location makes it important to the United States today? Give a reason for your answer.
5. Why was Puerto Rico called the "poorhouse of the Caribbean" in the first part of the 1900's?
6. List four improvements that have been made in Puerto Rico as a result of Operation Bootstrap.

Drawing Conclusions

Answer each of the following questions by drawing conclusions based on information given in the chapter. Write a short paragraph in answer to each question.

1. Most of the large cities of Puerto Rico are located along the coast. Why do you think this is so? The map on page 287 and the land and history sections of the chapter will help you answer this question.
2. Many Puerto Ricans have moved from rural areas to cities in recent years. How would you explain this? Consider the ways in which Puerto Ricans earn their living before you draw your conclusions.
3. Food processing is the main type of industry in Puerto Rico. Why do you think this is so? In answering this question, consider the mineral resources and other raw materials that are available on this island.

ATLANTIC

BAHAMA ISLANDS

OCEAN

GREATER

ANTILLES

CARIBBEAN SEA

LESSER ANTILLES

LESSER ANTILLES

Lesser Antilles

and Bahama Islands

26 Trinidad and Tobago

GEOGRAPHY

Land. Trinidad and Tobago are islands in the Lesser Antilles. (Compare map on pages 14 and 15 with map on page 16.) Together these islands form the smallest independent country in the Caribbean Lands. Trinidad is located only seven miles northeast of the South American country of Venezuela. Tobago, a much smaller island, lies about twenty-one miles northeast of Trinidad. The area of these islands is less than the area of the state of Delaware.

Trinidad is made up of low mountains, forested hills, and gently rolling lowlands. A range of low mountains stretches across the northern part of the island. The highest peak of this range is only 3,085 feet above sea level. Two ranges of hills also cross Trinidad. One range is located in the central part

Coconut trees on Trinidad. Much of this island consists of gently rolling lowlands. Tropical crops grow well in Trinidad's warm, humid climate.

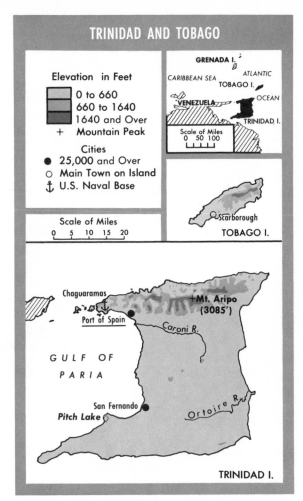

TRINIDAD AND TOBAGO

Elevation in Feet
0 to 660
660 to 1640
1640 and Over
+ Mountain Peak
Cities
● 25,000 and Over
○ Main Town on Island
⚓ U.S. Naval Base

Scale of Miles
0   5   10 15 20

GRENADA I.
ATLANTIC
CARIBBEAN SEA
TOBAGO I.
VENEZUELA
OCEAN
TRINIDAD I.
Scale of Miles
0 50 100

Scarborough
TOBAGO I.

Chaguaramas
+ Mt. Aripo (3085')
Port of Spain
Caroni R.
GULF OF PARIA
San Fernando
Pitch Lake
Ortoire R.

TRINIDAD I.

Trinidad and Tobago form the smallest independent country in the Caribbean Lands.

of the island, and the other is in the extreme southern part.

Between the ranges of mountains and hills are lowlands. These lowlands were once covered with tropical rainforest. Although much of this land has been cleared for farming, forests still cover about one half of Trinidad.

Tobago is a small, hilly island. It is heavily forested, except in valleys and coastal areas, where some land has been cleared for livestock grazing and farming.

Facts About Trinidad and Tobago

Area: 1,980 square miles.

Population: About 910,000.

Density of Population: About 460 people per square mile; about 1,279 people per square mile of arable* land.

Capital and Largest City: Port of Spain (population about 100,000).

Racial Composition: Almost half of the people of Trinidad and Tobago are Negro. More than one third are East Indian. The rest are white or of mixed ancestry.

Literacy: More than three out of every four people in Trinidad and Tobago can read and write.

Main Language: English is the official language.

Main Religion: About two thirds of the people are Roman Catholic or Protestant. Most of the East Indians are Hindu or Moslem.

Main Occupation: About one fourth of the workers in Trinidad and Tobago are farmers. People with jobs in the petroleum industry are the highest paid workers on the islands, but fewer than one tenth of the country's workers are employed in this industry.

Income: Yearly per capita income is about $595.

Important Farm Products: Sugarcane is the most important export crop. Cacao, citrus fruits, and bananas are also grown for export. Rice and other food crops are grown for domestic use.

Natural Resources: Petroleum, natural gas, and asphalt.

Manufacturing: Producing and refining petroleum is the most important industry.

Currency: Trinidad and Tobago's unit of money is the West Indian dollar, which is officially worth about 59 cents.

Climate. The weather in Trinidad and Tobago is warm and humid all year round. These islands are closer to the equator than any other islands in the Caribbean Lands region. Daytime temperatures are often more than ninety degrees. Nights, however, are usually comfortably cool.

The weather on Trinidad is very rainy, especially along the eastern coast of the island. Here, rainfall is more than one hundred inches each year. The heavy rainfall, combined with high temperatures, makes eastern Trinidad well suited for growing cacao. The amount of rainfall decreases toward the west. The western coast receives about sixty inches of rain each year. Sugarcane, which is Trinidad's most important crop, grows well in the western part of the island.

Natural resources. Trinidad and Tobago is one of the few Caribbean countries rich in mineral resources. The most valuable mineral by far is petroleum. It is produced from about three thousand oil wells on Trinidad. These wells are located mainly in the southern part of the island.

Natural gas is also found on Trinidad. This important mineral is often discovered in wells that are being drilled for oil. On Trinidad, natural gas is used mainly by manufacturing plants as a

Drilling for oil on Trinidad. The country of Trinidad and Tobago is rich in mineral resources. The most valuable mineral by far is petroleum.

Trinidad's Pitch Lake supplied most of the world's asphalt for many years. Today, only small amounts of natural asphalt are exported from Trinidad.

fuel. The large reserves of natural gas are attracting new industry to the island.

Trinidad has long been famous for a lake of natural asphalt, called Pitch Lake. This lake, which is located in southwestern Trinidad, is about one-half mile wide and 280 feet deep. Asphalt, or pitch, is a black, gummy substance which is used to pave roads and to make roofing and waterproofing materials. For many years, Pitch Lake supplied most of the world's asphalt. Today, however, most asphalt is refined from crude oil. Only small amounts of natural asphalt from Pitch Lake are exported from Trinidad.

HISTORY

A Spanish colony is founded on Trinidad. Christopher Columbus discovered Trinidad in 1498 and claimed the island for Spain. In the late 1500's, Spaniards established a small settlement near the site of what is now Port of Spain. However, very few people settled on Trinidad. The island lay far south of the

important Spanish trade routes, and there was no gold or silver to attract settlers. Two hundred years after the first Spaniards settled on Trinidad, the island was still almost uninhabited.

In 1783, the king of Spain issued a proclamation that brought many settlers to Trinidad. This proclamation offered free land to foreigners who would settle on the island. Ships soon arrived bringing settlers. Most of them were French farmers who came from other islands in the West Indies. Many of them were accompanied by their slaves. They established sugar plantations in the western part of the island. In other areas, the settlers grew coffee, cotton, and cacao.

Trinidad becomes a British colony. In 1797, a British fleet captured Trinidad during a war between Spain and Great Britain. Five years later, the island was ceded to Great Britain. New settlers came to Trinidad from Britain. They were mainly attracted by the large areas of land that could be used to grow sugarcane.

In the early 1800's, the colonists were faced with a serious shortage of workers. The sugar planters found it difficult to import slaves into Trinidad to do the plantation work because the British government had become opposed to slavery. The shortage of labor became even more acute after 1834, when slavery was abolished.

East Indians come to Trinidad. To replace the slaves, the colonists began to look elsewhere for workers. In India, which at that time was also a British colony, they found large numbers of laborers willing to work for very low wages. Many thousands of them were brought from India to work on Trinidad's plantations. In Trinidad, these people were called "East Indians."

The East Indians came to Trinidad under an agreement to work for a period of several years. After this period, the government encouraged them to settle on the island. Most of them remained on Trinidad and started small farms on which they grew sugarcane as well as other crops to feed their families. With the coming of the East Indians, the production of sugar on the island increased rapidly.

Trinidad and Tobago gains its independence. Toward the end of the 1800's Tobago joined with Trinidad to form a united colony. In 1958, Trinidad and Tobago, together with Jamaica and other British islands in the Caribbean, formed a union called the West Indies Federation. Port of Spain became the capital of this federation. The West Indies Federation officially broke up in May, 1962, and three months later, Trinidad and Tobago became an independent country within the British Commonwealth.

Oil brings wealth to Trinidad and Tobago. In the early 1900's, oil was discovered on Trinidad. In the years that followed, the production of petroleum became Trinidad and Tobago's most important industry. For a time, it was the leading oil producer of the British Empire.

The oil industry has brought prosperity to many of Trinidad and Tobago's people. Large oil refineries provide jobs for thousands of workers. The country's yearly per capita income is one of the highest in the Caribbean Lands.

THE PEOPLE AND HOW THEY LIVE

People. The population of Trinidad and Tobago is growing rapidly. It is now about 910,000. Most of the people live in the western part of Trinidad.

People of many different nationalities and races live in Trinidad and Tobago. Almost half of the people are Negro. They are descended mainly from slaves who were brought to Trinidad during the 1700's and early 1800's. Most of the Negroes of Trinidad now live and work in the cities.

East Indians make up more than one third of the population of Trinidad and Tobago. They form the largest group of Asian people in the Caribbean Lands. The East Indians are descendants of laborers brought from India by the British to work on sugar plantations in the 1800's. Today, most of them still work on large sugar estates or raise sugarcane on their own small plots of land. Many East Indians grow rice in flooded rice paddies, using water buffalo to plow the fields, much as their ancestors did in India.

Most other people in Trinidad and Tobago are mulatto. Only about three out of every hundred are white.

A Moslem mosque on Trinidad. East Indians make up more than one third of the population of Trinidad and Tobago. Most of them are Hindu or Moslem.

Earning a living. Trinidad and Tobago's most important industry is producing and refining petroleum. Thousands of workers earn their living in the oil fields and large refineries on Trinidad. One refinery on this island is among the largest in the world. It employs more than ten thousand workers. The oil wells and refineries on Trinidad are owned by large oil companies in the United States and other countries.

Less than half of the crude oil processed by Trinidad's refineries comes from oil wells on the island. Most of the oil is imported from Venezuela and other countries. Almost all of the gasoline, fuel oil, and other products of the refineries are exported, mainly to the United States and to countries in Europe. Petroleum products make up about four fifths of the total value of Trinidad and Tobago's exports.

In recent years, more than one hundred new factories have been built on Trinidad. New industries are being attracted to the island by cheap power provided by natural gas. They are also being encouraged by the government of

In a large oil refinery on Trinidad, a Negro worker instructs employees of European and of East Indian descent. Trinidad and Tobago's most important industry is producing and refining petroleum. Gasoline, fuel oil, and other petroleum products are exported.

Trinidad and Tobago, which offers low tax rates and other benefits to new industries. One large new factory on Trinidad uses petroleum and natural gas in the manufacture of petrochemicals. Another plant on this island makes fertilizer from some of these chemicals.

Only about one fourth of the workers of Trinidad and Tobago earn their living by farming. Many farm workers are employed on large sugar estates in the western part of Trinidad. Some farmers grow sugarcane on their own small farms and sell it to the estates. Often these farmers also cut sugarcane on the estates during the harvest season. Sugar mills on the estates process the cane to make raw sugar. Most of the sugar is exported to Britain, Canada, and the United States.

Other important crops raised in Trinidad and Tobago are cacao, citrus fruits, and bananas. Large quantities of these crops are exported. Coconuts are also raised. Coconut oil is used to make margarine, soap, and other products for people of the islands.

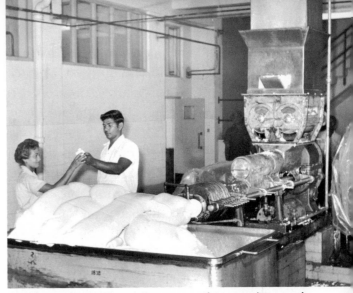

Testing margarine. Coconut oil is used to make margarine and other products. In recent years, many new factories have been built on Trinidad.

On small farms, rice and other food crops are grown for local use. However, the farmers of the country do not raise enough food for the growing population. Large quantities of rice, meat, milk, and other foods must be imported.

Transportation and communication. Trinidad and Tobago has a better system of roads than most other Caribbean countries. There are about 2,500 miles of roads, more than half of them paved. Many of these roads are paved with asphalt from Pitch Lake. Because the railroad system on Trinidad is very poor, most goods are transported by road.

Trinidad is a crossroads for air travel between North and South America and between Europe and South America. A modern international airport is located just outside Port of Spain.

Trinidad and Tobago has a poor communications system. Although there are more telephones here than in most other Caribbean countries, most of them are in Port of Spain. Very few people living in rural areas have telephones. There are two radio stations and one television station on Trinidad.

An East Indian with a herd of water buffalo. Many East Indians on Trinidad use water buffalo to plow the fields, much as their ancestors did in India.

305

Education. The people of Trinidad and Tobago have one of the highest literacy rates in the Caribbean Lands. More than three fourths of the people can read and write. The government has spent large sums of money on education in recent years. Today, there are enough schools and teachers for almost all children of elementary-school age to attend. Many new high schools have also been built, but more are still needed.

A branch of Jamaica's University College of the West Indies was opened on Trinidad in 1960. This school offers courses in engineering and tropical agriculture to students in Trinidad and Tobago.

Cities. There are few cities or large towns in Trinidad and Tobago. Scarborough, the largest town on Tobago, has fewer than 3,000 inhabitants. The largest city on Trinidad is Port of Spain.

Port of Spain (population about 100,-000) is the capital and largest city of Trinidad and Tobago. It is located along a sheltered harbor on the northwestern coast of the island of Trinidad.

Port of Spain is one of the busiest ports in the West Indies. Many ex-

A street in Port of Spain, the capital and largest city of Trinidad and Tobago. Port of Spain is one of the busiest ports in the West Indies.

porters and importers have their offices here. On the outskirts of the city are textile mills, sawmills, and other small factories.

The many different peoples who have settled in Port of Spain have influenced its architecture. Modern office buildings have been built next to old Spanish-style houses whose balconies overhang the narrow streets. Hindu temples and the rounded domes of Moslem mosques are evidence of the East Indian population.

Reviewing What You Have Learned
1. Why did few settlers come to Trinidad before 1783? Why did more come after 1783?
2. To whom does the name "East Indians" refer? Give two examples to show that these people still follow some of the ways of their ancestors.
3. What do you think are Trinidad and Tobago's two most important natural resources? List three ways in which these resources have affected industry in this country.

Finding More Information
East Indians make up more than one third of Trinidad and Tobago's population. Most of these people follow the teachings of Islam or Hinduism. Read about one of these religions in at least two outside sources. Then write a report about what you have learned. Your report should include the following main topics:
a. the religion's origin
b. its main teachings
c. customs and ceremonies related to the religion

In the great archipelago of the West Indies, there are more than one thousand islands that are controlled by Great Britain. Most of these islands are very small. They are grouped into twelve separate colonies. (See fact table on page 309.)

The British islands are scattered throughout the West Indies. (Compare the map on page 16 with the map below and the map on page 312.) Some of them lie at the eastern end of the Caribbean Sea. These islands are part of the Lesser Antilles. Three small islands, the

Three British colonies in the West Indies. The colonies of the Bahama Islands and the Turks and Caicos Islands together form an archipelago located north of the Greater Antilles, in the Atlantic Ocean. The colony of the Cayman Islands lies south of Cuba, in the Caribbean Sea.

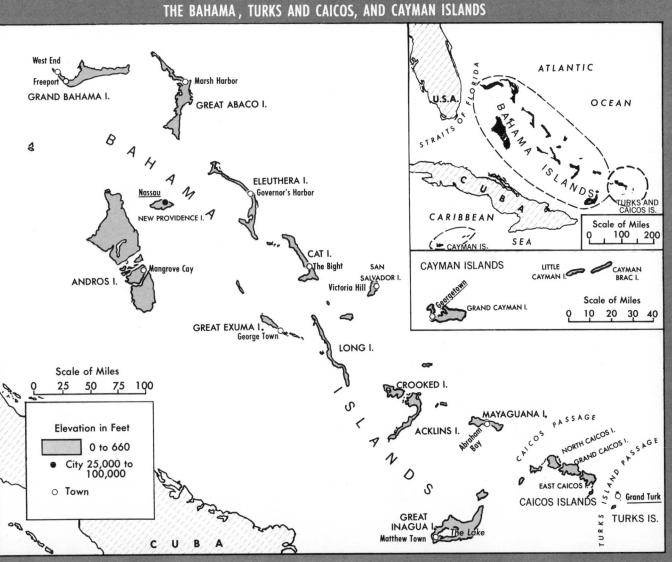

THE BAHAMA, TURKS AND CAICOS, AND CAYMAN ISLANDS

Caymans, are located in the Caribbean Sea south of Cuba. North of the Greater Antilles, in the Atlantic Ocean, are the Bahama Islands and the Turks and Caicos Islands.

THE BAHAMA ISLANDS

Land and climate. The Bahama Islands form an archipelago that extends from the Florida peninsula southeastward toward the island of Hispaniola. They lie farther north than any other part of the Caribbean Lands.

About seven hundred islands, most of them very small, make up the Bahamas. These islands are low and almost flat. Scattered among the islands are more than two thousand islets, or cays, and many coral reefs. (See page 27 to learn how the Bahama Islands were formed.)

Most Bahamians live on the small island of New Providence. Nassau, the capital and only city of the Bahamas, is located here. Bahamians call all of the islands except New Providence the "Out Islands."

The climate of the Bahama Islands is warm and pleasant. During the winter months, the average temperature is about seventy degrees. In the summer, the highest temperatures are usually between eighty and ninety degrees. The islands receive about forty to sixty inches of rain a year, which is generally enough for farming.

History. On October 12, 1492, Christopher Columbus stepped ashore on an island in the Bahamas. This was his first landing in the New World. He named

Islands in the Bahamas. About seven hundred low-lying islands make up the archipelago known as the Bahamas. These islands are almost flat, and most of them are very small. Scattered among the islands are many islets and coral reefs. The climate of the Bahamas is warm and pleasant.

Facts About the British Colonies in the West Indies			
Colony	**Area**	**Population**	**Capital**
Antigua	171 square miles.	About 58,000.	St. Johns (population about 21,600).
Bahama Islands	4,404 square miles.	About 111,000.	Nassau (population about 58,000).
Barbados	166 square miles.	About 235,000.	Bridgetown (population about 11,500).
British Virgin Islands	67 square miles.	About 8,000.	Road Town (population about 1,500).
Cayman Islands	100 square miles.	About 8,500.	Georgetown (population about 2,500).
Dominica	290 square miles.	About 62,000.	Roseau (population about 10,400).
Grenada	133 square miles.	About 90,000.	St. George's (population about 27,000).
Montserrat	32 square miles.	About 13,000.	Plymouth (population about 2,500).
St. Kitts-Nevis-Anguilla	138 square miles.	About 60,000.	Basseterre (population about 16,000).
St. Lucia	238 square miles.	About 92,000.	Castries (population about 24,500).
St. Vincent	150 square miles.	About 83,500.	Kingstown (population about 16,000).
Turks and Caicos Islands	166 square miles.	About 6,000.	Grand Turk (population about 2,500).

the island San Salvador, which means "Holy Savior." The map on page 58 shows the island that most historians believe is San Salvador. Although Columbus claimed several islands in the Bahamas for Spain, the Spanish never tried to settle here.

About 1650, English settlers arrived on the Bahama Islands. Some came directly from England. Others came from Bermuda, another British colony in the Atlantic Ocean. Like the Pilgrims in Massachusetts, these people had broken away from the Church of England. They were seeking freedom to worship as they pleased.

During the late 1600's, pirates began to use the Bahama Islands as bases. They hid their ships in secret harbors, or in narrow channels between the islands, and sailed out to attack passing cargo ships. Finally the British government sent troops to keep order. Several pirates were hanged. The rest were pardoned or were forced to leave the islands.

After the American Revolution, hundreds of people who were still loyal to Great Britain moved from the United States to the Bahamas. They brought Negro slaves with them, and established cotton plantations on some of the islands. However, cotton cultivation made

A Bahamian family making straw articles for sale to tourists. The tourist industry is the main source of income for the people of the Bahamas. In most places on the islands, the soil is too shallow for growing crops. There is little manufacturing on the Bahamas.

the thin soil infertile. After a few years, cotton could no longer be grown profitably.

About eighty years later, the Civil War in the United States brought prosperity to the Bahamas for a time. The Union navy blockaded southern ports to prevent ships from bringing badly needed supplies to the South. Because the Bahamas were close to these ports, blockade-running ships from the South often met British ships at Nassau and traded with them secretly.

Today, the Bahamas are important to the United States because of their location. Four missile-tracking stations have been established on the islands by the United States government. Workers at these stations use special instruments to record speed, altitude, and other information about missiles fired from Cape Kennedy in Florida.

Early in 1964, Britain granted internal self-government to the colony of the Bahama Islands. Bahamians now have the right to elect most of their government officials.

The people and their work. Only about twenty islands in the Bahamas are inhabited. Except for New Providence, these islands are thinly populated. About nine out of every ten people of the Bahamas are Negro or mulatto. Most Bahamians are members of the Church of England.

The tourist industry is the main source of income for the people of the Bahamas. Each year, more than 300,000 visitors come here from the United States and Canada to enjoy the pleasant climate and the fine beaches. Many Bahamians work in shops, restaurants, and hotels, or provide other services for tourists.

Fewer than one third of the workers of the Bahamas are farmers. In most places, the soil is too shallow for growing crops. Avocados, mangoes, pineapples, other fruits, and several kinds of vegetables are grown for local use. Tomatoes are exported to the United States and Canada. On Eleuthera Island, large numbers of chickens and cows are raised. Most of the milk, eggs, and poultry used in Nassau are produced here.

At present, there is little manufacturing on the Bahamas. However, industry here is growing. Among the goods manufactured are paper, textiles, and plastics. An industrial community is being developed at Freeport, on Grand Bahama Island. A deep harbor has been dredged, and land has been cleared for warehouses and factories. Manufacturing firms that build plants here will not have to pay taxes for a number of years.

Products from forests and fisheries are important to the Bahama Islands. Large areas on the islands of Great Abaco, Andros, and Grand Bahama are covered with pine forests. Trees cut here are made into lumber for export. In the waters near the Bahamas, people catch spiny lobsters and other sea animals. Large numbers of lobsters are shipped from the islands to Florida. On Great Inagua, salt is produced by evaporating seawater. Salt brings more money to Bahamians than any other export.

Cities. Each island or group of islands in the Bahamas has one main port town, where ships come to load and unload goods. Most of these towns are very small. The only city is Nassau, where about half of the people of the Bahamas live.

Nassau (population about 58,000) is the capital and main seaport of the Bahama Islands. It lies along a fine harbor on the northern coast of New Providence. The only international airport in the Bahamas is just outside Nassau. No important industries are located in or near the city.

Nassau is mainly a resort city. It has a pleasant climate and one of the loveliest beaches in the world. In the harbor, there are beautiful underwater coral formations that can be viewed from glass-bottomed boats.

THE TURKS AND CAICOS ISLANDS

The map on page 307 shows that the Turks and Caicos Islands are part of the Bahama archipelago. However, they are governed as a separate colony of Britain. There are about thirty islands in the colony. These low-lying islands receive only about thirty inches of rainfall a year, and even drinking water is often scarce. The main industry on the Turks and Caicos is producing salt from seawater. Some people earn their living by catching spiny lobsters.

A spiny lobster caught near the Turks and Caicos Islands. Some people on these islands and on the Bahamas earn their living as fishermen.

THE CAYMAN ISLANDS

About 150 miles south of Cuba are three small, low-lying islands called the Cayman Islands. (See map on page 307.) The soil on these islands is shallow, and the people do very little farming. Many of them earn their living by catching sharks and turtles in the Caribbean Sea. Sharkskin, turtle shells and skins, and live turtles are exported. Other important industries are lumbering, shipbuilding, and the making of rope from palm fibers. The Cayman Islands have a growing tourist industry.

THE "LITTLE EIGHT"

Land and climate. In the Lesser Antilles there are nine British colonies. One of these, the British Virgin Islands, is described in Chapter 30. The others are sometimes known as the "Little Eight." (See map at right.) All of the islands in the "Little Eight" are small. Some islands are rugged and mountainous. Others are almost flat and barely rise above sea level.

The "Little Eight" have a warm climate. The mountainous islands generally receive heavy rainfall, but the low-lying islands sometimes suffer from drought. (See page 45 to learn why this is so.) Between June and October, damaging hurricanes sometimes strike the islands.

History. The first settlement in the "Little Eight" was established by the English on the island of St. Kitts, in 1623. Both England and France claimed the islands in the "Little Eight" during the 1600's. For almost two hundred years, these two countries were rivals for control of the islands. By 1815, all of

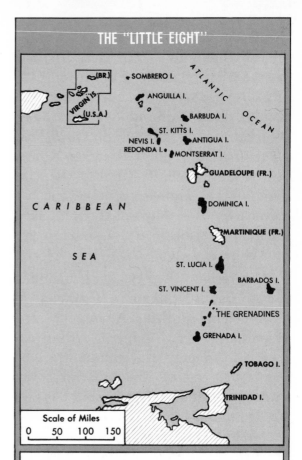

THE "LITTLE EIGHT"

Eight British colonies in the Lesser Antilles are sometimes known as the "Little Eight." The islands of St. Kitts, Nevis, Anguilla, and Sombrero together make up one colony. Antigua, Barbuda, and Redonda make up another. Each of four colonies in the "Little Eight" consists of a single island. These are Montserrat, Dominica, St. Lucia, and Barbados. The colony of St. Vincent includes the northern part of the Grenadines. The southern Grenadines are included in the colony of Grenada.

the islands in the "Little Eight" belonged to the British.

Between 1958 and 1962, the colonies in the "Little Eight" were members of the West Indies Federation. This federation also included the larger, more prosperous colonies of Jamaica and Trinidad and Tobago. It was expected that the federation would become an independent nation. In 1961, however, Jamaica decided to withdraw from the federation. Trinidad and Tobago followed in 1962. Shortly afterward, the federation officially broke up. Both Jamaica and Trinidad and Tobago became independent countries. The "Little Eight" remained British colonies.

Late in 1964, all of the "Little Eight" except Grenada decided to form a new West Indies Federation. This federation is expected to become independent as soon as it is organized. Its capital will be Bridgetown, on Barbados, the island with the largest population of the "Little Eight." Grenada is expected to join with the independent country of Trinidad and Tobago. (See Chapter 26.)

The people and their work. Most of the islands that make up the "Little Eight" are densely populated. Except for Dominica, all of these colonies have an average of more than three hundred people per square mile. (For the area, population, and capital of each colony, see fact table on page 309.) Many people in the "Little Eight" are very poor. There are not enough jobs for all of the workers.

Throughout the "Little Eight," farming is the main occupation. Some people work on large estates owned by a few wealthy men. Others cultivate their own small plots of land. There are few factories in the "Little Eight" to provide jobs.

Most of the people in the "Little Eight" are Negroes whose ancestors were brought from Africa as slaves. English is the official language.

St. Kitts-Nevis-Anguilla. In the northern part of the Lesser Antilles are the islands of St. Kitts (also called St. Christopher), Nevis, and Anguilla. Together

Cracking nutmegs on Grenada. The colony of Grenada is one of the world's leading producers of nutmeg and mace. These spices come from the fruit of the nutmeg tree. Throughout the "Little Eight," farming is the main occupation.

313

with the tiny islet of Sombrero, they make up a British colony. (See map on page 312.) St. Kitts and Nevis are mountainous islands, with peaks nearly four thousand feet above sea level. On St. Kitts, the average yearly rainfall is about fifty-five inches. Nevis is somewhat drier. Anguilla, a low-lying coral island, receives very little rainfall.

Raising and processing sugarcane are the most important occupations in the colony of St. Kitts-Nevis-Anguilla. Sugar and molasses are the leading exports of the colony. Most of the sugarcane is raised on St. Kitts. Cotton is the leading crop on Nevis, although sugarcane is also grown here. On Anguilla, most of the people earn their living by fishing, raising livestock, or producing salt.

Antigua. The islands of Antigua, Barbuda, and Redonda make up the colony of Antigua. (See map on page 312.) Nearly all of the people in the colony live on Antigua. Although this island has some hills that rise more than one thousand feet above sea level, most of

Fields of sugarcane on St. Kitts. The main export crops produced on the islands of the "Little Eight" are sugarcane, bananas, cotton, and cacao.

it is almost flat. The average yearly rainfall is about forty-five inches. Barbuda is a thinly populated coral island. It rises less than five feet above sea level in most places. Redonda, a rocky islet, is uninhabited.

Sugarcane is the main crop on Antigua, although the rainfall is barely enough for raising this crop. Sometimes the sugarcane is severely damaged by drought. Other food crops and cotton are also grown on Antigua. Processing farm products is the main kind of manufacturing on this island. Sugar, molasses, and cotton are exported. In recent years, the tourist industry has become important to the people of Antigua.

Montserrat. About thirty miles southwest of Antigua is the mountainous island of Montserrat. It is the smallest British colony in the Caribbean Lands. The highest point on the island is a volcanic peak that is more than three thousand feet above sea level. Much of the land on Montserrat is rocky and poor for farming. Rainfall is plentiful, sometimes totaling more than eighty inches a year.

Cotton is raised on about half of Montserrat's farmland. It is the colony's chief export. The main industries are cotton ginning and food processing. Soap, shingles, and a few other products are made on Montserrat. The colony is trying to increase its farm production and develop new products for export.

Dominica. Between the French islands of Guadeloupe and Martinique is Dominica. (See map on page 312.) Nearly all of the land on Dominica is very rugged. A range of forest-covered mountains extends across the island from north to south. One peak is nearly five thousand feet above sea level. Partly because of

On St. Lucia, steep-sided mountains rise high above the sea. In some places there are fertile valleys. Nearly every village along the coast has a fleet of small fishing boats. St. Lucia and other mountainous islands in the "Little Eight" generally receive heavy rainfall.

the high mountains, Dominica receives heavy rainfall. Some parts of the island receive about 250 inches of rainfall a year.

Nearly all of Dominica's people live along its coasts. A group of several hundred Carib Indians live in the rugged mountains. (See Chapter 3 for more information about the Carib Indians.)

Several crops grow well on Dominica. The island has rich soil, warm sunshine, and plentiful rainfall. Bananas are the main crop. Other important crops are limes, cacao, and coconuts. Most of the island's products are exported to Great Britain. Some people on Dominica earn their living by weaving floor mats and other articles from straw.

St. Lucia. St. Lucia is another mountainous island in the "Little Eight." It lies south of the French island of Martinique. On St. Lucia, steep-sided mountains rise high above the sea. In some places, there are fertile valleys, which are the main farming areas on the island. St. Lucia receives about ninety inches of rainfall a year. Because rainfall is heavy, dense forests cover many of the mountainsides.

Bananas are the main crop on St. Lucia. Sugarcane, coconuts, cacao, citrus fruits, and other crops are also grown. Many farm products are exported to Great Britain. A few products, such as rum and soap, are manufactured for use on the island. Nearly every coastal village has a fleet of small fishing boats. St. Lucia is trying to develop a tourist industry.

St. Vincent. The island of St. Vincent lies about twenty-five miles south of St. Lucia. A chain of rugged, thickly wooded mountains extends across the island from north to south. The highest peak is Mount Soufrière, a volcano that rises about four thousand feet above sea level. St. Vincent receives more than one hundred inches of rainfall a year. The colony of St. Vincent includes many small, thinly populated islands that are part of a group called the Grenadines. (See map on page 312.)

For many years, St. Vincent's most important export crop was arrowroot. The roots of this plant are used to make flour. Although bananas are now the main crop, large quantities of arrowroot are still produced. Most of the arrowroot flour made in factories on St. Vincent is exported to the United States and Great Britain. It is used in making baby food, biscuits, pudding, and some kinds of medicine. St. Vincent is the only place in the world that produces much arrowroot.

Harvesting arrowroot. St. Vincent is the only place in the world that produces much arrowroot. The roots of this plant are used to make flour.

Among other crops grown on St. Vincent are coconuts, cotton, sweet potatoes, and sugarcane. Products besides arrowroot flour that are manufactured here include rum, cigarettes, and concrete blocks.

Grenada. The island of Grenada lies farther south than any other British colony in the "Little Eight." Much of the island consists of low mountains. The most important farming area is in the eastern part of the island, where the land is fairly level. Rainfall is generally heavy. Some mountainous areas receive as much as 150 inches of rainfall a year. The colony of Grenada also includes the southern islands of the Grenadines.

Grenada is one of the world's leading producers of nutmeg and mace. Both of these spices come from the fruit of the nutmeg tree. Grenada exports these spices, mainly to the United States and Great Britain. In 1955, a hurricane struck the island and destroyed most of the nutmeg trees. Some farmers began to grow bananas instead, and production of this crop has increased rapidly.

Other crops grown on Grenada include cacao, sugarcane, and cotton. Cacao seeds, from which cocoa and chocolate are made, bring more money to the people of Grenada than any other export. Sugar, rum, soap, and a few other products are manufactured on Grenada.

Barbados. A comparison of the maps on pages 16 and 312 shows that Barbados is the easternmost island in the West Indies. It lies in the Atlantic Ocean, about one hundred miles east of St. Vincent. Most of the land on Barbados is gently rolling. The highest point is only about one thousand feet above sea level. Barbados has a warm, pleasant climate and moderate rainfall.

There are no large towns on Barbados except Bridgetown, the capital. However, Barbados is one of the most densely populated parts of the Western Hemisphere. An average of about 1,400 people live in each square mile. It is hard to provide jobs for everyone on this small, crowded island.

Most of the people on Barbados earn their living by raising or processing sugarcane. Several mills on the island produce raw sugar, which is exported mainly to Great Britain. Rum and molasses are also produced on Barbados, and small amounts of these are exported. Many workers are employed on sugar plantations only during the harvest season. The rest of the year, they make a living by raising vegetables or by fishing.

The second most important source of income on Barbados is the tourist industry. During the winter months, many people come from the United States and Great Britain to enjoy the warm, pleasant climate and fine beaches. During the summer, people from Venezuela like to

Bottling soft drinks on Barbados. It is hard to provide jobs for all the workers on this crowded island. Most people raise or process sugarcane.

vacation on Barbados because the weather is cooler here than in their own country.

Factories on Barbados produce cigarettes, beer, soap, furniture, and other goods. The island has supplies of clay, natural gas, and coral limestone. The coral limestone is used to make a variety of products, including building blocks and fertilizer.

Exploring Relationships
1. What would you consider the four most important natural resources of the Bahama Islands? List them. Then write a short paragraph explaining your choices.
2. Explain the relationship between the Bahamas and the United States at these times:
   a. after the American Revolution
   b. during the Civil War

Reviewing Important Facts
On a large piece of poster board, make a chart similar to the one on page 309. At the left, list the twelve British colonies in the West Indies. Then make columns with the following headings: Area, Population, Land Features, Climate, Earning a Living, Exports. Under the headings, list the important facts given in this chapter and in Chapter 30.

Visiting in the West Indies
The tourist industry is an important source of income for many of the British colonies in the West Indies. If you could visit one of the islands described in this chapter, which one would you choose? Write a report about your choice. Include the following information in your report:
a. the reason for your choice
b. what you would see and do on your visit to this island

Before writing your report, read about the island you have chosen in at least one outside source.

Facts About Guadeloupe and Martinique

Area: Guadeloupe, 687 square miles. Martinique, 425 square miles.

Population: Guadeloupe, about 289,000. Martinique, about 320,000.

Density of Population: Guadeloupe, 421 people per square mile; 1,500 people per square mile of arable* land. Martinique, 753 people per square mile; 1,378 people per square mile of arable land.

Capital and Largest City: Guadeloupe: Capital, Basse-Terre (population about 15,000). Largest city, Pointe-à-Pitre (population about 45,000). Martinique: Capital and largest city, Fort-de-France (population about 92,000).

Racial Composition: About three out of every four of Guadeloupe's people are Negro. Most of the people of Martinique are Negro or mulatto.

Literacy: About two thirds of the people of Guadeloupe can read and write. On Martinique, about three fourths of the people are literate.

Main Language: French.

Main Religion: Roman Catholicism.

Main Occupation: Most of the workers earn their living by farming.

Income: Yearly per capita income is about $420.

Important Farm Products: Sugarcane and bananas are the most important export crops of Guadeloupe and Martinique.

Manufacturing: Processing sugarcane and making rum are the most important industries.

Currency: The unit of money of Guadeloupe and Martinique is the *franc*. It is officially worth about 20 cents.

GEOGRAPHY

Land and climate. Guadeloupe and Martinique are overseas* departments of France in the Lesser Antilles. (See map on opposite page.) The department of Guadeloupe is made up of several islands. Martinique is a single island.

The two main islands of Guadeloupe, Grande-Terre and Basse-Terre, are separated by a narrow channel called the Rivière Salée. Grande-Terre is a low, flat island formed of coral limestone. Rainfall here is over sixty inches a year. However, rainwater evaporates quickly in the warm climate. Also, the soil does not hold moisture well. As a result, people must store rainwater in cisterns for drinking and other purposes.

Basse-Terre consists mainly of rugged volcanic mountains. The highest mountain, Soufrière, rises almost five thousand feet above sea level. In 1902, Mount Soufrière erupted and killed more than two thousand people. Rainfall is heavy on Basse-Terre. Some

Cutting sugarcane on Grande-Terre, one of the two main islands of Guadeloupe. Grande-Terre is a low, flat island formed of coral limestone.

mountain slopes receive more than two hundred inches of rainfall a year. The steep mountainsides are covered with dense forests.

Guadeloupe also includes several smaller islands. Marie-Galante and Désirade are low, flat, coral-limestone islands like Grande-Terre. South of the two main islands is a group of small, rocky islands called Les Saintes. About 130 miles northwest of Basse-Terre are the low but hilly islands of St. Martin and St. Barthélemy. The southern part of St. Martin belongs to the Netherlands. On most of the small islands, rainfall is light. Page 45 helps to explain why.

Martinique is a rugged, mountainous island. The highest peak, Mount Pelée, rises about 4,500 feet above sea level. Like Mount Soufrière, Mount Pelée erupted violently in 1902. The eruption destroyed the city of St. Pierre and killed about thirty thousand persons here. Between the steep-sided mountains of Martinique are narrow, fertile valleys. The largest lowland area is the Plain of Lamentin, near the middle of the island. On Martinique, rainfall differs greatly from place to place. Some mountain slopes facing the trade winds receive more than two hundred inches of rainfall a year. On the southern coast, the yearly rainfall is less than forty inches.

Volcanic eruptions are not the only dangers facing the people of Guadeloupe and Martinique. Occasionally the islands are shaken by earthquakes. Hurricanes sometimes strike the islands in summer and early fall, wrecking buildings and ruining crops.

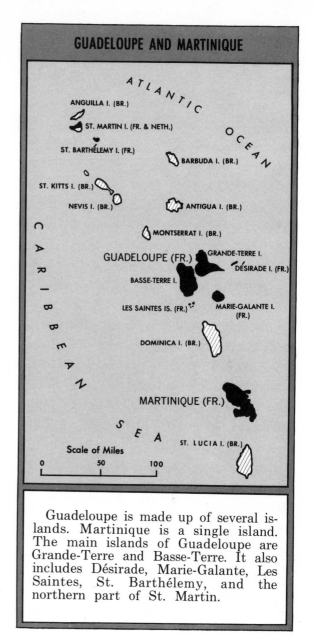

GUADELOUPE AND MARTINIQUE

ATLANTIC OCEAN

ANGUILLA I. (BR.)
ST. MARTIN I. (FR. & NETH.)
ST. BARTHÉLEMY I. (FR.)
BARBUDA I. (BR.)
ST. KITTS I. (BR.)
NEVIS I. (BR.)
ANTIGUA I. (BR.)
MONTSERRAT I. (BR.)
GUADELOUPE (FR.)
GRANDE-TERRE I.
BASSE-TERRE I.
DÉSIRADE I. (FR.)
LES SAINTES IS. (FR.)
MARIE-GALANTE I. (FR.)
DOMINICA I. (BR.)
CARIBBEAN SEA
MARTINIQUE (FR.)
Scale of Miles
0   50   100
ST. LUCIA I. (BR.)

Guadeloupe is made up of several islands. Martinique is a single island. The main islands of Guadeloupe are Grande-Terre and Basse-Terre. It also includes Désirade, Marie-Galante, Les Saintes, St. Barthélemy, and the northern part of St. Martin.

HISTORY

Christopher Columbus, exploring for Spain, discovered Guadeloupe in 1493 and Martinique in 1502. The Spanish never settled on these islands, partly because of the fierce Carib Indians who lived here. In 1635, the French started settlements on Guadeloupe and Martinique. They began to grow sugarcane and other crops for export. Thousands of Negro slaves were imported to work on the plantations. During the 1700's, the French islands were very prosperous.

Changes came to Guadeloupe and Martinique during the 1800's. The price of sugar dropped sharply. After slavery was abolished in 1848, the plantation owners had trouble finding workers. Many small plantations went out of business and were bought by the owners of large estates. Some farmers began growing bananas and other crops instead of sugarcane.

In 1946, Guadeloupe and Martinique became overseas departments of France. They are considered to be part of the French nation, just as Hawaii is part of the United States. Each department is ruled by a prefect appointed in Paris. However, the prefect is advised by a council elected by the people of the department. The people also elect deputies to represent them in the French parliament.

A banana plantation on Basse-Terre. Farming is the main occupation on Guadeloupe and Martinique. Leading export crops are sugarcane and bananas.

THE PEOPLE AND HOW THEY LIVE

The people and their work. Most of the people of Guadeloupe and Martinique are Negro or mulatto. Only about one person in every eight is white. On Les Saintes, most of the people are descended from early French settlers. The official language of Guadeloupe and Martinique is French, but most people speak a dialect that contains some African and English words. On St. Martin, nearly everyone speaks English.

Farming is the main occupation on Guadeloupe and Martinique. The most important export crops are sugarcane and bananas. Farmers who grow these crops have many problems. The price of sugar varies greatly and is often low. Banana plants are sometimes ruined by hurricanes or disease. Thousands of workers have jobs only during the harvest season. Each year, many islanders emigrate to France in search of employment.

On the level, fertile island of Grande-Terre, nearly all of the farmland is used for growing sugarcane. Rainfall here is

A country church on Martinique. Most of the people of Guadeloupe and Martinique are Negro or mulatto. Some are descended from early French settlers.

moderate, and comes mostly during the summer and fall. Sugarcane grows very well under these conditions.

Bananas are the main crop on Basse-Terre, where rainfall is heavy. Cacao and coffee are also grown here. These tree crops help to prevent soil erosion on steep slopes. Most of the farms and settlements on Basse-Terre are along the coast. Few people live in the rugged, forested interior.

Except for Marie-Galante, the smaller islands of Guadeloupe are too dry or too steep for growing much sugarcane. Cotton and food crops are grown by some farmers on St. Martin, St. Barthélemy and Désirade. On Les Saintes, most people earn their living by fishing or by making charcoal.

Sugarcane has been raised on Martinique for more than three hundred years. It is grown mainly on the fertile Plain of Lamentin and on lowlands along the eastern coast. Recently, bananas have become Martinique's most important crop. Pineapples and other tropical fruits are also raised on the island.

The processing of sugarcane is the leading industry on Guadeloupe and Martinique. There are more than twenty refineries that produce sugar for export. Distilleries on the islands make large quantities of rum from molasses, a by-product of sugar production. On Martinique, there are several pineapple-canning factories. Most other factories produce such goods as textiles and bricks for local use.

Guadeloupe and Martinique trade mostly with France. Because so much of their land is used for growing export crops, they must import large amounts

321

of food. They also buy most of their manufactured goods abroad, so imports are much larger than exports.

Cities. The largest city and chief port of Guadeloupe is Pointe-à-Pitre (population about 45,000), on the island of Grande-Terre. It is served by a large, modern airport. The capital of Guadeloupe is Basse-Terre (population about 15,000). This pretty town lies at the foot of Mount Soufrière, on the island of Basse-Terre.

Fort-de-France (population about 92,000) is the capital and largest city of Martinique. It lies along a deep harbor on the western coast. Most of the sugar, rum, and fruit produced on Martinique are exported from Fort-de-France. This colorful city resembles a town in France.

Reviewing What You Have Learned
1. Explain how Guadeloupe and Martinique are governed.
2. List three dangers faced by the people of Guadeloupe and Martinique.
3. State two reasons why there is not enough fresh water on Grande-Terre. How do the people here get water for drinking?

Fort-de-France, Martinique's capital and largest city, resembles a town in France. Guadeloupe and Martinique are overseas* departments of France.

29 Netherlands Antilles

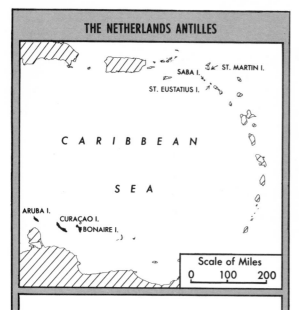

THE NETHERLANDS ANTILLES

Aruba, Bonaire, and Curaçao are the largest islands of the Netherlands Antilles. They are located off the coast of Venezuela. About five hundred miles to the northeast are the islands of St. Eustatius, Saba, and St. Martin. Part of St. Martin belongs to France.

GEOGRAPHY

The Netherlands Antilles is made up of five small islands and part of a sixth island in the West Indies. As the map above shows, the three largest islands are located about forty miles off the coast of Venezuela. These southern islands are named Aruba, Bonaire, and Curaçao. About five hundred miles to the northeast are the islands of St. Eustatius, Saba, and St. Martin. Only the southern part of St. Martin is in the Netherlands Antilles. The rest of this island belongs to France.

For many years, the Netherlands Antilles was a colony of the Netherlands.

322

In 1954, it became an equal partner with the Netherlands and Surinam in the Kingdom of the Netherlands. The Dutch queen appoints a governor to represent her in the Netherlands Antilles. Members of the lawmaking body are elected by the people of the islands.

Land and climate. The southern islands of the Netherlands Antilles are low and generally flat. In some places there are rolling hills. However, none of the hills rises much more than one thousand feet above sea level.

The climate of the southern islands is very dry. These islands have no mountains to force the trade winds to rise and drop their moisture. (See page 39 for more information about how mountains affect rainfall.) The southern islands often receive less than twenty inches of rain a year. Water for all purposes is very scarce. Most crops cannot be grown here without irrigation. In recent years, plants have been built on Curaçao and Aruba to make fresh water

Dry land on Aruba. The southern islands of the Netherlands Antilles are low and generally flat. Yearly rainfall is often less than twenty inches.

out of seawater. These plants have made more water available for homes and factories.

The northern islands of the Netherlands Antilles are more rugged than the southern islands. One mountain on St. Eustatius is nearly two thousand feet high. The island of Saba is a steep-sided volcano, rising about three thousand

St. Eustatius. The northern islands of the Netherlands Antilles are more rugged than the southern islands. They also receive more rainfall.

feet out of the sea. This volcano has not erupted for many years, and most of Saba's people live in its crater. The northern islands receive about forty inches of rainfall a year. Both the northern islands and the southern islands have warm weather all year round.

HISTORY

The islands of the Netherlands Antilles were discovered by Spanish explorers about 1500. A Spanish settlement was established on Curaçao. In the early 1600's, however, the Dutch took Curaçao from the Spaniards.

By 1650, the Dutch had settled on all of the islands that make up the Netherlands Antilles. Some of the settlers established plantations, where they grew such crops as sugarcane, cotton, and indigo. However, during the 1600's and 1700's, the islands of the Netherlands Antilles were chiefly important as trade centers. Trading ships often stopped at the Dutch islands to take on provisions. Curaçao became an important slave market. Thousands of Negroes were brought here from Africa

323

and sold as slaves to work on plantations in North and South America.

During the 1800's, the Dutch islands were less prosperous. The profitable slave trade came to an end because slavery was abolished throughout the Western Hemisphere. Fewer ships stopped at the islands to take on goods.

After 1900, oil became important to the Netherlands Antilles. Large oil deposits had been discovered in Venezuela, near Lake Maracaibo. This lake is only about two hundred miles from the islands of Aruba and Curaçao. Refineries were built on these islands to change the Venezuelan crude oil into gasoline, fuel oil, and other products. Large oil tankers carry these products to countries in many parts of the world.

The oil industry has brought prosperity to Curaçao and Aruba. Today the people of these islands have one of the highest standards of living of any people in the West Indies.

THE PEOPLE AND HOW THEY LIVE

People. People of many different races and nationalities live in the Netherlands Antilles. Most of the people on Curaçao, Bonaire, and the northern islands are Negro. On Aruba, most of the people are of mixed Carib Indian and European descent. Many people of Dutch descent live on Curaçao and Aruba. Also, people from Spain, Portugal, China, India, and many other countries have come to Curaçao and Aruba to work in the oil refineries or to find other jobs.

Earning a living. About one third of all the workers in the Netherlands Antilles make their living from the oil industry. There is one large refinery on Aruba and one on Curaçao. The refinery on Aruba is one of the largest in the

The oil refinery on Aruba is among the world's largest. Refineries on Aruba and Curaçao change Venezuelan crude oil into gasoline, fuel oil, and other products. The oil industry has brought prosperity to these islands. There are few other industries in the Netherlands Antilles.

world. Gasoline, fuel oil, and other petroleum products make up more than nine tenths of all exports from the Netherlands Antilles.

At the present time, there are few industries besides oil refining in the Netherlands Antilles. On the southern islands, small factories produce furniture, chocolate, cigarettes, clothing, and other products. Curaçao has a ship-building and ship-repair industry.

On Curaçao, some people earn a living by mining calcium phosphate. This is the only important mineral resource found in the Netherlands Antilles. Most of the calcium phosphate is exported to the United States, where it is used in making feed for poultry.

There is very little farming in the Netherlands Antilles, partly because of the lack of rainfall. Aloes, which will grow in a dry climate, are raised on Aruba and Bonaire. The southern islands import fruits, vegetables, and cereals from Venezuela. On the northern islands, people raise yams, sweet potatoes, and corn. Many farmers from these islands have moved to Curaçao or Aruba, where they can earn a better living by working at one of the refineries.

Many people in the Netherlands Antilles earn their living by working in shops or hotels or providing other services for tourists. The tourist industry brings more money to the Netherlands Antilles than any other industry except oil refining. Each year, more than 100,000 visitors come here to enjoy the warm climate, beautiful beaches, and interesting sights. In recent years, modern hotels have been built on each of the three southern islands and on St. Martin.

Willemstad is the capital and largest city of the Netherlands Antilles. It is built around a fine harbor and is one of the world's busiest ports.

Cities. The capital and largest city of the Netherlands Antilles is Willemstad (population about 44,000). It is built around a fine harbor on the southwestern coast of Curaçao. Near the city is Curaçao's huge oil refinery. Millions of tons of cargo enter and leave the port of Willemstad every year. Many ships bring food or oil here from Venezuela. Others take petroleum products to many different countries. A large number of ships stop at Willemstad to refuel. Willemstad is one of the busiest ports in the world.

The city of Willemstad is clean and colorful. Many of its buildings have red-tile roofs and are painted red, yellow, or other colors.

Facts To Review
1. Compare the northern and southern islands of the Netherlands Antilles with regard to (a) land features and (b) climate.
2. State two reasons why the islands of the Netherlands Antilles were important during the 1600's and 1700's.
3. What is the most important way of earning a living on the southern islands? Why are many farmers from the northern islands moving to the southern islands?

Facts About the Virgin Islands		
	United States	**British**
Area	133 square miles.	67 square miles.
Population	About 36,000.	About 8,000.
Capital and Largest City	Charlotte Amalie (population about 13,000).	Road Town (population about 1,500).
Racial Composition	Most of the people are Negro.	Most of the people are Negro.
Main Occupations	The largest number of workers have jobs in businesses that provide services for tourists. Many people work on sugarcane plantations or in factories that make rum.	Raising livestock is the most important occupation.
Important Farm Products	Sugarcane and livestock.	Livestock.
Manufacturing	Rum, the leading export, is made from molasses, a by-product of sugar production.	The British islands have little industry. Sailboats are made by hand, chiefly on Tortola.

Just east of Puerto Rico are about one hundred small islands and cays called the Virgin Islands. They are part of the Lesser Antilles. Only a few of the Virgin Islands are large enough to be of any importance. Most of the others are tiny and uninhabited.

The Virgin Islands are divided into two groups. More than half of the islands belong to the United States. They form a territory known as the Virgin Islands of the United States. The largest islands in this group are St. Croix, St. Thomas, and St. John. (See map on opposite page.)

East and north of the Virgin Islands of the United States are about thirty-five islands that belong to Great Britain. They make up a colony known as the British Virgin Islands. The largest islands in this group are Tortola, Virgin Gorda, and Anegada.

In the Virgin Islands, most of the land is rugged.

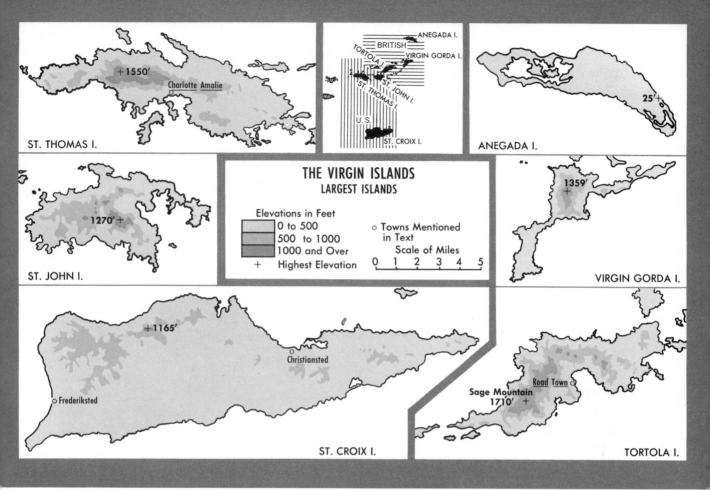

The Virgin Islands are part of the Lesser Antilles. They are divided into two groups. More than half of the islands belong to the United States, and the rest belong to Great Britain.

GEOGRAPHY

Land. Most of the land in the Virgin Islands is rugged and very hilly. The hillsides are generally steep, since the islands are the tops of tall mountains that rise from the ocean floor. However, few places are more than fifteen hundred feet above sea level. There is not much good farmland in the Virgin Islands. In many areas, the soil is so shallow that farming is almost impossible. Most of the land is covered with coarse grass and bushy plants. There are a few small patches of forest.

The only islands that have much level land are St. Croix and Anegada. The hills on St. Croix are less rugged than those on other islands. Much of the land is low and nearly level. This island has the best farmland in the Virgin Islands. Anegada is a coral island which rises barely twenty-five feet above the sea. Much of the soil here is not good for growing crops.

Climate. The climate of the Virgin Islands is warm and dry. Rainfall may vary greatly from year to year and from place to place. It averages about forty-five inches a year, but the moisture evaporates quickly in this warm climate. The shortage of water helps to make farming difficult. Often there is not enough water for drinking and other purposes. To help solve this problem, plants that make fresh water from seawater have been built on some of the islands.

HISTORY

Columbus discovered and named the Virgin Islands in 1493, on his second voyage to the New World. Although he claimed the islands for Spain, the Spanish did not settle here.

During the early 1600's, several European nations claimed one or more of the islands. Settlements were established by the Dutch, the French, and other peoples. None of these settlements lasted for more than a few years. There were no permanent settlements until 1666, when English planters arrived on Tortola. Plantations were established here and on the other Virgin Islands claimed by Great Britain. However, these plantations were never of much importance.

In 1672, Danish colonists landed on St. Thomas and claimed that island. By 1733, Denmark controlled St. John and St. Croix as well as St. Thomas. The Danes divided the land into plantations and imported Negro slaves to work for them. They produced sugar and cotton, which sold for high prices in Europe. Although the land was not very good for farming, the planters made large profits, especially from the sale of sugar.

Around the middle of the 1800's, sugarcane plantations on the Danish Virgin Islands became less profitable. By that time, Negro slaves far outnumbered white settlers. When the slaves on St. Croix started a rebellion in 1848, the governor freed all slaves on the Danish islands. Because the price of sugar had dropped in Europe, the plantation owners needed slave labor to operate at a profit. Faced with the loss of this cheap labor and with other problems, many Europeans moved away from the Danish islands.

In 1917, the United States bought the Danish Virgin Islands for 25 million dollars. These islands were considered valuable as bases for guarding shipping routes across the Caribbean Sea to the Panama Canal. At the end of World War II, the United States government set aside a large sum of money for building schools, roads, and hospitals, and for making other improvements on the islands.

THE PEOPLE AND HOW THEY LIVE

People. Only about 44,000 people make their homes on the Virgin Islands the year around. Most of them are Negro. About eight out of every ten people live on the United States islands of St. Thomas and St. Croix. Most of the rest live on the British islands.

Earning a living. The tourist industry is the main source of income for the people of the Virgin Islands of the United States. Each year, about 300,000 tourists come here to enjoy the beautiful scenery, fine beaches, and warm, pleasant climate. Many people on these islands work in hotels or shops, or provide other services for visitors. The tourist industry is also growing in the British Virgin Islands.

Grazing cattle. On the British Virgin Islands, raising livestock is the most important occupation.

A sugar mill on St. Croix processes cane grown on the island. The Virgin Islands have few factories.

Most of the farmers on the Virgin Islands grow sugarcane or raise livestock. Livestock raising is the most important occupation on the British islands. Nearly all of the sugarcane produced on the Virgin Islands is grown on St. Croix. The cane is processed in a mill on the island.

The Virgin Islands have very little manufacturing, partly because they lack natural resources. No valuable minerals have been found on any of the islands. Two leading manufactured products are rum and bay rum. Rum is an alcoholic beverage made from molasses, a by-product of sugar manufacturing. Bay rum is a skin lotion made from alcohol and the leaves of bayberry trees, which grow on St. John. On Tortola and some of the other islands, craftsmen make sailboats by hand. A plant to process imported bauxite is being built on St. Croix.

Cities. The largest town in the Virgin Islands is Charlotte Amalie (population about 13,000), which is located on the southern coast of St. Thomas. It is the capital of the Virgin Islands of the United States. Because Charlotte Amalie has a fine harbor, it has always been the Virgin Islands' most important seaport. During the 1700's and 1800's, sailing ships traveling between Europe and ports on the Caribbean Sea often stopped here to get water and supplies. Later, steamships stopped at Charlotte Amalie to refuel. Today, ships bring food and manufactured goods to Charlotte Amalie from Puerto Rico and the United States mainland. Some of these goods are then shipped to other ports in the Virgin Islands.

Christiansted and Frederiksted are the largest towns on St. Croix. They were founded by the Danes in the 1700's. Together they have fewer than eight thousand people.

Road Town, the capital of the British Virgin Islands, is located on Tortola. Its population is only about 1,500.

Think and Write
1. Why is farming difficult in most parts of the Virgin Islands?
2. State one reason why the United States bought the Danish Virgin Islands.
3. Why is there little manufacturing in the Virgin Islands? State one reason.
4. Why is the tourist industry important to the Virgin Islands of the United States?

Charlotte Amalie is the largest town in the Virgin Islands. Thousands of tourists come here each year.

329

Learning Map Skills

The earth is a sphere. Our earth is round like a ball. We call any object with this shape a sphere. The earth is, of course, a very large sphere. Its diameter* is about 8,000 miles, and its circumference* is about 25,000 miles. The earth is not a perfect sphere, however, for it is slightly flattened at the North and South poles.

A globe represents the earth. The globe in your classroom represents the earth. Since the globe is a sphere, it has the same shape as the earth. The surface of the globe shows the shapes of all the landmasses and bodies of water on the earth. By looking at the globe, you can see exactly where the continents, islands, and oceans are located. Globes are made with the North Pole at the top, but they are usually tilted to represent the way the earth is tilted. (See page 32.)

When you use a globe or a map, you need to know how many miles on the earth are represented by a given distance on the globe or map. This relationship, which is called the scale, may be expressed in numbers. For instance: 1 inch = 400 miles. Another way of expressing the scale is to include a small drawing that shows how many miles on the earth are represented by a certain distance on the globe or map. (See map on page 16.)

Locating places on the earth. Travelers, geographers, and other curious people have always wanted to know exactly where certain places are located on the earth. Over the years, a very accurate system has been worked out for giving such information. This system is used by people in all parts of the world.

A location system needs starting points and a unit of measurement. The North and South poles and the equator provide the starting points for the system we use to locate places on the earth. The unit of measurement is the degree, which is used in mathematics to measure circles. Any circle may be divided into 360 equal parts, called degrees.

Parallels show latitude. In order to locate a place on the earth, we first find out how far it is north or south of the equator. This distance, when measured in degrees, is called north or south latitude. The equator is the line of zero latitude. Since the North Pole is one fourth of the way around the earth from the equator, its location is one fourth of 360 degrees, or 90 degrees north latitude. Similarly, the South Pole is located at 90 degrees south latitude. A line that connects all points on the earth that have exactly the same latitude is called a parallel. This is because such a line is parallel to the equator. (See illustration A, below.)

Meridians show longitude. After we have determined the latitude of a place, we need to know its longitude. This is its location in an east-west direction. The lines that show longitude, called meridians, are drawn so as to connect the North and South poles. (See illustration B, below.) Longitude is measured from the meridian that passes through Greenwich, England. This line of zero longitude is called the prime meridian. Distance east or west of the prime meridian is called east or west longitude.

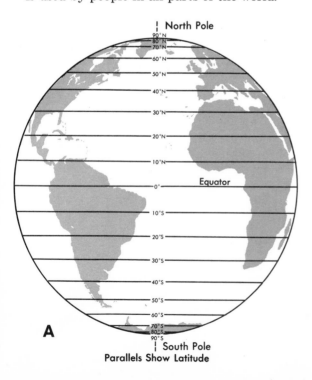

A
Parallels Show Latitude

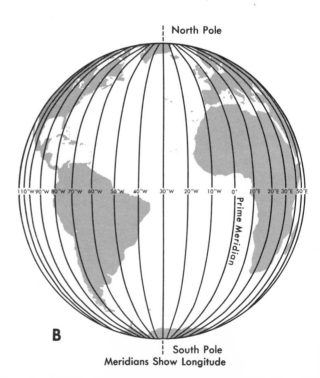

B
Meridians Show Longitude

A Round Globe on a Flat Surface

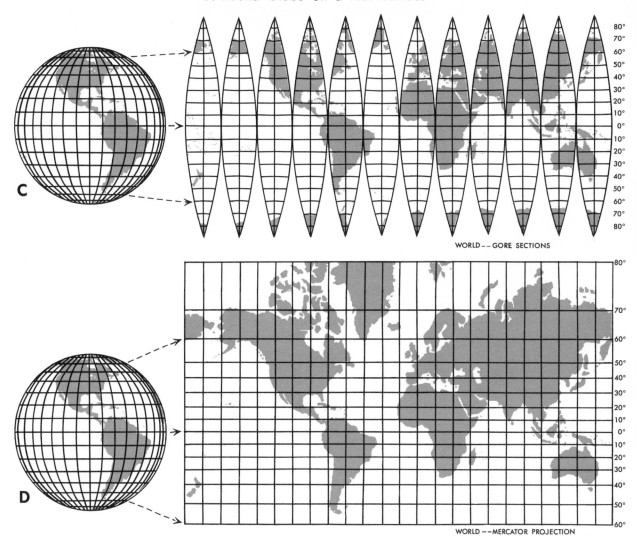

WORLD -- GORE SECTIONS

WORLD -- MERCATOR PROJECTION

Locating places on a globe. A parallel or a meridian can be drawn to represent any degree of latitude or longitude. On a globe, parallels and meridians are usually drawn every ten or fifteen degrees. The exact location of a place may be indicated like this: 30°N 90°W. This means that the place is located 30 degrees north of the equator, and 90 degrees west of the prime meridian. See if you can find this place on a globe.

The round earth on a flat map. An important fact about a sphere is that you cannot flatten out its surface perfectly. To prove this, you might perform an experiment. Cut an orange in half and scrape away the fruit. You will find that you cannot press either piece of orange peel flat without crushing it. If you cut one piece in half, however, you can press these smaller pieces nearly flat. Next, cut one of these pieces of peel into three sections, or gores, shaped like those shown in illustration C, above. You will find that you can press these small sections almost completely flat.

A map like that shown in illustration C can be made by cutting the surface of a globe into

twelve pieces shaped like the smallest sections of your orange peel. Such a map would be fairly accurate. However, an "orange-peel" map is not an easy map to use, because the continents and oceans are split. It would be difficult to measure distances across the splits.

A flat map can never show the earth's surface as truthfully as a globe can. On a globe, shape, size, distance, and direction are all accurate. Although a single flat map of the world cannot be drawn to show all four of these things correctly, a flat map can be made that will show one or more of these things accurately.

Illustration D, above, shows a world map drawn on a Mercator* projection. When you compare this map with a globe, you can see that the continents have almost the right shape. On this map, however, North America seems larger than Africa, which is not true. On Mercator maps, lands far from the equator appear much larger than they really are. These maps are useful to navigators because they show true directions.

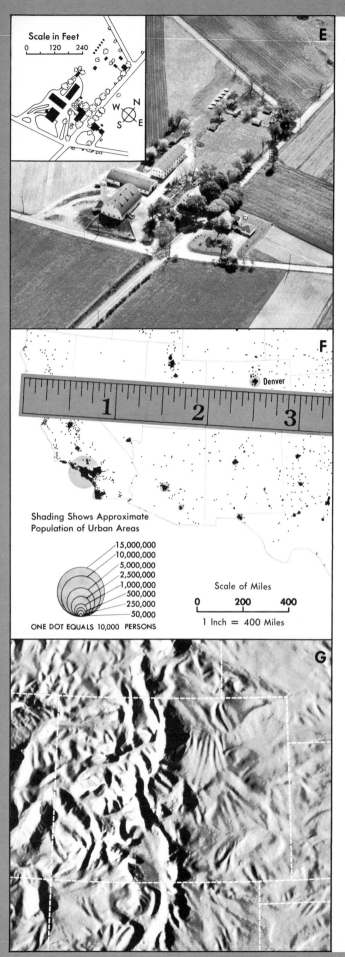

Scale in Feet
0   120   240

E

F

Denver

1   2   3

Shading Shows Approximate
Population of Urban Areas

15,000,000
10,000,000
5,000,000
2,500,000
1,000,000
500,000
250,000
50,000

ONE DOT EQUALS 10,000 PERSONS

Scale of Miles
0   200   400

1 Inch = 400 Miles

G

READING MAPS

Maps that show sections of our earth. For some purposes, we prefer maps that do not show the entire surface of the earth. A map of a very small area can be drawn with greater accuracy and can include more details than a map of a large area can.

Illustration E, at left, shows a photograph and a map of the same small section of the earth. Drawings on the map, called symbols, show the shape and location of things on the earth. The scale makes it possible to determine size and distance. Since north is not at the top of this map, a compass* rose has been drawn to show directions.

Maps for special purposes. Maps can show the location of many different kinds of things. For instance, they can show where volcanoes, mountain peaks, or ruins are located. A small chart listing the symbols and their meanings is usually included on a map. This is called the legend, or key. (See maps on pages 16 and 157.)

Symbols on some geography maps stand for the amounts of things in different places. Map F, at left, gives information about the population in the western part of the United States. The legend tells what the symbols stand for. If you will look at the maps on pages 112 and 113, you will see that a dot does not mean the same thing on all maps. The map on page 35 gives information about quantity in another way. Different designs, or patterns, cover areas that receive different amounts of yearly rainfall. (Compare the maps on pages 35 and 91.)

Maps also help us to understand the events that have occurred in history. The routes of early explorers in the Caribbean Lands are shown on the maps on pages 58 and 63. (See other history maps on pages 53 and 72.)

READING ELEVATIONS

Some maps show the earth's relief. When we fly over the earth in a jet plane, we can see mountains, valleys, and other landforms. We refer to such irregularities in the earth's surface as relief. For some purposes, we need maps and globes that show relief.

One way to show the earth's relief is to make a three-dimensional* model of the landforms on the surface of a globe or map. There is a problem, however, since a small model of the earth would be almost perfectly smooth.

If one inch on our globe or map equals one hundred miles on the earth, a mountain a mile high would rise only one hundredth of an inch above the surface of our map. Therefore, we use a different scale for the height of the landforms. If we let one inch equal a height of four miles, our mile-high mountain will now be one fourth of an inch high. It will show up clearly on the globe or map.

By photographing maps or globes with raised relief, we can make flat maps that show landforms. Map G, on the opposite page, is a photograph of a molded relief map. On page 8 is a photograph of a globe with raised relief. Photographs such as these help us to see what land areas really look like.

Topographic maps. Another kind of map that shows the earth's relief is the topographic, or contour, map. On a topographic map, lines are drawn to show different elevations of the earth's surface. These are called contour lines. The illustrations on this page help to explain how a topographic map is made.

Illustration H is a drawing of a hill. Around the bottom of the hill is our first contour line. This line connects all the points at the base of the hill that are exactly twenty feet above sea level. Higher up the hill, another contour line is drawn connecting all the points that are exactly forty feet above sea level. A line is also drawn at an elevation of sixty feet. Other lines are drawn at intervals of twenty feet until the top of the hill is reached. Since the hill is generally cone-shaped, each contour line is shorter than the one just below it.

Illustration I shows how the contour lines in the drawing of the hill (H) can be used to make a topographic map. This map gives us a great deal of information about the hill. Since each line is labeled with the elevation it represents, we can tell how high different parts of the hill are. It is important to remember that land does not rise in layers, as you might think when you look at a topographic map. Wherever the contour lines are far apart, we know that the land slopes gently. Where they are close together, the slope is steep. With practice, you can imagine the land in your mind as you look at such a map. Topographic maps are especially useful to engineers and architects.

On a topographic map, the spaces between the contour lines may be filled in with different shades of gray. Map J, at right, was made in this way. The four different shades of gray represent four different elevations of land, as indicated in the key box. This map shows about the same area as that in map G, on the opposite page. On some maps, colors are used to fill in the spaces between the contour lines.

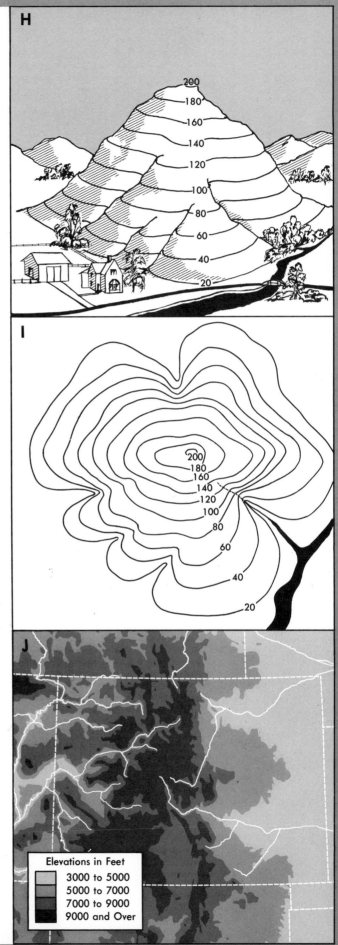

Elevations in Feet
3000 to 5000
5000 to 7000
7000 to 9000
9000 and Over

EDITORIAL AND MAP ACKNOWLEDGMENTS

Grateful acknowledgment is made to Scott, Foresman and Company for the pronunciation system used in this book, which is taken from the Thorndike-Barnhart Dictionary Series.

Grateful acknowledgment is made to the following for permission to use cartographic data in this book:

Aero Service Corporation relief map copyright: Page 332; Creative Arts: Pages 32 and 33; Panoramic Studios: Page 8; U.S. Department of Agriculture: Pages 91, 112, 113, and 114; U.S. Department of Commerce, Bureau of Weather: Page 46.

PICTURE ACKNOWLEDGMENTS

Grateful acknowledgment is made to the following for permission to use the illustrations found in this book: Alpha Photo Associates: Page 231; page 282 by Elizabeth Hibbs; page 143 by Max Hunn; Anne Bolt — London, England: Pages 25 (upper), 27 (upper), 99, 100, 110, 123, 154, 229 (upper), 284, and 304; Bahamas Development Board — Nassau, Bahamas: Page 27; page 56 by Frederic Maura; page 310 by Roland Rose; Bettmann Archive: Pages 50, 62, and 68; Black Star: Page 45; pages 37, 88, 140, and 268 (both) by Gordian Troeller; pages 22 (upper), 71 (left), 89 (upper), 95 (left), 114, 138, 177, 193, 200, 247, and 301 by Herbert Lanks; page 156 by Jim Mitchell; pages 87, 129, and 142 by Lee Lockwood; page 85 by Manfred Kreiner; page 196 by Owen;

Caterpillar News Service: Pages 127 and 225 (lower); Commonwealth of Puerto Rico, Dept. of Education — Hato Rey, Puerto Rico; Pages 285 and 295 (upper); Courtesy of Wyeth, Philadelphia: Page 236 (lower) by Jesse E. Hartman; Devaney: Page 295 (lower); page 168 by Herbert Lanks; Direccion General de Turismo — Santo Domingo, Dominican Republic: Page 254; Dominican Republic Embassy: Page 259; Eastfoto: Pages 12, 71 (right), 116 (top), 125, 244, 246, and 249; Estudio "Canossa" — San Salvador, El Salvador: Pages 121, 161, and 173; Frederic Lewis: Pages 26 (upper), 169, 197, and 300; pages 97, 162, and 211 (lower) by Max Hunn; pages 286 and 294 (upper) by Nat Norman; Freelance Photographers Guild: Pages 163, 179, and 276; page 30 by Dana Brown; page 318 by Esty Epstein; pages 17 and 19 by K. B. Roche; page 23 by Max Hunn; page 44 by Steinmetz; Galloway: Pages 24, 29, 33, 96, 132 (left), 158, 159, 183, 187, 189 (upper), 205, 209, 215, 223 (upper), 226, and 291; Hank Meyer Associates, Inc.: Page 41; Harvard College Library: Page 79; Historical Pictures Service: Pages 61, 64, 67 (lower), 73, 75, 77, 172, and 219; Hugh B. Cave: Pages 263, 264, 266, 270, and 271; Instituto Costarricense de Turismo — San José, Costa Rica: Pages 206, 207, and 213; International Bank for Reconstruction and Development: Pages 103, 109 (lower), 175, 176, 211 (upper), and 273; International Telephone and Telegraph: Page 293; Jamaica Tourist Board: Pages 126 and 283 (upper); Library of Congress: Page 57 repainted by Nichols; Monkmeyer Press Photo Service: Page 171; page 292 (lower) by Fujihara; pages 151, 274, 297 (upper), 299, 314, 316, 320 (upper), and 328 by Henle; pages 166 and 185 by Lanks; pages 178, 192, and 212 by Tiers; Panama Canal Co. — Balboa Heights, Panama: Pages 137, 220, and 221; Panamanian Institute of Tourism — Panama City, Panama: Page 227; Pan American Airways: Pages 3, 18, and 132 (right); Pan American Union: Pages 189 (lower), 251, and 253; Paul Popper, Ltd. — London, England: Pages 67 (upper), 83 (lower), 89 (lower), 92 (both), 95 (center), 98, 115, 132 (center), 145, 150, 152, 165 (lower), 167 (upper), 181 (lower), 182, 188, 194, 236 (upper), 252, 256, 257, 258 (both), 260, 261, 279, 280, 281, 283 (lower), 303, and 313; Photo Researchers, Inc.: Page 25 (lower); pages 48, 55, 101, and 272 by Bradley Smith; page 28 by Carl Frank; pages 51, 52, 149, 160, 164, 165 (upper), and 216 by George Holton; pages 83 (lower), 107, 111, 118, 153, 288, 297 (lower), 298, 305, 308, 320 (lower), 322, 323, 326, and 329 (both) by Fritz Henle; page 155 (upper) by Jean Speiser; page 325 by John Ross; pages 229 (lower) and 269 by Odette Mennesson-Riguad; pages 21, 26 (lower), 40, 54, 86, 95 (right), 131, 141, 144, 146, 167 (lower), 174, 180, 181 (upper), 190, 191, 199, 202, 203, and 223 (lower) by Tom Hollyman; Pix, Inc.: Page 276; Puerto Rico Cement Corp. — Ponce, Puerto Rico: Page 290; Puerto Rico Economic Development Administration: Page 294 (lower); Puerto Rico Information Service: Page 289; Radio Times Hulton Picture Library — London, England: Page 70; Raymond E. Fideler: Pages 10, 148, 225 (upper), and 228;

Roberts: Pages 22 (lower), 102, 106, 116 (lower), 130, 218, 235, 243, and 302; South Puerto Rico Sugar Co.: Page 120 by Francis Stopelman; Standard Oil Co.: Page 324; Texaco Trinidad, Inc.: Page 122;

Three Lions: Page 155 (lower); United Fruit Co.: Pages 81, 105 (right), 210, and 224; United Nations: Pages 36, 69, 105 (left), 201, 217, and 265; United Press International: Pages 109 (upper), 241, 242, and 278; University of Puerto Rico — Río Piedras, Puerto Rico: Page 296; Wide World Photos: Pages 222, 233, 238, 239, and 293 (upper).

GLOSSARY
COMPLETE PRONUNCIATION KEY

The pronunciation of each word is shown just after the word, in this way: **aqueduct** (ak'wə dukt). The letters and signs used are pronounced as in the words below. The mark ' is placed after a syllable with a primary or strong accent, as in the example above. The mark ' after a syllable shows a secondary or lighter accent, as in **archipelago** (är'kə pel'ə gō).

a	hat, cap	j	jam, enjoy	u	cup, butter
ā	age, face	k	kind, seek	ù	full, put
ã	care, air	l	land, coal	ü	rule, move
ä	father, far	m	me, am	ū	use, music
		n	no, in		
b	bad, rob	ng	long, bring		
ch	child, much			v	very, save
d	did, red	o	hot, rock	w	will, woman
		ō	open, go	y	young, yet
		ô	order, all	z	zero, breeze
e	let, best	oi	oil, voice	zh	measure, seizure
ē	equal, see	ou	house, out		
ėr	term, learn				
		p	paper, cup	ə	represents:
f	fat, if	r	run, try	a	in about
g	go, bag	s	say, yes	e	in taken
h	he, how	sh	she, rush	i	in pencil
		t	tell, it	o	in lemon
i	it, pin	th	thin, both	u	in circus
ī	ice, five	ŦH	then, smooth		

---

abaca (ä'bə kä'). A fiber obtained from the leaf stems of the abaca plant, which is related to the banana plant. Abaca is used to make rope.

active. When referring to a volcano, "active" means that the volcano constantly or from time to time emits steam, smoke, ashes, or lava.

adobe (ə dō'bi). Refers to brick made of earth that has been mixed with water and straw and then baked in the sun.

Africa. The second largest continent on the earth. (See map, page 60.)

aguardiente (ä'gwär dyen'tā). An alcoholic beverage, usually made from sugarcane. *Aguardiente* is a Spanish word meaning "burning water."

alloy (al'oi) **steel.** Steel made by combining iron and at least one other metal, such as nickel or manganese, with carbon.

aloes. A group of plants having thick, sharp-pointed leaves. Aloes grow in warm, dry climates. The leaves of some aloes contain a bitter juice used to make medicines.

Alvarado (al'və räd'ō), **Pedro de,** 1495?-1541. A leader in the Spanish conquest of America. He assisted Cortés in the conquest of Mexico in 1521. Between 1523 and 1527, Alvarado conquered southern Guatemala and all of El Salvador. (See page 63.)

American Revolution, 1775-1783. The war in which thirteen British colonies in North America won their independence from Great Britain. These thirteen colonies became the first states of the United States.

Anegada (an'ə gä'də) **Passage.** The waterway, about 40 miles wide, between the Virgin Islands and neighboring islands of the Lesser Antilles. It is one of the main passages between the Atlantic Ocean and the Caribbean Sea.

aqueduct (ak'wə dukt). A man-made canal, tunnel, or large pipe through which water travels to the place where it is to be used.

arable (ar'ə bəl). Refers to land that is suitable for cultivating crops.

Arawak (ä'rä wäk) **Indians.** A group of Indian tribes of South America and the West Indies. At one time, Arawak tribes occupied nearly all of the islands in the West Indies. By the time of the Spanish exploration of America, the Carib Indians had conquered the Arawak who lived in the Lesser Antilles. (See **Carib Indians.**) Today no pureblood Arawak Indians live in the Caribbean Lands, but Arawak tribes still live in South America. (Pages 54 and 55 give more information about the Arawak.)

archipelago (är'kə pel'ə gō). A group of islands, or a body of water that is dotted with islands.

Argentina (är'jən tē'nə). A country in the southern part of South America.

Asia. The largest continent on the earth. (See map, page 60.)

audiencia (ou dē en'sēə). In Spanish colonies in America, a council that served as a high court. Often it also had control over political and military affairs. The district that was served by this court was also called an *audiencia.* The *audiencia* of Guatemala included part of what is now Mexico, and all Spanish colonies in Central America except Panama. The *audiencia* of Santo Domingo included Spanish possessions in the West Indies.

avocado (av'ə kä'dō). A tropical fruit with a large seed and soft, oily flesh. It is often eaten in salads.

axis of the earth. An imaginary straight line that passes through the earth, joining the North and South poles. It takes the earth about twenty-four hours to rotate, or turn around, once on its axis.

bagasse (bə gas'). The pulpy or strawlike material that remains after sugarcane has been crushed to remove its juice. Bagasse is used as fuel in sugar mills and also is made into furfural. See **furfural.**

Bahama (bə hä'mə) **Islands.** A large group of islands that lie in the Atlantic Ocean north of the Greater Antilles. (See map, page 16.) Most of the Bahamas are united as an internally self-governing British colony. The Turks and Caicos Islands, at the southeastern end of the Bahamas, are a separate British colony.

Balboa (bal bō'ə), **Vasco Núñez de,** 1475-1519. A Spanish adventurer and explorer who discovered the Pacific Ocean. (See page 63 for more information.)

balsam of Peru. A fragrant, thick liquid obtained from a tree that grows chiefly in El Salvador. Balsam of Peru is used in making perfumes and medicines.

basin. An area of land that is largely surrounded by higher land.

Basse-Terre. See **Guadeloupe.**

Bastidas (bäs tē'däs), **Rodrigo de,** 1460?-? . A Spanish sea captain who explored the northern coasts of both South America and the Isthmus of Panama in 1501-1502.

bauxite (bôk'sīt). The ore that is the chief source of aluminum.

birthrate. The relationship between the number of births and the number of people in a given population. Usually the birthrate is stated as the number of births per hundred or per thousand persons during a year.

blockade (blo kād'). The use of armed forces by one nation to obstruct the trade and communications of another nation. Usually a blockade is carried out by patrolling a country's borders to prevent the transporting of goods to or from the blockaded nation. The blockade of Cuba, established by the United States in 1962, was a limited blockade. It stopped only the shipment of missiles and other military weapons to Cuba.

Brazil (brə zil'). A country in eastern South America.

British. Refers to Great Britain. See **Great Britain.**

British Commonwealth. The name commonly used to refer to the Commonwealth of Nations, an association of independent nations and their possessions, joined together for mutual benefit. The Commonwealth is headed by the British crown.

buccaneers (buk ə nirz'). Bold, adventurous sea raiders, or pirates, especially those who attacked Spanish ships and colonies in the Western Hemisphere in the 1600's.

cacao (kə kä'ō). Seeds from which chocolate and cocoa are made. Also refers to the tree on which these seeds grow.

calcium (kal'si əm). A soft, silvery-white metal. Combined with other substances, calcium is found in soil, in many rocks, and in most plants and animals.

336

calypso (kə lip′sō). A kind of folk music, using African rhythms, that originated in Trinidad. A calypso singer makes up verses that usually deal with news or gossip.

Caribbean (kar′ə bē′ən) **Lowland.** A flat, swampy lowland that extends along the Caribbean coast of Central America. (See map, page 20.) This lowland has a hot, humid climate and is mostly covered with dense rainforest.

Caribbean (kar′ə bē′ən) **Sea.** An arm of the Atlantic Ocean. (See map, page 16.)

Carib (kar′ib) **Indians.** A group of Indian tribes that originally lived in northeastern South America. About A.D. 1300, Carib tribes invaded the Lesser Antilles and seized the islands from the Arawak Indians. (See **Arawak Indians.**) Page 55 gives more information about the Carib Indians.

cativo (kə tē′vō). A large tree of Central America. Its wood is used for making plywood.

causeway. Generally, a causeway is a raised road built over water or over swampy land.

cay. A small, low island or reef.

central (sen träl′). A large mill that processes sugarcane.

Central America. The part of North America that lies south of Mexico. Central America is a long, narrow strip of land bordered on one side by the Caribbean Sea and on the other by the Pacific Ocean. (See map, page 16.) There are six independent nations and one European colony in Central America.

Central American Federation. Also called the United Provinces of Central America. This federation was established in 1823 by Costa Rica, El Salvador, Guatemala, Honduras, and Nicaragua. The federation broke up in 1838, and by 1841 each of the five member provinces had become an independent republic.

chicle (chik′əl). A gummy substance obtained from the latex, or juice, of the sapodilla tree. (See **sapodilla.**) Chicle is used to make chewing gum.

China. A large country in eastern Asia. See **Asia.**

chromium (krō′mi əm). A grayish metal that does not rust easily. It is used to make stainless steel and to coat, or plate, automobile parts and other metal articles.

Church of England. The Christian church that is established by law as the national church of England.

Cibao (si bä′ō). A broad valley in the northern part of the Dominican Republic. (See map, page 250.)

circumference (sər kum′fər əns). The distance around the outside of a circle or a sphere.

cisterns. Tanks or containers, usually underground, in which rainwater is stored.

citrus. Refers to oranges, lemons, grapefruit, and similar fruits.

civil war. A war fought between groups of people who are citizens of the same nation or country. The Civil War in the United States lasted from 1861 to 1865. This war was between the North, or Union, and the South, or Confederacy.

classical music. Music that has artistic communication rather than entertainment as its chief purpose. Classical music is sometimes described as "serious" music.

climate. The kind of weather that a place has over a period of many years. The most important conditions that determine climate are wind, sunshine, temperature, the amount of moisture in the air, and the amount of rain, hail, and snow that falls.

cobalt (kō′bôlt). A tough, silver-white metal often found in ores that contain iron and nickel.

Cold War. The conflict between the democratic nations of the world and the Communist nations. It is called a "cold" war because it is fought largely with propaganda and with economic and social pressures rather than with guns.

Colombia (kə lum′bi ə). A country in northwestern South America. (See map, page 16.)

colony. A territory outside the country that controls it.

---

common market. An association of countries formed to promote greater freedom of trade between the member nations and to help their industries grow. Most of the countries of Central America have joined in a common market. Before this common market was formed, many manufacturers in Central America were unable to sell enough goods to earn money for expanding their industries. It was difficult for a manufacturer to sell goods outside the borders of his country. This was caused partly by tariffs, or taxes, which each Central American country placed on goods coming in from outside its boundaries. Now the common-market countries of Central America are gradually lowering or eliminating the tariffs on products shipped between them. Manufacturers will be better able to sell their goods to customers in other common-market countries because the prices of these goods will be lower. These manufacturers will have more money to use for expanding their industries. They will be able to buy more machinery and provide jobs for more workers. It is hoped that the common market will help to raise the standard of living in Central America.

communism. Commonly, the teachings and actions of the Communist parties in the Soviet Union and other countries. The members of these parties are called Communists. A government controlled by a Communist party may also be described as "Communist." Communists believe that Communist governments must be established throughout the world, by force if necessary. Under communism, industry, farming, trade, transportation, communication, education, and most other activities are controlled by the government.

Communist. Refers to the theory of communism. Also, a person who belongs to or supports a Communist party. See **communism.**

compass rose. A small drawing included on a map to show directions. A compass rose is often used as a decoration. Here are three examples of compass roses:

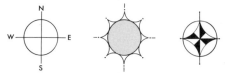

conquistadors (kon kwis′tə dôrz). The leaders of the Spanish forces that conquered vast areas in America, especially in Mexico and Peru. Conquistador means "conqueror" in Spanish.

Conservative. In Central America, Conservative refers to a certain set of political beliefs. A Conservative is a person having those beliefs. (See page 74 for more information.)

continent. One of the main landmasses on the earth. There are seven continents — Asia, Africa, North America, South America, Europe, Australia, and Antarctica. Some geographers consider that Asia and Europe together form one continent, called Eurasia.

contour. The outline of an object or surface.

convoy (kon′voi). A group of ships, vehicles, or persons protected by an armed escort during travel. Usually a convoy is a group of merchant ships protected by warships.

cooperative. In Cuba, a large, government-owned farm. Workers on a cooperative are supposed to receive a share of the profits.

copra (kop′rə). Dried coconut meat from which coconut oil is obtained.

coral. A rocklike limestone formation produced by huge colonies of tiny animals that live in the sea. (See page 27.)

Cordillera Central (kor′dəl yär′ə sen träl′). A range of mountains on the island of Hispaniola. (See map, page 250.) Cordillera Central is Spanish for "Central Range."

Cortés (kôr tez′), **Hernán,** 1485-1547. A Spanish soldier and adventurer. He led the expedition that conquered the Aztec Indians of Mexico. After this conquest, Cortés led other expeditions to extend Spanish rule in Mexico and Central America.

Creole (krē′ōl). In Central America and the West Indies, Creole generally refers to a person of European descent who was born in this region. Creole is also the name of the language spoken by most of the people of Haiti. (See page 269 for more information.)

crude oil. Petroleum before it has been refined.

customhouse. A building or office, often located in a port, where taxes are paid on goods being imported or exported.

Darien (där i en′). A region of dense jungle in eastern Panama and northwestern Colombia. (See map, page 214.)

Denmark. A country in northwestern Europe. See **Europe.**

density of population. Refers to the average number of people living in a given area. Usually this average is figured by dividing the total number of people living in an area by the total number of square miles in that area.

Department of State. A department of the government of the United States. The Department of State provides the president with information about other countries and advises him on policies toward these countries. It also conducts official business with other nations.

dialect (dī′ə lekt). A variety of a language that is somewhat different from the standard language. Usually dialect refers to spoken rather than written language.

diameter (dī am′ə tər). The length of a straight line that extends from one side of an object to the other. This line must pass through the exact center of the object.

diplomatic (dip′lə mat′ik) **relations.** The normal means of communication between nations, carried on peacefully by representatives of the governments.

divi-divi (div′i div′i). A small tropical American tree belonging to the pea family. Its pods yield a substance called tannin, used in tanning leather.

Drake, Sir Francis, 1540?-1596. A famous English sea captain. With the permission of the queen of England, he led raids on Spanish ships and towns in the Western Hemisphere. Drake was the first Englishman to sail around the world.

Dutch. Refers to the people and language of the Netherlands. See **Netherlands.**

emigration. Leaving a country or region to live permanently somewhere else.

England. Most of the southern part of Great Britain. See **Great Britain.**

Episcopalian (i pis′kə pāl′yən). Refers to a member of a Protestant church that is closely related to the Church of England.

equator (i kwā′tər). An imaginary line around the middle of the earth. It divides the earth into a northern half and a southern half.

equinox (ē′kwə noks). The time of the year when the sun shines directly on the equator, about March 21 and September 22. On these dates, day and night are of equal length everywhere on earth.

Eurasia (ūr ā′zhə). The largest landmass on earth. Eurasia is composed of the continents of Europe and Asia. Some geographers consider Eurasia itself to be a continent.

Europe. The sixth largest continent on the earth. (See map, page 60.) Europe is the western part of Eurasia. See **Eurasia.**

Europeans. Refers to the people of Europe. See **Europe.**

fiesta (fi es′tə). A festival, or holiday. Usually a religious celebration.

France. A country in the western part of Europe. See **Europe.**

French. Refers to the people and language of France. See **France.**

furfural (fėr′fə ral). A yellow or brown liquid made by treating plant materials, such as bagasse, with acid. (See **bagasse.**) Furfural is used in refining petroleum and in making drugs and synthetic fibers.

Gaillard (gāl′ärd) **Cut.** A channel that forms part of the Panama Canal. (See map, page 139.) Named after David Gaillard, the engineer who was in charge of excavating the channel.

Gama (ga′mə), **Vasco da,** 1469?-1524. A famous Portuguese navigator. He was the first European to reach the Indies by sailing around the southern tip of Africa (1497-1498).

Gatun (gä tün′) **Lake.** A large lake that was formed by building a dam across the Chagres River, in Panama. Gatun Lake provides the waterway for about half the length of the Panama Canal. (See map, page 139.)

general strike. A strike, or stoppage of work, that is carried out by all or a large number of the workers in several industries to achieve a political or economic goal.

PRONUNCIATION KEY: hat, āge, cãre, fär; let, ēqual, tėrm; it, īce; hot, ōpen, ôrder; oil, out; cup, put, rüle, ūse; child; long; thin; ŧHen; zh, measure; ə represents a in about, e in taken, i in pencil, o in lemon, u in circus. For the complete key, see page 335.

González (gôn sä′läs), **Gil,**   ?-1543. A Spanish soldier who explored parts of what are now Costa Rica, Nicaragua, and Honduras. (See page 63 for more information.)

Grande-Terre. See **Guadeloupe.**

grants. Gifts of land or money that are to be used for a special purpose.

Great Britain. The largest island in Europe. It lies off the western coast of the continent. Great Britain includes England, Scotland, and Wales. See **Europe.**

Greater Antilles (an til′ēz). A group of islands in the West Indies. (See map, page 16.) The Greater Antilles consists of the large islands of Cuba, Hispaniola, Jamaica, and Puerto Rico, and the small islands off their coasts.

Grenadines (gren′ə dēnz′). A group of about 600 small, thinly populated islands that lie between the British islands of St. Vincent and Grenada in the Lesser Antilles. (See map, page 312.) For purposes of government, the Grenadines are divided between the colonies of St. Vincent and Grenada.

Guadeloupe (gwä′də lüp′). A group of islands in the Lesser Antilles that make up an overseas department of France. (See Chapter 28.) Usually the name Guadeloupe is used to refer to the two main islands of the group, Grande-Terre and Basse-Terre. (See map, page 319.)

Guanacaste (gwä′nä käs′tä). A province of Costa Rica, located in the northwestern part of the country. Guanacaste is also the name of a range of mountains in this province.

guerrilla (gə ril′ə). Refers to warfare carried on by small groups of fighters who are not part of a regular army. Guerrilla forces make surprise attacks, destroy supplies, and cut lines of communication.

Gulf of Fonseca (fon sä′kä). An inlet of the Pacific Ocean. (See map, page 170.)

gypsum. A chalky mineral used in making cement and plaster and as a fertilizer.

hacienda (hä′si en′də). In Spanish-speaking countries, a large estate, such as a farm.

henequen (hen′ə kin). A strong fiber obtained from the leaves of a tropical plant, also called henequen. Used to make rope and coarse fabrics.

Hindu (hin′dü). Refers to a follower of Hinduism. See **Hinduism.**

Hinduism (hin′dü iz əm). The main religion of India and several other parts of Asia.

Hispaniola (his′pən yō′lə). The second largest island in the West Indies. Hispaniola is divided between the countries of Haiti and the Dominican Republic. (See map, page 250.)

Holy Week. The week before Easter Sunday.

hookworm. A disease caused by hookworms. These tiny worms enter the body through the skin, or in impure food or water.

humid (hū′mid). Moist. When referring to weather, humid means that the air contains much water vapor.

hurricane belt. The area in which hurricanes generally occur in the Caribbean Lands region. The hurricane belt includes the Greater Antilles, the northern islands of the Lesser Antilles, and the Caribbean coast of Central America north of Costa Rica. (See page 46 for more information about hurricanes.)

hydroelectric (hī′drō i lek′trik). Refers to hydroelectricity. See **hydroelectricity.**

hydroelectricity (hī′drō i lek′tris′ə ti). Electricity produced by waterpower. The force of rushing water runs machines called generators, which produce electricity.

hypotheses (hī poth′ə sēz). Possible solutions, or "educated guesses." A hypothesis may prove to be false, but it helps us in our search for the right solution to a problem.

immigration. Entering a country or region with the purpose of living there permanently.

inactive. When referring to a volcano, "inactive" means that the volcano is not active. (See **active.**) An inactive volcano may be either dormant or extinct. A dormant volcano is considered to be "sleeping" and is expected to become active again in the future. An extinct volcano has not erupted in recorded history and probably will not become active again.

India. A country in southern Asia. See **Asia.**

Indies. A name once used for the East Indies, a large group of islands off the southeastern coast of Asia. (See **Asia.**) India, the Indo-Chinese and Malay peninsulas, and the Philippine Islands were also sometimes considered to be in the Indies.

340

indigo (in'də gō). A plant from which a deep-blue dye, also called indigo, may be obtained.

Inter-American Highway. A highway that extends from Laredo, Texas, to Panama City, Panama. It is part of the Pan American Highway system. (See page 134 for more information.)

Irazú (ē'rä sü'). An active volcano in central Costa Rica. (See map, page 204.)

Islam (is'ləm). The religion founded by a prophet named Mohammed, who was born in Arabia in A.D. 570. Followers of Islam are called Moslems.

Isthmus (is'məs) **of Panama.** The strip of land that is occupied by the Republic of Panama. (See map on page 214.) An isthmus is a narrow strip of land that is bordered by water on each side and connects two larger areas of land.

jaguar (jag'wär). A large, tiger-like animal.

jungle. Dense, tangled plant life that grows in tropical areas where rainfall and warm sunshine are abundant.

junta (hùn'tə). A Spanish word meaning council or committee. In English, junta refers to a group of people who direct the government of a country. A junta usually gains control after a previous government has been overthrown.

Ladino (lə dē'nō). In some countries of Central America, a mestizo or an Indian who speaks Spanish and follows European rather than Indian customs.

Lake Atitlán (ä'ti tlän'). A large lake in the mountains of southwestern Guatemala. (See map, page 157, and pictures, pages 18 and 156.)

Lake Managua (mə nä'gwə). A lake about 40 miles long in western Nicaragua. (See map, page 195.)

Lake Maracaibo (mar'ə kī'bō). A large lake in northwestern Venezuela. Connected by a narrow channel to an inlet of the Caribbean Sea.

Lake Nicaragua (nik'ə rä'gwə). A large lake about 40 miles wide and 100 miles long in southwestern Nicaragua. (See map, page 195.)

land reform laws. Laws passed to improve the economic and social conditions of farmers. These laws aim to help farmers rent land at reasonable rates or to obtain farms of their own.

Latin America. Includes Mexico and the parts of Central America, the West Indies, and South America where Spanish, French, or Portuguese is the main language.

lava. Melted rock that flows out of a volcano, or opening in the earth. Lava becomes hard as it cools.

Lempa (lām'pä) **River.** A river about 200 miles long that begins in Guatemala, flows through southwestern Honduras, and then flows across El Salvador into the Pacific Ocean. (See map, page 170.)

Lenca Indians. A group of Indian tribes who live in northeastern El Salvador and southwestern Honduras. During the 1500's, the ancestors of these people occupied a larger part of Central America.

Lent. A period of fasting observed by some churches before Easter.

Lesser Antilles (an til'ēz). A group of small islands in the West Indies. (See map, page 16.)

Liberal. In Central America, Liberal refers to a certain set of political beliefs. A Liberal is a person having those beliefs. (See page 74 for more information.)

limestone. A rock that consists chiefly of a substance called calcium carbonate. Usually limestone is gray. It is used in building and in many other industries, especially in making steel and cement. Coral is one form of limestone. See **coral.**

literacy (lit'ər ə si). The ability to read and write. Usually only persons ten years of age and older are considered when determining the percentage of literate persons in a country.

lock. A section of a canal or river that is used to raise or lower ships to different water levels. A gate at each end permits ships to enter or leave the lock. When a ship is in the lock, the gates are closed. The water level in the lock is raised or lowered to the level of the other part of the canal or river. Then the ship passes out of the lock.

PRONUNCIATION KEY: hat, āge, cãre, fär; let, ēqual, tèrm; it, īce; hot, ōpen, ôrder; oil, out; cup, pùt, rüle, ūse; child; long; thin; ᴛHen; zh, measure; ə represents a in about, e in taken, i in pencil, o in lemon, u in circus. For the complete key, see page 335.

logwood. A tree of Mexico, Central America, and the West Indies that has very hard, brown wood in its center. A dye, also called logwood, is prepared from this wood.

mace. A fragrant spice prepared by drying the lacelike covering on the shell of a nutmeg. See **nutmeg.**

machete (mə shet′i). A large, heavy knife with a broad blade. Machetes are mainly used to cut sugarcane and to clear brush from land.

mahogany (mə hog′ə ni). A tropical tree that yields a valuable, hard, reddish-brown wood. Mahogany wood is often used to make furniture.

manganese (mang′gə nēs). A grayish-white metal that is added to iron in making steel. Manganese makes the steel stronger.

mango. A tropical fruit with yellowish-red, juicy pulp and a large, flat seed.

manioc (man′i ok). A tropical plant with starchy roots that are used for food. Also called cassava.

Maya (mä′yə) **Indians.** A group of civilized Indian tribes of northwestern Central America and southern Mexico. In the early 1500's, most of the Maya were conquered by the Spanish. Today there are more than two million descendants of the Maya living in Mexico and Central America. (See pages 49 to 54 for more information about the civilization of the Maya.)

Mercator (mėr kā′tər) **projection.** One of many possible arrangements of meridians and parallels on which a map of the world may be drawn. Devised by Gerhardus Mercator, a Flemish geographer who lived from 1512 to 1594. On a Mercator map, all meridians are drawn straight up and down, with north at the top. The parallels are drawn straight across, but increasingly farther apart toward the poles. If you will compare the first section, or gore, of the "orange-peel" map on page 331 with the section of the Mercator map directly below it, you will see how the Mercator map straightens out the meridians. Because the Mercator section has been stretched in an east-west direction, except at the equator, the landmass appears wider than it does in the "orange-peel" section. To make up for this east-west stretching, the Mercator map is also stretched in a north-south direction.

Therefore, on Mercator maps the shapes of landmasses and bodies of water are fairly accurate, but their sizes are not.

Meseta Central (mā sä′tä sen träl′). Spanish for "central tableland." The Meseta Central is a fertile, generally flat basin in the highlands of Costa Rica. (See map, page 204.) This basin covers about 3,500 square miles.

mestizo (mes tē′zō). Refers to a person of mixed Indian and white descent.

middle latitudes. Regions of the earth that lie generally between the 30 and 60 degree parallels of latitude in both the Northern and Southern hemispheres.

minimum wage laws. Laws that fix the lowest wage, or amount of money, that an employer is permitted to pay a worker.

Miskito (mis kē′tō) **Indians.** (Also spelled Mosquito.) A group of Indian tribes who live in the dense forests on the eastern coast of Nicaragua. Miskito Indians were living in this area at the time of Columbus' explorations. Today there are few pureblood Miskito Indians, because of intermarriage with other races.

Mona Passage. The waterway between Hispaniola and Puerto Rico. Mona Passage is about 75 miles wide and is one of the main passages between the Atlantic Ocean and the Caribbean Sea.

Monroe Doctrine. A policy of the United States that was stated in a message to Congress by President James Monroe in 1823. Monroe declared that the United States would not allow European nations to interfere with the nations of the Western Hemisphere. He also stated that no new colonies could be formed in the Western Hemisphere and that existing colonies could not be enlarged.

Morgan, Henry, 1635?-1688. An English pirate who attacked Spanish ships and settlements in America. Morgan carried out his raids from the English colony of Jamaica.

Moslem (moz′ləm). Refers to a follower of Islam. See **Islam.**

mosque (mosk). A Moslem temple of worship. See **Moslem.**

mother country. A country in relation to the colonies it controls.

mulatto (mə lat′ō). Refers to a person of mixed Negro and white descent.

natural resources. The things in nature that are useful to man. Natural resources include soil, water, minerals, forests, air, and sunshine.

Netherlands. A country on the North Sea coast of western Europe. See **Europe.**

Nicaraguan (nik'ə rä'gwən) **Lowland.** A level plain that extends southeastward from the Gulf of Fonseca, on the Pacific coast of Central America, to the Caribbean Sea. (See map, page 20.)

Nicoya (ni kō'yä) **Peninsula.** A peninsula in northwestern Costa Rica that extends into the Pacific Ocean. (See map, page 204.)

North America. The third largest continent on the earth. (See map, page 60.)

Northern Hemisphere (hem'ə sfir). The half of the world that is north of the equator. See **equator.**

nutmeg. A seed obtained from the fruit of the nutmeg tree. The seeds are grated and used as a spice.

offensive weapons. Weapons used for attacking rather than for defending.

"Operation Bootstrap." A program designed to raise the standard of living in Puerto Rico. (See **standard of living.**) This program includes industrial development, redistribution of farmland and improvement of farming methods, and construction of roads, power plants, housing projects, and schools. Also, new hotels have been built to attract tourists. Money for this program is provided by the government and by private investors.

orbit. The path followed by the earth as it moves around the sun.

overseas departments. French political divisions that are located outside of France. Departments are somewhat like the states of the United States. Each department is headed by a prefect. See **prefect.**

Pacific Lowland. A gently sloping plain that extends along the Pacific coast of Central America. (See map, page 20.)

papaya (pə pä'yə). A melon-like tropical fruit that varies in color from yellow to orange. It grows on the papaya tree, which looks somewhat like a small palm tree.

Papiamento (pä'pi ə men'tō). A language spoken on the southern islands of the Netherlands Antilles. Papiamento is a mixture of several languages, including Spanish, Dutch, English, and various African languages.

parallel (par'ə lel). One of the imaginary circles that are drawn east and west around the earth. (See page 330.) Parallel also means extending in the same direction and keeping the same distance apart. For example, the rails of a railroad track are parallel to each other.

parliament (pär'lə mənt). In some nations, the highest lawmaking body. Similar in some ways to the Congress of the United States.

peninsula (pə nin'sə lə). An area of land that is almost surrounded by water and is connected to a larger body of land.

people's farm. In Cuba, a government-owned farm on which workers earn daily wages. A people's farm is generally larger than a cooperative, but has fewer workers. See **cooperative.**

per capita income. A country's per capita income is the total income of all the people divided by the number of people in the country. Per capita figures are often rough guesses, for it is difficult to obtain correct figures.

Peru. A republic in western South America. At the time of the Spanish conquest of America, Peru was the center of the Inca Indian empire, which also included parts of what are now Chile, Argentina, Bolivia, and Ecuador. In the 1530's, Peru was conquered by Spaniards led by Francisco Pizarro. The Inca empire became the source of much of the treasure obtained by the Spanish in America.

Petén (pā tän'). A low, rolling plateau in northern Guatemala, mostly covered by dense rainforest. (See map, page 157.)

petrochemicals (pet'rō kem'ə kəlz). Chemicals obtained from petroleum or natural gas. Petrochemicals are used in making hundreds of products, such as paint, fertilizers, and synthetic rubber.

PRONUNCIATION KEY: hat, āge, câre, fär; let, ēqual, tėrm; it, īce; hot, ōpen, ôrder; oil, out; cup, pùt, rüle, ūse; child; long; thin; ᴛʜen; zh, measure; ə represents a in about, e in taken, i in pencil, o in lemon, u in circus. For the complete key, see page 335.

343

Pipil Indians. A group of Indian tribes who live in Guatemala and El Salvador. It is believed that the ancestors of the Pipil came from Mexico hundreds of years ago.

Pizarro (pi zär'ō), **Francisco,** 1470?-1541. The Spanish explorer who conquered Peru. See **Peru.**

plantain (plan'tən). A type of banana. Plantains are very large, hard, and starchy. They are an important food in tropical lands. Plantains are usually eaten cooked.

plateau (pla tō'). A large, generally level area of high land.

police state. A nation in which the government controls the economic, social, and political life of its people through a police organization that is not restrained by laws. In a police state, the ruler can carry out his wishes by issuing orders to the police. The citizens of the country do not have the protection of courts and legal processes.

Ponce de León (pän'sā dā lā ōn'), **Juan,** 1460?-1521. A Spanish soldier and explorer who conquered Puerto Rico and, in 1510, became governor of the island. In 1513, he led an expedition that discovered Florida.

Portugal. A country in southwestern Europe. See **Europe.**

prefect (prē'fekt). The chief administrative officer of a department, or regional division, of France.

"primitive" painting. A style of painting often used by artists who have had no training in their art. Usually this type of painting has simple designs and lacks perspective, or the impression of depth.

propaganda (prop' ə gan'də). Information or ideas spread for the purpose of influencing people's beliefs. Propaganda may be spread to help a cause or to hurt an opposing cause.

Protestant. Refers to a branch of Christianity. This branch includes many groups, such as the Church of England.

province. A governmental unit of a country or territory. A province is somewhat like a state of the United States.

radiotelephone. A telephone that uses radio waves instead of connecting wires.

rainforest. Commonly, a forest found in tropical areas that have no dry season, that receive more than 80 inches of rain each year, and that have average yearly temperatures between 68 and 85 degrees. A rainforest consists mostly of tall, broad-leaved evergreen trees.

rain shadow. An area that receives fairly light average rainfall because highlands prevent moisture-bearing winds from reaching it. (See "orographic rainfall" on page 39 for more information.)

raw sugar. The first form of sugar obtained from the processing of sugarcane. Raw sugar consists of yellowish-brown crystals covered with a film of molasses. Sugar bought in stores is made by refining raw sugar.

reefs. Ridges of rock, coral, or sand that are at or just below the surface of the sea. Usually reefs are formed of coral. See **coral.**

relief. The differences in altitude of a land surface.

republic (ri pub'lik). A nation having a form of government in which power rests with its citizens. The people govern themselves indirectly through the officers and representatives whom they elect to carry on the work of government.

Roman Catholic Church. A branch of Christianity. The head of the Roman Catholic Church is called the pope.

rosewood. The wood of various tropical trees. Used in making fine furniture.

Russia. See **Soviet Union.**

San Blas (sän bläs') **Islands.** A group of more than 300 coral islands near the northeastern coast of Panama. (See map, page 214.) These islands are inhabited by the primitive San Blas Indians.

Santo Domingo (san'tō də ming'gō). During colonial days, the name Santo Domingo referred to the island of Hispaniola, to the Spanish colony on that island, and to the capital city of that colony. This city is still called Santo Domingo, and is the capital of the Dominican Republic.

sapodilla (sap'ə dil'ə). A large, tropical evergreen tree. Its bark yields a juice that is used to make chicle. See **chicle.**

savanna (sə van'ə). An area of land covered with bunches of tall, stiff grass and scattered trees and bushes.

sesame (ses′ə mi). An herb that produces small, flattish seeds. These seeds, which are also called sesame, are used for their oil and as flavoring for food.

Sierra Maestra (si er′ə mä äs′trä). A range of mountains near the southeastern coast of Cuba. (See map, page 232.)

sisal (sī′səl). A plant from which a tough, white fiber is obtained. This fiber, which is also called sisal, is used to make twine and rope.

slums. Crowded residential areas in which the people are poor and their homes are unsanitary and in poor condition.

soccer. A game similar to the game of football. In the Caribbean Lands, soccer is called *fútbol*. (See page 152.)

solstice (sol′stis). The time of the year when the direct rays of the sun reach farthest north or south of the equator. This occurs about June 21, when the sun shines directly on the Tropic of Cancer, and about December 22, when the sun shines directly on the Tropic of Capricorn. See **Tropic of Cancer** and **Tropic of Capricorn.**

South America. The fourth largest continent on the earth. (See map, page 60.)

Southern Hemisphere (hem′ə sfir). The half of the world that is south of the equator. See **equator.**

Soviet Union. Short name for the Union of Soviet Socialist Republics, or U.S.S.R. Also called Russia. This country is located in Eurasia. See **Eurasia.**

Spain. A country in southwestern Europe. See **Europe.**

Spanish-American War. A war fought in 1898 between Spain and the United States. The treaty that ended this war freed Cuba from Spanish rule and gave the Spanish possessions of Puerto Rico, Guam, and the Philippines to the United States.

Spanish cedar. A tropical American tree from which a soft, light, fragrant wood is obtained.

spiny lobster. A large, spiny shellfish that lives in warm ocean waters.

square mile. An area of land or water equal to a square area that measures one mile on each side.

standard of living. The conditions that a person or group considers necessary in order to live properly. Among the factors considered in determining a standard of living are living conditions, working conditions, and the amount and kind of possessions of the person or group.

steel band. A group of musicians whose instruments are made from metal containers, such as oil barrels, which are played like drums.

stem. In referring to bananas, a stem is a banana stalk with the fruit attached. A stem has from 50 to 150 bananas in clusters of 10 to 20.

subsistence farming. Farming that usually supplies only the most basic needs of the farmer and his family. To subsist means to stay alive.

Surinam (sür′ə nam). A territory in northern South America that is part of the Kingdom of the Netherlands.

tenant farmers. Farmers who work land owned by someone else and pay rent to the owner, either in money or in shares of what they produce.

three-dimensional (də men′shə nəl). Having length, width, and depth.

tidal waves. Unusually high ocean waves, caused by earthquakes or hurricanes. Tidal waves rush against a shore and cause great damage as they wash inland.

tierra caliente (tyer′ə ka lyen′tə). Spanish for "hot land." Land in the tropics may be divided into three zones according to altitude. The *tierra caliente* is the lowest and warmest zone. It includes the land up to about 3,000 feet above sea level. See **tropics.**

tierra fría (tyer′ə frē′ə). Spanish for "cold land." Land in the tropics may be divided into three zones according to altitude. The *tierra fría* is the highest and coldest zone. It includes land that lies more than 6,000 feet above sea level. See **tropics.**

PRONUNCIATION KEY: hat, āge, cãre, fär; let, ēqual, tėrm; it, īce; hot, ōpen, ôrder; oil, out; cup, pùt, rüle, ūse; child; long; thin; ᴛʜen; zh, measure; ə represents a in about, e in taken, i in pencil, o in lemon, u in circus. For the complete key, see page 335.

345

tierra templada (tyer'ə tem plä'də). Spanish for "temperate land." Land in the tropics may be divided into three zones according to altitude. The *tierra templada* is the middle zone. It includes land that lies between about 3,000 and 6,000 feet above sea level. Temperatures in this zone are generally mild. See **tropics.**

topographic (top'ə graf'ik). Refers to the physical features of an area, such as lakes, rivers, and hills. A topographic map shows the elevation of these features and their location in relation to each other.

trade winds. Winds that blow steadily toward the equator in an area extending approximately 30 degrees north and 30 degrees south of the equator. (See explanation, pages 41, 42, and 43.)

tropical. Refers to anything located in, used in, or occurring in the tropics. See **tropics.**

Tropic of Cancer. An imaginary line around the earth, about 1,600 miles north of the equator. (See top chart, page 32.)

Tropic of Capricorn. An imaginary line around the earth, about 1,600 miles south of the equator. (See top chart, page 32.)

tropics. The part of the earth that lies between the Tropic of Cancer and the Tropic of Capricorn. (See top chart, page 32.) The weather in the tropics is generally hot all year round.

United Fruit Company. A United States company that raises bananas and other tropical crops in several countries of Central America, South America, and the West Indies. This company owns plantations, railroads, and a steamship line.

United Nations. An organization formed in 1945 to work for world peace. More than 100 nations are members. Agencies related to the United Nations work to solve problems in such fields as health, agriculture, and labor.

Vega Real (vā'gä rä äl'). Spanish for "Royal Plain." The Vega Real is a fertile plain in the northeastern part of the Dominican Republic. This area is the eastern part of the Cibao. See **Cibao.**

Venezuela (ven ə zwā'lə). A country in northern South America. (See map, page 16.)

voodoo. A form of religion that originated in Africa. Followers of voodoo believe that spirits influence the lives of human beings by either cursing or blessing them. Voodoo priests, or magicians, claim that they are able to bring people into communication with the spirits.

weathered. Refers to something that has been changed by exposure to the weather. For example, rock may be broken up into fine particles, or soil, by the action of wind, rainwater, or frost.

Western Hemisphere (hem'ə sfir). The half of the world in which the continents of North America and South America are situated.

West Indies. Islands lying north and east of Central America. The West Indies may be divided into three groups: the Bahama Islands, the Greater Antilles, and the Lesser Antilles.

West Indies Federation. An organization that included all of the British possessions in the West Indies except the Bahama Islands and the British Virgin Islands. This federation, officially called The West Indies, was established in 1958. It was dissolved four years later. In 1964, seven British colonies in the Lesser Antilles made plans to form a new federation.

World Bank. Short name commonly used for the International Bank for Reconstruction and Development. It has its headquarters in Washington, D.C. The governments of about one hundred countries are members of this bank and contribute money to it. When these nations need money for building highways, constructing dams, or making other improvements, they may borrow it from the World Bank.

World War I. A war that involved many parts of the world. It began in 1914 and ended in 1918.

World War II. A war that involved many parts of the world. It began in 1939 and ended in 1945.

wrought (rôt) **iron.** A form of iron that can be worked easily into artistic designs.

yaws. A tropical disease that causes sores on the skin. Very contagious.

yellow fever. An often fatal tropical disease caused by a virus that is spread from person to person, or from monkeys to people, by the bite of some kinds of mosquitoes.

Yucatán (ū'kə tan') **Peninsula.** A large peninsula that includes British Honduras, much of northern Guatemala, and part of southeastern Mexico.

Index

Explanation of abbreviations used in this Index:

p — pictures   *m* — maps

PRONUNCIATION KEY: hat, āge, câre, fär; let, ēqual, tėrm; it, īce; hot, ōpen, ôrder; oil, out; cup, pùt, rüle, ūse; child; long; thin; ᴛʜen; zh, measure; ə represents a in about, e in taken, i in pencil, o in lemon, u in circus. For the complete key, see page 335.

PRONUNCIATION KEY: hat, āge, cãre, fär; let, ēqual, tėrm; it, īce; hot, ōpen, ôrder; oil, out; cup, pu̇t, rüle, ūse; child; long; thin; ᴛHen; zh, measure; ə represents a in about, e in taken, i in pencil, o in lemon, u in circus. For the complete key, see page 335.

Panama Canal, 9, 11, 80, 137-138, 215, 220-222; *p* 10, 137, 138, 221, 225; *m* 139
Panama Canal Company, 225
Panama City, Panama, 227; *p* 226, 227; *m* 93, 214
Pan American Highway, 134; *m* 134
Pedro Miguel (pā′drō mē gel′) Locks, 138; *m* 139
people, 9, 85-94; *p* 85-89, 92; *m* 91. *See also* Indians *and* names of countries
Peralta Azurdia, Enrique, 162
per capita income, 11, 94, 343
petrochemicals, 122, 343
petroleum, *see* oil
Pico Duarte, 250; *m* 250
pirates, 66, 67, 218; *p* 67
Pitch Lake, Trinidad, 99, 302; *p* 99, 302; *m* 300
Pizarro, Francisco, 65, 218, 344
plantain, 108, 344
Pointe-à-Pitre (pwant′ ə pē′trə), Guadeloupe, 321
Ponce (pōn′sä), Puerto Rico, 297-298; *p* 298; *m* 93, 287
Ponce de León, Juan, 287-288, 344; *p* 288
population, 19, 90-92; *m* 91. *See also* names of countries
Port Antonio, Jamaica, 283; *m* 277
Port-au-Prince, Haiti, 274; *p* 33, 274; *m* 93, 250
Portobelo (pōrt′ə bel′ō), Panama, 218; *m* 214
Port of Spain, Trinidad and Tobago, 303, 306; *p* 306; *m* 93, 300
Port Royal, Jamaica, 279; *m* 277
pressure belts, *see* climate
Puerto Rico (pwert′ō rē′kō), 285-298; *p* 285, 286, 288-298; *m* 287
  area, 286
  cities, 297-298; *p* 297, 298; *m* 287
  climate, 47, 285-286
  communication, 296
  currency, 286
  earning a living, 293-294; *p* 293, 294
  education, 296; *p* 296
  exports, 127, 294
  farm products, 286, 294
  government, 291-292; *p* 292
  history, 287-291; *p* 288-291
  income, 286
  land, 26, 285, 298; *p* 26, 285, 286

  language, 286
  natural resources, 286-287
  "Operation Bootstrap," 290-291, 343; *p* 290, 291
  people, 292-293; *p* 292
  population, 286, 292
  religion, 286
  transportation, 295; *p* 295

Quezaltenango (kā säl′tə näng′ gō), Guatemala, 168; *m* 157

racial groups, *see* people
railroads, *see* transportation
rainfall, *see* climate
recreation, 152-154; *p* 152-154
Redonda Island, *see* "Little Eight"
religion, 65, 66, 89. *See also* names of countries
rice, 107-108; *p* 107; *m* 112
Rivera (rē vä′rä), Julio Adalberto, 173
roads, *see* transportation
Road Town, British Virgin Islands, 329; *m* 93, 327
rum, 121

Saba Island, *see* Netherlands Antilles
St. Barthélemy (san′bar′tāl′mē′) Island, *see* Guadeloupe
St. Croix (sānt kroi′) Island, *see* Virgin Islands
St. Domingue (san′dô′mang′), *see* Haiti
St. Eustatius (sānt yu̇ stā′ shəs) Island, *see* Netherlands Antilles
St. John Island, *see* Virgin Islands
St. Kitts Island, *see* "Little Eight"
St. Lucia Island, *see* "Little Eight"
St. Martin Island, 319, 320, 322, 325; *m* 319
St. Pierre, Martinique, 28
St. Thomas Island, *see* Virgin Islands
St. Vincent Island, *see* "Little Eight"
San José (san hō zā′), Costa Rica, 213; *p* 213; *m* 93, 204

San Juan (san hwän′), Puerto Rico, 31, 297; *p* 30, 92, 297; *m* 93, 287
San Pedro Sula, Honduras, 186, 193; *m* 184
San Salvador, El Salvador, 170, 177-178; *p* 178; *m* 93, 170
San Salvador Island, Bahama Islands, 58; *p* 29, 56; *m* 307
Santa Ana, El Salvador, 178; *m* 93, 170
Santiago, Guatemala, 161; *p* 161
Santiago de Cuba, Cuba, 248; *m* 93, 232
Santiago de los Caballeros, Dominican Republic, 262; *m* 250
Santo Domingo, Dominican Republic, 261-262, 344; *p* 260, 261; *m* 93, 250
Scarborough, Trinidad and Tobago, 306; *m* 300
Schick Gutiérrez (shik′gü tye′res), René, 199
schools, *see* education
seasons, *see* climate
sisal, 264, 271, 345; *p* 264
slavery, 76, 77-78
soil, *see* natural resources
Somoza (sō mō′sä), Anastasio, 199; *p* 199
Somoza, Luis, 199
Soviet Union, 240-241, 345
Spain,
  declines in power, 66-67
  economy of its colonies, 69-70
  explorers for, 57, 58, 59, 62-64, 65; *p* 57, 62; *m* 58, 63
  government of its colonies, 69
  loses its empire, 71, 72, 73; *m* 72
  rules the Caribbean, 59-66; *m* 72
Spanish-American War, 79, 235-236, 345; *p* 79, 236
Spanish treasure ships, 65-66; *m* 65
sports, *see* recreation
standard of living, 13, 345
sugar, *see* industry
sugarcane, 68, 111-113, 200, 224, 242, 258, 281, 294; *p* 111, 243, 289, 314, 318; *m* 112

Tegucigalpa (tə gü sə gal′pə), Honduras, 186, 192-193; *p* 193; *m* 93, 184
Ten Years' War, 235
textile, *see* industry

PRONUNCIATION KEY: hat, āge, cãre, fär; let, ēqual, tėrm; it, īce; hot, ōpen, ôrder; oil, out; cup, pu̇t, rüle, u̇se; child; long; thin; ᴛHen; zh, measure; ə represents a in about, e in taken, i in pencil, o in lemon, u in circus. For the complete key, see page 335.

PRONUNCIATION KEY: hat, āge, cãre, fär; let, ēqual, tėrm; it, īce; hot, ōpen, ôrder; oil, out; cup, pút, rüle, ūse; child; long; thin; ŦHen; zh, measure; ə represents a in about, e in taken, i in pencil, o in lemon, u in circus. For the complete key, see page 335.